IS CAPITALISM
CHRISTIAN?

IS CAPITALISM CHRISTIAN?

Toward a Christian Perspective on Economics

Edited by

Franky Schaeffer

CROSSWAY BOOKS • WESTCHESTER, ILLINOIS
A Division of Good News Publishers

Cover designed by Sarah Cioni/Cioni Artworks.

First printing, 1985.

Library of Congress Catalog Card Number 85-70471

ISBN 0-89107-362-0

The publisher would like to express appreciation for permission to reprint the following articles in this volume:

"The Enthusiasm for Spending," from *The Liberal Crack-up,* by R. Emmett Tyrrell, Jr. (New York: Simon & Schuster, 1984), Chapter 10.

"Goodness and the GNP," from *The Economy in Mind,* by Warren T. Brookes (New York: Universe Books, 1982), Chapter 9.

"The Ideal of Democratic Capitalism," from *The Spirit of Democratic Capitalism,* by Michael Novak (New York: Simon & Schuster, 1982), Chapter 4.

"The Bandung Generation," from *Modern Times: The World from the Twenties to the Eighties,* by Paul Johnson (New York: Harper & Row, 1983), Chapter 14.

"Western Guilt and Third World Poverty," from *Equality, The Third World, and Economic Delusion,* by P. T. Bauer (Cambridge: Harvard University Press, 1981), Chapter 4.

"The Two Kinds of Memory," from *How Democracies Perish,* by Jean-Francois Revel (New York: Doubleday, 1983), Chapters 25, 26.

"Central American Policies—What the Marxists Are Really Up to in South America," from *Imprimis* (journal of Hillsdale College, June 1984), by Humberto Belli.

"From Equal Opportunity to 'Affirmative Action,' " from *Civil Rights: Rhetoric or Reality,* by Thomas Sowell (New York: William Morrow and Company, 1984), Chapter 2.

"Comparable Worth: The Feminist Road to Socialism," from *Commentary* magazine (September 1984), by Michael Levin, pp. 13-19.

"The Media—Shield of the Utopians," from *The Coercive Utopians: Social Deception by America's Power Players,* by Rael and Erich Isaac (Chicago: Regnery Gateway, 1983), Chapter 11.

"The Dismal Science," from *The Doomsday Myth*, by Charles Maurice and Charles W. Smithson (Stanford: Hoover Institute Press, 1984), Chapter 2.

"Standing Room Only? The Demographic Facts," from *The Ultimate Resource*, by Julian L. Simon (Princeton: Princeton University Press, 1981), Chapters 11, 12.

"A Critique of Christian Marxism," from *Liberation Theology* (Ronald Nash, editor), by Dale Vree (Milford, Mich.: Mott Media, 1984), pp. 203-214.

"For the World Against the World," from *The Naked Public Square: Religion and Democracy in America*, by Richard John Neuhaus (Grand Rapids: Eerdmans, 1984), Chapter 14.

"A Pilgrimage in Political Theology: A Personal Witness," from *Liberation Theology* (Ronald Nash, editor), by Clark Pinnock (Milford, Mich.: Mott Media, 1984), pp. 101-120.

"Compassion and the Poor," from *The Generation That Knew Not Josef*, Billingsley (Portland: Multnomah Press, 1985), Chapters 17-19.

"Underdevelopment Revisited," from *Commentary* magazine (July 1984), by Peter L. Berger, pp. 41-45.

"The Networks vs. the Recovery," from *Commentary* magazine (July 1984), by Paul H. Weaver, pp. 35-40.

"Introduction," from *The Resourceful Earth: A Response to Global 2000*, by Julian L. Simon and Herman Kahn (New York: Basil Blackwell, 1984), pp. 1-49.

"The Goal Is Not to Describe: A Review of Nicholas Wolterstorff's *Until Justice and Peace Embrace*," by Richard John Neuhaus, from *This World* magazine, No. 9, pp. 105-110.

"Famine, Development & Foreign Aid," from *Commentary* magazine (March 1985), by Nick Eberstadt, pp. 25-31.

"Ecclesiastical Economics: Envy Legitimized," from *Reality and Rhetoric: Studies in the Economics of Development*, by P. T. Bauer (Cambridge: Harvard University Press, 1984), pp. 73-89.

This book is for the Newburyport "mafia": Harold and Mary Fickett, Steve and Barbara Hawley, Steve and Sheri Larson, John and Susie Skillen, Randy Cobler, Genie, Jessica, Francis, and John Schaeffer, and honorary members Tom and Lovelace Howard. With thanks for your friendship,

Franky

CONTENTS

Acknowledgments

First, I would like to thank all the authors who have contributed to this volume as well as their publishers. I would also particularly like to thank Susie Skillen for her invaluable help to me in editing this book. Lastly, I would like to thank Norman Podhoretz and his colleagues at *Commentary* for pursuing an editorial policy which over the course of a number of years has been of inestimable value to me in developing an awareness of the issues that this book represents.

Franky Schaeffer

IS CAPITALISM
CHRISTIAN?

Introduction

An abiding irony of the twentieth century is the willful credulity of the Western intellectual elites in the face of our century's most brutal and excessive failures. Afflicted with severe shortsightedness, bewildered Western leaders failed to respond effectively both to Nazi and Stalinist totalitarianism and the eugenics movement. Their acute myopia has been attended by a morbid fascination with Socialist and Marxist economic dogma—the dogma that has impoverished wealthy nations and retarded the growth of the emerging states.

The more troubling irony is that Christians, Roman Catholic and Protestant alike, have jumped on the bandwagon, either tagging along at the rear or attempting now and again to lead the parade. As Paul Johnson documents in *Modern Times*, the clergy led the pacifist movements which gave Hitler his head start. For instance, Dick Sheppard, leader of the pacifist clergy and founder of the "Peace Pledge Union," collected signatures to frighten off Herr Hitler and thus to avert war! Archbishop of Canterbury Hewlett Johnson wrote openly opposing rearmament just before Hitler attacked France and Great Britain. The gullible Archbishop also lauded Joseph Stalin's "internal reorganizaton" of his nation as a brave effort to take "his people down new and unfamiliar avenues of democracy." Jean-Francois Revel observes about totalitarian states: "concessions do not appease the gluttony of such systems; they stimulate [them]."

Flirtation with leftist ideology has sapped the internal convictions and sound judgment of the ruling elites in the West—its academics, bureaucrats, scientists, and media personalities. While the Western press unsympathetically scrutinized the minute by minute activities of the United States in Vietnam, Communist China's genocide against Tibet went unnoticed. Under media cries of a "new Vietnam," America cut back its miniscule aid to the Contras of Nicaragua and reduced to several dozen its advisors in El Salvador, while the Soviet Union quietly increased its army of liquidation in Afghanistan from one hundred thousand to two hundred and fifty thousand. The chemical industrial accident of Bhopal, India, which took the lives of over two thousand people resulted in loud calls for government industrial control, and prompted hordes of ambulance-chasing American "public interest" lawyers to pack their bags and head for lucrative percentages that could be won in damages. Yet when the Soviet Union in Afghanistan, Vietnam in Laos, and Thailand used chemical and biological weapons *deliberately* against innocent civilians, women, children, and soldiers, killing tens of thousands, the Western elites raised no notable or sustained objections.

To say that the West, or at least the West's elites, are biased towards the left is merely to state the obvious. This leftist bent takes many forms, from the conveniently closed eyes when Soviet aggression becomes too pronounced, to the bias for Socialist solutions to all economic problems.

In response to those (particularly in our own Christian circles) who would persuade us that socialism is Christian, the essays in this volume have been collected to address one question in particular: Is capitalism Christian? If the question is narrowly understood, the answer may seem obvious. Capitalism, like any economic system, is merely a tool and can therefore be no more "Christian" than the George Washington Bridge is "Christian." Nevertheless, economic systems have proven themselves to be better or worse at preserving Christian and humane values, and Christians, as people supposedly of justice and mercy, must be concerned with the *results* of economic systems in people's everyday lives. Posed more generally, the question asks: has any one economic system proven to be more amenable to Christian values? By analogy, were the George Washington Bridge to prove itself effective at transporting people safely and efficiently from Jersey to Manhattan, then at least for that reason we might call it more "Christian" than another bridge which collapsed.

Indeed to take the analogy one step further, if one should find that a particular engineering firm constructed nothing but bridges that collapsed, invariably taking the lives of thousands of innocent victims, one could go so far as to call the firm unChristian, indeed anti-Christian. Any human activity which inevitably brings unmitigated suffering to other human beings cannot be described as Christian, however benevolent those involved in such activities may feel themselves to be.

Every modern Communist and Socialist experiment, Western or Eastern, without exception, has brought economic disaster, hardship, and loss of freedom. One can only judge an economic system by the fruit it bears, not by the promises on the package. "Does it work?" is not an unreasonble question. The "progressive" revolutionary leftist societies have produced only poisonous fruits: the destruction of human lives, coercion, totalitarianism, poverty, and starvation.

What ought to be an obvious lesson of the twentieth century is that when economic freedoms are lost, all freedoms atrophy. Hence, while right-wing dictatorships—Franco's Spain and South America's Argentina, for instance—have rediscovered democracy, there is no instance of a nation which has gone into the orbit of the Soviet Union, China, or Cuba reversing its policies and rediscovering human freedom, dignity, and worth.

Indeed, the reverse is true: civil and religious freedom, progress, and the preservation of human rights are inextricably linked with economic freedom, with the right to own property, and with a minimum of state interference in economic affairs. And as Warren Brookes asserts in his essay "Goodness and the GNP," a healthy capitalist economy is in turn dependent on Christian moral standards: "Without the civilizing force of universal moral standards, particularly honesty, trust, self-respect, integrity, and loyalty, the marketplace quickly degenerates." The commitment to moral and spiritual values goes hand in hand with a prosperous economy.

Brookes asks, "Can business executives who routinely cheat on their spouses be expected not to cheat the consumer, the government, or their competitor?" Because ours is a fallen world, capitalism as a free economy leaves the door open to abuse, self-gratification, and greed. Nevertheless, it also has the greatest actual claim of success for alleviating human suffering. Michael Novak writes, "No better weapon against poverty, disease, illiteracy, and tyranny has yet been found than capitalism. The techniques, human skills, and changes of cultural habit necessary to expand the productive capacity of the earth have been pioneered by democratic capitalism. Its compassion for the material needs of humankind has not in history yet had a peer."

The essays gathered here document the bankruptcy—the sterility—of Socialist economic systems. They also demonstrate that free market economies, and the enterprise and invention they encourage, have not only produced economic prosperity, but have promoted the personal and social freedoms that all people long for, but which only a few, in these dark days of expanding

Socialist tyrannies, have tasted. Since utopian perfection cannot be achieved in a fallen world, three-quarters of a capitalist loaf is better than the whole loaf promised by Socialist dreamers but never delivered. One need only consider a few facts of our own time to realize how completely our own recent history has vindicated this premise. Compare the great jagged scar of minefields, barbed wire, booby traps, vicious dogs, and guard towers—the necessary paraphernalia of the Communist border patrol—with the United States-Mexico border. The one is a lethal contraption designed to keep a people enslaved, knowing that few would stay in the Soviet bloc by choice. The other is a porous border consisting of a few flimsy fences and several hundred overworked border guards attempting to keep hundreds of thousands of people *out* of the domain of the great "imperialist Satan," the United States of America.

From the boat people of Southeast Asia to the Mexicans crossing into Southern California, the poor of the world have seen and judged economic systems for themselves, with or without the approval of the leftist scholarly elites. Whenever they are given the opportunity, the poor, the underprivileged, and the working people of the world *vote with their feet* for capitalism and its partial loaf over the empty leftist promises which, unlike professors at Harvard, they have had to live with. From every starving, pot-bellied, gaunt-eyed Ethiopian child comes one mute message: Marxist centralized planning does not work! The message is substantiated by the East German border guards patroling the Berlin Wall who are sent two by two, each with the instruction to shoot the other should his comrade in arms attempt a desperate leap over the wall in a mad scramble for the "decadent capitalist West."

Marxist idealists, Western intellectuals, and other elitists claim to have an ear attuned to the needs of the poor. More often than not, they are merely listening to self-appointed totalitarian "representatives of the poor" who usually turn out in the end to be oppressors. The message that the world's poor have been sending for the last seventy years comes loud and clear. When given a real opportunity to vote, via the ballot box or their feet, they choose democratic government, free market ideals, capitalism, and the ability to travel and emigrate to countries in which work and prosperity can be found—the capitalist countries.

The irrational devotion to socialism among the educated Western elites in the face of the unrelieved failure of Socialist experiments can only be explained as a manifestation of our century's own secular religion. As G. K. Chesterton observed, if men will not believe in God, they will believe in anything. Like all false gods, the Socialist deity takes more than it gives, its yoke is heavy, its burden impossible to bear, its living waters are sour. Only its high priests—professors on government grants or ruling elites in Socialist countries—benefit from its service. The common people toil and groan in vain.

Unfortunately, those seduced by the Socialist-Communist idol are not entirely outside the fold of the church. The British churchmen confused by the Nazi movement and the Western intellectuals confused by Stalin may find their counterparts in the contemporary church who have been confused by leftist economic ideology.

In the 1984 elections, the majority of America's Roman Catholics, a group once considered safely in the clutches of the Democratic Party, voted overwhelmingly for Ronald Reagan and his conservative policies. Ironically, while a clear trend toward conservatism became apparent in the nation as a whole as well as in the rank and file membership of the U.S. Catholic Church, the U.S. Catholic bishops seemed to be moving steadily to the left on a range of social and economic issues (with their stand against abortion as an exception to this trend).

The bishops' leftward excursion became most obvious in the first draft of the bishops' Pastoral Letter on the U.S. economy released November 11, 1984. Stripped of the meager lip service the document paid to the Church's traditional opposition to "statism," the 112-page document proposed a series of measures that if actually implemented by the U.S. government would have gone a long way toward transforming the United States into a Socialist state.

For instance, implicit in the Pastoral Letter's specific statist utopian proposals were the following: Law should impose limits on personal income and personal family wealth. The government should regulate income to businesses it believes would "provide needed jobs." "Affirmative Action" programs in education and employment and other fields should be expanded and imposed by law. The concept of "comparable pay" for "comparable work" should be imposed by law. Supply-side incentives in the economy should be dismantled, and instead tax laws should be revised to bring about a new egalitarianism through "progressivity." Welfare benefits should be immeasurably enlarged as taxes are raised, and should no longer depend on "work requirements or work tests." All Americans should be guaranteed a job, with the government providing "direct public service employment and also . . . public subsidies for employment in the private sector." Concern over the

"East-West" struggle between the Communist bloc and the free nations of the world should be downplayed, with defense spending eventually abandoned, in favor of massive financial support for the Third World, administered by the U.N.

In fact, the draft Letter was so radically to the left that even the ultraliberal *Washington Post* in its story analyzing the Letter criticized it as "impractical" and more extreme than positions now taken, "even by many liberal economists and politicians." By contrast, the Communist Party newspaper *The Daily World* greeted the document with great enthusiasm, as did Ron Sider and several other leftist churchmen.

To a growing number of Catholics, this letter was the latest and most dramatic of many signs that the U.S. bishops and most especially their elite bureaucracy at the U.S. Catholic Conference had become largely dominated by far left ideologues. As *Human Events*, the Washington-based political analysis newspaper, noted in its November 24, 1984 issue, "the only effective way to fight back, many believe, is to boycott the collection basket at Sunday Mass." Why had the Catholic bishops turned their backs not only on the conservative drift of the nation as a whole, but on their own traditions as well?

Following the end of the Second Vatican Council, the "modernization" process of the Catholic Church began which has led from one crisis to another. The increase in bureaucratic meddling in the Catholic hierarchy occurred during the sixties, the same period of history as the increase of the bureaucratization (the "Great Society" Johnson years) of the nation as a whole. The Catholic Church's shift on economic and other issues simply followed the general shift in U.S. government bureaucracies towards the left and towards meddling in heretofore nonregulated affairs such as business and industry. James Hitchcock, Roman Catholic professor of history at St. Louis University, has noted,

> Largely unnoticed at first, the development of this [church] bureaucracy was both a cause and an effect of the decline of episcopal authority. Put simply, many bishops found the world of the late 1960's—both the religious and secular parts of it—daunting and bewildering, every familiar guidepost now obscured. Acutely aware that their own education and experience did not seem to fit them to exercise their authority in a radically changed world, many bishops began automatically to defer to their 'experts.' ("The Catholic Bishops, Public Policy and the New Class," in *This World*, Fall 1984)

During this same period of bureaucratization, the Catholic leadership began to engage in "ecumenical dialogue." One result was that the Catholic hierarchy and their bureaucrats began to take their cues from liberal Protestantism, which they saw at that time as much more "progressive" than the traditional Catholic Church. One might accurately say that the emergence of the left-wing Catholic Church hierarchy in America and its bureaucracies owes a good deal to its imitation of liberal, secularized, mainline Protestantism.

As the bishops began to depend more and more on "experts" for social relevance, these specialists were drawn increasingly from secular academic sources and were often only nominally Catholic or wholly secularized and antireligious. The academic world of the sixties and seventies from which these bureaucrats came was largely leftward in its thinking, as indeed the academic community still tends to be today.

Thus we find, more and more, that standing between the bishops and their flock are a group of leftist bureaucrats and specialists, typified by Father Brian Hehir. Father Hehir, an "expert" on political and economic issues, orchestrated the 1983 Pastoral Letter on war and peace, a Gandhian pacifist statement on nuclear weapons. He has also been the guiding light in putting together the leftist vision of America contained in the first draft of the Pastoral Letter on the economy. In both cases he was quite successful in seeing that moderate and traditional voices got little if any hearing in the process.

Many other writers and commentators have been distressed by the bishops' letter. George F. Will in his nationally syndicated column (Friday, November 16, 1984) writes,

> All the important social policy discussions of the last decade evidently occurred without the bishops noticing. . . .
> American capitalism is the most efficient anti-poverty machine the world has ever seen. It is arguable that, at this point, less government action would serve the poor by enhancing the general growth of the economy. . . . The Conference of Bishops is located in Washington. Small wonder it has come to sound like just another liberal lobby.

The tragic irony is how very far to the left of common sense (let alone the common good!) the Catholic bureaucrats surrounding the bishops have moved. While the U.S. Catholic bishops were drafting their utopian economical nonsense, Planned Parenthood Federation, headquartered in London, England, published a very similar booklet called *Human Numbers, Human Needs*. This propopulation planning, Socialistic, proabortion (and therefore anti-orthodox-Catholic) book presents an economic "analysis" almost identical to the Pastoral Letter issued by the bishops in America. The Planned Parenthood booklet states: "There is a clear need for long term planning, at national, and where possible, global levels." The authors then go on to plead for "redistribution of wealth" and "redistribution of incomes and resources." According to Planned Parenthood's analysis of the world, "the affluent consumers of the northern countries and the southern elites constitute perhaps the major threats to the world's oceans and fish stocks, tropical forests, genetic diversity and global climate."

The model for the future Planned Parenthood admires most is China! We read: "The most remarkable of all family planning policies, . . . Chinese parents are told that if action had been taken sooner it would have been acceptable for them to have two children—the need for the one child limit is, it is stressed, the price of delay." The booklet does not mention (let alone condemn) China's recent barbaric practice of forced third-trimester abortions and infanticide. The *Wall Street Journal* noted in an editorial on December 19, 1984, "Planned Parenthood's love affair with socialism has become more than a harmless upper middle class hobby and now borders on the ludicrous."

It also seems ludicrous that the bishops' Pastoral Letter so closely mirrors Planned Parenthood's leftist coercive utopian ideology in all their views except, for the time being, on abortion. Tragically the Catholic bishops have allowed themselves to be pushed by their "New Class" bureaucrats and "scholars" into squandering their moral capital by buying into the utopian and failed Marxist ideologies of the left.

The Roman Catholic Church is not alone in its problems. Within the evangelical community, too, leaders have emerged whose gullibility is made dangerous by their popularity. Though perhaps sincere in their Christian concern for the poor, Ronald Sider, Tony Campolo, Jim Wallis, and John Alexander, for example, have allowed their zeal for a socially conscientious gospel to lead them towards leftist dogma in one guise or another. Their common stock in trade is to nourish a kind of wallowing guilt and self-recrimination against the United States, capitalism, and prosperity. Campolo makes us feel guilty for eating too many potato chips; Sider, for having too many children and eating too many bananas. America's economic and agricultural miracle, which feeds not only the United States, but much of the world, becomes in the words of Ronald Sider a "grain monopoly" to be decried. John Alexander, another member of the evangelical Hate America Club, has referred to the United States as an evil empire comparable only to the Soviet Union.

Wallis, founder of the Washington-based Sojourners community, stated that America should have apologized to Iran for taking American hostages. America, says Wallis, is partly responsible for the Soviet attack on Korean Flight 007, and responsible as well for seducing the Vietnamese boat people with an addiction to Western consumerism. In his own publication Wallis wrote: "Many of today's [Vietnamese] refugees were inoculated with a taste for a Western lifestyle during the war and are fleeing to support their consumer habit in other lands" (*Sojourners*, September 1979).

Such a statement is staggering. With the exception of George Marchais, leader of the French Communist Party, no one in the West besides Jim Wallis went on record in defense of the Communists and in criticism of the boat people. Even the Italian Communist Party had the strength of mind to denounce the genocidal butchery of the North Vietnamese and later the Khmer Rouge. As Lloyd Billingsley points out in the final essay in this book, these "evangelical" purveyors of guilt are caught in a logical inconsistency:

> On the one hand, they say poverty is abominable, and God's wrath is called down on us for allowing it. . . . On the other hand, radical Christians lead us to believe that poverty is the only acceptable lifestyle for Christians and hence desirable. One cannot have it both ways.

A hyperactive guilt reflex seems to be the motivating force behind their reasoning, not true Christian compassion. As P. T. Bauer puts it in his essay included in this book, "Exponents of guilt are concerned with their own emotional state and that of their fellow citizens, and not with the results of the policies inspired by such sentiments." The self-proclaimed prophet handing out sackcloth and scattering ashes is one thing. More troubling is how the evangelical establishment, like a sort of penitent Nineveh responding abjectly to the disgruntled prophet, has flung open its doors to such voices. The lecture circuit is packed, the evangelical periodicals are loaded, with the purveyors of guilt. It is one thing to have wild-eyed doomsayers within the fold; it is another thing to make them our leaders.

Unfortunately the drift of the evangelical leadership towards socialism, or at least pop-New Age leftism, is not solely the preserve of a few isolated individuals such as Jim Wallis. Just before the 1984 election eighteen Wheaton College professors, joined by three administrators, signed an open letter which they distributed to the entire student body urging the students to vote for the Mondale-Ferraro presidential ticket. This was despite the fact that the Mondale-Ferraro ticket and the Democratic platform in that year's election clashed with the basic views of Bible-believing Christians concerning such issues as abortion, homosexuality, public funding of abortion, and the growing incidence of infanticide and other eugenic monstrosities. The rationale behind urging students at an evangelical college to vote for the most radically leftist presidential ticket in our history was that the Mondale-Ferraro ticket was more closely aligned with Christian ideas of "justice and compassion" in dealing with the "poor." But the fact of the matter was that even this claim was patently false.

The decline in the economy and the consequential increased suffering of America's poor under the Carter administration and its leftist economic policies should have provided tutelage enough. Evidence of the decline of living standards of every Western European power that has followed the Socialist path advocated by Walter Mondale and company provides ample warning. The coercive utopian and elitist influence in government planning, expansion, and bureaucracy in our own recent history are danger signals. That supposedly intelligent scholars at an evangelical institution could think it was in their best interests, or the nation's best interests, to vote for the policies of the American New Age liberal left is a testimony to the power of the desire to be fashionable, "with it," and "relevant."

Evangelical Christians have been open to parroting the "received wisdom" of secular liberalism—or, as Richard John Neuhaus remarks, trying to be "one of the boys"—in other areas as well. Many Christians—for instance, Campolo and Nicholas Wolterstorff—persist in worrying about a "population explosion" even though the claims of doomsayers such as Paul Erlich and the Club of Rome have long since been disproved. Many of the faculty on the campuses of evangelicaldom, bringing up the rear ten years behind the times, are little more than carbon copies of the New Age liberals churned out by the truckload in the sixties and seventies. Disgruntled, rejoicing not in success but in failure, viewing the scene through vaguely anti-American glasses, they romanticize poverty and decry the gluttony of the potato-chip eaters.

It is time to call a spade a spade. The evangelical elite's flirtation with leftist, Socialist ideology is at best a case of chasing after a will-o'-the-wisp and at worst a form of modern idolatry. We must denounce socialism. The *results* of the ever-expanding welfare state, of centralized economic planning, of government interference in the free market, and of communism itself are profoundly anti-Christian.

Ideas have consequences. In the hands of Lenin and Stalin, to speak only of his Russian disciples, the ideas of Marx have impoverished—when they haven't slaughtered—the half of the world which the Soviet Union, the greatest imperialist state in the history of mankind, has subjugated.

Nor can we ignore the fact that in the United States, free market economics, free enterprise, and capitalism have brought in their train a general prosperity unequaled in the history of mankind. If one claims to be "on the side of the poor," then, judging by who has helped the poor most, one must give all the credit to the United States—a wealthy nation built by the enterprising *formerly* poor of the world. America's definition of poverty on her own soil would be considered wealth in two-thirds of the world today. Indeed, America's poverty line is now $1000 above the average income in the Soviet Union.

How odd that some among us are so anxious to foist on the rest of the world the anticapitalist systems that we ourselves wisely refuse to accept. The leftist talk of "compassion" for the poor and the oppressed rings hollow in the face of the track record of "progressive" systems which inevitably impoverish and enslave their beneficiaries. Why is it that in searching books such as Sider's *Rich Christians in an Age of Hunger* or Wolterstorff's *Until Justice and Peace Embrace* one finds little or no coherent discussion of how wealth is produced, of what brings prosperity, or of how civil freedoms have historically been linked with economic freedom. Perhaps the reason is simply that their untenable pop-Socialist position cannot bear close scrutiny. With the millions of souls who have been slaughtered by leftist regimes crying for justice, with the demonstrable failure of Socialist economics in totalitarian states now being used to subjugate the Third World, one does well not to ask too many embarrassing questions.

Perhaps Christians have a peculiar susceptibility to appeals made to personal conscience. The journey towards Christ begins with an acknowledgement of sin and an admission of personal guilt in the face of Christ's perfection. That sense of guilt seems xxvi / IS CAPITALISM CHRISTIAN?

to cause a knee-jerk response to appeals made to conscience—
"we must be more compassionate," "we are too complacent," "we
are selfish materialists." While Christians certainly must be compassionate and self-sacrificing, the attempt to expiate one's guilt
through social or political action is a false gospel. The balanced
mind can appreciate the joy, beauty, diversity, creativity, and
abundance of God's world as well as recognize its fallenness. But
in the mind of those taken up with the idolatry of self-criticism,
guilt becomes manipulative and, indeed, dangerous. Dangerous
especially to all those on whom the results are showered: Third
World recipients of ill-conceived, guilt-motivated "assistance,"
the transient poor who are made permanently poor by attempts
to "help them."

In a sort of diabolical marriage between the worst of Puri-
tanism and socialism, Christian New Age liberals, evangelical
and Catholic alike, combine hatred of the flesh with coercive
utopianism. The result is pernicious ideology that tries to make
ordinary people feel guilty just for being alive. It is this joyless
spectacle unfolding on the world, impoverishing people and nations, which leads those who are thoughtful to abandon Socialistic concepts in favor of capitalistic ideals. In G. K. Chesterton's
seminal essay "Why I Am Not a Socialist" the drab sameness of
the whole dreary business seems to be the chief reason he rejects
Socialistic ideals. Chesterton was convinced, rightly so as it
turned out, that if the Socialists in Britain had their way the price
of beer would go up, jollity and gaiety would be forgotten.

C. S. Lewis also rejected the totalitarian impulses of socialism. One can see in Narnia's White Witch the winter of terminal
bureaucracy in which "it is always winter and never Christmas."
Father Christmas is banned and all luxuries and "useless items"
banished forever in favor of a well organized superstate. C. S.
Lewis, Chesterton, and more recently Malcolm Muggeridge have
all understood what George Orwell made clear in *Animal Farm*
and *1984*. Statist solutions to human problems simply lead to
more statist solutions and less humans.

Evangelicals pitifully scramble to be "one of the boys," yet
always lag ten years behind. The irony is keener when we realize
that much of the secular left has redrawn its own position; several
authors represented in this volume, both Christian and secular,
were former leftists (Michael Novak, Jean-Francois Revel, Clark
Pinnock, Peter Berger). One thinks also of the remarkable conversion of a former leftist such as Malcolm Muggeridge to the Christian faith itself. It is disturbing that even now evangelicals in

academia so studiously avoid the burgeoning growth of neoconservative literature, some of the finest of which appears in this book.

If these essays will introduce the reader to a new and cogent world of economic discourse, they will serve a valuable purpose. Evangelicalism will be the richer if it will add to its bookshelf the works of Paul Johnson, Michael Novak, Warren Brookes, P. T. Bauer, Thomas Sowell, R. Emmett Tyrrell, Jr. and other presently less well known in the evangelical hinterlands than Sider, Campolo, Wallis, and company. Ideas have consequences, and the ideas in this book may, if read widely enough, begin a process by which some very bad ideology is replaced with a truer, more lucid vision of the world.

Roman Catholics have reason to take heart. Authors such as Michael Novak and Paul Johnson, to name but two neoconservative Catholic writers, represent some of the most farsighted, clear-thinking people who are expressing ideas in the area of economics, politics, and history. In the evangelical world Ronald Nash, Herbert Schlossberg, Lloyd Billingsley, and others are making tremendous contributions. The point, therefore, as anyone who reads these essays will see, is not that there is no alternative to fashionable socialism. Rather, the point is will we listen, learn, act?

No economic plan, solution, or type of political arrangement will ever be perfect. Yet, having accepted man's fallen state as the only natural limit to the possibilities of man's creativity, we must then look about us and decide on the basis of evidence, not ideology, what economic systems presently and realistically available best provide for the needs of most people. Not just in one area, but in all areas, from free speech to the price of oatmeal. From the diversity represented in art galleries and movie theaters to the state of farm technology. From the freedom of worship of the most obscure sect to individual mobility.

Given the fact that individuals long for freedom and at the same time want a certain measure of economic security, no system has performed better in this century or any other than the American free enterprise system. It has had its casualties and lapses, but unlike the Socialistic collectivized systems of Eastern Europe, Russia, or China, it helps a much greater number of people than it hurts, allows freedom which is the creative basis of all wealth, and has provided and still does provide for the basic needs of a massive, growing, and vibrant population.

Free enterprise in countries lacking abundant natural resources, such as Switzerland and Japan, has also produced wealth and prosperity. Clearly the economic and political system of a country itself produces wealth or poverty, and not natural resources, a colonial past, or any other factor. Holland, for instance, has a higher population density than India, and yet no one regards Holland as a Third World nation. The most densely populated areas of the earth—Singapore, Japan, Hong Kong, and Holland—all prove that population density itself does not either make or break a nation—it is the economic system within that nation. Even if imposed or copied, the Judeo-Christian tradition of personal autonomy and freedom, hard work, and the right to invest and reap rewards from one's investment, with or without natural resources, will bear fruit.

The reverse is also true. The economic growth and prosperity of a nation with vast natural resources, a low population density, and plenty of agricultural reserves may be slowed or irreparably damaged by a long enough dose of Socialist claptrap. Many of the formerly prosperous African nations prove this. The stories of Uganda, Ghana, and more recently Zimbabwe come to mind. State interference can take a country full of minerals, fertile lands, and a hard-working population and reduce it to impoverishment. Yet freedom, free enterprise, and capitalism will enrich people with far less ideal natural surroundings. It is ideas and beliefs which finally determine the health and prosperity of a nation.

At the end of the twentieth century, as we look back over a seventy-year Socialist experiment and an equal period of capitalist Western prosperity, one thing becomes clear. Economic freedom is not a superfluous footnote to other freedoms, but a prerequisite to the existence of all other freedoms. Even liberal Sweden attests to this. As the years have gone by, Sweden's coercive Socialist economic policies have increasingly spilled over into other areas to the point that civil liberties of all kinds are threatened. Religious freedom, educational freedom, and the freedom to raise one's children according to one's own beliefs have in fact been lost to an extent that would shock an average American. Human planning and social engineering on a grand scale is a virus that will totally consume its host before the virus itself dies off.

The lesson of the twentieth century is that those whom we should fear most are those with the best intentions. Dictators come and go, but utopian ideology grows more and more virulent and destructive. Capitalism is no better or worse than the citizens who employ it as a system of commerce. Socialism, on the other hand, is always worse as a system than the collective sum of its people. Human beings deserve better than the endless gray and dreary grindstone to which Socialistic systems harness people. Creativity, freedom, growth, beauty, and the use of one's talents have a legitimate and crucial role, even in a fallen world.

Franky Schaeffer
1985

PART ONE: IN DEFENSE OF FREE ENTERPRISE: HOW FREEDOM PRODUCES PROSPERITY

ONE

The Enthusiasm
for Spending

R. EMMETT TYRRELL, JR.

Snicker at the Liberal if you will, but when it comes to economics he has been right about affluence. It is gruesome. Going back to Biblical times, fastidious observers of humanity have been familiar with its morbid capacities, and today anyone of average intellect who has given the subject any thought or, say, been imprisoned *à table* with the pretty daughter of the twelfth Earl of Blavidshire comes to suspect affluence's meretricious facade. Making money is an adventure; but being surrounded with the stuff is a malaise, which must be treated with an appropriate remedy lest the patient be overcome by idiocy.

In practice, affluence is second and third helpings of Beef Wellington when one would suffice. It is not one bottle of very good Bordeaux but several, and soon you are mistaking the waiter for the chef and then the washroom attendant for the newly promoted waiter. After the cognac you are boozily inviting the bewildered fellow home to admire your cheese vault. If he has his wits about him he will take you up on it; it is an easy way for a washroom attendant to lay hands on a nice stock of Port du Salut plus, perhaps, a silver setting or two. Riches cultivate their own ruin, leaving the fat cat crapulent and besotted. Let us give the Liberals their due: they have been aware of this for decades while the evangels of free enterprise have, to their discredit, usually ignored it.

R. EMMETT TYRRELL, JR. is founder and editor of *The American Spectator*, a creative, entertaining, and thought-provoking newspaper. He is also a syndicated columnist for King Features who appears regularly in *The Washington Post*. He also writes frequently for other journals such as *Commentary, National Review*, and *Harper's*. In 1979, *Time* magazine named him one of fifty future leaders of America. His books include *Public Nuisances* and, as editor, *The Future That Doesn't Work: Social Democracy's Failures in Britain* and *The Liberal Crack-up* (Simon & Schuster, 1984), from which the following chapter is taken.

Alas, in recent decades the Liberals have shown that they themselves are not free of the curse. These have been palmy times for them in and about the public sector, and many have become as unlovely as any bedizened rock-and-roll impresario. Clearly, Mammon fetched them. In fact Mammon sozzled them. In the 1970s they lost all sense of how economies work and how wealth is produced. Their tampering with the economy grew wild and extravagant. No industry was left unregulated, no group unsubsidized. To review a sampling of their economic pronunciamentos and reckless reforms is to witness the high jinks of a mob of happy drunks, all oblivious to the source of the riches in which they soaked. They seemed to think that wealth was the result of government distribution. They spoke of jobs as a matter of human rights and of work as an ignominy to be borne by no man. They harangued affluence as lustily as ever, but the affluence they harangued was always the affluence of others, particularly the affluence of the bourgeoisie.

The Liberals in their rush to vet affluence had dangerously underrated its toxicity. It is more horrible than these experts had estimated. It did the experts in.

Contrary to their welfarist notions, one cannot simply hand wealth over to the poor. To begin with, peremptorily grabbing it from the affluent imperils political liberty, discourages productivity, and destroys knowledge—to wit: the investment and entrepreneurial knowledge of those whose wealth is being grabbed; and bear in mind that this knowledge is at least one source of social progress. Then too, giving it to the poor is frequently as ruinous to them as a vast inheritance is to a prodigal youth. With depressing regularity the Liberals' welfare programs have actually enfeebled the poor and beguiled the working poor into indolence. Finally, doling out wealth even debauches the doler. It left the Liberals suffering advanced megalomania. From 1960 to 1980 the Liberals had increased transfer payments to the poor by $187.2 billion in 1980 dollars, yet their labors gave them no comfort; and their jeremiads on the poor's behalf grew nearly hysterical. By the early 1980s, having seen welfare's slice of the federal budget increase by nearly 100 percent,[1] they were bawling as though the poor were in worse condition than ever before. One could not argue them out of their gloom. As in so many other matters, the New Age Liberals had by this time become fanatics.

Affluence—only a handful of Medicis and Mellons, Rockefellers and Rothschilds have ever known how to handle the stuff. The Liberals of the New Age botched it totally, and by the late 1970s, as they uttered their last tantras to "small-is-beautiful" and "an era of limits," and as they heaved up their final reforms, it was apparent that they had changed radically. No longer were they mere critics of unfettered capitalism. Now they hated capitalism. Imagine a Medici loathing commerce or a Mellon hating banks. The Liberals hated both. In large numbers they became socialists by process of elimination. Socialism was the only economic system that did not set their blood to boiling.

In their fantasies they saw the poor as enduringly noble, competent, and—so one deduces from their twaddle—would-be millionaires were it not for the ceaseless oppressions of those brutes who had become millionaries first. The poor, in fact, became gods. Producers of wealth became society's enemies. In a fantasy that had grown for more than a decade, consumers became the human equivalent of baby seals.

In mild form the fantasy was simple consumerism: a sedate, self-serving delusion portraying all who engage in commerce as suspected swindlers and poisoners; the rest of us are consumers, gullible and almost destitute; over us all presides the Liberal, the consumer*ist*, who warily patrols every act of commerce. It was a very public-spirited delusion.

Its more virulent form, however, was not so benign, for it left its victims nearly violent and given to diabolizing capitalism with an amazing passion, the kind that transforms the gentle features of a Jane Fonda into armament. Suddenly she is a shouter of the "Internationale," a champion of the down-and-out, an unremitting opponent of Little Lord Fauntleroy and all his damn fripperies. Not all New Age Liberals became out-and-out socialists. When Dr. John Kenneth Galbraith, Harvard's millionaire economics journalist, made his historic acknowledgment, he was in the bold minority. The rest were tacit socialists, allowing them to be at one with him in *vivre à droite et voter à gauche*.

New Age Liberals ceased to view capitalism as a medium for exchanging goods and services. Rather they saw it in terms of depravities, fiends, and innocent victims—that is to say, in terms comprehensible to small children or to believers of the Marxist sciences. The sensible remonstrances the Liberals of yesteryear had borne against capitalism's excesses gave way in the 1970s to frightening *pensées* such as Harvard's Dr. Stephen Marglin served up in *The Saturday Review:* "War and poverty; imperialism and subversion of the political system; racism and sexism; destruction of the community and environment. Each and every one of these social ills is used by capitalists to maintain their hegemony. Is the price too high? More and more people are coming to think so."[2]

Were more and more people truly coming to this position? Was it the end of the line for the Chamber of Commerce, Rotary, and the Giant Corporation? If so, it was a curious way to end a dialectic, even a Marxist dialectic. About the time Dr. Marglin tapped out his grim judgment, capitalists were beginning to swarm all over the Republic. By the early 1980s venture-capital funds were booming at an unprecedented rate, and business starts hit a record pace—nearly 600,000 per year for 1981 and 1982.[3]

Even before Dr. Marglin's announcement, America was in the midst of its most apolaustic swirl since the 1920s. Despite episodic recession and inflation, almost all Americans were conspicuous consumers, even the poor of Liberal legend. America's poor lived more prosperously than all the middle classes of the socialist Third World, or even the Communist world. In fact many of America's poor were quite fat.[4] Properly dressed and shaven many could pass for German bankers or Dutch clergymen, though they had more leisure time. The rotundity of many of America's poor is an embarrassing detail for our welfarists; and if they refer to it at all they cite it as evidence of improper nutrition, which to their minds is as much a concomitant of capitalism as pollution and sexism.

As for the nonpoor, millions of them were pothering exuberantly in shopping malls, department stores, and boutiques—wherever capitalism displayed its garish wares. If they shared Dr. Marglin's premonitions, they betrayed no sign of it, and why should they? Even in times of economic unease they had an abundance of cash, which they willingly spent.

Americans were consuming rising percentages of their discretionary incomes on goods and services that in most societies would be considered luxuries and in some, miracles. Many Americans freely paid high prices for goods bearing esteemed logos. "Designers" put their marks on everything from automobiles to chocolates, and men and women from every walk of life paid top dollar to have the signature of one of these tenth-rate Michelangelos appear on their bedenimed rumps. Now, there was the mark of a happy commercial transaction! Yet the socialist dithyrambs of the New Age would not subside: "Capitalism kills. It is not just a matter of imperialistic wars or the treatment of human labor as expendable commodity. It is so vastly mistaken a way to organize human behavior that its cancerous costs are almost as great for the higher classes as for the lower," declared Dr. Hugh Drummond in another version of the hoary theme.[5] On the other hand, few who believed this tosh lived like stern Maoists or even like that abstemious old warhorse of American socialism, Norman Thomas. It is a mark of the corruption of the age—widely noted and never disputed—that most of capitalism's hostile forces would not turn their backs on Gucci or Pucci or a nice summer home on Martha's Vineyard, somewhere to get away from the pollution, sexism, and general tackiness of Capitalist America.

Though the anti-capitalist diatribes with their doomsday vaticinations were as incomprehensible to most Americans as the orphic gibbers of faith healers, they were hardly unfamiliar. Wherever the views of the New Age held sway, denigratory images of capitalism and business became dominant. This was particularly true in Hollywood, California.

In an evaluation of prime-time television drama from the 1979-1980 season, the Media Institute, a private Washington, D.C., research group, found that "Two out of three businessmen are portrayed as criminal, evil, greedy, or foolish; almost one-half of all work activities performed by businessmen involve illegal acts; most big businessmen are portrayed as criminals; and television almost never portrays business as a socially or economically useful activity."[6] Now, here is a tantalizing irregularity for you. Increasingly it had become *de mauvais goût* to utter any irreverence whatsoever against one's fellow American, no matter how absurd or unappealing he might be. America's high-minded pursuit of justice for all and prejudice toward none had swollen into a vast sentimentality, a phony scrupulosity against slighting the members of any group—neither the fat nor the deviant, the lazy nor the stupid. No one's vices or foibles were to be scoffed at or even noted. This scrupulosity was observed with particular intensity by the Liberals of the New Age, and naturally they were soon strangling on pent-up contempt. When they discovered that the money-makers and the moneyed were exempt from the sentimental niceties, they were greatly relieved, and they had at them with utmost fury. The idealists in the entertainment and intellectual industries were particularly effective, for they are very imaginative and arty. In fact, they showed a flair for invidious stereotyping not seen on these shores since the Renaissance days of the Ku Kluxers.

The comparison is based on scholarly research. Benjamin J. Stein, whose pioneering anthropological studies of America's entertainment capital meet the highest standards of social science, has discovered in Hollywood a state of mind surprisingly reminiscent of the 1920s Ku Kluxian *intellectuel* cerebrating in a hill-jack metropolis hundreds of miles from Eastern bankers, Jews, Catholics, and other frightening caballers. Dr. Stein's *The View from Sunset Boulevard* has preserved dozens of Hollywood *philosophes'* thoughts on such dark mysteries as capitalism, banking, and general commerce. All are right out of jerkwater America. Among the writers, producers, and directors interviewed by Dr. Stein, many believe business is in cahoots with the Pentagon. Others see connections with the Mafia. Still others believe in possibilities so hellish that they cannot even be portrayed on film. Yet these yahoos gladly earn hundreds of thousands, often millions, of dollars annually, and with no pangs of conscience they spend them on all the joys the capitalists can produce—or does one think that they buy their goods and services from some socialist paradise? Come, come, these clowns are the most avid conspicuous consumers in the Republic. I was once trapped in an airplane with a pigsty of them en route to the Cannes film festival. The racket of junk jewelry banging against junk jewelry, the stench of horrid perfumes and colognes, the idiot yakking—all were enough to make a civilized traveler beg for a parachute; and, as Dr. Stein observes, practically every Hollywood genius believes that those who produce the luxuries that he adores are Fagins.

The denigration of the businessman takes on an aura of special absurdity when one recalls that in the 1970s the businessman, though hounded by a swelling crowd of government marplots, developed and marketed products that revolutionized our lives, adding immeasurably to our pleasure and productiveness. What is more, all major media were ravenous for heroes to celebrate. Why not whoop it up for a few score entrepreneurs to go along with all those actors, singers, athletes, models, human guinea pigs, and victims of disaster and disease? The burgeoning communications industry and the burgeoning public relations industry combined to serve our natural nosiness and make celebrity a national pastime. Magazines were founded to celebrate the celebrated. Newspapers reported their doings with high seriousness. Television and radio devoted a huge amount of time to talking with them and about them. Yet no one ever thought to celebrate the developers and marketers of the semiconductor, the microchip, the drugs such as antibiotics, painkillers, and promising antivirals.

We were living through the first stages of celebrity's golden age, yet the denigration of the business ran *pari passu* with the solemnizing of two-legged nihilities and occasionally of scoundrels. Unlike sport's golden age in the 1920s, when the accomplishments of the athletes were genuine, the accomplishments of 1970s celebrities were mostly in the realm of public relations. "Celebrity is now a substitute for fame," Michael Novak noted in the early 1980s. "The latter is earned by extraordinary achievement. The former is manufactured by freakiness."[7] Wit was lost in this world, as were all the higher forms of intelligence. In fact intelligence could be one's undoing, for it might bring agitation to the simpletons who composed the age of celebrity's hard-core audience.

In the golden age of celebrity, vacuous mannequins like

Bianca Jagger or Brooke Shields were photographed and quoted and asked to make special appearances merely because at some happy moment earlier on they had been photographed and quoted and asked to make a special appearance. How often was Robert Noyce photographed and quoted and asked to make special appearances? He was the major developer of the microchip, which was not so much held against him as the fact that he actually made a bundle on this little discovery. In the golden age of celebrity the only acceptable way to earn a fortune was through sports or entertainment or grotesquerie.

Now, one need hold no romantic illusions about the capitalists to reject this image of them as paradigmatic fiends. Doubtless there are businessmen who are rascals and worse. Surely many are dunces and philistines. I do not doubt for a minute that the average chief executive when he comes home at night removes his pants and spends the rest of the evening watching television in his undershorts; but certainly the average businessman is a better sort of fellow than the scoundrel portrayed on the tube, and probably he is a better sort than the Hollywood *philosophe* who believes that socialist hooey about capitalism but lives a life awash in Mammon's pleasures. Such hypocrites consider wealth evil but loll in it anyway. It is a rare businessman who takes his profits and scorns profit-taking. Those who do very likely work in the entertainment business. The industry has never been esteemed for its business ethics.

In the 1970s the socialist critique of capitalism gained a powerful purchase on the minds of many and for a perfectly understandable reason: capitalism is almost wholly absorbed with economics; socialism has hardly anything to do with economics. Its concern is drama.

Economics is, as they say, a dismal science. Economists and an alarming number of capitalists give themselves over to such tiresome stuff as interest rates, productivity rates, exchange rates, prices, and profits. Only these last two items divert the true-blue socialist. The other stuff puts him to sleep. He lives for action and inspiration, preferably religious inspiration. Socialism is one of the longest-playing religious soap operas in history, with bankers and bosses enslaving and impoverishing the rest of us, compassion and sweetness struggling against greed and brute force, good against evil. If socialism were merely an economic system, it would long ago have been heaved aside to be replaced by barter, hunting-and-gathering, or some other more advanced economic system not so given to socialism's shoddy merchandise, shortages, and economic stagnation. If it were only a political system, it would have been dumped as a fossil on the order of feudalism, for its record of coercion, bellicosity, and brutal oligarchy is well known. But socialism is art, the art of self-delusion.

It is quite as misleading to speak of socialist economics as it is to speak of chiropractic science. The true socialist is not an economist but a storyteller, often a gifted storyteller but nothing more. Not one has ever been able to massage socialism into uttering anything that is true about economics or anything else. The most memorable of the socialist gogues remains Dr. Marx, and his contribution to knowledge is not in economics but in warfare. He provided men with a compelling new rationale for killing each other off, and since his passing more people have been slaughtered in his name than in the names of Allah or Jesus.

The socialist theory is a fable. The socialist reality is a very uncomfortable place to live: political tyrants having replaced the bosses of yore; coercion having vanquished liberty; shortages and want having replaced economic growth and self-reliance. Greed remains, but long ago it was surpassed in popularity and maliciousness by envy. Where there once was optimism there is now pessimism. The citizen who once hoped to be an entrepreneur now queues up like everyone else for a new pair of socks or a feast of moldy state-issued potatoes.

Wherever socialism has slithered into power there is either unspeakable cruelty or slow economic decomposition. Russia, the Socialist Motherland, offers its citizens both. The decrepitude of Britain, upon whose wealth the sun could not set four decades ago, is evidence of socialism's knack for despoiling an economy. More recently we have witnessed the amazing impoverishment of Germany under the Social Democrats and the almost instantaneous economic collapse of France's theretofore robust economy under François Mitterrand's Socialists.

By the late 1970s all the liberal welfare states of Europe were in a very dilapidated state. The most advanced of them, Sweden, had an average marginal tax rate of more than 60 percent and a deficit at 12 percent of GNP and rising. All the EEC nations combined exited the 1970s having created no more jobs than they had had at the beginning of the decade, and Germany under the Social Democrats ended 1980 with 2 percent less employment than in 1970.[8] Millions of immigrant laborers were now being booted from these progressive domains. Imagine if the United States treated its immigrants in this way! Imagine if we had the police power to search out and deport groups of people! In a socialist paradise, even a liberal socialist paradise, there is that kind of control.

The United States has suffered heavy bombardment from socialist critics for its economic problems, its low tax base, its rampant capitalism, and its renowned poverty class. Yet the United

States, as *The Wall Street Journal* has delighted in informing us, has been able to establish a poverty line that is perhaps $1,000 above the median family income of the Soviet Union, and only approximately 6 percent of the American population was below that line in 1980.[9] During the 1970s the U.S. economy produced a net gain of 19 million jobs, increasing employment five times as fast as the French economy, and three times as fast as Japan's. As George Gilder points out, "While the U.S. economy absorbed a baby-boom population bulge that did not occur in Europe, and accommodated an estimated 12 million legal and illegal immigrants, the E.E.C. countries stopped the influx of overseas workers and payed hundreds of thousands to return to their homelands."[10]

So obvious are socialism's economic and political failures that at times even some of the faithful are moved to doubt, and when the dubiety steals in there can be eloquence. Such an instance came sometime in 1979 when one of Dr. Marx's most faithful Yank disciples, Sidney Lens, reviewed the good-government policies of the socialist camp and lamented: "How can one justify, for instance, the forced migrations in People's Kampuchea (Cambodia)? . . . Or consider the current conflict between Kampuchea and Vietnam: How is it possible for two *socialist* states to wage war against each other? . . . Worse still, how can *socialist* China regard *socialist* Russia as its chief enemy and insist, in its domestic and foreign propaganda, war with the Soviet Union is 'inevitable'? . . . As for the Soviet Union, how can one explain its suppression of free speech, free press, and free trade unions years after the revolution? Perhaps a socialist regime must deny democratic prerogatives when it comes to power in order to forestall a counterrevolution—but for *sixty-one years?* . . . I wish I could resolve these contradictions for myself in simple, unambiguous terms." Yet the illumination is usually brief. "Like most people," Dr. Lens went on, "I would like to cherish the vision of a beautiful tomorrow. I would like to hold and share the conviction that there *is* a better alternative—for if socialism is not the alternative to the militarism, repression, instability, and injustice of capitalism, what is?"[11]

Militarism? Repression? Instability? Injustice? Is Dr. Lens talking about us? I fear that he is. We live in a world that has witnessed six decades of Soviet *gulags*, show trials, pogroms, despotism, and economic privation plus bellicosity on a worldwide scale. Every day enormities are committed against ordinary people in socialist and Third World lands that equal those reported in the Old Testament; yet in the New Age, capitalism's critics look across America and harangue ghosts ascertainable only through Marxist calculations. How does one account for it?

I return to affluence. The Sidney Lenses of America think of capitalism and begin hallucinating, their vision blurred by wild dollar signs undulating and running amuck just beyond their grasp, ticky-tacky homes carpeting the land as far as the eye can see, mounds of cheap manufactured products glistening in the sunshine. It is a fevered vision and a positively demented way to view an economic system; but twenty years of having things pretty much their own way—every reform, every regulation—and still not seeing heaven on earth left the New Age Liberals in this sorry state. Reality repulsed them. Complexity and uncertainty daunted them. They yearned for the happy tales of socialism where after the last titanic battle against the captains of industry a tidy little world would be secured free of militarism, repression, instability, and injustice.

The difference between socialism and capitalism is the difference between fiction and history: the one is a story invented irrespective of truth; the other follows closely the way men and women live. Socialism is a way of life that has never been satisfactorily lived, outside a few choice monasteries and communes. Capitalism is a way of life that grew out of the actions of tens of thousands of ordinary people availing themselves of the exhilarating intellectual currents of the eighteenth century, and has been successfully lived for generations, much to our enrichment and happiness.

One is distracted from the capitalist reality when one fastens upon the legendary dollar sign, and one is diverted from the socialist reality when one fastens on socialism's ideals. The socialist ideals are alluring. Peace, prosperity, cooperation, equality, community, freedom—it is a honeyed vision. Yet is it a reality in any of those gray lands under Dr. Marx's suzerainty? Let us not belabor the subject, but let us be bold and forthright. Prolonged observations of the species *Homo sapiens* suggests that the only places on this orb where one will see even an approximation of these socialist ideals are those few voluptuous lands where there is capitalism. The thought does occur that if the socialist were really serious about his lovely vision, well, he would be a capitalist.

There is more peace, freedom, prosperity, dignity, and even equality in Dubuque, Iowa, than in Moscow or Peking or poor Mitterrand's Paris. Moreover, the early analysts of capitalism foresaw as much. Unlike the dyspeptic Dr. Marx, who retired from the hurly-burly to the reading room of the British Museum, there to dream up a world that never was, thinkers like Adam Smith reported on an emerging world. Two centuries later the expectations of capitalism's early analysts have proved infinitely more accurate than Dr. Marx's prophecies for the socialist fairy tale.

Montesquieu saw that commercial activity would ameliorate

men's "destructive prejudices." From a continent recently torn by religious wars and the squabbles of pompous aristocrats, the French philosopher observed that commerce "polishes and softens barbaric morals." A long line of distinguished men of affairs followed, from James Madison to the twentieth-century secretary of state Cordell Hull, all sharing and championing Montesquieu's shrewd insight that "the spirit of commerce unites nations."[12] Doubtless the officers and customers of many modern-day multinational corporations would agree. Commerce was expected to usher in a more peaceful world because, as Thomas Paine could see, it "diminishes the spirit both of patriotism and military defense."[13] Beyond peace, commerce was seen as encouraging freedom, prosperity, and diversity not only for aristocrats but also for common folk. As Adam Smith noted, before the rise of capitalism men had "lived almost in a continual state of war with their neighbors, and of servile dependency upon their supervisors," but with the growth of capitalism men might experience "order and good government and, with them, the liberty and security of individuals."[14]

Capitalism was a new order brought into existence not by the clubs of thugs and the calculations of dreamers, but by ordinary men aided by a growing sense of personal liberty. Always, economic freedom had to overcome the resistance of the state, save in the whelp Republic across the Atlantic. In no other country was the new order given more encouragement than in early America, where the founding fathers had eloquently argued the merits of freedom and commerce. Tocqueville was particularly mindful of capitalism's merits, and when he toured America in the 1830s he was stimulated by what he saw: free citizens "calculating and weighing and computing" as they shoved back a wilderness to transform the land into a civilization where even the meanest would someday live in unprecedented comfort and freedom.[15]

Today's haranguers for peace, freedom, prosperity, and equality, then, have chosen fantasy over reality. They exalt Dr. Marx over Adam Smith and the founding fathers. They venerate a crank, who dreamed of a world that never was and never was to be, over men who studied and celebrated a real world, a world progressing toward the very desiderata they claim to admire. Today's socialist is not greatly different, in truth, from the reactionary. The latter idealizes a past that never was. The former idealizes a future that never will be. Both have an unscotchable and irrational yearning to escape the present or to destroy it.

Capitalism has fulfilled its analysts' expectations. It has created a world with a higher percentage of self-reliant, competent individuals than history has ever seen before. It has encouraged the rule of law and the enlargement of personal freedom by putting limits on both the bully and the state. It has allowed an unparalleled growth in the world's wealth, a blurring of class distinctions, and ever more comfort and opportunity for the poor. Of all the systems in history, only capitalism has allowed the ceaseless and relatively peaceful movement of huge numbers of people rising from poverty or falling from affluence. Capitalism is unsurpassed in allowing citizens to realize their potential. If some come out poor and others rich, at least the poor under capitalism are less poor than under other systems.

Liberating the competent to create wealth so that all benefit from the competent's industry was by the late 1970s so obviously a superior economic system that its New Age opponents could argue against it neither rationally nor on economic grounds. Thus they led jeers against it—*"trickle-down theory, trickle-down theory,"* they taunted. Did they believe that things trickle up? I believe they did. Many solemnly asserted that the proper prescription for economic vigor was to give wealth to the poor, thus increasing "purchasing power" and social justice. Yet where does wealth come from in the first place?

In the New Age the critics of capitalism never could explain how wealth is created. Most simply avoided the matter, taking the prosperity of America for granted. Others believed that wealth was stolen goods taken from the noble poor—else how did the poor become poor? Neither group confronted the hard little truth that wealth is created by work and faith, and that without work life is not only penurious but also tedious and barbaric. Any diligent observer of our species knows the truth of this. How many times have you encountered men and women who live intellectually, morally, and culturally at the level of animals? Only when one comes to the topic of their occupations does one begin to see a human being. It is by selling paint or by bringing the kids to basketball practice that these people begin to experience humanity. Here they learn about others and they learn the important things about themselves. Moreover, they avoid mischief. Dr. Freud understood that work is the best therapy. How he discovered this I cannot say, but he did, and it put him a step ahead of the economic wisdom of the New Age.

Ignorant of the value of work and of the source of wealth, the New Age critic of capitalism employed flamboyant rhetorical flourishes to lay practically all society's shortcomings to capitalism. "The efficient rapacity of our raider-rulers," Professor Garry Wills wrote in *The New York Review of Books,* "has made consumption expand at a dizzying rate, equaled only by the rate at which resources diminish—air, earth, fuel, and water."[16] Close textual analysis suggests that Dr. Wills is one of those New Age adepts who believe that capitalism is theft and presumably that a comfortable middle-class life is the natural condition for all if only the greed of the Business Roundtable could be thwarted. A research expedition through this nation's hoosegows, however, establishes clearly that a very high percentage of our prison population is composed of those who have never committed their first capitalist act. In fact, many prison inmates have performed no productive work whatsoever that is not *malum prohibitum*. Most of our nation's jailbirds share the socialists' delusions about how wealth is amassed, and I for one find it vastly reassuring to know that you can still be sentenced to ten-to-twenty for taking the socialists seriously. No wonder so many believers in the New Age have had a special solicitude for those behind bars. But all would have been better off had they realized that the surest path to riches is steady work and law-abidingness.

There is no doubt that beyond the prison bars, out in America where men sweat after dollars and perquisites, there is mischief and mayhem, but the fault lies not with the economic system that as aforementioned has encouraged law-abiding behavior and peaceful commerce. There is only so much an economic system can do for a society. Neither capitalism nor socialism is a substitute for higher cultural and moral commitments. As Michael Novak has asserted, "The commercial virtues are not . . . sufficient to their own defense. A commercial system needs taming and correction by a moral-cultural system independent of commerce. At critical points, it also requires taming and correction by the political system and the state. The founding fathers did not imagine that the institutions of religion, humanism, and the arts would ever lose their indispensable role. They did not imagine that the state would wither away. Each of the three systems needs the other. Yet they did understand that an economic system without profit is merely spinning its wheels, providing neither for the unmet needs of the poor nor for progress."[17] George Gilder goes further.

In the 1980s Gilder arrived at captalism's most subtle champion and possibly its most ardent. He endorsed what Walter Lippmann had written during the Great Depression in *The Good Society:* "for the first time in human history" there was a system that gave men "a way of producing wealth in which the good fortune of others multiplied their own," and in which "for the first time men could conceive a social order in which the ancient moral aspiration of liberty, fraternity, and equality was consistent with the abolition of poverty and the increase of wealth." Sounding as Gilder would fifty years later, Lippmann went on: "Until the division of labor had begun to make men dependent on the free collaboration of other men, the worldly policy was to be predatory. The claims of the spirit were otherworldly. So it was not until the industrial revolution had altered the traditional mode of life that the vista was opened at the end of which men could see the possibility of the Good Society on this earth. At long last the ancient schism between the world and the spirit, between self interest and disinterestedness, was potentially closed."[18]

The New Age critics' preoccupation with other people's wealth is deadly to an understanding of capitalism. What really matters is the capitalist's act of creation. It is the source of growth and riches. The capitalist, Gilder tells us, begins with a blank canvas and creates. Most who work in this world do so with the expectation of contractual remuneration, but the capitalist's expectation is based solely on faith. The capitalist is a bold, adventuresome, self-reliant citizen who looks ahead trying to ascertain what his fellow citizens' needs will be in the future. Economists, in the main, believe in *Homo economicus*, man as a slug moved to action solely by financial inducement. It is as gross a generalization as the belief that all redheads are hot-tempered or all fat people are jolly. Some men will roost under their favorite shade tree no matter what the economic inducement. Others will work until they have attained a certain level of material comfort and no more. Yet there are those whose restless gropings never end. This, Gilder tells us, is the true capitalist. Taking on Adam Smith's theory of the invisible hand, Gilder argues that the psychology of the eternal groper or tinkerer is more fundamental to economic growth than the existence of markets; only capitalism allows this fellow his opportunity to bring us material progress. Gilder's argument is audacious and perplexing, especially for the grim socialist.

Parting company even with most champions of capitalism, Gilder believes that capitalism is an eminently moral system. "Capitalism begins with giving," says Gilder in a buoyant humor. "Not from greed, avarice, or even 'self-love' can one expect the rewards of commerce, but from a spirit closely akin to altruism, a regard for the needs of others, a benevolent, outgoing, and courageous temper of mind. Such a universal trait as self-interest—altogether as prevalent in any socialist backwater or deadening bureaucracy as in the realms of great enterprise—will reveal virtually nothing of the rare sources of riches in human society. Not taking and consuming, but giving, risking, and creating are the characteristic roles of the capitalist, the key producer of the wealth of nations. . . ." Gilder asserts that capitalists are chiefly stimulated not by the desire to consume or to make pigs of themselves, "but by the freedom and power to consummate their entrepreneurial ideas." Even more important than hedonism or economic inducement, Gilder believes, is the capitalist's drive to tinker with the world and try to understand it. Here, he says, is the source of wealth, which is to say "value defined by others."[19]

Is Gilder right? I have no doubt that he is right to take on the notion of *Homo economicus*. As for the capitalist's altruism, I reserve judgment. It certainly is a lovely thought. For centuries those who have been most proficient at creating wealth have endured some of mankind's bloodiest atrocities. Wealth maddens the mob. It maddened the Nazis against Jews and the Soviets against Kulaks and Jews. It accounted for the slaughter of the Ibo in Nigeria, and the deaths of more than a million overseas Chinese in Indonesia. The record is long and horrible. Yet always the slaughter is undertaken for high ideals. If there is any truth in Gilder's claim about the capitalist's altruism, the greed and envy of others stands revealed as even stupider and uglier than it appears.

NOTES

1. *Survey of Current Business*, July 1961, p. 16, and *Survey of Current Business*, July 1981, p. 15.
2. "Embattled America: The Experts Polled," *Saturday Review*, July 7, 1979, p. 34.
3. George Gilder, "The Numbers Tell a Supply-Side Story," the *Wall Street Journal*, June 13, 1983, p. 22.
4. See George G. Graham in "Oversight on Nutritional Status of Low Income Americans in the 1980s," testimony delivered at a hearing before the Subcommittee on Nutrition of the Committee of Agriculture, Nutrition, and Forestry, United States Senate, April 6, 1983, p. 102.
5. Hugh Drummond, "Dr. Drummond Loses His Patience," *Mother Jones*, August 1977.
6. The Media Institute, *Crooks, Conmen and Clowns: Businessmen in TV Entertainment*, ed. Leonard J. Theberge (Washington: The Media Institute, 1981), p. vi.
7. Michael Novak, *Confessions of a Catholic* (San Francisco: Harper & Row, 1983), p. 101.
8. George Gilder, "A Supply-Side Economics of the Left," *The Public Interest*, Summer 1983, pp. 36, 38.
9. George Gilder, *Wealth and Poverty* (New York: Basic Books, 1981), p. 12.
10. *Op. cit.*, Gilder, "A Supply-Side Economics of the Left," p. 37.
11. Sidney Lens, "On the Contradiction of Socialism," *The Progressive*, March 1979, p. 24.
12. Baron de Montesquieu, *The Spirit of the Laws*, trans. Thomas Nugent (New York: Hafner Publishing Company, 1966), p. 316.
13. Thomas Paine, *The Complete Writings of Thomas Paine*, ed. Philip S. Foner (New York: Citadel Press, 1945), p. 36.
14. Adam Smith, *The Wealth of Nations* (New York: P. F. Collier & Son, 1905), II, p. 107.

15. Michael Novak, *The Spirit of Democratic Capitalism* (New York: Simon and Schuster, 1982), p. 118.
16. Garry Wills, "Carter and the End of Liberalism," *The New York Review of Books*, May 12, 1977, p. 18.
17. *Op. cit.*, Novak, *The Spirit of Democratic Capitalism*, p. 121.
18. *Op. cit.*, Gilder, *Wealth and Poverty*, p. 8.
19. George Gilder, "Capitalism Is for Givers," *The American Spectator*, February 1982, pp. 7, 9.

Goodness and the GNP

WARREN T. BROOKES

> To the masses of the Western world the news that all men are more than things was proclaimed by the Christian gospel and was celebrated in its central mysteries . . . For in the recognition that there is in each man a final essence— that is to say, an immortal soul—which only God can judge, a limit was set up on the dominion of men over men in the long ascent out of the morass of barbarism. Upon this rock they have built the rude foundations of the Good Society.
>
> Walter Lippmann

Although liberty is the supreme end of a democratic society, and fundamental to economic development, we must not naively think that more liberty and less government, alone, will solve our economic ills and produce endless wealth, nor should we be beguiled by the more extreme libertarian point of view that morality itself has nothing to do with the common wealth.

This attitude reflects a legitimate rejection of the legislated theocracy of the religious right (as well as the excessive regulations of the left), but it also reflects a failure to understand that, at its roots, economics is a metaphysical rather than a mathematical science, in which intangible spiritual values and attitudes are

---

WARREN T. BROOKES, an economic columnist for the *Boston Herald-American*, is known for his easy-to-read style of discussing complex economic issues. He also writes a weekly column, "The Economy in Mind," which appears in more than forty newspapers. It is widely read and quoted in influential circles, from the *Wall Street Journal's* editorial page to the White House. He recently published a book, also titled *The Economy in Mind*, from which the following essay is taken.

at least as important as physical assets and morale more fundamental than the money supply. Products, after all, are the assembly of qualities, and their value derives directly from the innate character and ideals of those who create them and the workmanship of those who produce them. Things are, in their final analysis, the expression of thoughts. Quality products derive from quality thoughts, shoddy products from shoddy thoughts.

Plainly, then, a national economy, like an individual business or a specific product, is the sum of the spiritual and mental qualities of its people, and its output of value will be only as strong as the values of society. There are many examples of barbaric societies which practiced the "free market" of the jungle and finally perished in the poverty of hedonism. Without the civilizing force of universal moral standards, particularly honesty, trust, self-respect, integrity, and loyalty, the marketplace quickly degenerates. A society that has no values will not produce much value; a nation whose values are declining should not be surprised at a declining economy. As Ralph Waldo Emerson postulates, "A dollar is not value, but representative of value, and, at last, of moral values."

In this present age of intense libertarianism, we can see that Epicureans and hedonists are not given to work and savings; and in our urban ghettos the freest of Huns and vandals are unlikely to produce many goods and services. It takes serious self-discipline to contribute more than we take. Our national epidemic of crime in both offices and streets is far more indicative of our economic ills than we care to admit—not merely for the direct damage that is done to victims, but for what it says about the values and the morale of a nation. Can we really expect economic revival without spiritual revival? Can economic regeneration be spawned in the soil of moral degeneration?

Take, for example, the appalling breakdown in the family over the past decade or so. Not only is the family the basic social unit, it is the most fundamental economic force in society, the key to work, consumption, savings, investment, and the whole future thrust of any nation. Yet it is also the economic force most vulnerable to deteriorating moral and spiritual values. Marriage itself is after all a moral commitment. So the continuing, ever-mounting assault on traditional family values may well be more destructive to our economic well-being as a nation than any of our faulty fiscal or monetary policies. As William Barrett argues, "The violent dissatisfaction with the prosaic and workable arrangements of society (from the family on up) that permit liberty, is part of the general spiritual sickness of modernity"; and Norman Podhoretz rightly contends, "It cannot be cured by any set of economic or political arrangements."

That was the theme of the 1981 Connecticut Mutual Life "Report on American Values in the 80's," which found that more than half of all Americans now doubt that politics or economic policies alone can solve our basic societal problems such as energy shortages, inflation, and crime; and that, more than we have suspected, Americans are seeking a new level of spiritual and religious commitment as the solution. "Bewildered by the confusion of the present, large numbers of citizens now find solace in the firm conviction of their ancestors." The Report also found that these firm convictions of religious commitment have a direct bearing on *economic* values, particularly work and family:

- "The 'most religious' Americans are more likely [than the 'least religious'] to feel a sense of dedication to their work" (97% vs. 66%).
- "The 'most religious' are more likely to find that their work contributes to society" (91% vs. 53%).
- "The 'most religious' are more likely to find their work interesting and rewarding" (92% vs. 68%).
- The 'most religious' are more likely to believe financial security can be obtained by hard work" (88% vs. 70%).
- "The 'most religious' are much more likely to say they would reconcile marital problems at all costs rather than seek divorce (60% vs. 33%).

LEADERS AND PUBLIC ON MORAL ISSUES

(in percentages)

Issues considered morally wrong	Public	Leaders	News media
Abortion	65	36	35
Homosexuality	71	42	38
Lesbianism	70	42	37
Adultery	85	71	72
Premarital sex	40	31	20
Sex before 16	71	55	54
Cohabitation before marriage	47	32	24
Pornographic movies	68	56	46
Hard drugs	84	73	66
Marijuana	57	33	22

SOURCE: *Report on American Values* (Connecticut Mutual Life Insurance Company, April 1981).

In short, the study affirms a growing public recognition that the spiritual and metaphysical are more basic to our economic progress and prosperity than the physical and political; that spiritual values are fundamental to economic values; that goodness does have to do with the GNP.

Unfortunately, the study also found that on a whole range of specific moral issues, "American leaders are substantially out of tune with the public they are supposed to represent." The moral ethic of our culture, then, is being directed, particularly in the media, by leaders of thought whose personal values are moving against the spiritual and moral currents of the public at large.

The study found that "the reemergence of America's religious strain represents far more than a recent response to national concern about Vietnam and Watergate. It symbolizes nothing less than a determined effort to revitalize American self-confidence in the face of adversity"—and, it would seem, in the face of determined opposition from the movers and shakers of American public debate and conciousness.

During the 1980 election campaign, the distinguished American political commentator David Broder told a Public Television audience, "People have the feeling that the country has lost its greatness," and he observed that "for many, the return to greatness means a return to traditional spiritual values."

More than one hundred and fifty years before, another great observer of the American scene, Alexis de Tocqueville, recognized the direct connection between this nation's economic strength and its moral ethos, when he wrote in *Democracy in America:*

I searched for America's greatness in her matchless constitution and it was not there.

I searched for America's greatness in her halls of Congress and it was not there.

I searched for America's greatness in her rich and fertile fields and teeming industrial potential and it was not there.

It was not until I went into the heartlands of America and into her churches and met the American people that I discovered what it is that makes America great.

America is great, because America is good, and if America ever ceases to be good, America will cease to be great.

Following Tocqueville's hypothesis to its logical conclusion, the current decline in this nation's economic as well as strategic strength ultimately may have more to do with a decline in our "goodness" than with the failure of specific policies or leaders.

When Moses went up Mount Sinai in search of direction out of the wilderness, he did not come back down with a road map but with a set of moral laws. The central theme of the Old Testament is that when the Hebrew people, the Children of Israel, were obedient to those Ten Commandments, they prospered and found their way. When they departed from them and "worshipped other gods" they failed, and lost their freedom. A clear moral code thus became the foundation of a great, though small, nation and, in turn, the cradle of Western civilization itself. Spiritual values were understood to be precedent to economic and social well-being.

But today most of these Ten Commandments have been regarded by an increasingly permissive and corporate society (particularly its leadership) as slightly outmoded, or at least irrelevant. Most of them are being violated more casually than ever before in our own nation's history. We now seem as a nation far more preoccupied with private sensual fantasies than with dreams of glory, far more prepared to defend the pornographers than to glorify the prophets.

Yet people ask, what do these personal moral and ethical standards have to do with the Gross National Product and a failing economy? I would answer with a number of rhetorical, metaphysical questions of my own:

- When we abandoned the gold standard in 1971, was this simply a faulty economic decision or was it an outward expression of the wholesale abandonment of traditional internal moral standards?
- Is it reasonable to expect a nation absorbed in existential self-gratification to save for the future?
- Can young people routinely "spaced out" on dope really be expected to be productive or to strive for excellence in academic or economic endeavor? Is our productivity falling prey more to "pot" than to policies?
- Is there not some definite connection between moral pollution, the miasma of white-collar crime and greed, and the physical pollution of hazardous wastes and foul air?
- Can business executives who routinely cheat on their spouses be expected not to cheat the consumer, the government, or their competitors?

- Can the 58 percent of minority children now born out of wedlock be expected to grow up to lead productive and stable economic lives when 80 percent of child abuse and teenage crime now can be traced to fatherless homes?
- Can a society where abortions have become a more and more routine form of birth control (and outnumber live births in many major cities) be expected not to throw away its natural resources, too?
- Can we expect people who "want something for nothing" in their private affairs not to get the same thing from their government in the form of inflation?
- Is the steady devaluation of our currency merely the outward expression of the steady devaluation of our lives?

I ask these questions not because I agree with those who would again tie up our nation in a strict Puritan straitjacket. Prohibition didn't work and censorship is abhorrent. Although our laws must be deeply rooted in our moral standards, it is difficult to legislate private behavior without potential totalitarian abuse. On the other hand, when we speak of our economic product, we call it "*goods* and services." We do not call it "*bads* and ripoffs"! Yet that is what it becomes if this product derives from a culture that has lost its moral moorings and its innate sense of goodness. We look at Japan and marvel at its productivity and examine its economic policies, but do we also examine the kind of strict lifestyles, disciplined family values, and work ethic that dominate most Japanese lives?

These concerns are not being raised only by Christian fundamentalists. They are troubling some of this nation's deepest non-Christian thinkers. Irving Kristol told an American Enterprise Institute Conference on "Capitalism and Socialism: A Theology Inquiry":

> Until 20 or 25 years ago, it was thought natural for liberal governments to interefere in matters pertaining to individual morality, and it was thought to be wrong for such governments to interfere too much in economic matters. We have turned these two propositions around. We now think it right for government to intervene in economic matters and wrong for government to intervene in matters of individual morality. This is the great disaster of our age. Government can be productive in interfering with morality, but it is likely to be counterproductive when it interferes with economic affairs.

It is Kristol's concern that capitalism and the free market-place, without the inspiration and moral framework provided by Judeo-Christian values, will degenerate into ugliness and repression and lose its dynamic character: "To the degree that organized religion has decayed and the attachment to the Judeo-Christian tradition has become weaker, to that degree capitalism has become uglier and less justifiable."

Today it seems self-evident that because of our decline in values, our economy is paying an enormous price in lost productivity and higher social costs—shifting from the production of "goods and services" to the promotion of "bads and ripoffs" in both our public and private sectors. Capitalism without the moral underpinning of the Decalogue and the inspiration of the Beatitudes soon degenerates into self-destructive greed.

CHRISTIANITY AND CAPITALISM

The unpleasant confrontation between Iran and the United States indicates the degree to which in this nuclear age, human warfare has been shifted from the battlefield to the mind, from the physical to the mental realm. Almost as never before, the Judeo-Christian (and mostly capitalistic) West is engaged in a warfare of ideas, not only with the forces of atheistic Communism in the Warsaw Pact nations, but also with the Islamic East.

It is not unduly pessimistic to observe that in this metaphysical arena, the West (including Israel) seems to be losing some ground and finding itself hostage to a world that is increasingly non-Jewish, non-Christian, and noncapitalistic. Superficially, we can blame this loss of leadership on the economics of energy dependence and the erosion of Western military preparedness. Yet most of us realize that dry rot within is always more hazardous than assault from without.

As virtually every public opinion poll still shows, there is also an alarming uncertainty, a malaise, among Americans as to whether there is not a fundamental conflict between our spiritual values on the one hand and our institutional economic arrangements on the other—whether, in fact, capitalism and Christianity can continue successfully to coexist. The evidence suggests that a substantial share, if not the majority, of our academic and religious leadership now believes that it cannot. In a 1981 issue of *Harvard Business Review*, Norman Podhoretz writes, "Most intellectuals have always looked upon capitalism as an evil: a sys-

tem unsound in itself and the cause of moral and spiritual depre-
dations throughout society as a whole."

It was this pervasive mental uncertainty among American
opinion-makers that the Ayatollah Khomeini exploited so skill-
fully during the hostage siege, calling on the whole nation of
Islam to wage "holy war" against what he called "the satanic
forces" of the Judeo-Christian world and its "oppressive and exploitive economic system." In the context of the abject poverty of
most of Islam today, with its gaping polarization between the
ludicrously rich and the incredibly poor, Khomeini's charges certainly had a hollow ring, coming as they did from that part of the
world which was the very last to be forced (by the West) to give
up slavery, and which still practices unconscionable religious and
intellectual persecution and mass political murder.

Yet in the context of the aggressively sensual hedonism and
crass commercialism which now drives so much of our own capitalistic system, Khomeini's attack in 1980 touched sensitive
nerves. There is, for example, little connection between the purity and simplicity of the Bethlehem babe's appearance on earth and
the merchandising madness that annually turns the U.S. Christmas season into a frenzy of frustration and robs us of much of its
potential holiness and inspiration. This is a sorry annual remind-
er that while it is true that capitalism seems to have flourished
most from the impetus of the Judeo-Christian ethic of individual
self-betterment, its economic affluence and prosperity have not
always brought spiritual well-being. Quite often it has generated
the opposite. Good Christians may become successful capitalists,
but successful capitalists are not necessarily good Christians (in
spite of what Dale Carnegie may argue).

This may explain why, in this most capitalistic of all nations, there now seems to be even more theological distrust of
capitalism than there is of atheistic socialism and, indirectly, why
no other nation in the West, except Great Britain, has more severely punished capitalism's economic lifeblood (savings and
profits) than the United States has (at least until 1981). Not
surprisingly, no other Western nation saves as little—or is experiencing slower growth in productivity.

Irving Kristol thinks this American "love-hate" relationship
with capitalism is due to the overwhelming dominance of traditional Christianity in our cultural and economic institutions:
"Orthodox Jews have never despised business, Christians have.
The act of commerce, the existence of a commercial society, has
always been a problem for Christians." The reason, Kristol contends, is that Judaism and Islam provide mankind with laws

which help them adapt to and live in an imperfect human world. Christianity, on the other hand, is more "gnostic," or prophetic, in character, calling on mankind to *change* the world we live in. "It tends to be hostile to all existing laws and all existing institutions . . . to insist that this hell in which we live, this 'unfair' world can be radically corrected."

It is this material utopianism which draws so many Christians to socialism, which seems to rest on the Christian ideal of the essential spiritual brotherhood, equality, goodness, and perfection of man, and which theorizes that it is only the iniquitous and discriminatory economic forces of capitalism that make man behave badly. Remove these forces, the Christian socialist promises, and mankind's inherent goodness will flourish in a kind of kingdom of heaven right here on earth.

Socialist experiments have always enticed Christians, from the ill-fated Brook Farm of the nineteenth century to the tragic Jonestown of 1978. Almost without exception, these experiments have foundered on the shoals of unredeemed human nature (i.e., sin) and on economic fallacies dominated by distribution, not production—fallacies that succeed only in spreading poverty, not in producing wealth. This utopianism arises from a rather superficial demand-side view both of religion (or metaphysics) and of economics. Kristol suggests that "Socialist redistribution bears some resemblance to Christian charity," but charity is no more the be-all of Christianity than distribution is the whole of economics. Charity without redemption becomes itself an expression of poverty and futility, as does distribution without production to replenish it.

Moreover, economy itself is the creation and production of *value*. Since, at its root, value is an expression of spiritual qualities with moral implications, religion, which is the teaching and promulgation of values, is intimately connected to the economy. From this perspective religion can be seen as supply-side in nature, because without a strong and flourishing value system, economic output must inevitably languish. Most religions, and especially Christianity and Judaism, also teach that a basic source of our daily supply can be found in the spiritual ideas, inspiration, and qualities of thought and character that come from a relationship to God. From this standpoint, true economy becomes the active expression of God-derived qualities in human endeavor, including the process by which we give raw matter value and purpose, and turn it into economic "goods."

Faith in the Infinite—which St. Paul calls "the substance of things hoped for"—leads directly to the Christian and Judaic teaching that giving is its own reward, since the more one gives the more one has to give. As St. Luke presents Christ's teaching, "Give, and it shall be given unto you; good measure, pressed down, and shaken together, and running over, shall men give unto your bosom. For with the same measure that ye mete withal it shall be measured to you again." The Golden Rule, actively followed, would wholly destroy both individual and collective poverty. And if everyone is busy giving (contributing and producing), then we have the ultimate underpinning for Say's law that supply generates its own demand and rewards its own effort.

Further, what we have to give, whether in our work lives or our home lives, is, in the last analysis, also qualities of thought and attitudes. Integrity, loyalty, responsibility, trustworthiness, inspiration are powerful economic and social assets in any endeavor. Yet they are not elicited simply by financial incentives. They are the product of spiritual search, self-discipline, and teaching. They are also the positive wealth which millions of religious refugees and immigrants brought with them to America. Spiritual disciplines undergirded the development of our common wealth.

Unfortunately, however, just as the nation has turned away from its first economic and libertarian principles, from supply to demand, so too has the focus of the Church shifted gradually from the teaching of faith to secular political action, from turning men to the search for metaphysical supply—the true wealth of divine ideas—to the reallocation of material demand and apparently limited material resources. Redistribution has replaced contribution as the dominant theme.

GOD AND THE WELFARE STATE

Over the past two decades, to the horror of some and the joy of others, the organized Church, Protestant, Catholic, and Jewish, has moved forthrightly into broad areas of economic, political, and social concern, as if in delayed response to Walter Raushenbush's New Social Gospel, which in its day (1917) seemed wildly radical, but today seems quaintly moderate.

It is no longer unusual to find such venerable organizations as the National Council of Churches and the U.S. Roman Catholics' Campaign for Human Development taking strong leftist stands on such controversial issues as tax reform, rent control, subsidized public housing, welfare, national health insurance, and even vertical divestiture of the oil companies.

The underlying theme of most of this activity seems to boil down to the demand-side premise that income redistribution and the fully socialized welfare state are the highest human expressions of the Judeo-Christian ethic of compassion, that distribution is in some way more Christian than production, that one (distribution) equates with compassion and the other (production) with exploitation. With all due respect to these religious leaders, at best they seem guilty of a shallow interpretation of their own Biblical teachings (not to mention economic reality), and, at worst they appear to have a strange kind of death wish, through the sacrifice of the metaphysical initiative for the frustrations of power politics.

It must be transparently clear to any thinking person that the ultimate effect of the creation of the fully socialized welfare state is not merely the destruction of human liberty (and true economy—the unfoldment of ideas), but the shift of human trust from dependence on God to dependence on the state—the exchange of the worship of Deity for the idolatry and tyranny of Leviathan.

As the theologian Peter Berger admonishes, "Whatever socialism may be as an ideal, its empirical realization removes from the scene yet another limiting factor to the power of the modern state"; and this modern state is fundamentally dangerous because it represents "the most massive concentration of power in human history." "Since the demise of Nazi Germany," he notes, "all totalitarian societies have been socialist."

Even so-called democratically socialist countries annihilate what Michael Novak calls the mediating role of the Church, as the state and its welfare programs become the repositories of an increasingly secular faith.

If religious leaders doubt this, they need only consider what has happened to the Christian Church (both Protestant and Catholic) in Great Britain's democratically socialist welfare state. In 1947, a public opinion poll showed that about 90 percent of the public claimed to believe in God. But by 1975, after 30 years of welfare-state development, another poll showed that belief in God in Britain had dropped to less than 27 percent of the population, while in the United States it had remained over 90 percent. Actual church membership and attendance, which has drifted down to 44 percent in the United States, is now down to less than 15 percent in Great Britain. The same decline has taken place in socialist Sweden, where religion has almost ceased to be a serious issue. The same can be said, to a lesser extent, of Roman Catholicism in socialist Italy, France, and Germany.

Why has this taken place? Can it not be because the Church, in stressing human material needs so completely (needs which it has neither the resources nor the mandate to fulfill), has abdicated its unique role as spiritual feeder and focused the thought of the people, instead of on God, even more assiduously on the state (and therefore on material things and relationships) as the source of all good? As William Barrett suggests, the turn to socialism among religious intellectuals "represented a displacement of moral and religious values which had not found their outlet elsewhere, and here came to distorted expression." The distortion, however, lay in failing to understand the essentially spiritual and metaphysical nature of wealth and supply and the consequent drift to humanitarianism.

That could be why, today, we hear so much about "Christian humanism" and "Christian humanitarianism." Yet these very terms seem to be contradictions, since humanism and humanitarianism are ethical beliefs that specifically deny the existence or aid of God. Webster defines "humanitarianism" as "The doctrine that man may perfect his own nature without the aid of divine grace; the doctrine that denies the divinity of Jesus."

James Curry, former president of the American Humanist Association, admitted in 1970 that "Humanism is a polite term for atheism." In other words, humanism is an approach to life (albeit charitable and compassionate) that relieves mankind from the necessity to establish any relationship with God or to look to Him as the fundamental source of all good. It totally denigrates the supply side of faith and spirit. Corliss Lamont, a leader of the humanist movement, declares that "Humanism believes in a naturalistic metaphysics . . . that considers all forms of the supernatural a myth. Humanism is the viewpoint that men have but one life to live, and that human happiness is its own justification and needs no sanction or support from supernatural sources: that, in any case, the supernatural does not exist."

Compare this antifaith, man-centered humanist (and ultimately entropic) view of the universe with the essential spiritual concept of God and man that permeates both the Old and New Testaments of the Bible, both the Torah and the Gospels. It was Moses, for example, who spurned the comparative comfort and security of the Egyptian "welfare state" (and its bondage) to lead a national tribe out into a cruel and dangerous wilderness to find a "promised land," because he deeply believed God had commanded his way toward greater human freedom and abundance ("milk and honey"). Yet through that tough experience, both Jews and Christians believe, Moses was able to prove for all time that God "could set a table in the wilderness" and that even the most basic human needs could be met by putting God first—that faith indeed is *real substance.*

It was this essential message that permeated the Sermon on the Mount, when Jesus admonished man to "Take no thought, saying what shall we eat, or what shall we drink, or wherewithal shall we be clothed. For your Heavenly Father knoweth that ye have need of these things. But, seek ye first the Kingdom of God and His righteousness, and all these things shall be added unto you."

When the Pharisees came to him, wondering just what kind of "kingdom" (welfare state?) was to be established and where it would appear on earth, Jesus rebuked their materialistic utopianism, saying, "The kingdom of God cometh not with observation. Neither shall ye say lo here, nor lo there, but the kingdom of God is within you," within human consciousness. It was in a way the first formal expression of supply-side thinking. He did not say that first you take care of all human needs, and *then* you will find God. He told them that if they would search for the individual understanding of God, this understanding and resulting inspiration would in turn give them all the "things" they would need. He put spiritual causation in individual consciousness first, and material results second. Thoughts, Jesus taught, were fundamental to things. Emerson put it succinctly: "Great men are they who see that spiritual is stronger than any material force, that thoughts rule the world."

Humanism (a demand-side view) reverses all that, putting man's material needs first as the prerequisite of the good society. It places the pursuit of immediate material comfort and security first, and the search for freedom and spiritual dominion second. Where the Talmudic philosopher argues, "The noblest charity is to prevent a man from accepting charity; and the best alms is to show and enable a man to dispense with alms," the welfare state would encourage even greater tyranny over the human spirit.

As Professor Howard Parsons, a member of the American Humanist Association and a scholar at the University of Bridgeport, declares: "Marxism [socialism] is the most effective and influential form of atheism to appear in history, and the most formidable non-religious challenge to Christianity for the commitment of men." This may explain why the left-leaning "liberal" establishment churches are not benefiting from the current spiritual and religious revival in the United States, which is taking place in the more fundamentalist denominations. In 1979 virtually all of the "liberal" church denominations lost members, while almost all of the "conservative" churches gained. Also in growing numbers, individuals are apparently turning not so much to organized religion, but directly to God and the power of prayer for answers to their human problems—on an individual level rather than through collective religious or political action.

Ironically, just when a growing share of the public sees the direct connection between spiritual and moral values and real economic well-being, the mainstream liberal Christian Church has all but abandoned primary emphasis on moral teaching. Yet without this teaching, capitalism loses its enormous potential to bless. It is no accident that capitalism rose to world economic leadership only as a byproduct of the spread of Judeo-Christian spiritual values and laws; and to the extent that these values dissipate in hedonistic, amoral humanism, capitalism itself will decline. As Kristol charges, "Capitalism is facing today not an economic crisis but a crisis of belief." The same humanist-socialists who hate the market hate Christianity and Judaism with equal intensity, because the God of Israel requires individual spiritual growth and freedom.

Instead of lying down with these "strange bedfellows," the Church liberals should stop their ideological war on democratic capitalism, and instead renew their commitment to the spiritual and moral teaching of metaphysical qualities which have always in the past made capitalism the most effective weapon against the poverty they contend is their chief human concern. The fact that they do not do this suggests that too much of the liberal church is more intent on cultivating the poor than on healing them of poverty. If healing poverty were really their goal, they would support and redeem capitalism with even more enthusiasm than they now seem to show for the dialectics of Marx.

CAPITALISM AND HEALING POVERTY

One day in 1979 the front pages of many newspapers featured a haunting picture of the frail Mother Theresa receiving the Nobel Peace Prize for her magnificent but frustrating work among the very poorest of Calcutta's impoverished seven million—where up to 50 percent are unemployed and hundreds routinely die of starvation in the streets each night, defying the most heroic efforts at relief.

Mother Theresa's saintly life and grand humilities present a clear and implicit rebuke to the opulence of an uncaring West, more concerned for the price of oil and gold than for the cost of human suffering. But that, too, could be a superficial view, since nothing could do more for Calcutta's starving millions than a vital economy, freed from the shackles of centuries of religious superstition and pagan mysticism. Buried deep in the business sections of the same newspapers that carried Mother Theresa's story was the news that despite a much-heralded recession, U.S. unemployment had dropped, once more, to 6 percent, while the "troubled U.S. economy" was still employing 60 percent of its adult population, the highest employment percentage of any nation in recorded economic history (and nearly 20 points higher than in India).

In spite of spiraling inflation and energy costs (and after all benefits), less than 7 percent of all Americans in 1982 live below the comparatively high U.S. poverty line; and even this 7 percent live better than 80 percent of the rest of the world's population. As Michael Novak wrote, "No better weapon against poverty, disease, illiteracy, and tyranny has yet been found than capitalism. The techniques, human skills, and changes of cultural habit necessary to expand the productive capacity of the earth have been pioneered by democratic capitalism. Its compassion for the material needs of humankind has not in history, yet, had a peer."

There are, however, no Nobel Peace Prizes for democratic capitalism or for American industry and its fabulously successful assault on poverty. Instead, only brickbats, as the media daily parade industry's more unseemly excesses on page 1 and bury its successes on page 40, while "profit" has become an ugly epithet and capitalism itself is scorned as "trickle-down" economic theory.

It is ironic that the same Christian Church which was once the strongest apologist for the "Babbittry" of unrestrained nineteenth-century capitalism and the so-called Protestant work ethic has now turned with such savage scorn on the affluent society which this "ethic" has produced. Although some of this radical shift in American Christian thought has been spurred by a long-overdue awakening to the real plight of the poor and minorities, it also seems to represent a more fundamental change in today's Christian models.

The "new world" ethic of productivity and industry, which has done so much to alleviate human suffering, has apparently been traded in for the "old world" model of poverty as being synonymous with Christian piety and "no growth" as synonymous with "Christian stewardship." In this new-old model, so graphically and repeatedly presented on the television screen, to be poor (regardless of cause) is automatically to be deserving of social reverence and concern (and absolved of responsibility), while to be well-off (by this same semi-Marxist/pseudo-Christian logic) is to be guilty of exploiting the poor both at home and abroad, or at the very least "destroying the environment"!

In the process, observers now suggest, the Church may have fallen prey to a total reversal of the Christian message. In Dostoevsky's novel *The Brothers Karamazov*, the Grand Inquisitor argues that when the Antichrist comes, his message will be *first* to feed the people and *then* to ask of them virtue—thus abandoning the teaching that spiritual values precede material well-being and giving up the war against sin.

One of the tragedies of our time is that even as U.S. material poverty has been statistically reduced (by more than two thirds since 1963), the evidence of spiritual poverty and human degradation has steadily mounted. Between 1960 and 1979, while social spending soared from 10 percent of the GNP to 22 percent, the nation's crime rates more than doubled, the percentage of fatherless homes more than tripled, and whole sections of great cities disappeared in the violent rubble of what passes for "social compassion." Irving Kristol writes, "The conventional Christian wisdom of today is that the poor—what we call underprivileged people—need not be expected to behave virtuously (or rationally) until their material situation has been remedied." Yet this conventional wisdom is a mockery of Christ's teaching, which demands the relinquishment of sin as the precursor to the reception of good, placing primary stress on the metaphysical, rather than the physical, as the source of supply.

Curiously, aside from the fundamentalists, most of the established churches in America have been actively downplaying individual sin as it relates to the overcoming of social ills. Collective victimology seems to have replaced individual salvation as the central message of liberal theology. As a direct result, too many of our social programs have been predicated on the "nofault" principle that an individual should not have to suffer even for his own irresponsibility. The state must act as protector and insurer against failure regardless of cause. Unfortunately, while the irresponsible benefit, the vast majority who do act responsibly are penalized by rapidly growing taxation and programs, which, in turn, subsidize even more no-fault actions and higher costs for all. Sin succeeds while good purpose is punished by the vast array of no-fault government policies:

- no-fault unemployment compensation available even to those who leave their jobs and stay off them voluntarily, or to

employers who "schedule layoffs" simply because compensation is available;
- no-fault, tax-subsidized, private health-insurance programs which most economists now agree are unnecessarily promoting exaggerated use of hospital care and are mainly responsible for skyrocketing costs of U.S. medical care and insurance;
- no-fault compulsory car insurance in which the 10 percent who cause 90 percent of the accident losses pay no more for coverage than the 90 percent who drive responsibly—a program which has driven damage claims and insurance rates to all-time highs—30 percent to 40 percent higher than in states that do not have this program;
- no-fault criminal justice which tends to blame "society" for crime and, by 1975, reduced the level of punishment to less than 2 percent of all crimes committed, helping to triple the crime rate in the country in less than ten years, with enormous economic and social costs;
- no-fault divorce laws and "sexual liberation" which have contributed to the highest divorce and family breakup rates in history, an epidemic in venereal disease, and the highest rate of teenage illegitimate pregnancy ever; and
- no-fault education policies which have downplayed individual achievement and performance and discouraged the whole concept of individual moral responsibility and the work ethic.

What worries the social scientists, economists, and political theorists is not only the enormous economic costs of such no-fault living, but its deeper psychological costs to the nation's morale. Dr. Karl Menninger suggests that one of the principal reasons for the rapid rise in mental illness in our society is the decline in a sense of individual responsibility and personal worth—a feeling of helplessness and lack of direction. He argues that people have always learned more from their mistakes than from their success; but when the "price" of mistakes is eliminated, the result is confusion and a loss of motivation to "do better."

What is now being recommended, even by many liberal economists and social scientists, is the introduction into most of our social programs of elements of restraint which put a greater premium on individual responsibility and provide penalties for errant behavior. A good example is the recent decision in several states to withhold unemployment compensation from those who quit work voluntarily and to take individuals off welfare who refuse repeated offers of employment. The intent of these efforts is not to be harsh or merely fiscally prudent, but to take a more reasonable approach to providing generous help to those who really do need it, while restoring the positive economic assets of individual responsibility and worth to the substantial number who really don't—to encourage the satisfaction of work over the degradation of chronic dependence on the state.

In Massachusetts, for example, where 55 percent of the population in 1980 was directly dependent on government (up from 41 percent in 1960), and where a nearly $3-billion welfare budget barely kept over 500,000 recipients from starving or freezing, the most serious impediment to the future of the state's economy was not energy but severe and chronic shortages of both skilled and unskilled labor! Yet the strongest opponents of attempts to move individuals from welfare to work have included not only the bureaucracies, but the Church.

This institutionalization and subsidization of poverty threatens the very productivity and prosperity that could heal it—and the Christian church, both Protestant and Catholic, too often looms as the staunchest defender of this system of curious compassion, vigorously opposing even the mildest efforts to reform it or tighten it. This arises, it would seem, not only from a shallow sense of true compassion but from an even more superficial reading of the actual teachings of Christ Jesus.

Although it is plain that the Master ministered to the poor (and urged us to imitate Him in this), nowhere can He be found glorifying poverty as an end in itself. Instead, Jesus promised that the very quest for spiritual understanding and faith in God would itself bring the increase: "I am come that ye might have life, and that ye might have it more abundantly."

While Jesus lifted up the poor, the halt, and the sick, it was also plain that He did not tolerate the self-pity, helplessness, or ingratitude that would make such conditions worse. "Take up thy bed and walk," He commanded the pitiable invalid as He healed him. One startling indication of this came when Judas challenged the Master to sell off the bag of provisions and ointments which the disciples carried with them and to give the proceeds to the poor. Jesus rebuked this contrivance of compassion by telling Judas, "The poor ye have always with you, but me, ye have not always with you," thus ascribing more power for healing poverty to the spiritual ideas He presented than to the "petty cash" of temporary charity. He even rebuked the do-gooding Martha, "thou art careful and troubled about many things," while praising the contemplative Mary. Reflection was shown to be more valuable than reaction.

And in His parable of the talents, Jesus taught mankind to use their God-given talents, faith, and understanding to overcome limitation and lack instead of submitting to them, concluding with the disturbing warning: "unto every one that hath [i.e., those who use their talents] shall be given, and he shall have abundance: but from him that hath not [those who do not use their talents] shall be taken away even that which he hath."

That is hardly a model of sentimental Christian compassion or pious poverty. That such a stern but loving supply-side lesson in individual responsibility and productivity should come from the lips of the same Teacher who preached the parable of the Good Samaritan shows that Jesus saw no essential conflict between the Old Testament image of God as Lawgiver or Principle and His own revelation of God as Love. He understood that it is Love's purpose to compel progress and that mankind often learns more from adversity than from success.

Without the demand to strive and grow, implicit in the ideal of God as Father (or divine Principle), would mankind continue its search for a higher human standard and for the perfection the Gospels urge as our birthright? Without God as Principle, would not compassion merely become a self-justifying trap for human stagnation and defeat? Can we really have a genuine sense of God as Love without a sense of Him as lawgiver?

While each of us, theoretically, has the capacity to be both strongly principled and warmly compassionate, both fatherly and motherly at the same time, the fact is that few of us achieve this balance easily, regardless of gender. Most families still need both a father and a mother, in qualities at least—father qualities which produce, provide, and discipline, and mother qualities which care, love, and nourish. As it is with the family, so it is with nations which throughout history have tended to swing back and forth between extremes. Whenever they became too captive of any one extreme for too long, the opposite had tended to reassert itself. But balance and completeness have never come without hard work to nations or individuals.

Human beings soon discover that principle without love or compassion ceases to be principle and becomes oppression. Contrariwise, love or compassion without the strength of self-discipline and principle soon ceases to be very loving and becomes the "smotherhood" of domination. There is nothing very loving about a family or a society that fails to discipline its children in order to prepare them to live responsibly on their own. Thus the failure of permissive education and the social-welfare state.

On the other hand, there is nothing very principled about a

family or a society that deals out harsh discipline without compassionate and rational support. Thus the failure of the narrow "law-and-order" mentality that practices autocracy and usually generates only more resentment and rebellion. Human political systems are, at their very best, imperfect efforts to find the balance between these two main aspects of Deity—the righteous lawgiver and the judge of the Old Testament and the God who is Love in the New—between Moses' Commandments and the Beatitudes of Jesus Christ.

Unfortunately, for too many years Western democracies, in particular, have believed that liberal compassion was all good while conservative restraint and discipline were all bad—that they could forever have unlimited demand and distribution without worrying about production and supply. In the process they have fostered a whole "me" generation of takers and nearly destroyed a generation of producers. The demand side of our country has been eating up the supply side, in religious expression as well as economics. We love to talk about "caring," but we don't like to think about sin or responsibility. The time has come, therefore, not to throw out compassionate liberalism, but to tame it somewhat by reasserting some of the restraints of principled conservatism on the body politic.

But beyond this, it seems to me, Americans need to understand why neither ideological extreme should ever dominate completely as the left has been doing or as the extreme right might like to do in the future. The utopian moral absolutes presented by both left and right are impossible to realize in human experience, unless consciousness is redeemed far beyond its present level.

GOVERNMENT AS GOD?

Above all, we must avoid the worse result of giving godlike powers to any government, left or right. Not only does this lead to arbitrary tyranny, but it undermines our most powerful metaphysical and economic assets—our morale, our individual sense of self-worth, indeed, morality itself. It should not surprise us that in direct proportion as we have traded in our original commitment to individual self-government of law for centralized government of men (bureaucracies), we have seen lawlessness, chaos, and corruption rise.

As Leonard Read warns: "We find in a growing statism the explanation for our double standard of morality. The same person to whom stealing a penny from a millionaire would be unthinkable will, when the state apparatus is put at his disposal, join in taking billions from everybody, including the poor. . . ." The Church itself now runs the risk of publicly admitting its own failure to generate spontaneous sharing, contribution, and giving as acts of faith inspired by love. It is too gladly substituting the force of compulsory institutionalized government for spiritual leadership and persuasion. Read continues:

> As this is done, man loses his wholeness; he is dispossessed of responsibility for self, the very essence of his manhood. The more dependent he becomes, the less dependable. . . .
>
> Thus, the state inflicts itself as a dangerous centrifuge on society; man violently spun from the center which is his wholeness, his self-reliance, his integrity, and thrown in fragments onto an ever-widening periphery of unnatural specializations; man disoriented in unnatural surroundings, lost in detail and trivia; man from whom integrity has taken flight; man minus responsibility for self, the state his guardian and master.

It seems no accident that just at this moment of spiritual crisis, Providence should provide the Roman Catholics with a pope, John Paul II, who clearly appreciates this danger and the need to dampen the fires of secular socialism, who knows firsthand the failure of government to "stand in" for God. It is no easy task. As he discovered in Puebla, Mexico, in 1979, a growing share of Catholic clergy both here and abroad are falling for the exciting lure of Marxist political activism as the way to better the lot of their parishioners; and given their impoverished lot, the lure is entirely understandable, if not credible, since too often these helpless people find they have merely traded one human tyranny for another.

"We believe we should not be satisfied with just prayer," one of the activist rebels said. To which Pope John Paul II had the courage to respond: "The idea of Christ, as a political figure, does not tally with the Church's catechesis. Clerical involvement in radical politics is counterproductive. You are not social managers, political leaders, or functionaries of a temporal power," he warned his rebel clerics. His recipe for true spiritual activism: "A soul living in habitual contact with God will know how to care for the poor without surrendering to sociopolitical radicalisms, which in the end are shown to be inopportune and counterproductive. Whatever the miseries or suffering that afflict man," he concluded, "it is not through violence, the interplay of power and political systems, but *through the truth concerning man, that he journeys toward a better future.*"

What the new pope so vividly expresses is his clear understanding of the one thing that separates Christianity from both Marxism and materialistic capitalism: the idea of spiritual causation—that the way to human triumph and freedom is not through material systems, but through spiritual and metaphysical understanding; that spiritual ideas do indeed have the power and substance to effect material betterment and peaceful social reformation and revolution. But the notion of world redemption through individual spiritual salvation is anathema to the Marxist humanism beguiling many materialistically minded clergy, who are looking only for an earthly utopia. Not that capitalism has any special claim on Christian virtue. It certainly does not. A greedy capitalist is no more spiritual than an imperious Marxist ideologue. Both have equally materialistic views—and goals. The difference is that while capitalism thrives on the political and religious freedom also essential to Christianity, Marxism relies on tyranny for survival.

"Where the spirit of the Lord is, there is liberty," wrote St. Paul. And wherever there is such spiritually supported liberty, capitalism invariably flourishes; but where Marxist totalitarianism rules, all religious experience is automatically threatened and spiritual inspiration stagnates. As Pope John Paul found out from his experience in Poland, while Christianity can live (albeit critically and disapprovingly) with capitalism, it withers in Communist states, which, he says, "produce only oppression, intimidation, violence, and terrorism."

On the other hand, while Christ Jesus plainly rejected the materialistic utopianism which seems to characterize so much of the rhetoric of present-day populist Christianity, He also rejected the human pursuit of material wealth for its own sake, the "bottom-line" thinking that has become so self-defeating, economically and morally, to present-day capitalism.

THE PROFIT MOTIVE IS NOT ENOUGH

Although capitalism may not be essential to the survival of Christianity, the metaphysical insights of Christianity and Judaism are essential if we are to keep capitalism from destroying itself. The troubled state of the American private economy, with slackening productivity, uncertain profitability, and growing public distrust, mandates a fresh vision for capitalists in the 1980s and beyond.

It is in no way to denigrate the essential role of profits in our economy to suggest that the profit motive, alone, is simply no longer enough—indeed, it never was. There is, after all, nothing particularly sacred or inspired about the profit motive. It is as natural to apes and squirrels as it is to human beings—as endemic to unredeemed human nature as raw greed. The most selfish infant often displays as much of it as the largest corporate conglomerate.

Yet, it often escapes the notice of some religionists that both individuals and corporations with the most intense expressions of the profit motive often fail in the long run, while some of the greatest business successes (and profits) have come to men and women with the most generous and unselfishly motivated natures. This would seem to confirm the validity of the Christian teaching that "It is more blessed to give than to receive," more rewarding to contribute than to exploit, and to point to an ideal for the conduct of private enterprise and the true "market economy."

Throughout the economic history of this nation, we can see that those companies survive and succeed the longest which have done the best job of identifying real human needs and filling them—and thereby contributing to our general well-being by responding to the market. Conversely, we observe again and again that those companies which systematically abuse and exploit both workers and consumers (markets) for the sake of short-term gain tend to have very poor survival rates. There is nothing in this that is inconsistent with the fundamental metaphysical principles and laws which permeate most religious doctrines, which teach that evil motives produce their own failures, while good inevitably produces its own generous rewards. Capitalism, then, can survive only if it is leavened by the insights of the spiritual sense which tempers greed and promotes genuine vision.

Among these insights is the realization that profits, while they are the natural and legitimate result of business well run to serve the public, cannot be the exclusive goal of business. When the single-minded pursuit of profit dominates corporate thinking, it can tend to exclude vision, hinder true creativity and productivity, debilitate the dynamism of enterprise, and ultimately reduce wealth itself.

In exact proportion as corporate America has in recent years come to be dominated by "profit maximization," its innovation and invention have been inhibited, its productivity sapped, and, curiously enough, its real growth and profitability reduced. It is easy enough to blame this on the impact of rising government regulations and stultifying federal tax, spending, and inflationary policies, which have turned most American business toward "defensive" economic thinking, putting more emphasis on this year's gain than on building for the future.

Although government must share the blame for this situation, so must the boardrooms of corporate America, which have allowed the ethically neutral business-school mentality to substitute its accounting manipulation, cash-flow thinking, and the tax-accounting logistics of mergers for the real vision of growth through the metaphysical process of creativity, invention, and true enterprise. It is this decline in creative vision that has led to the increasing spiritual impoverishment of executive suites.

It has also affected the relative success of the corporations and the country as well. The Preacher's warning that "Where there is no vision the people perish" applies especially to business.

The American economic scene is littered with the wreckage and evident deterioration of companies that for too long have ignored creative thinking and basic research and development, as well as the changing pattern of real human needs, while fixating on this year's balance sheet. Automobile companies, railroads, and the steel industry are examples of how excessive profit orientation has produced not more growth and profits, but less. This could also be said of those labor unions that have overextended their reach beyond productivity.

There is a profound metaphysical reason for this experience. It arises from a failure to understand the real nature of profits as savings and their basic purpose, not as an overarching goal in and of themselves, but as an ethical and moral discipline, a standard of efficient performance, and ultimately the product of self-denial. Savings (including profits) are the result of the willingness to put aside immediate gratification and consumption for the purpose of increasing future good. In this sense, then, profits, like savings, are the economic expression of the spiritual and moral ethic of self-control, the willingness to check our purely animal instincts for short-term pleasure, and to sacrifice our most selfish desires in order to achieve a much larger reward—specifically, more real dominion over our human experience and more secure well-being.

The most successful companies in this country have been

built, by and large, out of the self-discipline and creative faith in the future of a comparatively few men and women who, had they been motivated purely by short-term greed or "bottom lines," could never have achieved what they did. I think for example of Bradley Dewey, Sr., who helped give this nation synthetic rubber during World War II when we needed it most, and in the process contributed valuable private inventions for the public good.

Dewey's greatest achievement was the plastic packaging process known as Cryovac, which, along with subsequent imitators, revolutionized the production, distribution, and consumption of meat and poultry in this country. The process has saved consumers literally tens of billions of dollars in reduced waste, distribution costs, and spoilage, and has been the basis of the creation of tens of thousands of new jobs.

It took Dewey nearly twenty difficult years before Cryovac finally became a profitable venture—during which time he continually confounded his accountants and controllers by sacrificing nearly his entire capital investment and lifesavings to bring this idea through all its technical and marketing problems to fruition. Dewey's long-range vision ultimately produced a major new and profitable business that has blessed millions; yet there never was a man, in my experience, who was less preoccupied with "profit maximization" or more occupied with genuine service to his country. For Dewey, profits were a secondary and disciplinary measure of performance, only a means to the larger end of enabling his company to carry out other new ideas that would improve human welfare.

We should not be surprised that the nation's healthiest industry today, high technology, is one of the few places in American business where one will find lots of visionary Deweys. Real economic growth and vitality depend on this imaginative and courageously trusting type of mentality—the kind that, for a good example, will rise above nearly three years of million-dollar a-month losses to produce the billion-dollar success that is now Federal Express.

Unfortunately, the corporate-conglomerate scene is all too often dominated by the myopic slide-rule mentality that is interested primarily in the next stockholders meeting, the next merger move, the next hearing in Washington. The substitution of short-term self-gratification for the self-denial of genuine creativity (which is the true compassion of the entrepreneur) is cause for alarm.

THE COMPASSIONATE CAPITALIST

In all the sentimental folderol that characterizes so much social and political commentary today, we almost never hear the term "compassionate" applied to a business executive or an entrepreneur. Yet in terms of results in the measurable form of jobs created, lives enriched, communities built, living standards uplifted, and poverty healed, a handful of "compassionate capitalists" have done infinitely more for their fellowmen than all the self-serving politicians, academics, social workers, or religionists who claim the adjective "compassionate" for themselves.

I had, for example, the special privilege of coming into direct contact with an obscure Austrian immigrant to this country by the name of Ernst Mahler, who had come to work for Kimberly Clark shortly after World War I. Mahler was an entrepreneurial genius whose innovative ideas and leadership, over a period of about thirty years, transformed this once-small, insular newsprint and tissue manufacturer into one of the largest paper corporations in the world, which gives prosperous employment to more than one hundred thousand and produces products (which Mahler helped innovate) that are now used by more than two billion people. Mahler became enormously wealthy, of course. Yet his personal fortune was insignificant when compared with the permanent prosperity he generated, not only for his own company but for the hundreds of thousands who work for industries which his genius ultimately spawned and which long outlived him—not to mention the revolutionary sanitary products that have liberated two generations of women, or the printing papers that completely transformed international publishing and communications for fifty years.

I can safely predict that you have never heard of him up to this moment. Not one person in one hundred million has. Yet his contribution has permanently uplifted the lives of millions and far exceeds in real compassion most of our self-congratulatory politicians and "activists" whose names are known to all. What is so troubling is that those who cloak themselves in this "compassion mantle" are so often the very people who are hedging in the economic freedom that made Earnst Mahler's life and contribution possible.

As Michael Novak so ably expresses it,

> The motive of this system [democratic capitalism] is to concentrate upon improving the material base of humankind; but its higher purpose in doing so is to empower

individuals to use their native liberty as they see fit. For democratic capitalism, liberty is at once the means to greater productivity, and the end thereof. Unlike pretentious socialism, democratic capitalism does not presume to take the place of archbishops, philosophers, and poets in instructing individuals how to use their liberty. Instead such a system permits individuals to find, or to lose their own way.

Or, as St. Paul suggests, to work out their own salvation.

The "liberal" Christian clergy routinely condemns men like Earnst Mahler and the market they have created as exploitive and selfish and calls for a "more compassionate society," based on statist regulation and a forced redivision of wealth that obviates Christian charity. But who among these theologians has contributed a scintilla as much practical good for their fellowmen? Where is there more effective Christian compassion—in the truly creative capitalist or in the sympathetic social worker? In the "invisible hand" that guides the market or in the heavy bureaucratic hand that stifles it?

THEOLOGY VS. ENTROPY

Even more troubling is the utter failure of most of America's spiritual leadership to challenge the "scientific determinism" that would impose growing limitations on compassionate capitalism and on the upward hopes and mobility of the American people. Even as technology itself daily breaks new ground into the exhilarating realm of the metaphysical and cosmic sciences, the liberal Church seems more and more earthbound in its outlook as it embraces what Jeremy Rifkin archly calls "the theology of entropy."

This new liberal-theological "entropic world view" argues that mankind, having received a material creation as a gift from a spiritual God, must now redefine its hopes and dreams in the context of finite limits. It must accept all of the unspiritual premises these limits imply, from environmental extremism to zero population growth, from abortion to the "right to die"; it must see itself merely as transitory stewards of an untouchable earth environment.

Not only do such views come perilously close to adopting Rousseau's noble savage as a model for Christian living, but, in implicitly accepting entropy as "the supreme governing law," they are denying the immorality of God and His image, man, and, in particular, the prophets from Moses to Jesus who preached and demonstrated the triumph of the metaphysical (or spiritual) over the physical and material.

The Entropy Law, after all, is the essence of materialism. It posits the case for growing disorder, destruction, inharmony, disintegration, and death. As Jeremy Rifkin argues, "We desperately search for immortality in this finite world, while *knowing there is none*. There is a nihilism in our search." Is it not precisely that search for immortality that is the central theme and cause of Christianity and, indeed, of most of the great Hebrew prophets as well? Can there be any greater illustrations of "anti-entropy" than manna from heaven, water struck from a rock, oil continually provided out of what had seemed to be an empty barrel, the myriad spiritual healings of the most horrendously advanced deteriorative diseases, the feeding of the multitude, the walking on water, the cleansing of leprosy in the river Jordan—to mention but a few of the Biblical miracles?

And what is the meaning of the Resurrection if not the triumph over entropy? Was Jesus so enamored of this finite material world that He wished all mankind (except Himself) to accept its fatalistic premises and limits? "In the world ye have tribulation," He said, "but be of good cheer, I have overcome the world."

The central theme of Biblical prophecy is this "overcoming" and the bringing of order, healing, harmony, and peace of God to bear on individual human lives. "We shall overcome" is not merely a civil-rights spiritual, but the paradigm of Christian salvation summed up so gloriously by St. Paul in his first Epistle to the Corinthians:

> Now if Christ be preached that he rose from the dead, how say some among you [entropicists?] that there is no resurrection of the dead?
> But if there be no resurrection of the dead, then is Christ not risen:
> And if Christ be not risen, your faith is also vain. . . .
> For as in Adam [entropy] all die, even so in Christ [spiritual anti-enthropy] shall all be made alive.

The growing number of Christian theologians who now embrace the limits-of-growth view are apparently prepared to reject spiritual reality and its potential for "overcoming" and instead are lending their religious authority to a movement and viewpoint whose purpose Rifkin smugly spells out: "By radically redefining humanity's relationship to the rest of God's creation, contemporary Christian scholars are thrusting a theological dagger directly into the heart of the expansionist epoch"—and, in so doing, condemning the poor of the world to permanent despair.

They are also of necessity giving up on the Church's basic mission to purify and reform mankind of sin. If there is no ultimate tomorrow, then why strive for perfection today? If there is no immortality, then mortality and sin become the models for human behavior, the market does indeed become a jungle, and the only alternative is totalitarian government to distribute the resulting impoverishment "equitably."

It is no accident that precisely in proportion as the established liberal church has abandoned its prophetic purifying role in favor of "political solutions" the national moral fabric has tattered and poverty has grown, while the production of wealth has languished. Since wealth is at its root metaphysical (the product of ideas and the promotion of useful qualities and values), purification and spiritualization of thought are not merely Christian ideals; they are at once the keys to human prosperity and economic progress, and the disciplines that make human freedom possible and capitalism compassionate.

In other words, goodness and purity of thought are not merely the stuff of Pollyanna religion or of positive thinking; they are substantial economic assets, the most fundamental components of our real GNP; and they will grow even more important as this nation moves progressively into an economy based on the components of mind more than on the elements of matter. It seems ironic that at the very moment in human history when mankind appears poised for a leap away from a things-based economy to the cybernetic realm of ideas and logic (from the physical to the metaphysical sense of wealth)—that is, to follow Buckminster Fuller's challenge to "dare to spread our wings of intellect and fly by the generalized principles governing the universe"—the Church establishment should seem to be moving so determinedly in the opposite direction, from prophecy back to politics.

Ultimately this new economy depends on the creative inspiration that comes to enlightened thought; and it is the prophet's primary role to uplift and enlighten, to "shepherd" this creative upreach. In this sense, the Church, indeed all religious expression, is central to the economic well-being of the nation and the genuine relief of human poverty. Although simple human prosperity can never be the primary goal of moral and spiritual teaching, it is the inevitable result. Without this teaching, mankind is doomed to moral and economic decline, no matter what system of government or economics it chooses.

As Alexis de Tocqueville suggested, the greatness of our economy can continue only as a reflection of the goodness of our people.

SOURCES

Walter Lippmann, *The Good Society* (Boston: Little, Brown, 1943).

William Barrett, in *Capitalism, Socialism and Democracy*, a symposium that first appeared in *Commentary*, April 1978, and was reprinted by the American Enterprise Institute, Washington, D.C., 1979.

Research and Forecasts, Inc., New York City, *Report on American Values in the 80's: The Impact of Belief* (Hartford: Connecticut Mutual Life Insurance Company, April 1981).

David Broder made his comment on a PBS telecast, "Washington Week in Review," September 12, 1980.

Alexis de Tocqueville, *Democracy in America*.

Michael Novak (ed.), *Capitalism and Socialism: A Theological Inquiry* (Washington, D.C.: American Enterprise Institute, 1979). Contains papers by Irving Kristol, Seymour Martin Lipset, Peter Berger, Muhammad Abdul-Rauf, Ben J. Wattenberg, and Penn Kemble. See also Irving Kristol, *Two Cheers for Capitalism* (New York: Basic Books, 1978).

For further background, see my four-part series, "Capitalism and Christianity: Can They Coexist?" *Boston Herald American*, December 18, 20, 21, and 25, 1979.

Norman Podhoretz, "The New Defenders of Capitalism," *Harvard Business Review*, March-April 1981.

Hebrews 11:12.

Luke 6:38.

Gallup Poll on religious belief, 1975. A new Gallup study for the Center of Applied Research in the Apostolate (CARA), Washington, D.C., includes over fifteen thousand interviews in Europe and over two thousand in the United States. Assembled for public release in September 1982, its preliminary findings show consistency with the Connecticut Mutual Life poll cited above.

Peter Berger's paper appeared in Novak (ed.), *Capitalism and Socialism*, cited above.

Corliss Lamont, *The Philosophy of Humanism*, 6th edition (New York: Ungar, 1982).

Matthew 26:31-33.

Luke 17:20.

Ralph Waldo Emerson, *Progress and Culture*, A Phi Beta Kappa address, July 18, 1876.

Michael Novak, "The Myth of Compassion," *National Review*, December 7, 1979, p. 1564.

Karl Menninger, *Whatever Became of Sin?* (New York: Hawthorne, 1973).

John 10:10.

John 12:3-8.

Luke 10:40-42.

Matthew 25:14-30.

Leonard E. Read, "Statism and Goodness," *Notes from FEE* (Foundation for Economic Education, Irvington-on-Hudson, N.Y.), March 1981.

Juan A. Tamay, UPI story on Pope John Paul's visit to Mexico City and Puebla, January 28, 1979. See also "A Church for the Poor," *Newsweek*, February 26, 1979.

2 Corinthians 3:17.

Proverbs 29:18.

Jeremy Rifkin, *Entropy* (New York: Viking Press, 1980).

John 16:33.

1 Corinthians 15:12, 13, 17, 22.

THREE

The Ideal of Democratic Capitalism

MICHAEL NOVAK

> Why wouldst thou be a breeder of sinners? I am myself indifferent honest; but yet I could accuse me of such things that it were better my mother had not borne me. I am very proud, revengeful, ambitious; with more offences at my beck than I have thoughts to put them in, imagination to give them shape, or time to act them in. What should such fellows as I do crawling between heaven and earth? We are arrant knaves all; believe none of us.

> —*Hamlet*, Act 3, Scene 1

A free political economy wears sin like a scarlet letter. Soft neon lights beckon, alas, to massage parlors and "adult" (that is, adolescent) magazines. Democratic capitalist societies exhibit the lives of human beings not perhaps as they should be but as they are, for they have been conceived in due recognition of the errant human heart, whose liberty they respect. In this, they follow the example of the Creator who knows what is in humans—who hates sin but permits it for the sake of liberty, who suffers from it but remains faithful to his sinful children.

MICHAEL NOVAK is Resident Scholar in Philosophy, Religion, and Public Policy at the American Enterprise Institute in Washington, D.C. He was educated at Holy Cross Seminary, Stonehill College, and Gregorian University in Rome. He did his graduate studies in history and philosophy of religion at Harvard University. Mr. Novak has taught at Union Theological Seminary, Stanford University, the State University of New York, Syracuse University, and the University of California at Santa Barbara. He has published several influential books, including *Belief and Unbelief*, *The Experience of Nothingness*, *Ascent of the Mountain*, *Flight of the Dove*, *The Rise of the Unmeltable Ethnics*, and *The Guns of Lattimer*. The following essay is taken from his recent book *The Spirit of Democratic Capitalism* (Simon & Schuster, 1982).

Three points must be made about the special sense of sin which informs democratic capitalism. First, it regards sin as rooted in the free personality, beyond the reach of any system, an ineradicable given from which all realistic thinking about political economy must begin. Secondly, a way to defeat sin—a way to transform its energy into creative use (and thus to take on Satan the best revenge)—is offered by the workings of unintended consequences. A system trying to put ineradicable sin to creative purposes need neither rely on perfect virtue nor aim directly at pure intentions. Thirdly, moral virtue is a significant part of self-interest. Thus, a free society, without aiming so high as perfect virtue, must insist upon a core of common indispensable morality and can under suitable checks and balances wrest a reasonable degree of goodness, decency, and compassion from less than perfect materials. One must be satisfied in systems, Aristotle once wrote, with "a tincture of virtue," even though rather more than that may sometimes be obtained.

FREEDOM AND SIN

Political economy must deal with humans as they are. Yet remarkably different hypotheses are entertained about human beings. Who are we? What may we hope? What ought we to do? These, Immanuel Kant suggested, are the perennial questions behind political economy. Every system of political economy represents at least an implicit answer to them. Each system allows only so much scope to individuals. Each favors some instincts in the human breast and penalizes others. Each embodies a conviction about the most dangerous evils, which need to be watched with care or carefully repressed.

Consider for a moment three different forms of political economy. Traditional societies are aimed against disorder. Socialist societies are aimed against inequality. Democratic capitalist societies are aimed against tyranny.

Traditional societies are preoccupied by problems of order and stability. Their enemy is "the war of all against all."[1] They have vivid memories of plunder, murder, rape, riot, and civil war. Cities have been sacked, the countryside terrorized by marauding bands, economies disrupted, daily life rendered desperate. Leaders who have brought order out of chaos, united peoples, and created conditions of stability are highly praised. Their work may seem like God's work, as if they had brought about on earth the harmony and regularity which humans observe at night in the quiet patterns of the stars. God, then, is often imagined to be a God of order, of lawlike rationality, of harmony and peace. Sins against order are regarded as sins against God. Punishments for acts of disorder—as in medieval European societies—have been direct and brutal. Hands are cut off. Tongues are cut out. Adulterers are stoned.

In socialist societies, the enemy of human development is thought to lie in inequalities of economic wealth and power. These being removed, it is imagined that society will be cooperative and the human breast at peace with itself. In extreme forms of socialism, all forms of private ownership are to be abolished, as the source of inequalities and restlessness. The gap between rich and poor is regarded as the mainspring of injustice. In moderate forms, which respect the connection between liberty and private property, income differentials still seem to be a scandal. The assumption seems to be that envy is the central passion in the human breast. Socialists seem to think that humans *should* feel envy, even if they don't. For socialism, the fundamental evil is the conflict between classes. "Socialism," writes R. H. Tawney, "would end the conflict by ending the economic and legal conditions by which it is produced. Its fundamental dogma is the dignity of man; its fundamental criticism of capitalism is, not merely that it impoverishes the mass of mankind—poverty is an ancient evil—but that it makes riches a god, and treats common men less than man."[2]

Democratic capitalism has a rather different understanding of itself from the one imputed by Tawney. Far from impoverishing the mass of humankind, it has intended to generate a greater improvement in the material conditions of every portion of humankind. Far from making riches a god, democratic capitalism promotes a pluralism of interests and purposes. The ideal in whose light it judges the bigness of corporations is pragmatic: does bigness promote or injure the common goal? Democratic capitalism is not identical with corporatism—a system of large corporations.

What democratic capitalism fears is tyranny, most notably by the state, but also by excessive private power. It fears the mean pettiness of regimented equality. It propounds an openness about economic wealth and power. It regulates the trusts. It foments rapid mobility, recognizing that old fortunes decline and new ones arise. In some forms of disparity in wealth and power, it sees utilities from which all benefit. For other forms of disparity, it establishes several correctives: a plural scheme of checks and balances; legitimate power in the political system and in the moral-cultural system to restrain, temper, and check the economic system; and stimulation of the due circulation of elites and the economic mobility of individuals.

Under democratic capitalism, inequalities of wealth and power are not considered evil in themselves. They are in tune with natural inequalities which everyone experiences every day. Nature itself has made human beings equal in dignity before God and one another. But it has not made them equal to one another in talent, personal energy, luck, motivation, and practical abilities. On the other hand, inequalities of every sort are potential sources of evil and abuse. Human beings are insecure. Often, even as little children, they engage in petty rivalries and tear one another down. Long before the rise of democratic capitalism, even in Biblical times, envy was potent. Nature itself generates inequalities of looks, stature, intellect, and heart. Should a good society repress inequalities, or should it respect them, while teaching cooperation and respect? Democratic capitalism is loathe to repress natural human energies which manifest obvious inequalities. Such energies are perennial, universal, and irrepressible; the attempt to repress them breeds yet more dangerous evils. Yet even persons in many ways unequal to one another may respect one another in other ways as equals, may cooperate, and seek mutual benefit.

Any society which does not promote and support its best natural leaders punishes itself and weakens its probabilities of survival and progress. In all fields, genius is rare and high talent is in relatively short supply. Any political economy which wishes to be as creative as possible must try to invent a system which permits persons of talent in all fields to discover their talents, to develop them, and to find the social positions in which their exercise bears maximal social fruit. Necessarily, such a system must encourage massive programs of self-discovery and self-improvement. Such a system must promote considerable fluidity and mobility. It must reward performance and learn to seek out talent wherever it may be found. Such a system requires vital local communities which identify and promote talents appearing in their midst. Under the pressures of high technology and its demands, democratic capitalist societies (like others) face keen difficulties, stemming from government, business, and even the mass media, in keeping subsidiary communities* vital, in not

---

*The evangelical subculture is such a community and is increasingly undercut.

overwhelming them, and in promoting their self-reliance and creativity. Too little thought flows in this direction, and then the
ideals of democratic capitalism are themselves undercut.

Democratic capitalism does not promise to eliminate sin. It
certainly does not promise equality of results (an outcome which,
in any case, would run counter both to nature and to justice). It
does not even promise that all those who have wealth or who
acquire wealth will do so according to moral merit. Its sense of
meritocracy is not a judgment upon individuals but is based upon
the system *qua* system. It holds that a system which permits
individual families over time to rise and to fall in wealth in
accord with their own actions and circumstances will, *on the
whole*, better reward familial performance than any other form
of society.[3] The judgment of individual cases may be left to God.

It is, so to speak, the chief virtue of democratic capitalism
that, in giving rein to liberty, it allows tares to grow among the
wheat. Its political economy is not designed for saints. Whereas
socialists frequently promise, under their coercive system, "a new
socialist man" of a virtuous sort the world has never seen before,
democratic capitalism (although it, too, depends upon and nourishes virtuous behavior) promises no such thing. Its political
economy, while depending upon a high degree of civic virtue in
its citizens (and upon an especially potent moral-cultural system
separated from the state), is designed for sinners. That is, for
humans as they are.

Most social revolutions promise a reign of the saints. Most
promise a new type of moral man. And most intend to produce
this higher type of morality through the coercive power of the
state. This is precisely the impulse in the human breast which
democratic capitalism finds to be the most productive of evil.
Against it, tolerating other evils, it most resolutely sets its face.

There are, in this respect, two main traditions of revolutionary thought, the utopian and the realist. Utopian revolutionaries imagine that the source of human evil lies in social structures and systems, and that in removing these they will remove
evil and virtue will flourish. By contrast, realists hold that the
source of human evil lies in the self and in the necessary limitations of every form of social organization. Realists hold that no
real or imagined social structures and no system, however ingeniously designed, will banish sin from the field of human liberty.
"The revolution," Charles Péguy once wrote, "is moral or not at
all."[4] But what makes a revolution moral? For the utopians, morality flows from structures and systems. (At one extreme, Stalin-

ists hold that any act by individuals to bring about socialism is objectively a moral act.) For the realists, morality flows from individual will and act.

In the realist tradition, a moral revolution in political economy depends upon creating a system within which, to the maximum extent history makes possible, liberty for individuals will flourish. Such a system necessarily means that sin will flourish too. Yet the system *qua* system will be moral if two conditions are met. First, the design must include pluralistic institutions which permit both liberty and virtue to prosper. Second, the system of moral and religious culture must instruct individuals in the ways of liberty and virtue. Such a design rests upon an exact diagnosis of human frailty on the one hand, and of the effects, intended and unintended, of institutional arrangements on the other.

The realist revolutionary does not believe that the overthrow of an evil system will guarantee a better to replace it. He does not glorify the revolutionary struggle or the revolutionary moment, for he does not conceive that the source of evil lies in the system to be overthrown. The realists do not imagine that there has been, is now, or ever will be a political economy from which evil will be banished. Wherever there are human beings, there will be evil. Because they do not believe in a paradise on earth, or in an innocent system, the realists are often dismissed as mere "reformers." In fact, their vision is revolutionary precisely because they reject the moral pretenses both of ancient traditional orders and of contemporary utopian orders. The utopias of the modern age strike them as too like the theocracies and moral tyrannies of the past.

Theological traditions ground both the utopian and the realist strains of revolutionary theory. Many scholars trace both to Calvinism. One strain arises from the humility involved in recognizing, as John Wesley did, inevitable differences in individual conscience. The other arises from the millennialism of Joachim of Flora and the Muenster Rebellion. Both strains begin with a profound awareness of the sinfulness of this world. From one strain comes a realism which concentrates moral attention upon checking the evil always present in the human heart. The other is fired by a passion for purification from evil, through the destruction of evil institutions and the dawn of a new era. Karl Marx traces the origins of scientific socialism to the latter. Democratic capitalism has its origins in the former. Both speak of a "new order of the ages." Each is the ground of a new sort of liberation theology.[5]

In Latin America today, the utopian strain has been gaining ground among Catholics and Protestants alike. Thus, when liberation theologian Juan Luis Segundo describes the choice between capitalism and socialism as the "theological crux" for Latin America, he explicitly prefers the utopianism of socialism to the realism of democratic capitalism.[6] The economic successes of the realist tradition have changed the material horizon of the peoples of the Third World. But the *ideas* of the realist tradition have had surprisingly little impact upon its intellectual elites. For theologians reflexively hostile to democratic capitalism, the socialist vision seems all the more commendable for being utopian. They see in it the perfectionism of Christianity. They dream about a new society of equality, justice, autonomy, and brotherhood. One reads them in vain for descriptions of the exact institutional structures by which these dreams will be realized.

Democratic capitalism places its strongest emphasis upon practice. The British empiricists and American pragmatists alike highly praised "the experimental method." In a sense quite different from that of Karl Marx, they held that the point of philosophy is not merely to reflect the world but to change it. Since what they feared most was the abuse of public power through state tyranny, they developed a theory of the limited state. Since they were mindful that men are not angels, they tried to design a system that would diffuse power broadly through a system of differentiation. Since they did not believe that parchment alone governs men, they tried to establish a dynamic system of competing interests of many sorts, political, economic, and moral-cultural. Since history showed that not even the church of Christ can be purified of sin, they did not expect the earthly city to be pure. Instead of trying to cleanse the earth of sin, they set out to construct a framework of laws, institutions, and plural purposes, within which no one sector, and no one interest, might impose unitary dominance.

The seminal thinkers who set democratic capitalism upon its historic course were exceedingly practical men, thoroughly sobered by the human capacity for sin and illusion. While some scholars interpret their work as though they were sunny rationalists,[7] the opposite is nearer the truth. Thinkers like Montesquieu, Adam Smith, and James Madison were counter-rationalists. They were not optimistic about the human capacity for reasonableness or virtue. Ironically, the modest virtue they claimed for democratic capitalism laid the system open to charges that it encourages the worst in the human breast. Some have accused it of licensing greed and making riches god. Still others accuse it of radical individualism, moral anarchy, and destructive competitiveness. Some sunny rationalism.

THE DOCTRINE OF UNINTENDED CONSEQUENCES

In political economy, there are two self-frustrating ways to defeat sin. One is to convert individual hearts. The other is to construct a system which imposes virtue by force. Democratic capitalism chose a third way. Through close study, its founders observed that in political economy personal intentions characteristically lead to unintended consequences. There is a gap between "moral man" and "not-so-moral society."[8] Thus, political economists must pay less attention to individual intentions and more attention to systemic even if unintended consequences. In free societies, at least, there are so many agents, intentions, and actions that the line between intentions and results is too complex for the human mind to discern in advance.[9] If there is a social order, its rationality may become apparent after the fact. Its order cannot be planned or commanded in advance.

This doctrine of unintended consequences is central in the theory of democratic capitalism. It represents the conservative strain within the Enlightenment. It is counter-rationalist. By contrast, socialism is clearly rationalist, depending as it does on the ability of the human mind to ram its own intentions through social reality. Equally by contrast, anti-capitalist conservatives resist the dynamism, change, and progress which democratic capitalists favor. Friedrich Hayek is probably correct in his essay "Why I Am Not a Conservative" in identifying democratic capitalism as an inheritance of the Whig tradition—of Montesquieu, Smith, Burke, de Tocqueville—rather than of the conservative tradition.[10]

The doctrine of unintended consequences turns the eyes of the political economist away from the moral intentions of individuals and toward the final social consequences of their actions. More than that, it turns his attention to systems *qua* systems. This led to the insight that, among competing alternatives, the hopes for a good, free, and just society are best reposed in a system which gives high status to commerce and industry.

Consider the alternatives. The clergy had a demonstrated record of fanaticism, intolerance, and misuse of power. The military had a record of despoliation. Lords and nobles had a record of hauteur, luxury, and indolence on the one hand, and of martial adventure on the other. The state and its bureaucracies, through the system of royal privileges and grants, had long been parasitic upon the prosperity of nations. Bureaucracies of state and church, producing nothing, drove away producers by their arrogance. To which central activity, to which class, then, ought those who favor liberty to turn? Men of manufacturing and commerce might be an unsavory and disagreeable lot. Yet certain features in the formal structure of their own activities allied their own interests to those of liberty.

Men of manufacturing and commerce often have their origins outside existing establishments. Once successful, they may be scorned as *nouveaux riches*, but nonetheless social mobility is important to them. Their activities, moreover, depend upon stability and law, for they must make investments long before the fruits of manufacturing and trading bring them return; their instruments are trust and contract. For another thing, men of manufacturing and commerce have an interest in small increments and marginal savings; their habits of mind incline them to productivity and to moderation. Finally, they have an interest in expanding prosperity for many others, in reaching out to other nations and peoples, and in maintaining ties of peace and order abroad (lest their overseas investments be confiscated by powers suddenly turned hostile).

For all these reasons (and others), the founders of democratic capitalism looked to the formal structures of manufacturing and commerce for real interests that might undergird a political economy of liberty. Perhaps it is worth singling out yet another attractive feature of the world of trade. Its medium is money— cold, impersonal, insensitive to station, class, creed, race, or person. The very qualities which some find so unattractive in money led the partisans of liberty to see in it a respecter not of persons but of laws. The ancient proverb *Radix malorum cupiditas* was often translated in the vernacular as "Money is the root of all evils." The evil uses to which money can be put need no stress. But money has within it moral as well as immoral potency, and its use opens the political economy to men of every class, race, and creed. Its impersonality has good as well as ill effects in societies historically battered by class and religious strife.

The founders of democratic capitalism had a further structural reason for giving greater scope to men of manufacturing and commerce than had obtained under any previous form of political economy. They wished to build a center of power to rival the power of the state. They separated the economy from the state not only to unleash the power of individual imagination and initiative, but also to limit the state from within and to check it from without. They did not fear unrestrained economic power as much as they feared political tyranny. For they believed that restraints upon economic power are many, partly from competitors, but even more from the hazards of economic mortality. Business ventures frequently fail, nature is unpredictable, markets fluctuate, and new technologies make old centers of power obsolete. One may imagine "economic power" in the abstract as formidable, but enterprise by enterprise, industry by industry, it is always subject to swift and sudden failure. Like states, centers of economic power are tempted to abuse their power. That is precisely why the state retains ultimate legal and coercive power, and why the moral-cultural system is kept free of direct dependence either upon the state or upon the economic system.

Neither Montesquieu nor Smith nor Madison was a merchant or an industrialist. None had a high opinion of merchants or industrialists, or pictured the latter as moral idealists. Smith in particular cited evidence that such men, as a class, were often vulgar and crass. Still, it was not to the motivation or virtue of merchants and industrialists that democratic capitalism looked for the social basis of a law-abiding, dynamic, free society. It is the *structure* of business activities, not the intentions of businessmen, that are favorable to rule by law, to liberty, to habits of regularity and moderation, to a healthy realism, and to demonstrated social progress—demonstrably more favorable than the structures of churchly, aristocratic, or military activities. It is in the interests of businessmen to defend and to enlarge the virtues on which liberty and progress depend.

This view stands on its head the usual accusation against democratic capitalism. Those who prefer ecclesiastical, aristocratic, or martial values commonly deplore the values of a society undergirded by the moral imperatives of business. Yet democratic capitalism looks to the record, rather than to the intentions, of rival elites. None had produced an equivalent system of liberties. None had so loosed the bonds of station, rank, peonage, and immobility. None had so raised human expectations. None so valued the individual.

Under democratic capitalism, individual persons began receiving and using proper names.[11] They began to enjoy rights of privacy. They began thinking of themselves as agents responsible for altering their own future and that of the world. De Tocqueville observed how all through the United States a kind of spiritual energy coursed through mechanics and artisans, farmers and carpenters, men and women of every station, who felt charged to make their own world.[12] Under all other systems of political economy, traditional or socialist, priority is given to collectives: orders human and divine, station and rank, classes and systems. Uniquely, democratic capitalism makes the insight and choice of the human person the determining power of history.

Yet democratic capitalism is not a system of radical individualism (as is often alleged). Parties and factions loom large in it. Family is central to it. Structures, institutions, laws, and prescribed procedures are indispensable to its conception. In economic matters, its chief social inventions are the business corporation and the free labor union. Its theory of sin makes such complexity necessary. Its theory of sin makes creative use even of self-interest.

VIRTUOUS SELF-INTEREST

R. H. Tawney described the age of capitalism as the age of acquisitiveness. Marx described it as the reduction of every human relation to the cash nexus. Pamphleteers for generations have denounced its licensing of greed. Yet simple reflection upon one's own life and the life of others, including the lives of those critics who denounce the system from within, suggests that there are enormous reservoirs of high motivation and moral purpose among citizens in democratic capitalist societies. The history of democratic capitalism is alive with potent movements of reform and idealistic purpose. As the world goes, its people do not in fact seem to be more greedy, grasping, selfish, acquisitive, or anarchic than citizens in traditional or in socialist societies. If democratic capitalism is to be blamed for sins it permits to flourish, the virtues it nourishes also deserve some credit.

In practice, the bone of contention seems most often to be the central concept of self-interest. A system committed to the principle that individuals are best placed to judge their real interests for themselves may be accused of institutionalizing selfishness and greed—but only on the premise that individuals are so depraved that they never make any other choice.

The founders of democratic capitalism did not believe that such depravity is universal. Furthermore, they held that the laws of free economic markets are such that the real interests of individuals are best served in the long run by a systematic refusal to take short-term advantage. Apart from internal restraints, the system itself places restraints upon greed and narrowly construed self-interest. Greed and selfishness, when they occur, are made to have their costs. A firm aware of its long-term fiduciary responsibilities to its shareholders must protect its investments for future generations. It must change with the times. It must maintain a reputation for reliability, integrity, and fairness. In one large family trucking firm, for example, the last generation of owners kept too much in profits and invested too little in new technologies and new procedures, with the result that their heirs received a battered company unable to compete or to solve its cash-flow problems. Thus a firm committed to greed unleashes social forces that will sooner or later destroy it. Spasms of greed will disturb its own inner disciplines, corrupt its executives, anger its patrons, injure the morale of its workers, antagonize its suppliers and purchasers, embolden its competitors, and attract public retribution. In a free society, such spasms must be expected; they must also be opposed.

The real interests of individuals, furthermore, are seldom merely self-regarding. To most persons, their families mean more than their own interests; they frequently subordinate the latter to the former. Their communities are also important to them. In the human breast, commitments to benevolence, fellow-feeling, and sympathy are strong. Moreover, humans have the capacity to see themselves as others see them, and to hold themselves to standards which transcend their own selfish inclinations. Thus the "self" in self-interest is complex, at once familial and communitarian as well as individual, other-regarded as well as self-regarding, cooperative as well as independent, and self-judging as well as self-loving. Understood too narrowly, self-interest destroys firms as surely as it destroys personal lives. Understood broadly enough, as a set of realistic limits, it is a key to all the virtues, as prudence is.

Like prudence in Aristotelian thought, self-interest in democratic capitalist thought has an inferior reputation among moralists. Thus it is necessary to stress again that a *society* may not work well if all its members act always from benevolent intentions. On the other hand, democratic capitalism as a system deliberately enables many persons to do well by doing good (or even purporting to do good). It offers incentives of power, fame, and money to reformers and moralists.[13]

The economic system of democratic capitalism depends to an extraordinary extent upon the social capacities of the human person. Its system of inheritance respects the familial character of motivation. Its corporate pattern reflects the necessity of shared risks and shared rewards. Its divisions both of labor and of specialization reflect the demands of teamwork and association. Its separated churches and autonomous universities reflect the importance of independent moral communities. The ideology of individualism, too much stressed by some proponents and some opponents alike, disguises the essential communitarian character of its system.

Regrettably, the theory of democratic capitalism was left too long to economists. While economists are entitled to specialize, theologians also have such rights. A theology of democratic capitalism requires a larger view, of which economists freely concede the legitimacy. Thus, Milton and Rose Friedman in their best-selling *Free to Choose* consciously stress

> . . . the broad meaning that must be attached to the concept of "self-interest." Narrow preoccupation with the economic market has led to a narrow interpretation of self-interest as myopic selfishness, as exclusive concern with immediate material rewards. Economics has been berated for allegedly drawing far-reaching conclusions from a wholly unrealistic "economic man" who is little more than a calculating machine, responding only to monetary stimuli. That is a great mistake. Self-interest is not myopic selfishness. It is whatever it is that interests the participants, whatever they value, whatever goals they pursue. The scientist seeking to advance the frontiers of his discipline, the missionary seeking to convert infidels to the true faith, the philanthropist seeking to bring comfort to the needy—all are pursuing their interests, as they see them, as they judge them by their own values.[14]

Under self-interest, then, fall religious and moral interests, artistic and scientific interests, and interests in justice and peace. The interests of the self define the self. In a free society, persons are to choose their own interests. It is part of the function of a free economy to provide the abundance which breaks the chains of the mere struggle for subsistence, and to permit individual persons to "find themselves," indeed to define themselves through the interests they choose to make central to their lives.

In brief, the term "self-interest" encodes a view of human liberty that far exceeds self-regard, selfishness, acquisitiveness, and greed. Adam Smith attempted to suggest this by speaking of *rational* self-interest, by which he meant a specification of human consciousness not only intelligent and judgmental, beyond the sphere of mere desire or self-regard, but also guided by the ideal of objectivity. In *The Theory of Moral Sentiments* (1759), he argued that what is truly rational must be seen to be so not merely from the point of view of the self-interested party but from that of a disinterested rational observer as well. He called the achievement of such realistic judgment "the perfection of human nature." The whole system, as he imagined it, is aimed toward the acquisition of such realism: "We endeavour to examine our own conduct as we imagine any other fair and impartial spectator would examine it." Again: "To feel much for others, and little for ourselves . . . to restrain our selfish, and to indulge our benevolent, affections, constitutes the perfection of human nature."[15]

Democratic capitalism, then, rests on a complex theory of sin. While recognizing ineradicable sinful tendencies in every human, it does not count humans depraved. While recognizing that no system of political economy can escape the ravages of human sinfulness, it has attempted to set in place a system which renders sinful tendencies as productive of good as possible. While basing itself on something less than perfect virtue, reasoned self-interest, it has attempted to draw from self-interest its most creative potential. It is a system designed for sinners, in the hope of achieving as much moral good as individuals and communities can generate under conditions of ample liberty.

Can human society imitate Providence?

NOTES

1. Thomas Hobbes vividly described the difficulties of establishing social order in his description of the life of man in a mythical state of nature: ". . . no Arts; no Letters; no Society; and which is worst of all, continuall feare, and danger of violent death; and the life of man, solitary, poore, nasty, brutish, and short." Hobbes's Leviathan, ed. W. G. Pogson Smith (London: Oxford University Pres, 1929; reprint of 1651 ed.), p. 96.
2. R. H. Tawney, Equality, 4th ed. (London: Allen & Unwin, 1952; originally published in 1931), p. 222. Tawney complained that the working class is lacking in moral indignation over the conditions of capitalist society: "As it is, though they resent poverty and unemployment, and the physical miseries of a proletariat, they do not always resent, as they should, the moral humiliation which gross contrasts of wealth and economic power necessarily produce" (p. 29).
3. Michael Walzer criticizes the meritocratic aspect of democratic capitalism in his Radical Principles: Reflections of an Unreconstructed Democrat (New York: Basic Books, 1980); see esp. pp. 250-51. See my review in Commentary 71 (February 1981), pp. 78-80.
4. Charles Péguy once placed these words on the door of his room. Another famous line of his runs: "Socialism is a new life, not just a policy" (Letter to Camille Bidault, February 27, 1887). Three useful biographies are Daniel Halévy, Péguy and the Cahiers de la Quinzaine, trans. Ruth Bethell (London: Denis Dobson, 1946; translation of the 1919 ed.); Marjorie Villiers, Charles Péguy: A Study in Integrity (New York: Harper & Row, 1965); and Hans A. Schmitt, Charles Péguy: The Decline of an Idealist (Baton Rouge, La.: Louisiana State University Press, 1967).
5. For a comparison of the two paths, see Michael Novak, ed., Liberation South, Liberation North (Washington, D.C.: American Enterprise Institute, 1981).

6. Juan Luis Segundo, "Capitalism—Socialism: A Theological Crux," in *The Mystical and Political Dimensions of the Christian Faith*, eds. Claude Geffré and Gustavo Gutiérrez (New York: Herder & Herder, 1974), pp. 105-123. This essay is reprinted in the text cited in the preceding note.

7. Robert Heilbroner's interpretation of Adam Smith is typical: "As regularly and as inevitably as a series of interlocked mathematical propositions, society is started on an upward march. . . . In a sense the whole wonderful world of Adam Smith is a testimony to the eighteenth-century belief in the inevitable triumph of rationality and order over arbitrariness and chaos." The truth is that Smith's conceptions of rationality and order are simply different from Heilbroner's, and far less utopian. *The Worldly Philosophers*, 5th ed. (New York: Simon & Schuster, 1980), pp. 64, 68.

8. Late in his career, reconsidering the title of his early classic *Moral Man and Immoral Society* (New York: Charles Scribner's Sons, 1932), Reinhold Niebuhr wrote: "A young friend of mine recently observed that, in the light of all the facts and my more consistent 'realism' in regard to both individual and collective behavior, a better title might have been *The Not So Moral Moral Man in His Less Moral Communities*." *Man's Nature and His Communities* (New York: Charles Scribner's Sons, 1965), p. 22.

9. Eric Voegelin, *Order and History*, 4 vols. (Baton Rouge, La: Louisiana State University Press, 1956-1975); see esp. vol. 1, preface, and introduction.

10. See Friedrich A. Hayek, *The Constitution of Liberty* (Chicago: Henry Regnery, 1960), pp. 397-411.

11. See Paul Johnson, "Is There a Moral Basis for Capitalism?" in *Democracy and Mediating Structures: A Theological Inquiry*, ed. Michael Novak (Washington D.C.: American Enterprise Institute, 1980), p. 56.

12. See Alexis de Tocqueville, *Democracy in America*, ed. J. P. Mayer (Garden City, N.Y.: Doubleday, 1969), pp. 544-546.

13. See Kathleen Nott, *The Good Want Power: An Essay in the Psychological Possibilities of Liberalism* (New York: Basic Books, 1977).

14. Milton and Rose Friedman, *Free to Choose* (New York: Harcourt Brace Jovanovich, 1980), p. 27.

15. Adam Smith, *The Theory of Moral Sentiments* (Indianapolis: Liberty Classics, 1969), pp. 204, 71.

PART TWO: DEATH OF THE "SOCIALIST EXPERIMENT"

FOUR

The Bandung Generation

PAUL JOHNSON

The same historical process which created the superpowers placed traditional powers in a dilemma. What was their role? The defeated nations, France, Germany and Japan, were driven by necessity to a fundamental reappraisal. But Britain had not been defeated. She had stood alone and emerged victorious. Could she not carry on as before? Churchill had fought desperately for British interests. He rejected utterly Roosevelt's notion of America and Russia as the two "idealist" powers and Britain as the greedy old imperialist. He knew of the bottomless cynicism reflected in Ambassador Maisky's remark that he always added up Allied and Nazi losses in the same column.[1] He pointed out to the British Ambassador in Moscow that Russia had "never been actuated by anything but cold-blooded self-interest and total disdain for our lives and fortunes."[2] He was somberly aware that Russia was anxious to tear the British Empire to pieces and feast on its members, and that America too, aided by the Dominions and especially Australia and New Zealand, favoured "decolonization." H. V. Evatt, Australia's cantankerous Foreign Minister, got such notions written into the UN charter.[3] Churchill snarled at Yalta: "While there is life in my body no transfer of British sovereignty will be permitted."[4]

Six months later Churchill had been thrown out by the electorate. His Labour successors planned to disarm, decolonize, make

PAUL JOHNSON was educated at Stonyhurst College, Lancashire, and Magdalen College, Oxford. He has made over forty television films and has written for many newspapers and magazines, including the *Times* of London, the *New York Times*, *Wall Street Journal*, *Washington Post*, *Time*, *L'Express*, and *Die Welt*. He is author of *The History of Christianity, Enemies of Society, Journey into Chaos* and *Modern Times: The World from the Twenties to the Eighties* (Harper & Row, 1983) from which this chapter is taken. Johnson was the inaugural holder of the DeWitt Wallace Chair in Communications in a Free Society at the American Enterprise Institute.

friends with Russia and build a welfare state. In practice they found themselves at the mercy of events. In August 1945 Lord Keynes presented them with a paper showing the country was bankrupt. Without American help, "the economic basis for the hopes of the country is non-existent."[5] Ernest Bevin, the trades union leader turned Foreign Secretary, began with the slogan "Left can talk to Left" and hoped to share atomic secrets with Russia. But he was soon telling his colleague Hugh Dalton: "Molotov was just like a Communist in a local Labour Party. If you treat him badly, he makes the most of the grievances, and if you treat him well he only puts his price up and abuses you the next day."[6] Gradually Bevin came to embody Britain's determination to organize collective security. He told Molotov in 1949, "Do you want to get Austria behind your Iron Curtain? You can't do that. Do you want Turkey and the Straits? You can't have them. Do you want Korea? You can't have that. You are putting your neck out and one day you will have it chopped off."[7]

Bevin's foreign policy meant Britain had to stay in the strategic arms race. Exactly a year after Keynes delivered his bankruptcy report, the Chief of Air Staff indented with the government for nuclear bombs. Specifications for the first British atom bomber were laid down January 1, 1947.[8] Britain's leading nuclear scientist, P. S. M. Blackett, opposed a British bomb, but then he thought that Britain could and should adopt a posture of neutrality vis-à-vis America and Soviet Russia.[9] The chief scientific adviser, Sir Henry Tizard, was also against an independent nuclear force: "We are not a great power and never will be again. We are a great nation, but if we continue to behave like a Great Power we shall soon cease to behave like a great nation."[10] But Tizard was staggered by the Soviet success in exploding an A-bomb as early as August 1949: he attributed it to theft of the material. At all events the decision to make the bomb was taken in January 1947, at the height of the desperate fuel crisis just before Britain handed over the burden of Greece and Turkey to Truman. Only Attlee, Bevin and four other ministers were present.[11] The expenditure was "lost" in the estimates and concealed from parliament. When Churchill returned to office in 1951, he was astounded to find that £100 million had been thus secretly laid out and the project well advanced.[12]

The decision to make the bomb, and the brilliant success with which it was developed and deployed, undoubtedly kept Britain in the top club for another thirty years. It was the first British A-bomb test off Monte Bello Island in October 1952 which led the Americans to resume the atomic partnership. The first British H-bomb test at Christmas Island in May 1957 formalized this partnership by persuading Congress to amend the 1946 McMahon Act: the bilateral agreements of 1955 and 1958 could not have been obtained without a British nuclear capability. Once in the club, Britain was able to play a leading part in the test-ban negotiations of 1958–63 and the process which produced the Non-Proliferation Treaty of 1970. In 1960, in a famous phrase, Aneurin Bevan defended the British bomb to his Labour Party colleagues on the grounds that without it a British Foreign Secretary would "go naked into the council chambers of the world." But this was a misformulation. Without it, Britain would not have been a party to these and other negotiations in the first place: for, like other gentlemen's clubs, the nuclear one does not admit nudes into its council chamber. In 1962 the Anglo–US Nassau agreement gave Britain title to sixty-four modern nuclear launching-platforms as opposed to 1,038 for the USA and about 265 for Soviet Russia. By 1977 the relative figures were America 11,330, Russia, 3,826, and Britain 192. It was this fall in the British ratio which excluded her from the Strategic Arms Limitation Talks (SALT), even though at that time the British "deterrent" could destroy all the major industrial and population centers in Soviet Russia and inflict twenty million casualties.[13]

In 1945–1946, then, it became an axiom of British policy to engage, in conjunction with the Americans, in collective security arrangements to contain Soviet expansion, and to contribute to- wards them a British nuclear force. Through all the changes of mood and government, that consistent thread ran through British policy right into the 1980s. But it was the only stable element. All else was confusion and irresolution. There was a failure of vision, a collapse of will. In the late summer of 1945 the British Empire and Commonwealth seemed to have returned to the meridian of 1919. British power was stretched over nearly a third of the globe. In addition to legitimate possessions, Britain administered the Italian empire in North and East Africa, many former French colonies, and many liberated territories in Europe and Asia, including the glittering empires of Indo-China and the Dutch East Indies. No nation had ever carried such wide-ranged responsibilities. Twenty-five years later, everything had gone. History had never before witnessed a transformation of such extent and rapidity.

It was often to be said, as the disintegration took place, that the collapse of the Empire was foreshadowed by the fall of Singapore early in 1941. But that is not true. There was no ignominy in 1941. Though there was a failure of leadership in the defense of the city, there was no shame in the campaign as a whole. The British in Malaya were not guilty of *hubris* in despising the Japanese. On the contrary they predicted accurately what would happen unless the garrison was reinforced and, above all, rearmed. Instead the decision was taken to save Russia. As it was, two hundred thousand well-equipped and very experienced Japanese troops, with an overwhelming superiority in sea- and airpower, were held at bay for seventy days by elements of only three and a half divisions of Commonwealth fighting troops. In any event, the image of Asiatic victory was wholly erased by the magnitude of Japanese defeat. Britain surrendered at Singapore with ninety-one thousand men. When General Itagaki handed his sword to Admiral Mountbatten in 1945 he had six hundred and fifty-six thousand men in the Singapore command. Elsewhere the British received the capitulation of more than a million. More than 3,175,000 Japanese men at arms came in from the cold, the greatest defeat any Asian or nonwhite nation has ever undergone. In every department, Western (i.e., white) technology and organization had proved not marginally but overwhelmingly superior. It was not only a characteristic but the very archetypal colonial-style victory of firepower over muscle-power.[14]

Nor was there any physical evidence of a collapse of loyalty towards the British empire among the subject peoples. Quite the contrary. The intense efforts made by the Japanese to establish an "Indian National Army" and an independent regime were a total failure. A "government" was established in October 1942 under Chandra Bose, which declared war on Britain and set up its capital in Rangoon. The INA disintegrated immediately when it went into action against the Indian Army. The Japanese were never able to persuade or force more than thirty thousand Indians, civil and military, to serve against Britain. Many thousands of Indian POWS preferred torture and death to changing allegiance: for instance, of the two hundred officers and men of the 2/15 Punjabs captured at Kuching, virtually all were murdered by April 1945, some being beaten to death, others beheaded or bayoneted. Opposition to the war by part of India's "political nation" had no effect on the "military nation." Whereas 1,457,000 Indians served in the army in 1914–18, during the Second World War the number passed the 2,500,000 mark; Indians awarded Victoria Crosses rose from eleven to thirty-one.[15]

Who spoke for India? The "political nation"? The "military nation"? Could anyone speak for India? In 1945 India was over four hundred million people: two hundred and fifty million Hindus, ninety million Muslims, six million Sikhs, millions of sectarians, Buddhists, Christians; five hundred independent princes and maharajahs; twenty-three main languages, two hundred dialects; three thousand castes, with sixty million "untouchables" at the bottom of the heap; 80 percent of the nation lived in five hundred thousand villages, most of them inaccessible even by surfaced road. Yet for all practical purposes the decision had been taken in 1917, under the Montagu reforms, to begin the process of handing power over this vast and disparate nation not to its traditional or its religious or racial or economic or military leaders—or all combined—but to a tiny elite who had acquired the ideology and the techniques and, above all, the vernacular of Western politics. The decision had been confirmed by the reaction to Amritsar. That indicated the British Raj was no longer determined to enforce the rule of law at all costs. The 1935 Act set the process of abdication in motion. The British establishment, whatever public noises it might make, knew exactly what was happening. As Baldwin's *eminence grise*, J. C. C. Davidson, reported to him:

> The fact is that the British government, the Viceroy and to a certain extent the states have been bounced by Gandhi into believing that a few half-baked, semi-educated urban agitators represent the views of 365 million hard-working and comparatively contented cultivators. It seems to me that the elephant has been stampeded by the flea.[16]

India illustrates the process whereby the full-time professional politician inherited the earth in the twentieth century. Reforms created an alien system of representation. A class of men, mainly lawyers, organized themselves to manipulate it. In due course the governing power was handed over to them. The dialogue was entirely between the old and the new elites. The ordinary people did not come into play, except as a gigantic walk-on crowd in the background. The process was to be repeated all over Asia and Africa. The forms of the Westminster, Paris, or Washington model were preserved. The substance was only tenuously present, or absent entirely. Lenin's Bolsheviks of 1917, Mao's CCP cadres of 1949, and the Congressmen of India came to power by different routes. But they had this in common. All three new ruling groups were men who had never engaged in any other occupation except politics and had devoted their lives to the exploitation of a flexible concept called "democracy."

Lenin had asserted his mandate to rule by the methods of a caudillo; Mao by those of a warlord. Gandhi and Nehru stepped into a vacuum created by the collapse of the will to rule. The 1935 Act had made the Raj unworkable, except by permanent repression. In 1942, partly under pressure from Roosevelt, Churchill agreed to a declaration giving India self-government after the war. On July 28 he lunched with George VI, whose diary records: "He amazed me by saying that his colleagues & both, or all 3, parties in Parlt. were quite prepared to give up India to the Indians after the war."[17] This proved to be completely accurate. The arguments in 1945–47 were entirely about the manner and timing, not the fact, of Britain's departure. The actual Indian Independence bill, which became law July 18, 1947, was passed by both Houses of Parliament without a division and against a background of almost complete public indifference.

Indeed, had Britain not abdicated, quickly and wearily, it is difficult to see quite how Indian independence could have been secured. Gandhi was not a liberator but a political exotic, who could have flourished only in the protected environment provided by British liberalism. He was a year older than Lenin, with whom he shared a quasi-religious approach to politics, though in sheer crankiness he had much more in common with Hitler, his junior by twenty years. In his local language, Gujarati, Gandhi means "grocer," and both he and his mother, from whom he inherited chronic constipation, were obsessed by the bodily functions and the ingress and egress of food. This preoccupation was intensified when he went to London and moved in vegetarian circles. We know more about the intimacies of his life than that of any other human being in history. He lived in public in his *ashram* or religious camp, attended by a numerous entourage of devoted women, most of them willing to describe his ways in the most minute detail. By the mid-1970s more than four hundred biographies of him were in existence, and the English edition of his utterances, compiled by fifty researchers and thirty clerks of the Indian Information Ministry, which set up a special department for this purpose, will fill eighty volumes averaging five hundred and fifty pages each.[18]

Gandhi's first question, on rising, to the women who waited on him every morning was "Did you have a good bowel movement this morning, sisters?" One of his favorite books was *Constipation and Our Civilization*, which he constantly reread. He was convinced that evil sprang from dirt and unsuitable food. So although he ate heartily—"He was one of the hungriest men I have ever known," a disciple said—his food was carefully chosen and prepared. A mixture of bicarbonate of soda, honey, and lemon juice was his drink, and all his vegetarian dishes were assisted by munching quantities of crushed garlic, a bowl of which stood by his plate (he had no sense of smell, a useful attribute in India).[19] In middle age, Gandhi turned against his wife and children, indeed against sex itself. He thought women were better than men because he assumed they did not enjoy sex. He carried out his so-called *Brahma-*

charya experiments of sleeping with naked girls solely for warmth. His only seminal emission in his middle and later years was in his sleep in 1936, when he was aged sixty-six; it disturbed him a great deal.[20]

Gandhi's eccentricities appealed to a nation which venerates sacral oddity. But his teachings had no relevance to India's problems or aspirations. Hand-weaving made no sense in a country whose chief industry was the mass production of textiles. His food policy would have led to mass starvation. In fact Gandhi's own *ashram*, with his own very expensive "simple" tastes and innumerable "secretaries" and handmaidens, had to be heavily subsidized by three merchant princes. As one of his circle observed: "It costs a great deal of money to keep Gandhiji living in poverty."[21] About the Gandhi phenomenon there was always a strong aroma of twentieth-century humbug. His methods could only work in an ultraliberal empire. "It was not so much that the British treated him forbearingly," George Orwell wrote,

> as that he was always able to command publicity. . . . It is difficult to see how Gandhi's methods could be applied in a country where opponents of the regime disappear in the middle of the night and are never heard of again. Without a free press and the right of assembly, it is impossible not merely to appeal to outside opinion but to bring a mass-movement into being. . . . Is there a Gandhi in Russia at this moment?[22]

All Gandhi's career demonstrated was the unrepressive nature of British rule and its willingness to abdicate. And Gandhi was expensive in human life as well as money. The events of 1920–21 indicated that though he could bring a mass movement into existence, he could not control it. Yet he continued to play the sorcerer's apprentice, while the casualty bill mounted into hundreds, then thousands, then tens of thousands, and the risks of a gigantic sectarian and racial explosion accumulated. This blindness to the law of probability in a bitterly divided subcontinent made nonsense of Gandhi's professions that he would not take life in any circumstances.

There was a similar element of egregious frivolity in Jawaharlal Nehru. He was a brahmin, from a priestly caste which had in modern times (characteristically) turned to law and politics. He was an only son, a mother's boy, brought up by governesses and theosophists, then as an expatriate at Harrow, where he was known as Joe, and Cambridge. As a young man he led a fashionable life in London and the spas, on £800 a year. He was easily bored. He allowed his father, a hard-working Allahabad lawyer, to pick a wife for him, another Kashmiri brahmin. But he never (like Lenin) showed the smallest desire to take a job to support his family. As his father complained:

> Have you had any time to attend to the poor cows . . . reduced to the position of cows by nothing short of culpable negligence on your part and mine—I mean your mother, your wife, your child and your sisters? . . . I do not think that a man who is capable of starving his own children can be much good to the nation.[23]

Nehru drifted into politics in the wake of Gandhi's campaign, and in 1929 the Mahatma made him Congress president. He dabbled in peasant life: "I have had the privilege of working for them, of mixing with them, of living in their mud-huts and partaking in all reverence of their lowly fare," as he put it. He was in jail for agitation at the same time as Hitler's spell in Landsberg: "It will be a new experience, and in this blasé world it is something to have a new experience." India, he thought, might be saved by "a course of study of Bertrand Russell's books." In many ways he was a Bloomsbury figure, a politicized Lytton Strachey, transplanted to an exotic clime. "An intellectual of the intellectuals," wrote Leonard Woolf. "The last word in aristocratic refinement and culture dedicated to the salvation of the underdog," enthused Mrs. Webb.[24] He swallowed the European Left pharmacopoeia whole, enthusing for Republic Spain, accepting Stalin's show-trials at their face-value, an Appeaser and a unilateral disarmer. He spent most of the war in jail following a putative revolt in 1942 which received very little support, and thus acquired an extensive knowledge of Indian penology. But of the process of wealth-creation and administration, by which four hundred million people were fed and governed, he knew nothing. Until the end of the 1940s he seems to have thought that India was underpopulated.[25] Almost until the last minute he refused to believe—because he knew so little about the real India—that if the British Raj handed over power to Congress the Muslims would demand a separate state. Even more astounding was his view that violent sectarianism, which had been endemic before the nineteenth century and had begun again only after the Gandhi movement and Amritsar, had been essentially created by British rule. He told Jacques Marcuse in 1946: "When the British go, there will be no more communal trouble in India."[26]

In fact, the postwar Indian elections, in which the Muslim

League captured virtually all the seats reserved for Muslims with its program of partition, indicated that division was inevitable and large-scale violence probable. The transfer of power has been presented as a skillful exercise in Anglo-Indian statesmanship. The reality is that the British government simply lost control. Lord Mountbatten was appointed Viceroy on February 20, 1947, with the British economy on the verge of collapse, and told to do what he liked ("*carte blanche*" as he told the King) provided he stuck to the June 1948 deadline for independence.[27] The massacres had begun even before he reached India. Churchill took the view that "a fourteen-month time interval is fatal to an orderly transfer of power" since it gave extremists on both sides time to organize. Lord Wavell, the previous Viceroy, felt Britain should hand over a united country, leaving it to the Indians themselves to divide it if they wished. General Sir Francis Tuker, who had prepared a contingency plan for division, judged that partition was inevitable if the transfer was rushed. Mountbatten rushed the transfer. He made a decision in favor of partition within a fortnight of his arrival. Sir Cyril Radcliffe, who headed the boundary commission, had to make the awards alone as the Hindu and Muslim members were too terrified to make independent decisions.

The result was like the breakup of the Habsburg Empire in 1918–19: the unifying principle was removed, and the result created more problems than it solved. The princes were abandoned. The minority sects and clans were simply forgotten. The untouchables were ignored. All the real difficulties—the Punjab, Bengal, Kashmir, the North-West Frontier, Sind, British Baluchistan—were left to resolve themselves. Mountbatten had a genius for public relations and kept up a brave front. But the transfer and partition were catastrophic shambles, an ignominious end to two centuries of highly successful rule based on bluff. Some five to six million people ran for their lives in each direction. A procession of terrified Hindus and Sikhs, for instance, stretched for fifty-seven miles from the West Punjab. The boundary force of twenty-three thousand was too weak, and some of its troops may have joined the killing themselves.[28] The carnage reached even into Lutyens's incomparable palace, for many of Lady Mountbatten's Muslim staff were murdered; she helped to move their corpses into the mortuary. Gandhi, who had made it all possible, confessed to her: "Such a happening is unparalleled in the history of the world and it makes me hang my head in shame."[29] Nehru, who had seen liberated Indians as so many Bloomsberries, now admitted to Lady Ismay: "People have lost their reason completely and are behaving worse than brutes."[30]

Gandhi was among the victims, murdered in January 1948 by

one of the fanatics whose hour had come. How many went with him will never be known. Estimates of the dead at the time ranged from one to two million. More modern calculations are in the two hundred thousand to six hundred thousand range.[31] But there has been a general desire to minimize and forget the event for fear of repeating it. In the anarchy, other great injustices took place. In Kashmir, Nehru's home state, he used troops to enforce Indian rule, despite the fact that most Kashmiris were Muslims, on the grounds that the ruler was a Hindu: the Muslims there were "barbarians." In Hyderabad, where the majority were Hindus and the ruler a Muslim, he reversed the principle and again used troops on the grounds that "madmen are in charge of Hyderabad's destinies."[32] Thus Kashmir, the most beautiful province of India, was itself partitioned and remains so more than thirty years later; and the ground was prepared for two wars between India and Pakistan.

Nehru ruled India for seventeen years and founded a parliamentary dynasty. He was a popular ruler, though not an effective one. He did his best to make India's parliament, the Lok Sabha, work and spent much time there. But he was too autocratic to allow cabinet government to flourish: his rule was a one-man show—"I think my leaving might well be in the nature of a disaster," he admitted complacently.[33] The view was generally shared abroad: "The greatest figure in Asia," wrote Walter Lippmann. "If he did not exist," said Dean Acheson, "he would have to be invented." "A world titan," pronounced the *Christian Science Monitor.* "Mr. Nehru, without boasting, may say that Delhi is the School of Asia," echoed the *Guardian.* Adlai Stevenson thought him one of the few men entitled "to wear a halo in their own lifetimes."[34] Privately Nehru came to doubt it all. "It is terrible to think that we may be losing all our values and sinking into the sordidness of opportunist politics," he wrote in 1948. He put through a land reform, but it benefited only a few richer peasants and did nothing for agricultural productivity. As for planning, he thought it would "change the picture of the country so completely that the world will be amazed." But nothing much happened. In 1953 he confessed that on economics "I am completely out of touch." At one time he liked to open a dam or two; later his interest waned. In general "We function more and more as the old British government did," he wrote to Governor-General Rajagopalachari, "only with less efficiency."[35] Nehru did not seem to know how to rule. He spent four to five hours every day just dictating to as many as eight typists answers to the two thousand letters which Indians with grievances wrote daily to his office.[36]

What Nehru really enjoyed was holding forth about international morality on the world stage. In the 1950s he became the leading exponent of the higher humbug. At home he practiced acquisitiveness. In 1952 he subdued the Naga tribesmen by using the army (though he vetoed machine-gunning them from the air). When the Portuguese Goans obstinately refused to rise and unite themselves with India, he sent in "volunteers" and liberated them by force. Abroad, however, he denounced "imperialism," at any rate when practiced by the West. He thought that their behavior in Korea showed the Americans to be "more hysterical as a people than almost any others, except perhaps the Bengalis" (who continued to massacre each other into the 1950s). The Anglo-French operations against Egypt in 1956 were "a reversal of history which none of us can tolerate." "I cannot imagine a worse case of aggression."[37]

But for the Communist world he adopted a quite different standard. To the end, his bible on Russia remained the Webbs' mendacious volumes: "the great work," as he termed it. Visiting the country in 1955 he found the people "happy and cheerful . . . well fed." He thought civil liberty was not missed. There was a "general impression" of "contentment," with everyone "occupied and busy"; and "if there are complaints they are about relatively minor matters."[38] He never showed the slightest interest in Soviet colonialism or even recognized that it existed. When Sir John Kotelawala, Prime Minister of Ceylon, criticized the Soviet system of puppet-states in Eastern Europe, Nehru turned on him furiously. He refused to condemn the Soviet invasion of Hungary in 1956, pleading "lack of information," and contented his conscience with a tiny private complaint.[39] Of course there was nothing Nehru could do about Hungary. But he might have saved Tibet from invasion and absorption by China, whose claims were purely imperialistic. Many Indians wanted him to take action, but he did nothing. He thought the aggression had to be understood in terms of "Chinese psychology" with its "background of prolonged suffering."[40] He did not explain why the suffering Chinese needed to take it out on the helpless Tibetans, whose ancient society was smashed like a matchbox and whose people were hustled off into central China, being replaced by Chinese "settlers." The arguments Nehru used to defend China were identical with those used on Hitler's behalf in the mid-1930s: Nehru was not only the last of the Viceroys, he was also the last of the Appeasers.

At the time Nehru was anxious to act as impresario and introduce the new China to the international community. He basked in Chou En-lai's oily flattery ("Your Excellency has more knowledge of the world and Asia than I have"). He hero-worshipped the virile and militaristic Mao, and was quite taken by his fierce and sinister neighbor, Ho Chi Minh ("Fine, frank face, gentle and benign"). In China, he was "amazed" by the "tremendous emotional response from the Chinese people" to his visit.[41] It does not seem to have occurred to him that China and India had fundamental conflicts of interest, and that in building up Chinese prestige he was knotting an almighty scourge. The first punishment came in 1959 when the Chinese, having got everything they needed out of the Pandit, started to rectify their Himalayan frontier and build military roads. Nehru was hoist with his own petard of respecting China's "rights" in Tibet. The big crisis came in 1962 when the harassed Nehru, misled by the overconfidence of his own generals, blundered into war and was badly beaten. He was then driven to the humiliation of asking for immediate American aid, for in his panic he feared a Chinese paratroop drop on Calcutta. So the "neo-colonialist" C130s were provided by Washington, and the "imperialist" Seventh Fleet moved to his succour up the Bay of Bengal. Then, mysteriously, the Chinese steamroller halted and Nehru, mopping his anxious brow, was glad to take U.S. advice and accept a cease-fire.[42] But by then he was an old man who had ceased to count much.

Up to the mid-1950s, however, he was the cynosure of a new entity which progressive French journalists were already terming *le tiers monde.* The concept was based upon verbal prestidigitation, the supposition that by inventing new words and phrases one could change (and improve) unwelcome and intractable facts. There was the first world of the West, with its rapacious capitalism; the second world of totalitarian socialism, with its slave-camps; both with their hideous arsenals of mass destruction. Why should there not come into existence a third world, arising like a phoenix from the ashes of empire, free, pacific, nonaligned, industrious, purged of capitalist and Stalinist vice, radiant with public virtue, today saving itself by its exertions, tomorrow the world by its example? Just as, in the nineteenth century, idealists had seen the oppressed proletariat as the repository of moral excellence—and a prospective proletarian state as Utopia—so now the very fact of a colonial past, and a nonwhite skin, were seen as title-deeds to international esteem. An ex-colonial state was righteous by definition. A gathering of such states would be a senate of wisdom.

The concept was made flesh at the Afro-Asian Conference held April 18-24, 1955 in Bandung, at the instigation of Indonesia's President Sukarno. Some twenty-three independent states from Asia and four from Africa were present, plus the Gold Coast and the Sudan, both soon to be free. The occasion was the apogee of Nehru's world celebrity, and he chose it as a brilliant opportunity to introduce Chou En-lai to the world. But the many other stars include U Nu of Burma, Norodom Sihanouk of Cambodia, Mohammed Ali of Pakistan, Kwame Nkrumah, Africa's first black president-to-be, Archbishop Makarios of Cyprus, the black Congressman Adam Clayton Powell, and the Grand Mufti of Jerusalem.[43] It was calculated that one thousand and seven hundred secret police were in attendance. Some of those present were subsequently to plot to murder each other; others to end their lives in jail, disgrace, or exile. But at the time the Third World had not yet publicly besmirched itself by invasions, annexations, massacres, and dictatorial cruelty. It was still in the age of innocence when it was confidently believed that the abstract power of numbers, and still more of words, would transform the world. "This is the first inter-continental conference of colored peoples in the history of mankind," said Sukarno in his opening oration. "Sisters and brothers! How terrifically dynamic is our time! . . . Nations and states have awoken from a sleep of centuries!" The old age of the white man, which had ravaged the planet with its wars, was dying; a better one was dawning, which would dissolve the Cold War and introduce a new multiracial, multireligious brotherhood, for "All great religions are one in their message of tolerance." The colored races would introduce the new morality: "We, the people of Asia and Africa . . . far more than half the human population of the world, we can mobilize what I have called the *Moral Violence of Nations* in favor of peace."[44] After this striking phrase, a Lucullan feast of oratory followed. Among those overwhelmed by it all was the black American writer Richard Wright: "This is the human race speaking," he wrote.[45]

Sukarno was eminently suited to preside over this gathering. No one illustrated better than he the illusions, the political religiosity, and the inner heartlessness of the postcolonial leadership. The Dutch East Indies had been cobbled together into an administrative unit from thousands of islands. It was an empire in itself. Until 1870 it had been run on principles of pure cupidity. Thereafter, under the inspiration of the great Islamic scholar C. Snouck Hurgronje, a combination of Westernization, "association," and the creation of native elites was introduced under the name of "ethical policy."[46] It was well-intended, but it was really a reflection of Dutch nationalism; it had no answer when a rival, Javanese nationalism appeared in the 1930s. This seems to have been worked out from 1927 onwards, by Sukarno and others, in the internment camp for native agitators at Upper Digul in New Guinea.[47] It was an unimpressive mixture of Islamic, Marxist, and European liberal clichés, but garnished by resounding phraseology. Whatever else he was, Sukarno was the great phrase-maker of his time. When the

Dutch were ousted in 1941, their will to rule collapsed. In 1945 the Javanese nationalists began to take over. The Dutch left, taking 83 percent of the mixed races with them. The Chinese became an unrepresented and increasingly persecuted minority. The non-Javanese majority, many of them in primitive tribal confederations, found themselves colonial subjects of a Javanese empire named "Indonesia."

Sukarno had no more moral mandate to rule one hundred million than Nehru had in India; rather less in fact. He too was devoid of administrative skills. But he had the gift of words. Faced with a problem, he solved it with a phrase. Then he turned the phrase into an acronym, to be chanted by crowds of well-drilled illiterates. He ruled by *Konsepsi*, concepts. His party cadres painted buildings with the slogan "Implement President Sukarno's Concepts." His first concept in 1945 was *Pantja Sila*, or the Five Fundamental Principles: Nationalism, Internationalism (Humanitarianism), Democracy, Social Prosperity, Belief in God. These were "the Essence of the Indonesian Spirit."[48] The cabinet was NASAKOM, uniting the three main streams of the "revolution": *Nasionalisme*, *Agama* (religion), and *Komunisme*. The constitution was USDEK. His political manifesto was MANIPOL. A cabinet coalition was *gotong-rojong*, "mutual help." Then there were *musjawarah* and *mufakat*, "Deliberation leading to Consensus" and "functional representation" (his term for corporatism). Dissatisfied with party government, he made a "Bury the Parties" speech, followed by the introduction of what he termed "guided democracy" or *Demokrasi Terpimpin*. This introduced a "Guided Economy" or *Ekonomi Terpimpin* which expressed "Indonesian identity," *Kepribadian Indonesia*. He felt himself called to do the guiding or, as he put it, "President Sukarno has called on Citizen Sukarno to form a government."[49]

As Sukarno's internal difficulties mounted in the 1950s, he spent more time and words on foreign matters. He spoke of "Free and active neutralism"; then of the dichotomy of "old established" and "new emerging forces"; then of the "Djakarta–Phnom-Penh–Peking–Pyongyang Axis." He harassed his Chinese subjects. He attacked the international Boy Scout movement. One of his axioms was "A Nation Always Needs an Enemy." So he introduced another *Konsepsi*, "Greater Indonesia," which meant expansion into Dutch New Guinea, which he rechristened West Irian, Malaysia, Portuguese Timor, and the Australian territories. For this purpose he invented the term "confrontation," coined the phrase *Ganjang Malaysia*, "Crush Malaysia!" and developed a technique of staging "controlled demonstrations" outside foreign embassies, occasionally letting them become "overenthusiastic" (as in 1963 when the British Embassy was burned down). The crowd was given a slogan for every occasion. For foreign abuse there was NEKOLIM ("Neo-Colonialism, Colonialism and Imperialism"). When foreign aid was cut off or he was criticized by the UN, there was BERDIKARI ("standing on one's own feet"). 1962, when he got hold of West Irian, was "the year of triumph"; 1963, when he failed with Malaysia, was "the year of living dangerously." This last, *Tahun Vivere Pericoloso*, and his stock RESOPIM ("Revolution, Indonesian socialism, natural leadership") reflect the curious amalgam of Dutch, Indonesian, French, Italian and English words (and ideas) with which Sukarno kept his tottering empire going.[50]

If anyone believed in living dangerously, it was the talkative, hyperactive, pleasure-loving Sukarno. Practicing multiracialism, he acquired a notably varied collection of wives and mistresses, and extended his research still further on his numerous foreign jaunts. The Chinese secret police filmed him in action and so preserved his sexual *Konsepsi* for posterity. Khrushchev, already briefed in this respect by private Tass reports, was still deeply shocked, on his visit in 1960, to see the President chatting gaily with a naked woman.[51] But as the 1960s progressed, the Indonesian economy moved closer to collapse. The virtual extinction of the Chinese minority destroyed the internal distribution system. Food rotted in the countryside. The towns starved. Foreign investment vanished. Apart from oil, which still flowed, industry was nationalized and slowly subsidized under a rapacious bureaucracy. By autumn 1965, foreign debt amounted to over $2,400 million, and credit was exhausted. Sukarno had run out even of slogans. Not knowing what to do, Sukarno appears to have given the go-ahead to a *coup* by the Indonesian Communist Party (PKI).

The *putsch* took place in the early hours of October 1. The plan was to destroy the leadership of the armed forces. General Abdul Yani, the Army Chief of Staff, and two other generals were shot on the spot. The Defense Minister, General Nasution, escaped by climbing over the wall of his house, though his daughter was murdered. Three other generals were captured and then tortured to death, in ritual fashion, by the women and children of the PKI: their eyes were gouged out and their genitals sliced off, then their bodies thrown into the Lubang Buaja, the Crocodile Hole.[52] The events were later investigated by a special military tribunal, whose voluminous transcripts leave no doubt about Communist guilt.[53] But the movement, termed *Gestapu*, was a failure. General Suharto, the Strategic Reserve Commander, took over. A fearful retribution followed. The revenge killings began on October 8, when the PKI Djakarta headquarters was burned. The massacres were organized in the local collective fashion, so that all were equally involved in responsibility, and entire families expiated the guilt. It was one of the great systematic slaughters of the twentieth century, the age of slaughter. The toll may have been as high as one million, though the consensus of authorities puts it in the region of two hundred thousand to two hundred and fifty thousand.[54] Sukarno, under house arrest in his palace, repeatedly but impotently called for an end to the killing, for the dead were essentially his supporters. But he was ignored, and his offices gradually stripped from him by a process of slow political torture. At each progressive stage in his degradation, one of his wives left him, and only one remained when he died of kidney disease on June 21, 1970, forgotten and speechless.

But this, too, was in the future. At Bandung in 1955 the all-conquering word still held sway. Among those present was the Egyptian president, Gamal Abdul Nasser, a handsome newcomer to the new humbug but already an accomplished rhetorician in his own right. Israel, undoubtedly an Afro-Asian state, was not represented at the Conference. Therein lay a long and complex tale, produced by the bisection of two of the strongest and most paranoid twentieth-century forces: the insatiable demand for oil and the evil of anti-Semitism.

Britain had moved into the Middle Eastern oilfields in 1908 and had been followed by America in 1924. By 1936 Britain controlled 524 million tons of proven reserves, against 93 million by America; in 1944 the figures had jumped to 2,181 million and 1,768 million; and by 1949 American output, coming chiefly from the richest fields of all in Saudi Arabia, had passed British.[55] By the early 1940s it was already recognized that the Middle East held most of the world's oil reserves: "The center of gravity of world oil production," said Everett De Golyer, head of the U.S. Petroleum Commission in 1944, "is shifting until it is firmly established in that area." At the same time there were the first hints that America might run out of domestic oil—by 1944 the calculation was that only fourteen years' supply remained.[56] Four years later Defense Secretary Forrestal was telling the oil industry: "Unless we had access to Middle East oil, the American automobile companies would have to devise a four-cylinder motor car."[57] European dependence increased much faster. By the time of Bandung its oil consumption was growing by 13 percent annually, and the Middle East proportion had jumped from 25 percent in 1938 to 50 percent in 1949 and now stood at over 80 percent.[58]

The growing dependence of U.S. and European industry on a single source of oil was itself worrying. What turned it into an intractable problem was its conflation with the irreconcilable claims of Arabs and Jews to Palestine. The Balfour Declaration and the idea of a Jewish National Home was one of the post-dated checks Britain signed to win the Great War. It might conceivably have been honored without detriment to the Arabs—for it did not imply a Zionist state as such—but for one critical British mistake. In 1921 they authorized a Supreme Muslim Council to direct religious affairs; and it appointed Mohammed Amin al-Husseini, head of the biggest landowning clan in Palestine, to be senior judge or Mufti of Jerusalem for life. It was one of the most fatal appointments in modern history. The year before, he had been given ten years' hard labor for provoking bloody anti-Jewish riots. He had innocent blue eyes and a quiet, almost cringing manner, but he was a dedicated killer who devoted his entire adult life to race-murder. There is a photograph of him taken with Himmler: the two men smile sweetly at one another; beneath, a charming inscription by the ss chief to "His Eminenece the Grossmufti": the date was 1943 when the "Final Solution" was moving into top gear.

The Mufti outrivaled Hitler in his hatred for Jews. But he did something even more destructive than killing Jewish settlers. He organized the systematic destruction of Arab moderates. There were many of them in 1920s Palestine. Some of them even welcomed Jewish settlers with modern agricultural ideas, and sold land to them. Arabs and Jews might have lived together as two prosperous communities. But the Mufti found in Emile Ghori a terrorist leader of exceptional ability, whose assassination squads systematically murdered the leading Arab moderates—the great majority of the Mufti's victims were Arabs—and silenced the rest. By the end of the 1930s Arab moderate opinion had ceased to exist, at least in public, the Arab states had been mobilized behind Arab extremism, the British Foreign Office had been persuaded that continued access to oil was incompatible with continued Jewish immigration, and the 1939 White Paper virtually brought it to an end and, in effect, repudiated the Balfour Declaration: "a gross breach of faith," as Churchill put it.[59]

Then in 1942 came the first authenticated reports of the "Final Solution." They aroused not pity but fear. America tightened its visa regulations. Seven Latin-American countries followed suit; so did Turkey.[60] At this stage Chaim Weizmann still believed agreement could be reached with Britain to resume the flow of immigrants. In October 1943, Churchill (with Attlee present to represent the Labour Party) told him that partition was acceptable, and on November 4, 1944 he promised Weizmann that one to one and a half million Jews could go to Palestine over ten years.[61] But Chur-

chill was virtually the only Zionist at the top of British politics.
More worthwhile, because concrete and immediate, was his creation, within the British army, of an independent Jewish brigade,
whose members ultimately formed the processional nucleus of the
Haganah, the defense force of the Jewish Agency, when it turned
itself into an army.

At this stage Churchill still thought Britain could control the
destiny of Palestine. In fact, it was already slipping from her grasp.
There were two main factors. The first was Jewish terrorism. This
was created by Abraham Stern, a Polish Jew who had become a
Fascist and an Anglophobe at Florence University, and later tried to
get Nazi finances for his organization through Vichy Syria. Stern
was killed by police in 1942, but his gang continued, as did a much
bigger terrorist group, the Irgun, commanded from 1944 by Mena-
chem Begin. This was a fateful development, because for the first
time modern propaganda was combined with Leninist cell structure
and advanced technology to advance political aims through murder.
During the next forty years the example was to be followed all over
the world: a cancer of modern times, eating at the heart of humanity. Churchill, with his unfailing gift for driving to the root of
events, warned of the tragedy "if our dreams of Zionism are to end
in the smoke of an assassin's pistol and the labors for its future
produce a new set of gangsters worthy of Nazi Germany." Weizmann promised that the Jewish people "will go to the utmost limits
of its power to cut off this evil from its midst."[62] Haganah, in fact,
attempted to destroy both Irgun and the Stern gang. But as the war
ended and the efforts of Jews to reach Palestine became more fran-
tic, it devoted its energies to the legitimate object of assisting illegal
immigration. The "Final Solution" did not end anti-Semitism. Thus,
on July 5, 1946 in the Polish town of Kielce, a rumor that Jews
were engaged in the ritual killing of Gentile children stirred up a
mob which, with the connivance of the Communist police and
army, beat to death forty Jews.[63] This was one of many incidents
which accelerated the stampede.

With Haganah preoccupied, the gangs flourished, egged on by
the rabid elements in the American press. Typical was what Ruth
Gruber wrote in the *New York Post* of the Palestine police:

> These men who loathed the idea of fighting their friends,
> the Nazis, embraced with passion the idea of fighting
> Jews. They walked around the streets of Jerusalem and Tel
> Aviv, the city built by Jews, singing the *Horst Wessel Song*.
> They marched into crowded markets giving the *Heil Hitler*
> salute.[64]

On July 22, 1946 Irgun blew up Jerusalem's principal hotel, the King David, killing forty-one Arabs, twenty-eight British, seventeen Jews, and five others. Part of the hotel was a British government office, and Begin claimed that the object of the bomb was to destroy secret records. But in that case, as Haganah pointed out, the bomb should have been exploded outside office hours. Begin claimed a warning was given: in fact it reached the phone operator two minutes before, and as he was telling the hotel manager the bomb went off.[65] This crime became the prototype terrorist outrage for the decades to come. The first to imitate the new techniques were, naturally, the Arab terrorists: the future Palestine Liberation Organization was an illegitimate child of Irgun.

Jewish terrorism was counterproductive in other respects. On July 30, 1947 two captured British sergeants were murdered in cold blood, and their bodies booby-trapped. The Jewish Agency called it "the dastardly murder of two innocent men by a set of criminals."[66] There were anti-Semitic riots in Manchester, Liverpool, Glasgow, and London; in Derby a synagogue was burnt down. But the effect of this particular episode, coming on top of others, was to turn the British Army anti-Jewish. As in India, Britain had used too little severity. The figures show that, from August 1945 to September 18, 1947 (leaving out the King David deaths), 141 British died, forty-four Arabs, twenty-five Jewish nonterrorists; in addition thirty-seven Jewish terrorists were killed in gunfights, but only seven executed (two committed suicide in prison).[67] The British troops knew they were being unjustly judged. As a result, when the evacuation took place, officers and men conspired to hand over weapons, posts, and supplies to the Arabs. The military consequences were very serious. In effect, Jewish terrorism cost the Jewish state the Old City of Jerusalem and the West Bank of the Jordan, which were not taken until 1967, and then without legal title.

Terrorism led Britain to wash her hands, like Pilate, of the Palestine problem. Ernest Bevin, in charge from July 1945, was an old-fashioned, working-class anti-Semite, though not a vicious one. He told the Labour Party congress in 1946 that the American idea for another one hundred thousand immigrants in Palestine was proposed from "the purest motives—they did not want too many Jews in New York."[68] Terrorism made him bitter. He thought that if Britain pulled out, the Jews would all be massacred, and that British troops were being murdered by those whose lives they were protecting. But by the beginning of 1947 he had had enough. The fuel crisis tipped the balance in favour of scuttle. On February 14—the same month Attlee decided to get out of India straightaway and hand over responsibility for Greece and Turkey to America—Bevin had the Jewish leaders into his office and told them he was transferring the problem to the UN. There was no electricity; only candles. Bevin joked, "There's no need for candles as the Israe*lites* are here."[69]

The second factor was the impingement of America. David Ben-Gurion visited the U.S. in 1941 and felt "the pulse of her great Jewry with its five millions."[70] For the first time he sensed that, with the help of America's Jews, Zionism could be achieved in the immediate future, and thereafter he hustled Weizmann along towards this object. Whether it was right to turn the concept of a Jewish national home into a state is still a matter of argument. Weizmann had the magnanimity to recognize that the cost to the Arabs must be heavy. He told the Anglo-American Committee of Inquiry set up after the war that it was not a choice between right and wrong, but between greater and lesser injustice. Ben-Gurion took a deterministic view: "History had decreed that we should return to our country and re-establish here the Jewish state."[71] But this was to speak with the voice of Lenin or Hitler. There is no such person as History. It is human beings who decree.

The truth is, during the war years the American Jewish community first developed its collective self-confidence and began to exert the political muscle its numbers, wealth, and ability had created. In the immediate postwar it became the best-organized and most influential lobby in America. It was able to show that it held the voting key to swing states like New York, Illinois, and Pennsylvania. Roosevelt had a strong enough political base to ignore this pressure. With characteristic frivolity, he seems to have turned anti-Zionist when, on returning from Yalta, he had a brief meeting with the King of Saudi Arabia. "I learned more about the whole problem," he told Congress, ". . . by talking with Ibn Saud for five minutes than I could have learned in an exchange of two or three dozen letters."[72] David Niles, the passionately pro-Zionist presidential assistant, testified: "There are serious doubts in my mind that Israel would have come into being if Roosevelt had lived."[73]

Truman was politically much weaker. He felt he had to have the Jewish vote to win the 1948 election. He was genuinely pro-Zionist too, and distrusted the Arabism of "the 'striped-pants boys' in the State Department."[74] In the event it was his will which pushed the partition scheme through the UN (November 29, 1947) and recognized the new Israeli state which Ben-Gurion declared the following May. There were vast forces against it. Max Thornburg of Cal-Tex, speaking for the oil interests, wrote that Truman had "prevailed upon the Assembly to declare racial and religious criteria the basis of political statehood" and thereby "extinguished" the "moral prestige of America" and "Arab faith in her ideals."[75] The State

Department prophesied ruin. Defense Secretary Forrestal was appalled: "no group in this country," he wrote bitterly of the Jewish lobby, "should be permitted to influence our policy to the point where it could endanger our national security."[76]

It is likely, indeed, that if the crisis had come a year later, after the Cold War had really got into its stride, the anti-Zionist pressures on Truman would have been too strong. American backing for Israel in 1947–48 was the last idealistic luxury the Americans permitted themselves before the Realpolitik of global confrontation descended. The same time-scale influenced Russia. It backed Zionism in order to break up Britain's position in the Middle East. It not only recognized Israel but, in order to intensify the fighting and the resultant chaos, it instructed the Czechs to sell it arms.[77] These considerations would not have prevailed a year later, when the rush for Cold War allies was on. Israel slipped into existence through a crack in the time continuum.

Hence the notion that Israel was created by imperialism is not only wrong but the reverse of the truth. Everywhere in the West, the foreign offices, defense ministries, and big business were against the Zionists. Even the French only sent them arms to annoy the British, who had "lost" them Syria. The Haganah had twenty-one thousand men but, to begin with, virtually no guns, armor, or aircraft. It was the Communist Czechs, on Soviet instructions, who made Israel's survival possible, by turning over an entire military airfield to shuttle arms to Tel Aviv.[78] Virtually everyone expected the Jews to lose. There were ten thousand Egyptian troops, forty-five hundred in Jordan's Arab Legion, seven thousand Syrians, three thousand Iraqis, three thousand Lebanese, plus the "Arab Liberation Army" of Palestinians. That was why the Arabs rejected the UN partition scheme, which gave the Jews only fifty-five hundred square miles, chiefly in the Negev Desert. By accepting it, despite its disadvantages (it would have created a state with five hundred and thirty-eight thousand Jews and three hundred and ninety-seven thousand Arabs), the Zionists showed they were willing to abide by the arbitration of international law. The Arabs chose force.

It was a small-scale, heroic struggle. Like the Trojan War, it involved many famous personalities: General Neguib, Colonel Nasser, Hakim Amir, Yigal Allon, Moshe Dayan. At the heart of the Arab failure was the hatred between their field commander, Fawzi al-Qawukji, and the Mufti and his gruesome family. The Mufti accused Qawukji of "spying for Britain . . . drinking wine and running after women."[79] The Iraqis and the Syrians had no maps of Palestine. Some of the Arab armies had good equipment, but all were badly trained except for the Jordanians, and King Abdullah of

Jordan only wanted Old Jerusalem, which he got. He had no desire to see an Arab Palestinian state with the Mufti in charge. As he told Golda Meir at a secret meeting: "We both have a common enemy— the Mufti."[80] In retrospect it is clear that the only chance the Arabs had was an overwhelming success in the first days of the war. Ben-Gurion took this from them by a preemptive strike in April 1948, the most important decision of his life, which he was able to carry through with Czech Communist weapons.[81] Thereafter, despite anxious moments, Israeli power increased steadily: by December it had a properly equipped army of one hundred thousand and had established a military ascendency it retained into the 1980s.

The creation of Israel finally ended European anti-Semitism, except behind the Iron Curtain. It created the Arab refugee problem. This was the work of extremists, on both sides. The Arab population of Palestine was 93 percent in 1918, when the Balfour Declaration first began to take effect, and 65 percent in 1947, when the crisis broke. The Arabs could then have had their independent state, plus a major share in the running of Israel. But by then the Mufti and his assassination squads had done their work. On October 14, 1947, when Azzam Pasha, Secretary-General of the Arab League, met the Jewish negotiator Abba Eban in London, he told him bluntly that the time for reason was past: if he accepted the partition he would, he said, be "a dead man within hours of returning to Cairo."[82]

Here we see a classic case of the evil which political murder brings. For by the beginning of the actual fighting, Azzam himself was speaking the language of horror on the radio: "This will be a war of extermination and a momentous massacre," he announced.[83] Even before the fighting began, thirty thousand mainly well-to-do Arabs had left Palestine temporarily, expecting to return in triumph. They included the muhktars, judges, and caids. With no administration to protect them, many poor Arabs fled. When the Jews captured Haifa, twenty thousand Arabs had gone, and most of the remaining fifty thousand left afterwards despite Jewish pleas to remain. Elsewhere the Arab League ordered the Arabs to remain in their homes; there is no evidence to justify Jewish claims that Arab governments were responsible for the flight of the refugees.[84] The Arab exodus was undoubtedly assisted by the fearful massacre carried out by the Irgun at the village of Deir Yassin on April 9, 1948, right at the start of the fighting. About two hundred and fifty men, women, and children were murdered. An Irgun spokesman said on the evening of this atrocity: "We intend to attack, conquer and keep until we have the whole of Palestine and Transjordan in a greater Jewish state. . . . We hope to improve our methods in future and make it possible to spare women and children."[85] The Irgun units were thrown out of the Israeli Army during the June truce in the middle of the fighting; and it was the honorable soldiers of the Haganah who, for all practical purposes, created and saved Israel.

By then the damage had been done. When the smoke cleared there were over half a million Arab refugees (the UN figure was about six hundred and fifty thousand; the Israeli figure five hundred and thirty-eight thousand).[86] To balance this, five hundred and sixty-seven thousand Jews in ten Arab countries were forced to flee in the years 1948–57.[87] Nearly all went to Israel, and all who did had been resettled by 1960. The Arab refugees might likewise have been resettled, as were comparable numbers of refugees, on both sides, after the Greek-Turkish conflicts of 1918–23. Instead the Arab states preferred to keep the refugees in the camps, where they and their descendants remained, as human title-deeds to a Palestinian reconquest, and the justification for further wars in 1956, 1967, and 1973.

Granted Abdullah's willingness to compromise, the Arab-Israeli conflict might have been quickly resolved. He had the best historical title to leadership of the Arab cause. But his country had only three hundred thousand indigenous inhabitants and an income of less than £1,200,000. It was the British who, to assist their war effort, had encouraged the Arabs to create a League; and since they directed the war from Cairo, and since Egypt was the largest country in the area, the League had become an essentially Egyptian and Cairene institution. Hence Egypt led the pack against Israel. This was both an anomaly and a tragedy. For geographical reasons, Egypt and Israel were natural allies, and in antiquity they had been so. The "pure" Arabs of the Hejaz, like Abdullah, did not regard Egyptians as Arabs at all: he said they were poor, miserable, and backward Africans. Egypt's playboy king, Farouk, aroused his particular contempt: when he mentioned his name to visitors, Abdullah would spit into the corner of his carpeted tent.[88] The Egyptians, by contrast, saw themselves as the inheritors of the oldest civilization in the world and the natural leaders of the Arab cause: Farouk had a vision of Egypt as an authoritarian Muslim state embracing gradually all Arabs, even all Muslims. Hence he identified the continuing campaign against Israel with Egypt's own self-respect and aspirations for leadership in the region. From this essentially frivolous set of notions sprang the tragedy which turned Egypt into Israel's bitter enemy for a quarter-century.

The element of instability was increased by Britain's growing disinclination to act as paramount power in the area. As early as October 1946 Britain decided to pull most of its troops out of the

Middle East to East Africa, with Simonstown near Capetown replacing the big naval base at Alexandria. Attlee disliked the Arab leaders: "I must say I had a very poor view of the governing classes."[89] The Palestine mess, even more than the debacle in India, disgusted British public opinion with the whole idea of imperial responsibilities. It shook even Churchill: "Simply such a hell-disaster," he told Weizmann in 1948, "that I cannot take it up again . . . and must, as far as I can, put it out of my mind."[90] But that was only the start. Farouk's grotesquely luxurious lifestyle and the corruption of his regime (the 1948 defeat was blamed on an arms scandal) had led to growing criticism, which came to a head when he married a new queen, Princess Narriman, and took her on a much-publicized honeymoon during Ramadhan in 1951. To distract the public, he unilaterally abrogated the Anglo-Egyptian Treaty on October 8. Early the next year he began guerrilla warfare against the Canal Zone, where Britain had a vast base: thirty-eight camps and ten airfields, capable of accommodating forty-one divisions and thirty-eight squadrons. Old-style monarchs are ill-advised to invite the mob on stage. On January 26, it took over Cairo, murdering Europeans, Jews, and the rich of all nations. The young officers, who had bitterly resented the higher direction of the war against Israel, saw an opening. Six months later their Free Officers Committee sent Farouk packing on his yacht, loaded with his lifetime collection of trinkets and pornography.

The leading spirit was Colonel Gamal Abdul Nasser, who soon elbowed aside the popular general, Mohammed Neguib, initially set up as figurehead. The son of a postal-clerk and a coal-merchant's daughter, he began with some radical ideas. In the disaster of 1948 he told an Israeli staff officer that he envied the socialist *kibbutz* system of farming, which he contrasted with Egypt's absentee landlordism. As this stage he blamed the British, not the Jews: "They maneuvered us into this war. What is Palestine to us? It was all a British trick to divert us from their occupation of Egypt."[91] His *Philosophy of the Revolution* was a frothy mixture of Marxist tags, Western liberalism, and Islam: good, flatulent stuff. He was an archetypal member of the "Bandung generation": adept at words, but not much else. Like Sukarno, he was brilliant at devising slogans and titles: he often changed the name of the party he created and of the gimcrack Arab federations he negotiated. His particular specialty was crowd manipulation. His windy rhetoric went down well, especially with the students, and he seems to have been able to goad the Cairo mob into changing any slogans he wished, often changing them from day to day.[92]

Once in power, Nasser was soon corrupted by it. Like Sukarno, he dissolved the parties. He set up People's Courts and accumulated three thousand political prisoners. He always maintained a modest degree of terror. It was "necessary." Egypt was a poor country with a rapidly growing population (forty million by the 1970s) and a cultivable area smaller than Belgium. Nasser's philosophy did not embrace workable ideas for the creation of wealth. Such ideas as he had promoted its consumption. So terror was not enough. Like Sukarno, he needed a foreign enemy, preferably several. His rule was a deafening series of overseas crises to cover the sad silence of misery at home. First he intensified the campaign against the Suez base. But the British agreed to evacuate it, leaving behind only care and maintenance units. The agreement signed July 27, 1954 gave Nasser almost everything he asked for. When Churchill's colleagues defended it in the Commons, the old man sat with his head bowed. So Nasser turned on the Sudan, a potential satellite. But it slipped from his grasp and moved towards independence.

Then Nasser went to Bandung. It completed his corruption, as it did for other young nationalist politicians. Why sweat at the thankless task of keeping a poor country fed and clothed when the world stage beckoned? Bandung opened Nasser's eyes to the opportunities the age offered to an expert publicist and sloganizer, especially one prepared to play the anticolonialist card. And he had been holding one in his hand all the time: the Jews! Israel was easily rationalized into a general imperialist conspiracy theory. Azzam Pasha had produced the exculpatory mythology as long ago as July 16, 1948. The Arabs had lost because of the West: "England and America followed every Arab effort to obtain arms and opposed it with all their force, while at the same time they worked resolutely and vigorously to assure the flow of war materials and troops to the Jews."[93] After Bandung, then, Nasser reversed his earlier analysis. He worked to build up a coalition of "anti-imperialist" Arab states, to overthrow the decision of 1948, and then to create an Arab superstate with himself at the helm.

The Cold War played into his hands. As part of the containment of the Soviets, Britain and America had been constructing a Middle Eastern alliance, embracing Turkey, Iran, and Pakistan. It was known as the "northern tier." Much against America's will, Britain was anxious to tie this grouping to its own system of Arab clients, notably Iraq and Jordan. Anthony Eden, who had at last succeeded Churchill as Prime Minister, wanted to bolster Britain's sagging leadership in the area with American assistance. The new regime in Russia of Nikita Khrushchev, eager to retrieve Stalin's mistakes in 1948, saw Nasser's emergence as a chance to leap over the northern tier and create client states of their own. The Russians offered to back Nasser's anti-Israeli coalition with a huge supply of Iron Curtain arms on credit. Nasser was delighted. So at one bound, the Russians were over the tier, and he was in business as a Third World soldier-statesman.

Nasser did not forget the other lesson of Bandung: nonalignment. The idea was to play off East and West against each other. That meant dealing with both and being the property of neither. The Bandung philosophy was for the new nations to create their own industrial bases as fast as possible, making themselves independent of "imperalism." Provided the money is there, it is actually easier and quicker—and of course much more spectacular—to build a steel plant than raise agricultural productivity. Nasser returned from Bandung determined to hasten a project to build a giant high dam on the Nile at Aswan. It would provide power for industrialization and extra water for irrigation, raising the cultivable area by 25 percent.[94] But the dam required a World Bank loan of $200 million, mainly from America. There were a great many economic and environmental objections to the scheme, objections which in the end proved fully justified—the net effect of the dam, completed by the Russians in 1970, was actually to increase unemployment and lower agricultural productivity. At all events, after much wavering, the Americans turned down the project on July 19, 1956. This was the kind of blow a high-risk regime like Nasser's could not suffer in silence. He retaliated by nationalizing the Anglo-French Suez Canal.

The Suez crisis of 1956–57 was one of those seriocomic international events, like Abyssinia in 1935, which illustrate historical trends rather than determine them. Britain's decline as a world power was perhaps inevitable. The rate of decline, however, was determined by its own national will. Postwar events had suggested the will was virtually nonexistent. Relative industrial decline had also been resumed, with a vengeance, as the economic crisis of autumn 1955 suggested. Sir Anthony Eden, who had waited so long in Churchill's shadow, was not the man to retrieve a lost game. He was nervous, excitable, intermittently sick, and with a fatal propensity to confuse the relative importance of events. In the 1930s he had, at one time, considered Mussolini more formidable than Hitler. Now, obsessed with the need for Britain to play a Middle Eastern role independently of America, he saw Nasser as another Duce. "I have never thought Nasser a Hitler," he wrote to Eisenhower, "but the parallel with Mussolini is close."[95] This was the wrong way to play it. Nasser needed and wanted dramas. Indifference was the easiest way to shrivel him. That was Eisenhower's tactic, mainly because it was election year and "peace" has always proved the highroad to

American voters' hearts. The difficulty was that Eden needed a drama himself. His first year in power out of Churchill's shadow had been a letdown. He was criticized, especially in his own party, for lacking "the smack of firm government." As the *Daily Telegraph* put it: "There is a favourite gesture with the Prime Minister. To emphasize a point, he will clench one fist to smack the open palm of the other hand. But the smack is seldom heard." It was a measure of Eden's unfitness that he allowed himself to be mortally rattled by this jibe, which evoked from him "a pained and pungent oath."[96] He would give them a smack all right!

The evening Eden got the news of Nasser's nationalization decree, he called the service chiefs to Downing Street. He asked them to prepare an invasion of Egypt. They reported back that it was impossible in under six weeks. That should have settled the matter. A country which cannot invade a small Arab state in less than six weeks is not a great power and had better devise other ways of pursuing its interests. Besides, it was not clear that Nasser had done anything illegal. He had not broken the 1888 convention which governed the Canal. To nationalize foreign assets with due compensation (as he proposed) was the right of every sovereign state. When the Iranian regime of Mohammed Mussadeq had nationalized the British oil refinery at Abadan in 1951, Britain—after, it must be said, much huffing—had sensibly left it to the CIA to knock Mussadeq off his perch. In any case the Canal agreement was due to run out in twelve years. By the time the first flush of anger had worn off, all this had become clear. Eden should have tied Nasser up in negotiations, waited until Eisenhower was reelected, and then concerted with him means to pick the Colonel off. But the Prime Minister wanted his smack. The French were of like mind. The Fourth Republic was on its last legs. It had lost Indo-China; it had lost Tunisia and was in the process of losing Morocco; it was embroiled in an Algerian revolt which Nasser was noisily abetting. The French wanted to pull him down, and they preferred to do it by frontal assault rather than intrigue. They, too, wanted a drama.

An Anglo-French seizure of Alexandria, termed "Operation Musketeer," was ready for September 8.[97] This scheme, though crude, would probably have worked if pursued with resolution. But Eden kept postponing and eventually scrapped it, in favor of a much slower and more difficult occupation plan for the Canal itself, which seemed to him more legal. The truth is, Eden could not make up his mind either to go right outside legality, or stick firmly within it. A perfect viable alternative was to allow the Israelis to dislodge Nasser. She and the Arab states were still technically at war. The Egyptians were blockading Israel's access to the Indian Ocean, in itself an act of war, and they refused her ships passage through the Canal, in flagrant breach of the 1888 convention. Much more serious, however, was that Nasser was clearly building up military strength, with Soviet help, and systematic military and diplomatic alliances, to launch a concerted assault on Israel, which would end in genocide. The process was actually concluded on October 25, 1956, when he formed a unified Egypt-Syria-Jordan command. This process provided moral justification for an Israeli preemptive strike at Egypt. The French approved such a course and were in fact supplying Israel with arms to pursue it, including modern fighters. But she lacked the bombers to knock out Egypt's air force and so guarantee her cities from air attack. Only Britain could supply those. But Eden turned this option down too. It went against his deepest instincts, which were pro-Arab.

The scheme he finally settled for, after much dithering, might have been calculated to get him the worst of all possible worlds. On October 22-24, at secret meetings in Sèvres, near Paris, British, French and Israeli representatives cooked up an immensely complicated plot, under which Israel would attack Egypt on October 29. This would provide Britain with a righteous pretext to reoccupy the Canal to protect lives and shipping there. Britain would issue an ultimatum which Israel would accept. Egypt's refusal would allow Britain to bomb the airfields. Then the Anglo-French would land by force at Port Said. Much ink has been spilt over this "collusion," which both Eden and his Foreign Secretary Selwyn Lloyd denied to their dying day.[98] But the French and Israeli participants later insisted there was a concerted scheme. General Moshe Dayan, the Israeli army commander, reported Lloyd as urging "that our military action not be a small-scale encounter but a 'real act of war,' otherwise there would be no justification for the British ultimatum and Britain would appear in the eyes of the world as an aggressor."[99]

Even this absurd scheme might have worked if Eden had possessed the will to go through with it to the bitter end. But he was an honorable man. He made a half-hearted Machiavelli. As a proxy-aggressor he was wholly incompetent. The transparency of the plot was obvious to all. The Labour opposition repudiated it and set up an uproar. The cabinet, kept imperfectly informed, was uneasy from the start and terrified at the violence of the American reaction once the invasion got under way. In letters of September 2 and 8 Eisenhower had warned Eden in the most emphatic terms not to use force, which he was sure would be counterproductive: "Nasser thrives on drama."[100] He was infuriated by Eden's springing this ill-conceived mine beneath him in the last stages of his election campaign. He litterly ground his teeth, a habit of his when angry, and instructed the U.S. Treasury to sell sterling, something a great many other people were already doing. This had an immediate effect on Eden's cabinet, where he was already sandwiched between two would-be successors: the old Appeaser, R. A. Butler, who wished to pull the party in the direction of the Left, and Harold Macmillan, who wished to pull it in the direction of himself. Both behaved in character. Butler said nothing but opposed the scheme behind the scenes. Macmillan urged boldness, then, when failure loomed, switched sides and, as Chancellor of the Exchequer, urged that there was no alternative but to comply with Eisenhower's wishes for a cease-fire. Eden collapsed on November 6, only a week after the adventure was launched and twenty-four hours after the first Anglo-French landings took place. His capitulation followed a particularly fierce message from Eisenhower, which may have included the threat of oil sanctions.[101] Thereafter he retreated into sickness and resignation.

The episode was a striking victory for the Bandung generation. Nehru, administering moral rebukes all round, was in his element. Nasser emerged with enhanced prestige because in all the excitement it was scarcely noticed that the Israelis had inflicted a shattering defeat, in less than a week, on his large, Soviet-armed forces. Any Egyptian discomfort was attributed to the Anglo-French forces. Thus what might have been a fatal blow to Nasser's prestige actually enhanced it, for "collusion" gave solid substance to the Arab mythology that Israel was merely an imperialist proxy. Suez confirmed the Bandung view of the world, mythology made flesh.

Suez is often said to have dealt the final blow to Britain's status as a great world power. That is not true. The status had been lost in 1947. Suez simply made it plain for all the world to see. The underlying cause was a failure of will, not of strength, and the Suez fiasco merely reflected that failure, of which Eden was a pathetic sacrificial victim. Macmillan, who succeeded him, drew the moral that in a world of superpowers, a medium-sized power survives by virtue of good public relations rather than battleships. The real loser in the long term was the United States. Eisenhower appeared to act decisively, and he got his way fast enough. Britain came to heel. He preserved his reputation as a man of peace. But in the process he helped to prepare a mighty scourge for America's own back, in the shape of the tendentious concept of "world opinion" first articulated at Bandung and now, by Eisenhower's own act, transferred to the UN.

Until the early 1950s, the Americans had controlled the UN. Their first mistake was to involve it in Korea, especially through the forum of the General Assembly, a pseudo-representative body which spoke only for governments, a growing proportion of which were undemocratic. Korea broke Trygve Lie, the Norwegian Secretary-General, who was loyal to the principles of the old Western alliance. He resigned when the Russians boycotted him and got the Left to stir up his own Secretariat against him. At this point the Western democracies should have dropped the UN and concentrated instead on expanding NATO into a worldwide security system of free nations.

Instead, after much bad temper, the powers appointed a senior Swedish diplomat called Dag Hammarskjöld. A worse choice could not be imagined. He came from a highly successful family of public servants in a nation uneasily aware that it had grown immensely prosperous by staying out of two world wars. He was guilt personified, and he was determined that the West should expiate it. Severe, well-read, humorless, unmarried (though not homosexual: "In Hammarskjöld's life," wrote his official biographer, "sex played little or no part"[102]), he exuded a secular religiosity. It was characteristic of him and of the advanced fifties good taste he faithfully reflected, that he transformed the old UN Meditation Room, a plain and unpretentious chamber, into a dark and dramatic cavern, with striking perspective and lighting and, in its center, a vast rectangular block of iron-ore illuminated by a single shaft of light. What did it symbolize? Relative morality perhaps. It was Hammarskjöld's manifest intention to cut the umbilical cord which linked the UN to the old wartime Western alliance, and to align the organization with what he regarded as the new emergent force of righteousness in the world: the "uncommitted" nations. In short, he too was a member of the Bandung generation, despite—or rather because of—his pallid face. When Eisenhower turned on Eden at Suez, broke him, and handed the whole problem to the UN, he gave Hammarskjöld exactly the opportunity he had been waiting for.

The Secretary-General set to work to oust the Anglo-French force and the Israelis and replace them with a multination UN "peace-keeping" contingent. He saw a role for himself as a world statesman, driven by the engine of nonalignment. Hence, though affecting impartiality, he threw his weight entirely behind the Afro-Asian camp. That meant treating Israel not as a small and vulnerable nation, but as an outpost of imperialism. There was on record a 1951 UN resolution, passed before his time, calling on Egypt to allow Israeli vessels through the Canal. At no point did Hammarskjöld make any attempt to get the resolution implemented. Nor would he allow that Arab denial of freedom of navigation to Israeli shipping in the Gulf of Aqaba was a threat to peace—though in fact it was this denial, tightened by the three-power Arab military pact of October 25, 1956, which was the immediate cause of the Israeli attack. He repeatedly declined to condemn Nasser's seizure of the Canal, and other arbitrary acts. So far as he was concerned, the Israeli attack and the Anglo-French intervention were wholly unprovoked acts of aggression. He said he was "shocked and outraged" by such behavior. On October 31, he took the unprecedented step of publicly rebuking the British and French governments. The Soviet invasion of Hungary, which took place under cover of the Suez crisis, he treated as a tiresome distraction. His friendliness to the Egyptians throughout, and his cold hostility to Britain, France, and Israel, made it plain where his emotional sympathies lay. He set his heart on the public humiliation of the three powers, and he got it. In deploying the UN emergency force to move into the vacuum created by the three-power withdrawal, he insisted that its presence was by grace and favor of Egypt: as he put it, "the very basis and starting point has been the recognition by the General Assembly of the full and unlimited sovereign rights of Egypt."[103] It had therefore to be withdrawn at Egypt's simple request, a right exercised by Egypt in 1967 as soon as it believed itself strong enough to destroy Israel. Hammarskjöld thus bequeathed another Middle Eastern war to his successors. More important still, however, was his demonstration of the way in which the UN could be used to marshal and express hatred of the West. In 1956 it was the turn of Britain and France. Soon it would be America's own.

America was also the loser by the impact of Suez on France. If Suez simply pushed Britain slightly faster down its chosen slope, in France it helped to bring to a head the national crisis created by the agony of French Algeria. Algeria was the greatest and in many ways the archetype of all the anticolonial wars. In the nineteenth century the Europeans won colonial wars because the indigenous peoples had lost the will to resist. In the twentieth century the roles were reversed, and it was Europe which lost the will to hang onto its gains. But behind this reality of wills there are demographic facts. A colony is lost once the level of settlement is exceeded by the growth rate of the indigenous peoples. Nineteenth-century colonialism reflected the huge upsurge in European numbers. Twentieth-century decolonization reflected European demographic stability and the violent expansion of native populations.

Algeria was a classic case of this reversal. It was not so much a French colony as a Mediterranean settlement. In the

1930s there were only one and a half million Arabs there, and their numbers were dwindling. The Mediterranean people moved from the northern shores to the southern ones, into what appeared to be a vacuum: to them the great inland sea was a unity, and they had as much right to its shores as anyone, provided they justified their existence by wealth-creation. And they did: they expanded two thousand square miles of cultivated land in 1830 to twenty-seven thousand by 1954.[104] These *pieds noirs* were only 20 percent French in origin (including Corsicans and Alsacians). They were predominantly Spanish in the west, Italian (and Maltese) in the east. But rising prosperity attracted others: Kabyles, Chaouias, Mzabite, Mauritanians, Turks, and pure Arabs, from the mountains, the west, the south, the east. And French medical services virtually eliminated malaria, typhus, and typhoid and effected a prodigious change in the non-European infant mortality rates. By 1906 the Muslim population had jumped to four and a half million; by 1954 to nine million. By the mid-1970s it had more than doubled again. If the French population had risen at the same rate, it would have been over three hundred million by 1950. The French policy of "assimilation," therefore, was nonsense since by the year 2000 Algerian Muslims would have constituted more than half the French population, and Algeria would have "assimilated" France rather than the reverse.[105]

By the 1950s there were not enough *pieds noirs* for long-term survival as a dominant class or even an enclave. Only a third of Algiers' nine hundred thousand inhabitants were Europeans. Only in Oran were they in a majority. Even in the most heavily settled part, the Mitidja, the farms were worked by Muslim labor. In 1914 two hundred thousand Europeans had lived off the land; by 1954 only ninety-three thousand. By the 1950s most *pieds noirs* had ordinary, poorly paid city jobs Arabs could do just as well. The social structure was an archaeological layer-cake of race prejudice: "the Frenchman despises the Spaniard, who despises the Italian, who despises the Maltese, who despises the Jew; all in turn despise the Arab."[106] There was no pretense at equality of opportunity: in 1945 fourteen hundred primary schools catered for two hundred thousand European children, 699 for 1,250,00 Muslims. Textbooks began: "Our ancestors, the Gauls. . . ."

More serious, however, was the fraudulence of the electoral system. Either the reforms passed by the French parliament were not applied at all, or the votes were cooked by the local authorities themselves. It was this which cut the ground beneath the many well-educated Muslim moderates who genuinely wanted a fusion of French and Muslim culture. As one of the noblest of them, Ahmed Boumendjel, put it: "The French Republic has cheated. She has made fools of us." He told the Assembly: "Why should we feel ourselves bound by the principles of French moral values . . . when France herself refuses to be subject to them?"[107] The elections of 1948 were faked; so were those of 1951. In such circumstances, the moderates had no effective role to play. The men of violence moved forward.

There was a foretaste in May 1945, when the Arabs massacred one hundred and three Europeans. The French reprisals were on a savage scale. Divebombers blew forty villages to pieces; a cruiser bombarded others. The Algerian Communist Party journal *Liberté* called for the rebels to be "swiftly and pitilessly punished, the instigators put in front of the firing-squad." According to the French official report, one thousand and twenty to thirteen hundred Arabs were killed; the Arabs claimed forty-five thousand. Many demobilized Arab soldiers returned to find their families dead, their homes demolished. It was these former NCOs who formed the leadership of the future Front de Libération Nationale (FLN). As the most conspicuous of them, Ahmed Ben Bella, put it: "The horrors of the Constantine area in May 1945 persuaded me of the only path: Algeria for the Algerians." The French commander, General Duval, told the *pieds noirs:* "I have given you peace for ten years."

That proved to be entirely accurate. On November 1, 1954, the embittered NCOs were ready: Ben Bella, by now an experienced urban terrorist, linked forces with Belkacem Krim, to launch a national rising. It is important to grasp that the object, from start to finish, was not to defeat the French Army. That would have been impossible. The aim was to destroy the concept of assimilation and multiracialism by eliminating the moderates on both sides. The first Frenchman to be murdered was a liberal, Arabophile schoolteacher, Guy Monnerot. The first Arab casualty was a pro-French local governor, Hadj Sakok. Most FLN operations were directed against the loyal Muslim element: employees of the state were murdered, their tongues cut off, their eyes gouged out, then a note, "FLN", pinned to the mutilated bodies.[108] This was the strategy pioneered by the Mufti in Palestine. Indeed many of the rebel leaders had served him. The ablest, Mohamedi Said, commander of "Wilaya 3" in the Kabyle mountains, had joined the Mufti's "Muslim SS legion," had parachuted into Tunisia as an *Abwehr* agent, and declared: "I believe that Hitler would destroy French tyranny and free the world." He still wore his old SS helmet from time to time. His disciples included some of the worst killers of the twentieth century, such as Ait Hamouda, known as

Amirouche, and Ramdane Abane, who had sliced off breasts and testicles in the 1945 massacres, read Marx and *Mein Kampf* in jail, and whose dictum was: "One corpse in a suit is always worth more than twenty in uniform."

These men, who had absorbed everything most evil the twentieth century had to offer, imposed their will on the villages by sheer terror; they never used any other method. Krim told a Yugoslav paper that the initiation method for a recruit was to force him to murder a designated "traitor," *mouchard* (police spy or informer), French gendarme or colonialist: "An assassination marks the end of the apprenticeship of each candidate." A pro-FLN American reporter was told: "When we've shot [the Muslim victim] his head will be cut off and we'll clip a tag on his ear to show he was a traitor. Then we'll leave the head on the main road." Ben Bella's written orders included: "Liquidate all personalities who want to play the role of *interlocuteur valable*." "Kill any person attempting to deflect the militants and inculcate in them a *bourguibien* spirit." Another: "Kill the *caids*. . . . Take their children and kill them. Kill all those who pay taxes and those who collect them. Burn the houses of Muslim NCOs away on active service." The FLN had their own internal *reglements des comptes*, too: the man who issued the last order, Bachir Chihani, was accused (like Roehm) of pederasty and sadistic sex-murders, and chopped to pieces along with eight of his lovers. But it was the Muslim men of peace the FLN killers really hated. In the first two-and-a-half years of war, they murdered only one thousand and thirty-five Europeans but six thousand three hundred and fifty two Arabs (authenticated cases; the real figure was nearer twenty thousand).[109] By this point the moderates could only survive by becoming killers themselves or going into exile.

The FLN strategy was, in fact, to place the mass of the Muslims in a sandwich of terror. On one side, the FLN killers replaced the moderates. On the other, FLN atrocities were designed to provoke the French into savage reprisals, and so drive the Muslim population into the extremist camp. FLN doctrine was spelt out with cold-blooded precision by the Brazilian terrorist Carlos Marighela:

> It is necessary to turn political crisis into armed conflict by performing violent actions that will force those in power to transform the political situation of the country into a military situation. That will alienate the masses, who, from then on, will revolt against the army and the police. . . . The government can only intensify its repression, thus

making the lives of its citizens harder than ever . . . police
terror will become the order of the day. . . . The population
will refuse to collaborate with the authorities, so that the
latter will find the only solution to their problems lies in
the physical liquidation of their opponents. The political
situation of the country will [then have] become a military
situation.[110]

Of course this odious variety of Leninism, if pursued ruth-
lessly enough, has a certain irresistible force. The French government in 1954 was composed, on the whole, of liberal and civilized men, under the Radical-Socialist Pierre Mendès-France. They
shared the illusion—or the vision—that Algeria could become a
genuine multiracial society, on the principles of liberty, equality,
and fraternity. Mendès-France, who had happily freed Indo-China
and Tunisia, told the Assembly: "The Algerian *départements* are
part of the French Republic . . . they are irrevocably French . . .
there can be no conceivable session." On Algeria, said his Interior
Minister, François Mitterrand, "the only possible negotiation is
war."[111] Both men believed that if France's own principles were
now at last fully and generously turned into an Algerian reality,
the problem would be solved. They sent out as Governor-General
Jacques Soustelle, a brilliant ethnologist and former resistance-
fighter, to create this reality. What they did not realize was that
the FLN's object was precisely to transform French generosity into
savagery.

Soustelle saw the FLN as Fascists. He thought he could defeat them by giving the Arabs genuine democracy and social justice. He created four hundred detachments of *Képis bleus* (SAS) in
remote areas to protect loyalists. He brought in dedicated liberals
like Germaine Tillion and Vincent Monteil to set up networks of
centres sociaux and maintain contacts with Muslim leaders of
opinion.[112] He sought desperately to bring Muslims into every
level of government. His instructions to the police and army
forbade terror and brutality in any form and especially collective
reprisals.[113] It is unlikely that Soustelle's policy of genuine integration could have succeeded anyway, once the French themselves
realize what it involved: France did not want to become a half-
Arab, half-Muslim nation, any more than most Arabs wanted to
become a French one. But in any case the FLN systematically
murdered the instruments of Soustelle's liberal policy, French and
Arab. They strove hardest to kill those French administrations
who loved the Arabs, and usually succeeded. One such victim was
Maurice Dupuy, described by Soustelle as a "secular saint." At his

funeral Soustelle was in tears as he pinned the *Légion d'honneur* on the eldest of Dupuy's eight orphaned children, and it was then he first used the word "revenge."[114]

In the summer of 1955 the FLN went a stage further and adopted a policy of genocide: to kill all French without distinction of age or sex. On August 20 the first massacres began. As always, they embraced many Arabs, such as Allouah Abbas, nephew of the moderate nationalist leader Ferhat Abbas, who had criticized FLN atrocities. But the main object was to provoke French army reprisals. At Ain-Abid near Constantine, for instance, thirty-seven Europeans, including ten under fifteen, were literally chopped to pieces. Men had their arms and legs cut off, children their brains dashed out; women were disembowled— one *pied-noir* mother had her womb opened, her five-day-old baby slashed to death, and then replaced in her womb. This "Philippeville massacre" succeeded in its object: French paratroopers in the area were given orders to shoot all Arabs and (by Soustelle's account) killed 1,273 "insurgents," which FLN propaganda magnified to twelve thousand. It was the 1945 massacre over again. As Soustelle put it, "there had been well and truly dug an abyss through which flowed a river of blood." French and Muslim liberals like Albert Camus and Ferhat Abbas, appearing on platforms together to appeal for reason, were howled down by all sides.[115]

From this point the Soustelle experiment collapsed. The war became a competition in terror. The focus switched to the Algiers Casbah, where every square kilometer housed one hundred thousand Algerians. It began with the execution of a crippled murderer, Ferradj, who had killed a seven-year-old girl and seven other civilians. The FLN commander, Ramdane Abane, ordered one hundred French civilians to be murdered for every execution of an FLN member. On June 21–24, 1956, his chief killer, Saadi Yacef, who controlled a network of bomb factories and fourteen hundred "operators," carried out forty-nine murders. The violence grew steadily through the second half of 1956—parallel with the buildup to the Suez adventure. The French Mayor of Algiers was murdered, and a bomb carefully exploded in the middle of the funeral ceremony. Yacef secretly ordered all his operators out of the area in advance, to make certain that in the subsequent wild reprisals only innocent Muslims were killed.[116]

The Suez debacle was important because it finally convinced the army that civilian governments could not win the war. Robert Lacoste, Soustelle's socialist successor, conceded the point. On January 7, 1957 he gave General Jacques Massu and his forty-six hundred men absolute freedom of action to clean the FLN out of Algiers. For the first time all restraints on the army, including the banning of torture, were lifted. Torture had been abolished in France on October 8, 1789. Article 303 of the Penal Code imposed the death penalty for anyone practicing it. In March 1955 a secret report written by a senior civil servant recommended the use of supervised torture as the only alternative to prevent much more brutal unauthorized torture. Soustelle had flatly rejected it. Now Massu authorized it, as he later admitted: "In answer to the question: 'was there really torture?' I can only reply in the affirmative, although it was never either institutionalized or codified."[117] The argument was that successful interrogation saved lives, chiefly of Arabs; that Arabs who gave information would be tortured to death, without restraint, by the FLN, and it was vital for the French to make themselves feared more. It was the Arab belief that Massu operated without restraints, as much as the torture itself, which caused prisoners to talk. But non-Muslims were tortured too. One, a Communist Jew called Henri Alleg, wrote a best-selling book which caused an outburst of moral fury throughout France in 1958.[118] Massu claimed that interrogations by his men left no permanent damage. On seeing Alleg, looking whole and well, on the steps of the Palais de Justice in 1970, he exclaimed:

> Do the torments which he suffered count for much along-
> side the cutting off of the nose or of the lips, when it was
> not the penis, which had become the ritual present of the
> *fellaghas* to their recalcitrant 'brothers'? Everyone knows
> that these bodily appendages do not grow again![119]

But the notion that it was possible to supervise limited torture effectively during a war for survival is absurd. In fact, the liberal Secretary-General of the Algiers Prefecture, Paul Teitgen, testified that about three thousand prisoners "disappeared" during the Algiers battle. At all events Massu won it. It was the only time the French fought the FLN with its own weapons. Algiers was cleansed of terrorism. Moderate Arabs dared to raise their voices again. But the victory was thrown away by a new policy of *regroupement* of over a million poor *fellahs*, a piece of crude social engineering calculated to play into FLN hands. Besides, the Massu experiment set up intolerable strains within the French system. On the one hand, by freeing army units from political control and stressing the personalities of commanders, it encouraged private armies: colonels increasingly regarded themselves as proprietors of their regiments, as under the monarchy, and began to manipulate their generals into disobedience. In the moral confusion, officers began to see their primary obligation as towards their own men rather than the state.[120]

At the same time, news leaking out of what the army had done in Algiers began to turn French liberal and center opinion against the war. From 1957 onwards, many Frenchmen came to regard Algerian independence, however distasteful, as preferable to the total corruption of the French public conscience. Thus the demand for the restoration of political control of the war—including negotiations with the FLN—intensified just as the French army was, as it believed, winning by asserting its independence. This irreconcilable conflict produced the explosion of May 1958 which returned General de Gaulle to power and created the Fifth Republic.

De Gaulle was not a colonialist. He thought the age of colonies was over. His body seemed in the past, but his mind was in the future. He claimed that at Brazzaville in 1944, when marshalling black Africa behind the Resistance, he had sought "to transform the old dependent relationships into preferential links of political, economic and cultural co-operation."[121] He saw the half-hearted continuation of French colonialism as the direct result of the weakness of the Fourth Republic's constitution, which he despised, and the "regime of the parties," incapable of "the unequivocal decisions decolonization called for." "How could it," he asked, "have surmounted and if necessary broken all the opposition, based on sentiment, habit or self-interest, which such an enterprise was bound to provoke?" The result was vacillation and inconsistency, first in Indo-China, then in Tunisia and Morocco, finally and above all in Algeria. Naturally, he said, the army "felt a growing resentment against a political system which was the embodiment of irresolution."[122]

The *coup* was detonated, probably deliberately, by the FLN decision on May 9, 1958 to "execute" three French soldiers for "torture, rape and murder." Four days later, white students stormed the government headquarters in Algiers. Massu asked Lacoste, who had fled to France, whether he had permission to fire on the white mob. He was not given it. That night, at a Brecht play attacking generals, a left-wing audience applauded deliriously.[123] But not one was actually prepared to fight for the Fourth Republic. In Algiers, the generals took over, and called for de Gaulle's return. Some thirty thousand Muslims went to the government forum to demonstrate their approval. They sang the *"Marseillaise"* and the army song, *"Chant des Africains"*: a spontaneous demonstration in favor of French civilization and against the barbarism of the FLN. Massu said: "Let them know that France will never abandon them."[124] When the generals called for de Gaulle they were lying, for they saw him merely as a battering-ram, to smash the Republic and take power themselves. De Gaulle thought Algeria was untenable and would destroy the French army. Indeed, he feared even worse might happen. On May 24 a detachment from Algeria landed in Corsica. The local authorities fraternized. Police sent from Marseilles allowed themselves to be disarmed. De Gaulle took over to avert an invasion of France itself, which would probably have succeeded or, alternatively, produced civil war. He saw ominous parallels with the beginning of the Spanish catastrophe in 1936. It would, he thought, finally destroy France as a great civilizing power. If Paris was worth a mass, France herself was worth a few lies.

So, having taken power, he went to Algiers to deceive. On June 4 he told the howling *colon* mob in Algiers: "*Je vous ai compris.*" "I tossed them the words," he wrote, "seemingly spontaneous but in reality carefully calculated, which I hoped would fire their enthusiasm without committing me further than I was willing to go."[125] He had said the previous year, privately: "Of course independence will come, but they are too stupid there to know it." "Long live French Algeria!" he chanted publicly in June 1958; privately: "*L'Afrique est foutue et l'Algérie avec!*" He called French Algeria "a ruinous Utopia." Publicly he continued to reassure the *colons* and the army. "Independence? In twenty-five years" (October 1958). "The French army will never quit this country and I will never deal with those people from Cairo and Tunis" (March 1959). "There will be no Dien Bien Phu in Algeria. The insurrection will not throw us out of this country." "How can you listen to the liars and conspirators who tell you that in granting free choice to the Algerians, France and de Gaulle want to abandon you, to pull out of Algeria and hand it over to the rebellion?" (January 1960). "Independence . . . a folly, a monstrosity" (March 1960).[126]

Meanwhile, he got an ever-tighter grip on the state. On September 28, 1958 the French adopted the constitution of the Fifth Republic, concentrating power in the president. On December 21 he was elected president. The same referendum which created the new constitution gave all French overseas territories the right of association or departure. The notion of consent thus became universal. One by one, de Gaulle broke or removed the men who had hoisted him to office. In February 1960 he demanded and received "special powers." Four months later he opened secret talks with the FLN leaders. In January 1961 he held a referendum offering Algeria freedom in association with France, and got an overwhelming "Yes" vote. It was the end of *Algérie francaise*, and it brought its extremist supporters out into the open, bombs in hand.

If the army leadership had insisted on taking power in May 1958, it could have done so, with or without de Gaulle. By April 1961, when it finally grasped de Gaulle's deception and sought to overthrow him, the chance had been missed. French opinion had moved on. The conscripts had transistor radios; they could hear the news from Paris; they refused to follow their officers. The revolt collapsed; its leaders surrendered or were hunted down and jailed. That left the way open for a complete scuttle. Captured FLN leaders were released from prisons to join the talks just as the rebel French generals were beginning their sentences.

White terrorism, the OAS *(Organization de l'Armée Secrète)*, took longer to deal with. It operated at full blast for over a year, using bombs, machine-guns and bazookas, killing over twelve thousand civilians (mainly Muslims) and about five hundred police and security men. It illustrates the fearful power of political violence to corrupt. Indeed, in many ways it was the mirror-image of the FLN. On February 23, 1962, its leader General Salan, who had had a distinguished career as an honorable soldier, issued orders for

> a generalized offensive. . . . The systematic opening of fire against CRS and gendarmerie units. "Molotov cocktails" will be thrown against their armoured vehicles . . . night and day. . . . [The objective is] to destroy the best Muslim elements in the liberal professions so as to oblige the Muslim population to have recourse to ourselves . . . to paralyse the powers that be and make it impossible for them to exercise authority. Brutal actions will be generalized over the whole territory . . . at works of art and all that represents the exercise of authority in a manner to lead towards the maximum of general insecurity and the total paralysis of the country.[127]

Nor did the corruption stop at the OAS. For in order to beat them and to protect de Gaulle himself (twice nearly murdered), the state built up its own official terror units, which murdered and tortured prisoners with impunity, and on a wide scale.[128] In this case, neither liberal France nor the international community raised a whisper of protest. OAS terrorism finally killed the idea of a white settlement. At the end of 1961 de Gaulle's closest adviser,

Bernard Tricot, reported back from Algiers: "The Europeans . . . are so hardened in opposition to everything that is being prepared, and their relations with the majority of the Muslims are so bad, that . . . the essential thing now is to organize their return."[129]

The end came in March 1962, in an orgy of slaughter and intolerance. The Muslim mob, scenting victory, had already sacked the Great Synagogue in the heart of the Casbah, gutting it, ripping the Torah scrolls, killing the Jewish officials and chalking on the walls "Death to the Jews" and other Nazi slogans. On March 15 the OAS raided Germaine Tillion's social center, where handicapped children were trained, took out six men, and shot them to death, beginning with the legs. One of them was Mouloud Feraoun, friend of Camus, who had termed him "last of the moderates." He had written: "There is French in me, there is Kabyle in me. But I have a horror of those who kill. . . . *Vive la France*, such as I have always loved! *Vive l'Algérie*, such as I hope for! Shame on the criminals!"[130] The cease-fire with the FLN, March 19, 1962, brought a further burst of OAS killing: eighteen gendarmes and seven soldiers were murdered. The French commander, General Ailleret, retaliated by destroying the last redoubt of Algérie *française*, the *pied noir* working-class quarter of Bab-el-Oued, with its sixty thousand inhabitants. He attacked it with rocket-firing divebombers, tanks firing at point-blank range, and twenty thousand infantry. It was the suppression of the 1870 Commune all over again; but this episode does not figure in the Marxist textbooks.[131] That was effectively the end of Algeria as a multiracial community. The exodus to France began. Many hospitals, schools, laboratories, oil terminals, and other evidence of French culture and enterprise—including the library of the University of Algiers—were deliberately destroyed. About 1,380,000 people (including some Muslims) left in all. By 1963, of a large and historic Mediterranean community, only about thirty thousand remained.[132]

The Evian Agreements, under which France agreed to get out, contained many clauses designed to save France's face. They were meaningless. It was a straight surrender. Not even paper protection, however, was given to two hundred and fifty thousand Muslim officials, many of a very humble kind, who had continued to serve France faithfully to the end. De Gaulle was too busy saving France by extricating itself from the horror, to give them a thought. When a Muslim deputy, ten of whose family had already been murdered by the FLN, told de Gaulle that, with self-determination, "we shall suffer," he replied coldly: "*Eh, bien—vous suffrirez.*" They did. Only fifteen thousand had the money and means to get out. The rest were shot without trial, used as human mine-detectors to clear the minefields along the Tunisian border, tortured, made to dig their own tombs and swallow their military decorations before being killed; some were burned alive, castrated, dragged behind trucks, fed to the dogs; there were cases where entire families including tiny children were murdered together. The French army units that remained, their former comrades-in-arms, stood by, horrified and powerless, for under the Agreements they had no right to interfere. French soldiers were actually employed to disarm the Muslim *harkis*, telling them they would be issued with more modern weapons, although in fact they were about to be slaughtered. It was a crime of betrayal comparable to the British handing over Russian POWs to Stalin's wrath; worse, indeed. Estimates of the number put to death vary from thirty thousand to one hundred and fifty thousand.[133]

Who knows? A great darkness descended over many aspects of the new Algeria, a darkness which has never been lifted since. The lies continued to the end. "France and Algeria," said de Gaulle on March 18, 1962, would "march together like brothers on the road to civilization."[134] The truth is, the new nation owed its existence to the exercise of cruelty without restraint and on the largest possible scale. Its regime, composed mainly of successful gangsters, quickly ousted those of its members who had been brought up in the Western tradition; all were dead or in exile by the mid-1960s.

Exactly twenty years after the independence agreement was reached, one of the chief signatories and Algeria's first president, Ben Bella himself, summed up the country's first two decades of independent existence. The net result, he said, had been "totally negative." The country was "a ruin." Its agriculture had been "assassinated." "We have nothing. No industry—only scrap iron." Everything in Algeria was "corrupt from top to bottom."[135] No doubt Ben Bella's bitterness was increased by the fact that he had spent most of the intervening years imprisoned by his revolutionary comrades. But the substance of his judgment was true enough. And unfortunately the new Algeria had not kept its crimes to itself. It became and for many years remained the chief resort of international terrorists of all kinds. A great moral corruption had been planted in Africa. It set a pattern of public crime and disorder which was to be imitated throughout the vast and tragic continent which was now made master of its own affairs.

NOTES

1. E. L. Woodward, *British Foreign Policy in the Second World War* (London 1970), I, p. XLIV.
2. 16 June 1943; quoted in David Dilks (ed.), *Retreat from Power* (London 1981), II *After 1939*.
3. William Roger Louis, *Imperialism at Bay: the United States and the Decolonization of the British Empire 1941-1945* (Oxford 1978).
4. Entry in Admiral Leahy's diary, February 9, 1945, quoted in Terry Anderson, *The United States, Great Britain and the Cold War 1944-1947* (Columbia 1981).
5. W. K. Hancock and Margaret Gowing, *The British War Economy* (London 1949), pp. 546-549.
6. Dalton Diary, September 10, 1946.
7. *Harold Nicolson: Diaries and Letters 1945-1962* (London 1968), pp. 115-16.
8. A. Goldberg, "The Military Origins of the British Nuclear Deterrent," *International Affairs*, XL (1964).
9. Edward Spiers, "The British Nuclear Deterrent: Problems, Possibilities," in Dilks, *op. cit.*, II, pp. 183-184.
10. M. H. Gowing, *Independence and Deterrence, Britain and Atomic Energy 1945-52*, 2 vols (London 1974), I, p. 131.
11. *Ibid.*, pp. 182, 183.
12. *Ibid.*, p. 406.
13. Dilks, *op. cit.*, II, p. 161.
14. For end of war statistics see David James, *The Rise and Fall of the Japanese Empire* (London 1951).
15. *Ibid.*, 251-3.
16. Robert Rhodes James, *Memoirs of a Conservative: J. C. C. Davidson's Letters and Papers 1910-1937* (London, 1969), p. 390.
17. John Wheeler-Bennett, *King George* VI: *His Life and Times* (London 1958), p. 703.
18. Ved Mehta, *Mahatma Gandhi and His Apostles* (New York 1976), p. 33ff.
19. *Ibid.*, pp. 13-16.
20. *Ibid.*, p. 44.
21. *Ibid.*, p. 56.
22. Orwell, *Collected Essays, etc.*, IV, p. 529.
23. Quoted in Sarvepalli Gopal, *Jawaharlal Nehru: A Biography* (London 1965), I, pp. 38, 39.
24. *Ibid.*, pp. 79, 98, 236; Leonard Woolf, *Downhill All the Way* (London 1967), p. 230.
25. Speech by Nehru at Ootacamund, June 1, 1948; Gopal, *op. cit.*, II, p. 308.
26. Richard Hughes, *Foreign Devil* (London 1972), pp. 282-292.
27. Richard Hough, *Mountbatten* (London 1980), p. 216.
28. R. Jeffrey, "The Punjab Boundary Force and the Problem of Order, August 1947," *Modern Asian Studies* (1974), pp. 491-520.
29. M. Masson, *Edwina Mountbatten* (London 1958), pp. 206-7.
30. Gopal *op. cit.*, II, p. 13.
31. Penderal Mood, *Divide and Quit* (London 1961), gives 200,000; G. D. Khosla, *Stern Reckoning* (Delhi n.d.), 4-500,000; Ian Stephens, *Paki-*

stan (London 1963), 500,000; M. Edwardes, *Last Years of British India* (London 1963), 600,000.

32. Gopal, *op. cit.*, II, p. 21, 42.
33. Letter from Nehru to Krishna Menon, August 24, 1949.
34. Walter Lippmann in *Herald Tribune*, January 10, 1949; Dean Acheson, *Present at the Creation* (New York 1969), p. 336; *Christian Science Monitor*, October 26, 1949. *Manchester Guardian*, May 26, 1954; W. Johnson (ed.), *The Papers of Adlai E. Stevenson* (Boston 1973), III, p. 181.
35. Nehru, letter dated June 9, 1951.
36. Gopal, *op. cit.*, p. 311.
37. Letter from Nehru to Rajagopalachari, July 3, 1950; cable to President Nasser, October 31, 1956; cable to J. F. Dulles, same date.
38. Quoted Gopal, *op. cit.*, II, p. 246.
39. S. Dutt, *With Nehru at the Foreign Office* (Calcutta 1977), p. 177.
40. Letter from Nehru to Ernest Bevin, November 20, 1950.
41. Gopal, *op. cit.*, II, pp. 194, 195, 227.
42. J. K. Galbraith, *A Life in Our Times* (London 1981), chapter 27, p. 420ff.
43. Keith Irvine, *The Rise of the Coloured Races* (London 1972), p. 540ff.; G. McT. Kahin, *The Asian-African Conference, Bandung* (Ithaca 1956).
44. J. D. Legge, *Sukarno: A Political Biography* (London 1972), pp. 264-5.
45. Richard Wright, *The Colour Curtain* (London 1965), p. 15.
46. Harry J. Benda, "Christian Snouck Hurgronje and the Foundation of Dutch Islamic Policy in Indonesia," *Journal of Modern History*, xxx (1958), pp. 338-347.
47. E. H. Kossman, *The Low Countries, 1780-1940* (Oxford 1978), p. 672ff.
48. See Sukarno's book, *The Birth of Pantja Sila* (Djakarta 1950).
49. D. S. Lev, *The Transition to Guided Democracy: Indonesia Politics 1957-1959* (Ithaca 1966).
50. For slogans, see Legge, *op. cit.*, pp. 288-290, 324, 332-333, 359 and *passim*.
51. Talbot (ed.), *op. cit.*, p. 322.
52. Legge, *op. cit.*, p. 387; John Hughes, *The End of Sukarno* (London 1968), p. 44.
53. J. R. Bass, "The PKI and the Attempted Coup," *Journal of SE Asian Studies*, March 1970; for critical bibliography of the *coup* see Legge, *op. cit.*, p. 390, footnote 45.
54. Hughes, *op. cit.*, chapter 16.
55. Howard M. Sachar, *Britain Leaves the Middle East* (London 1974), p. 391.
56. *Petroleum Times*, June 1948; *Oil Weekly*, March 6, 1944.
57. *Forrestal Diaries*, pp. 356, 357.
58. Sachar, *op. cit.*, p. 395.
59. Churchill, *Second World War*, IV, p. 952.
60. Sachar, *op. cit.*, p. 442.
61. Chaim Weizmann, *Trial and Error* (Philadelphia 1949), II, p. 437.
62. Yehudah Bauer, *From Diplomacy to Resistance: A History of Jewish Palestine 1939-1945* (Philadelphia 1970), p. 230.
63. Sachar, *op. cit.*, p. 447.
64. *New York Post*, 21 May 1946.

65. Nicholas Bethell, *The Palestine Triangle: The Struggle Between the British, the Jews and the Arabs, 1935-1948* (London 1979), pp. 254, 255.
66. Bethell, *The Palestine Triangle*, p. 261ff., based on records released in 1978.
67. *Jerusalem Post*, 1 August 1947.
68. Bethell, *op. cit.*, pp. 243, 244.
69. Jon and David Kimche, *Both Sides of the Hill: Britain and the Palestine War* (London 1960), pp. 21, 22.
70. Bauer, *op. cit.*, p. 230.
71. *The Jewish Case for the Anglo-American Committee of Inquiry on Palestine* (Jerusalem 1947), pp. 6, 7, 74-5.
72. Joseph Schechtman, *The U.S. and the Jewish State Movement* (New York 1966), p. 110.
73. Quoted in Alfred Steinberg, *The Man from Missouri: The Life and Times of Harry S. Truman* (New York 1952), p. 301.
74. Truman, *Memoirs*, II, p. 135.
75. *Petroleum Times*, June 1948.
76. *Forrestal Diaries*, pp. 324, 344, 348.
77. Howard Sachar, "The Arab-Israeli Issue in the Light of the Cold War," *Sino—Soviet Institute Studies* (Washington D.C.), 1966, p. 2.
78. Sachar, *Europe Leaves the Middle East*, pp. 546, 547.
79. *Ibid.*, p. 518ff.
80. Kimche, *op. cit.*, p. 60.
81. Netanel Lorch, *The Edge of the Sword: Israel's War of Independence 1947-1948* (New York 1961), p. 90.
82. David Horowitz, *State in the Making* (New York 1953), pp. 232-235.
83. Rony E. Gabbay, *A Political Study of the Arab—Jewish Conflict* (Geneva 1959), pp. 92, 93.
84. Sachar, *op. cit.*, pp. 550, 551; Walid Khalidi, "Why Did the Palestinians Leave?" *Middle East Forum*, July 1955; Erkine B. Childers, "The Other Exodus," *Spectator*, May 12, 1961. Arab League instructions were printed in *Al-Kayat* (Lebanon, April 30, May 5-7, 1948).
85. Colonial Office transcript (CO 733 477) quoted in Bethell, *The Palestine Triangle*, p. 355.
86. Walter Pinner, *How Many Arab Refugees?* (New York 1959), pp. 3, 4.
87. Sachar, *op. cit.*, p. 191; for distribution of Jewish exodus, see Martin Gilbert, *The Arab—Israeli Conflict: Its History in Maps* (London 1974), p. 50.
88. John Kimche, *Seven Fallen Pillars* (London 1954), p. 46.
89. Francis Williams, *A Prime Minister Remembers* (London 1961), pp. 175, 176.
90. Bethell, *The Palestine Triangle*, p. 358.
91. Sachar, *Europe Leaves the Middle East*, p. 51.
92. For an incisive portrait by a fellow-Muslim ruler see Mohammed Ahmed Mahgoub, *Democracy on Trial: Reflections on Arab and African Politics* (London 1974).
93. Constantine Zurayak, *The Meaning of the Disaster* (Beirut 1956), p. 2.
94. For the dam project see P. K. O'Brien, *The Revolution in Egypt's Economic System* (London 1966) and Tom Little, *High Dam at Aswan* (London 1965).
95. David Carlton, *Anthony Eden* (London 1981), p. 416.

96. *Ibid.*, p. 389.
97. André Beaufre, *The Suez Expedition 1956* (tr. London 1969), pp. 28-34; Hugh Stockwell, "Suez: Success or Disaster?" *Listener*, 4 November 1976.
98. See Eden's own account in *Memoirs: Full Circle* (London 1960); Selwyn Lloyd, *Suez 1956: A Personal Account* (London 1978).
99. Moshe Dayan, *Story of My Life* (London 1976), p. 181.
100. Dwight D. Eisenhower, *The White House Years: Waging Peace 1956-1961* (New York 1965), pp. 666, 667.
101. Carlton, *op. cit.*, pp. 451-453.
102. Brian Urquhart, *Hammarskjöld* (London 1973), p. 26.
103. *Ibid.*, pp. 170, 174, 185-189.
104. Alistair Horne, *A Savage War of Peace: Algeria 1954-1962* (London 1977), p. 60.
105. See Robert Aron et al., *Les Origines de la Guerre d'Algérie* (Paris 1962).
106. Albert-Paul Lentin, *L'Algérie des Colonels* (Paris 1958).
107. Horne, *op. cit.*, p. 72.
108. *Ibid.*, pp. 91, 92, 101; Pierre Leulliette, *St. Michael and the Dragon* (tr. London 1964).
109. Horne, *op. cit.*, pp. 132-135.
110. C. Marighela, *For the Liberation of Brazil* (Penguin 1971).
111. Horne, *op. cit.*, pp. 98, 99.
112. Germaine Tillion, *L'Algérie en 1957* (Paris 1957); Vincent Monteil, *Soldat de Fortune* (Paris 1966).
113. Jacques Soustelle, *Aimée et Souffrante Algérie* (Paris 1956).
114. Horne, *op. cit.*, pp. 117, 118.
115. Albert Camus, *Chroniques Algériennes 1939-1958* (Paris 1958).
116. Horne, *op. cit.*, p. 187.
117. Jacques Massu, *La Vrai Bataille d'Alger* (Paris 1971).
118. Henri Alleg, *La Question* (Paris 1958).
119. Horne, *op. cit.*, p. 201.
120. For examples, see J. R. Tournoux, *Secret d'Etat* (Paris 1960); J. J. Servan-Schreiber, *Lieutenant en Algérie* (Paris 1957).
121. Charles de Gaulle, *Memoirs of Hope* (tr. London 1970-71), I, p. 12.
122. *Ibid.*, p. 15.
123. Simone de Beauvoir, *La Force des Choses* (Paris 1963).
124. Horne, *op. cit.*, p. 291.
125. De Gaulle, *op. cit.*, p. 47.
126. Horne, *op. cit.*, pp. 376-378.
127. *Ibid.*, pp. 515, 516.
128. *Ibid.*, p. 495.
129. *Ibid.*, p. 506.
130. Mouloud Feraoun, *Journal 1955-1962* (Paris 1962).
131. Horne, *op. cit.*, p. 524.
132. *Ibid.*, pp. 540-543.
133. *Ibid.*, pp. 537, 538
134. De Gaulle, *op. cit.*, I, p. 126.
135. Ben Bella, interview with Radio Monte Carlo, *Daily Telegraph*, March 19, 1982.

FIVE

Western Guilt and Third World Poverty

P. T. BAUER

Come, fix upon me that accusing eye.
I thirst for accusation.

W. B. Yeats

1

Yeats' words might indeed have been written to describe the wide, even welcome, acceptance by the West of the accusation that it is responsible for the poverty of the Third World (i.e., most of Asia, Africa and Latin America).[1] Western responsibility for Third World backwardness is a persistent theme of the United Nations and its many affiliates.[2] It has been welcomed by spokesmen of the Third World and the Communist bloc, notably so at international gatherings where it is often endorsed by official representatives of the West, especially the United States. It is also widely canvassed in the universities, the churches, and the media the world over.

Acceptance of emphatic routine allegations that the West is responsible for Third World poverty reflects and reinforces Western feelings of guilt. It has enfeebled Western diplomacy, both towards the ideologically much more aggressive Soviet bloc and also towards the Third World. And the West has come to abase

---

P. T. BAUER, one of the world's leading economists, is Professor of Economics at the London School of Economics and fellow at Cambridge University. He received a peerage from the British government in 1983 in recognition of a life of impeccable scholarship in economics. The following article is taken from his book *Equality, The Third World, and Economic Delusion* (Harvard University Press, 1981).

itself before countries with negligible resources and no real power. Yet the allegations can be shown to be without foundation. They are readily accepted because the Western public has little firsthand knowledge of the Third World, and because of widespread feelings of guilt. The West has never had it so good, and has never felt so bad about it.

2

A few characteristic examples will illustrate the general theme of Western responsibility. To begin with, academics. The late Paul A. Baran, Professor of Economics at Stanford, was a highly regarded development economist. He was a prominent and influential exponent of Western guilt in the early days of contemporary development economics. He contributed the chapter on economic development to the *Survey of Contemporary Economics* published by the American Economic Association, and his book *The Political Economy of Growth* is a widely prescribed university textbook. In it Baran wrote:

> To the dead weight of stagnation characteristic of pre-industrial society was added the entire restrictive impact of monopoly capitalism. The economic surplus appropriated in lavish amounts by monopolistic concerns in backward countries is not employed for productive purposes. It is neither plowed back into their own enterprises nor does it serve to develop others.[3]

This categorical statement is wholly and obviously untrue because throughout the underdeveloped world large agricultural, mineral, commercial, and industrial complexes have been built up through profits reinvested locally.

Professor Peter Townsend of Essex University is perhaps the most prominent British academic writer on poverty. In his book *The Concept of Poverty*, he wrote:

> I argued that the poverty of deprived nations is comprehensible only if we attribute it substantially to the existence of a system of international social stratification, a hierarchy of societies with vastly different resources in which the wealth of some is linked historically and contemporaneously to the poverty of others. This system operated crudely in the era of colonial domination, and continues to operate today, though more subtly, through sys-

tems of trade, education, political relations, military alliances, and industrial corporations.[4]

This again cannot be so. The poorest and most backward countries have until recently had no external economic contacts and often have never been Western colonies. It is therefore obvious that their backwardness cannot be explained by colonial domination or international social stratification. And there are no industrial corporations in the least developed countries of the Third World (the so-called Fourth World) such as Afghanistan, Chad, Bhutan, Burundi, Nepal and Sikkim.

In this realm of discourse university students echo what they have learnt from their mentors. About ten years ago a student group at Cambridge published a pamphlet on the subject of the moral obligations of the West to the Third World. The following was its key passage:

> We took the rubber from Malaya, the tea from India, raw materials from all over the world and gave almost nothing in return.

This is as nearly the opposite of the truth as one can find. The British took the rubber *to* Malaya and the tea *to* India. There were no rubber trees in Malaya or anywhere in Asia (as suggested by their botanical name, *Hevea braziliensis*) until about one hundred years ago, when the British took the first rubber seeds there out of the Amazon jungle. From these sprang the huge rubber industry—now very largely Asian-owned. Tea-plants were brought to India by the British somewhat earlier; their origin is shown in the botanical name *Camilla sinensis*, as well as in the phrase "all the tea in China."

Mr. Charles Clarke, a former President of the National Union of Students, said in his presidential address delivered in December 1976: "For over a hundred years British industry has been draining wealth away from those countries." Far from draining wealth from the less developed countries, British industry helped to create it there, as external commerce promoted economic advance in large areas of the Third World where there was no wealth to be drained.

Western churches and charities are on the same bandwagon. Professor Ronald J. Sider is a prominent American churchman. In an article entitled "How We Oppress the Poor" in *Christianity Today* (July 16, 1976), an influential evangelical magazine, he wrote about the "stranglehold which the developed

West has kept on the economic throats of the Third World" and
then went on to say, "It would be wrong to suggest that 210
million Americans bear sole responsibility for all the hunger and
injustice in today's world. All the rich developed countries are
directly involved . . . we are participants in a system that dooms
even more people to agony and death than the slave system did."
These are evident fantasies. Famines occur in Third World countries largely isolated from the West. So far from condemning
Third World people to death, Western contacts have been behind
the large increase in life expectation in the Third World, so often
deplored as the population explosion by the same critics.

Many charities have come to think it advantageous to play
on the theme of Western responsibility. According to a widely
publicized Oxfam advertisement of 1972:

> Coffee is grown in poor developing countries like Brazil,
> Colombia and Uganda. But that does not stop rich coun-
> tries like Britain exploiting their economic weakness by
> paying as little for their raw coffee as we can get away
> with. On top of this, we keep charging more and more for
> the manufactured goods they need to buy from us. So? We
> get richer at their expense. Business is Business.

A similar advertisement was run about cocoa. Both advertise-
ments were subsequently dropped in the face of protests by actual and potential subscribers. The allegations in these advertise-
ments are largely meaningless, and they are also unrelated to
reality. The world prices of coffee and cocoa, which were as it
happens very high in the 1970s, are determined by market forces
and not prescribed by the West. On the other hand, the farmers in
many of the exporting countries receive far less than the market
prices, because they are subject to very high export taxes and
similar government levies. The insistence on the allegedly low
prices paid by the West to the producers and the lack of any
reference to the penal taxation of the producers locally are examples that this guilt literature is concerned more with the flagella-
tion of the West than with improving the conditions of the local
population.

The intellectuals outside the academies and churches are
also well to the fore. Cyril Connolly wrote in an article entitled
"Black Man's Burden" (*Sunday Times*, London, February 23,
1969):

> It is a wonder that the white man is not more thoroughly
> detested than he is. . . . In our dealings with every single

> country, greed, masked by hypocrisy, led to unscrupulous
> coercion of the native inhabitants. . . . Cruelty, greed and
> arrogance . . . characterized what can be summed up in one
> word, exploitation. . . .

If this were true, Third World countries would now be poorer
than they were before Western contacts. In fact, they are generally much better off.

Insistence that the West has caused Third World poverty is
collective self-accusation. The notion itself originated in the
West. For instance, Marxism is a Western ideology, as is the belief
that economic differences are anomalous and unjust, and that
they reflect exploitation. But people in the Third World, especially articulate people with contacts with the West, readily believed
what they were told by prominent academics and other intellectuals, the more so because the idea accorded with their interests
and inclinations.

Inspired by the West, Third World politicians have come
habitually to insist that the West has exploited and still exploits
their countries. Dr. Nkrumah, a major Third World figure of the
1950s and 1960s, was a well-known exponent of this view. He
described Western capitalism as "a world system of financial enslavement and colonial oppression and exploitation of a vast majority of the population of the earth by a handful of the so-called
civilized nations."[5] In fact, until the advent of Dr. Nkrumah,
Ghana (the former Gold Coast) was a prosperous country as a
result of cocoa exports to the West, with the cocoa farmers the
most prosperous and the subsistence producers the poorest
groups there.

Julius Nyerere, President of Tanzania, is a highly regarded,
almost venerated, world figure.[6] He said in the course of a state
visit to London in 1975: "If the rich nations go on getting richer
and richer at the expense of the poor, the poor of the world must
demand a change. . . ." When the West established substantial
contact with Tanganyika (effectively the present Tanzania) in the
nineteenth century, this was an empty region, thinly populated
with tribal people exposed to Arab slavers. Its relatively modest
progress since then has been the work primarily of Asians and
Europeans.

The notion of Western exploitation of the Third World is
standard in publications and statements emanating from the Soviet Union and other Communist countries. Here is one example.
The late Soviet academician Potekhin was a prominent Soviet
authority on Africa. He is worth quoting because Soviet economic writings are taken seriously in Western universities:

> Why is there little capital in Africa? The reply is evident. A considerable part of the national income which is supposed to make up the accumulation fund and to serve as the material basis of progress is exported outside Africa without any equivalent.[7]

No funds are exported from the poorest parts of Africa. Such remittances as there are from the more prosperous parts of the continent (generally very modest in the case of Black Africa, to which Potekhin refers) are partial returns on the resources supplied. In the most backward areas there are no foreigners and no foreign capital. It is the opposite of the truth to say that the reason there is little capital in Africa is that much of the national income is "exported . . . without any equivalent." In Africa, as elsewhere in the Third World, the most prosperous areas are those with most commercial contacts with the West.

3

Far from the West having caused the poverty in the Third World, contact with the West has been the principal agent of material progress there. The materially more advanced societies and regions of the Third World are those with which the West established the most numerous, diversified, and extensive contacts: the cash-crop producing areas and entrepôt ports of South-East Asia, West Africa and Latin America; the mineral-producing areas of Africa and the Middle East; and cities and ports throughout Asia, Africa, the Caribbean and Latin America. The level of material achievement usually diminishes as one moves away from the foci of Western impact. The poorest and most backward people have few or no external contacts; witness the aborigines, pygmies, and desert peoples.

All this is neither new nor surprising, since the spread of material progress from more to less advanced regions is a commonplace of history. In medieval Europe, for instance, the more advanced regions of Central and Eastern Europe and Scandinavia were the areas with most contacts with France, the Low Countries and Italy, the most advanced parts of Europe at the time. The West was materially far ahead of the present Third World countries when it established extensive and diverse economic contacts with them in the nineteenth and twentieth centuries. It was through these contacts that human and material resources, skills, capital, and new ideas, including the idea of material progress itself (and, incidentally, that of Western guilt too), flowed from the West to the Third World.

In recent times the role of external contacts in promoting economic advance in the Third World has been much more significant than that of similar contacts in the earlier history of Europe. To begin with, and as just noted, the very idea of material progress in the sense of sustained, steady, and increasing control over man's environment is a Western concept. People in the Third World did not think of these terms before the advent of Western man. Scholars of such widely differing philosophical and political persuasion as, for instance, J. B. Bury and Christopher Dawson, have for long recognized the Western origin of the idea of material progress. The Western impulse behind economic advance in the Third World has also been acknowledged by writers who recognized this progress but warned against the disturbing, even corrosive, results of the sudden impact of contact with materially much more advanced societies.[8]

The West developed multifarious contacts with the Third World in the nineteenth and twentieth centuries, when the difference in economic attainment between the West and these regions was very wide, much wider than such differences had been in the past. Thus these contacts offered correspondingly greater opportunities, especially in view of the great improvements in transport and communications over the last two hundred years or so.

Since the middle of the nineteenth century commercial contacts established by the West have improved material conditions out of all recognition over much of the Third World, notably in Southeast Asia; parts of the Middle East; much of Africa, especially West Africa and parts of East and Southern Africa; and very large parts of Latin America, including Mexico, Guatemala, Venezuela, Colombia, Peru, Chile, Brazil, Uruguay, and Argentina. The transformation of Malaya (the present Malaysia) is instructive. In the 1890s it was a sparsely populated area of Malay hamlets and fishing villages. By the 1930s it had become the hub of the world's rubber and tin industries. By then there were large cities and excellent communications in a country where millions of Malays, Chinese and Indians now lived much longer and better than they had formerly, either in their countries of origin or in Malaya.

Large parts of West Africa were also transformed over roughly the same period as a result of Western contacts. Before 1890 there was no cocoa production in the Gold Coast or Nigeria, only very small production of cotton and groundnuts, and small exports of palm oil and palm kernels. By the 1950s all these had become staples of world trade. They were produced by Africans on African-owned properties. But this was originally made possible by Westeners who established public security and introduced modern methods of transport and communications. Over this period imports both of capital goods and of mass consumer goods for African use also rose from insignificant amounts to huge volumes. The changes were reflected in government revenues, literacy rates, school attendance, public health, life expectation, infant mortality, and many other indicators.

Statistics by themselves can hardly convey the far-reaching transformation which took place over this period in West Africa and elsewhere in the Third World. In West Africa, for instance, slave trading and slavery were still widespread at the end of the nineteenth century. They had practically disappeared by the end of the First World War. Many of the worst endemic and epidemic diseases for which West Africa was notorious throughout the nineteenth century had disappeared by the Second World War. External contacts also brought about similar far-reaching changes over much of Latin America.

The role of Western contacts in the material progress of Black Africa deserves further notice. As late as the second half of the nineteenth century Black Africa was without even the simplest, most basic ingredients of modern social and economic life. These were brought there by Westerners over the last hundred years or so. This is true of such fundamentals as public security and law and order; wheeled traffic (Black Africa never invented the wheel) and mechanical transport (before the arrival of Westerners, transport in Black Africa was almost entirely by human muscle); roads, railways and man-made ports; the application of science and technology to economic activity; towns with substantial buildings, clean water, and sewerage facilities; public health care, hospitals, and the control of endemic and epidemic diseases; formal education. These advances resulted from peaceful commercial contacts. These contacts also made easier the elimination of the Atlantic slave trade, the virtual elimination of the slave trade from Africa to the Middle East, and even the elimination of slavery within Africa.

Although peaceful commercial contacts had nothing to do with the Atlantic slave trade, in the contemporary climate it is impossible not to refer to that trade in a discussion of Western responsibility for Third World poverty. Horrible and destructive as was the Atlantic slave trade, it cannot be claimed legitimately as a cause of African backwardness, still less of Third World poverty. Asia was altogether untouched by it. The most backward parts of Africa, such as the interior of Central and Southern Africa and most of East Africa, were largely unaffected by it.[9]

The slave trade between Africa and the Middle East antedated the Atlantic slave trade by centuries, and far outlasted it. Slavery was endemic over much of Africa long before the emergence of the Atlantic slave trade, and it was eventually stamped out by the West. Arabs and Africans do not seem to feel guilty about slavery and the slave trade; but Western Europeans and Americans often do and are made to do so. And yet it was due to their efforts that these practices were largely eliminated. Guilt is a prerogative of the West.

Western activities—supplemented at times by those of non-Western immigrants, notably Chinese, Indians, and Levantines whose large-scale migration was made possible by Western initiative—have thus transformed material conditions in many parts of the Third World. All this is not to say that over the past hundred years there has been substantial material advance uniformly throughout the Third World. Large areas, especially in the interior of the Third World, have had few contacts with the West. Moreover, in much of the Third World the political, social, and personal determinants of economic performance are often uncongenial to economic achievement. And the policies of many governments plainly obstruct economic achievement and progress. Again, people often refuse to abandon attitudes and mores which obstruct economic performance. They are not prepared to give up their established ways for the sake of greater prosperity. This is a preference which is neither unjustified nor reprehensible.

Such considerations in no way warrant the allegations that Western contracts have obstructed or retarded Third World progress. Wherever local conditions have permitted it, commercial contacts with the West, and generally established by the West, have eliminated the worst diseases, reduced or even eliminated famine, extended life expectation and improved living standards.

4

Many of the assertions of Western responsibility for Third World poverty imply that the prosperity of relatively well-to-do persons, groups and societies is achieved at the expense of the less well-off. These assertions express the misconception that the incomes of the well-to-do have been taken from others. In fact, with a few clearly definable exceptions, which do not apply to the relations between the West and the Third World, incomes whether of the rich or of the poor are earned by their recipients. In the Third World it is an article of faith of the most influential and articulate groups that their societies have been exploited by the West, both by Western individuals and Western companies, and also by locally resident ethnic minorities such as the Chinese in Southeast Asia, Asians in East Africa, and Levantines in West Africa. The appeal of these misconceptions is all too familiar. They are especially useful to politicians who have promised a prosperity which they cannot deliver. But they are also useful to other influential local groups who expect to benefit from policies inspired by these ideas, especially from the expropriation of foreign enterprises or discrimination against minorities.

In recent decades certain readily recognizable influences have reinforced the notion that the prosperity of some group means that others have been exploited. The impact of Marxist-Leninist ideology has been one such influence. In this ideology any return on private capital implies exploitation, and service industries are regarded as unproductive. Thus, earnings of foreign capital and the incomes of foreigners or ethnic minorities in the service industries are evidence of forms of exploitation. Further, neo-Marxist literature has extended the concept of the proletariat to the peoples of the Third World, most of whom are in fact small-scale cultivators. In this literature, moreover, a proletariat is exploited by definition, and is poor because it is exploited.[10]

The idea of Western responsibility for Third World poverty has also been promoted by the belief in a universal basic equality of people's economic capacities and motivations. This belief is closely related to egalitarian ideology and policy which have experienced a great upsurge in recent decades. If people's attributes and motivations are the same everywhere and yet some societies are richer than others, this suggests that the former have exploited the rest.[11] Because the public in the West has little direct contact with the Third World, it is often easy to put across the idea that Western conduct and policies have caused poverty in the Third World.

The recent practice of referring to the poor as deprived or underprivileged again helps the notion that the rich owe their prosperity to the exploitation of the poor. Yet how could the incomes of, for example, people in Switzerland or North America have been taken from, say, the aborigines of Papua, or the desert peoples or pygmies of Africa? Indeed, who deprived these groups and of what?[12]

5

The principal assumption behind the idea of Western responsibility for Third World poverty is that the prosperity of individuals and societies generally reflects the exploitation of others. Some variants or derivatives of this theme are often heard, usually geared to particular audiences. One of these variants is that colonialism has caused the poverty of Asia and Africa. It has particular appeal in the United States where hostility to colonialism is traditional. For a different and indeed opposite reason, it is at times effective in stirring up guilt in Britain, the foremost ex-colonial power.

Whatever one thinks of colonialism, it cannot be held responsible for Third World poverty. Some of the most backward countries never were colonies, as for instance Afghanistan, Tibet, Nepal, Liberia. Ethiopia is perhaps an even more telling example (it was an Italian colony for only six years in its long history). Again, many of the Asian and African colonies progressed very rapidly during colonial rule, much more so than the independent countries in the same area. At present one of the few remaining European colonies is Hong Kong—whose prosperity and progress should be familiar.[13] It is plain that colonial rule has not been the cause of Third World poverty.

Nor is the prosperity of the West the result of colonialism. The most advanced and the richest countries never had colonies, including Switzerland and the Scandinavian countries; and some were colonies of others and were already very prosperous as colonies, as for instance North America and Australasia. The prosperity of the West was generated by its own peoples and was not taken from others. The European countries were already materially far ahead of the areas where they established colonies.

In recent years the charges that colonialism causes Third World poverty have been expanded to cover "colonialism in all its forms." The terms "economic colonialism" and "neo-colonialism" have sprung up to cover external private investment, the activities of multinational companies, and indeed almost any form of economic relationship between relatively rich and relatively poor regions or groups. Reference to "colonialism in all its forms" as a cause of Third World poverty is a major theme at UNCTAD meetings. This terminology has become common currency in both academic literature and in the media. It regularly confuses poverty with colonial status, a concept which has normally meant lack of political sovereignty.

One unusually direct formulation of these ideas (which are

normally expressed in much more convoluted form in the academic and official literature) was provided in an editorial in the June 1978 issue of *Poverty and Power* published by War on Want, a British charity:

> We see poverty in the Third World as a result of colonial looting in the past and neo-colonial exploitation in the present.

The demise of political colonialism has probably been another important factor behind the shift in terminology. Disappearance of colonial rule has forced the accusers of the West to find new ground for their charges. Hence the terminology of neo-colonialism and economic colonialism. The usage represents a shift in the basis of accusation and at the same time it retains the benefits of the older, familiar terminology. The influence of Marxist-Leninist doctrine has also promoted the new terminology. According to Marxist-Leninist ideology, colonial status and foreign investment are by definition evidence of exploitation. In fact, foreign private investment and the activities of the multinational companies have expanded opportunities and raised incomes and government revenues in the Third World. Reference to economic colonialism and neo-colonialism both debase the language and distort the truth.[14]

6

The West is now widely accused of manipulating international trade to the detriment of the Third World. This accusation is a major theme of the demands for a New International Economic Order. In particular, the West is supposed to inflict unfavorable and persistently deteriorating terms of trade on the Third World. Among other untoward results, this influence is said to have resulted in a decline in the share of the Third World in total world trade, and also in a large volume of Third World foreign debt. These allegations are again irrelevant, unfounded and often the opposite of the truth.[15]

The poorest areas of the Third World have no external trade. Their condition shows that the causes of backwardness are domestic and that external commercial contacts are beneficial. Even if the terms of trade were unfavorable on some criterion or other, this would only mean that people do not benefit from foreign trade as much as they would if the terms of trade were more favorable. People benefit from the widening of opportunities which external trade represents. Besides this last and basic conclusion, there are many other objections to the notion that the terms of trade are somehow inherently unfavorable to the Third World, and external commercial contacts damaging to it.

As the Third World comprises most of the world, the aggregation of the terms of trade of all its countries has a very limited meaning. The terms of trade of some Third World countries and groups of countries move differently and often in opposite directions from those of others; the effect of the OPEC price increases on many Third World countries is only one recent and familiar example.

Again, except over very short periods, changes in the terms of trade as conventionally measured are of little welfare significance without reference to changes in the cost of production of exports, the range and quality of imports, and the volume of trade. Insofar as changes in the terms of trade do affect development and welfare, what matters is the amount of imports which can be purchased with a unit of domestic resources. This figure cannot be inferred simply from the ratio of import and export prices because these do not take into account the cost of production of exports. (In technical language, the comparisons relevant to economic welfare and development are the factoral terms of trade, which allow for changes in the cost of production, and not the simple ratio between import and export prices—i.e., crude commodity terms.) Further, expressions such as unfavorable terms of trade are meaningless except by reference to a base period. In recent decades, however, even the crude commodity terms of trade of Third World countries have been exceptionally favorable. When changes in the cost of production, the great improvement in the range and quality of imports, and the huge increase in the volume of trade are taken into account, the external purchasing power of Third World exports is now relatively high, probably more so than ever before. This situation has made it easier for governments to retain a larger proportion of export earnings through major increases in mining royalty rates, export taxes, and corporation taxes. The imposition of substantial export taxes, often very high in the Third World, makes clear that the terms of trade of a country do not determine people's ability to buy imports, much less their living standards.

The exponents of the idea that the terms of trade of the Third World deteriorate persistently rarely specify the period they envisage for this process. Yet it must come to an end at some stage before the terms of trade decline to zero.[16] Nor is it usually made clear why there should be such a deterioration. It is often implied that the West can somehow manipulate international prices to the disadvantage of the Third World. But the West cannot prescribe international prices. These prices are the outcome of innumerable individual decisions of market participants. They are not prescribed by a single individual decision-maker, or even by a handful of people acting in collusion.[17]

The share of a country or group of countries in total world trade is by itself no index of prosperity or welfare. Similarly, reduction in this share has by itself no adverse economic implications. It often reflects the expansion of economic activity and trade elsewhere, which does not normally damage but usually benefits those whose relative share has declined. For instance, since the 1950s the large increase in the foreign trade of Japan, the reconstruction of Europe, and the liberation of intra-European trade have brought about a decline in the share of other groups in world trade, including that of the United States and the United Kingdom. Furthermore, the share of a country or group of countries in world trade is often reduced by domestic developments, and in particular by policies unrelated to external circumstances such as increased domestic use of previously exported products, or domestic inflation, or special taxation of exporters, or the intensification of protectionist policies. Merely as an aside, it is worth noting that since the Second World War the Third World's share of total world trade has in fact much increased compared with earlier times. It is evident that this share has increased hugely under Western influence in the modern period. Before then, the areas forming the present Third World had little external trade. Of course, if international trade harmed the peoples of the Third World as the critics of the West so often allege, then a decline in the share of the Third World in this trade would be beneficial. Ultimate economic bliss would be attained when the Third World no longer had external economic relations, at any rate with the West.

The external debts of the Third World are not the result or reflection of exploitation. They represent resources supplied. Indeed, much of the current indebtedness of Third World governments consists of soft loans under various aid agreements, frequently supplemented by outright grants. With the worldwide rise in prices, including those of Third World exports, the cost even of these soft loans has diminished greatly. Difficulties of servicing these debts do not reflect external exploitation or unfavorable terms of trade. They are the result of wasteful use of the capital supplied, or inappropriate monetary and fiscal policies.

Again, the persistent balance of payments deficits of some Third World countries do not mean that they are being exploited or impoverished by the West. Such deficits are inevitable if the government of a country, whether rich or poor, advancing or stagnating, lives beyond its resources and pursues inflationary policies while attempting to maintain overvalued exchange rates. Persistent balance of payments difficulties mean that external resources are being lent to the country over these periods.

The decline of particular economic activities, as for instance the Indian textile industry in the eighteenth century as a result of competition from cheap imports, is habitually instanced as an example of the damage caused to the Third World by trade with the West. This argument identifies the decline of one activity with the decline of the economy as a whole, and the economic interests of one sectional group with those of all members of a society. Cheap imports extend the choice and economic opportunities of people in poor countries. These imports are usually accompanied by the expansion of other activities. If this were not so, the population would be unable to pay for the imports.

The so-called brain drain, the migration of qualified personnel from the Third World to the West, is another allegation of Western responsibility for Third World poverty or stagnation. This is a somewhat more complex issue than those noted so far, but it certainly does not substantiate the familiar accusation. The training of many of the emigrants was financed by the West. Again, formal education is not an indispensable instrument, nor even a major instrument of emergence from personal poverty or economic backwardness—witness the rapid progress to prosperity of untrained or even illiterate people in many Third World countries. The enforced exodus or outright expulsion of many enterprising and skilled people from many Third World countries, the maltreatment of ethnic minorities or tribal groups, and the refusal of many Third World governments to allow foreigners to work inhibit development much more than do voluntary departures. And many of these emigrants leave because their own governments cannot or will not use their services. It is not the West nor the emigrants who deprive the society of productive resources; it is these Third World governments.[18]

The West is also said to have damaged the Third World by ethnic discrimination. But the countries in which such discrimination occurred were those where material progress was initiated or promoted by contact with the West. The most backward groups in the Third World (aborigines, desert peoples, nomads, and other tribesfolk) were quite unaffected by ethnic discrimination on the part of Europeans. Many communities against which discrimination was often practiced—the Chinese in Southeast Asia, Indians in parts of Southeast Asia, Asians in Africa, and others—have progressed greatly. In any case, discrimination on the basis of color or race is not a European invention. In much of Africa and Asia and notably in India it has been endemic for many centuries. Finally, any ethnic discrimination by Europeans was negligible compared with the massive and sometimes brutal persecution of ethnic and tribal groups systematically practiced by the governments of many independent Asian and African states.

Altogether, it is anomalous or even perverse to suggest that external commercial relations are damaging to development or to the living standards of the people of the Third World. They act as channels for the flow of human and financial resources and for new ideas, methods, and crops. They benefit people by providing a large and diverse source of imports and by opening up markets for exports. Because of the vast expansion of world trade in recent decades, and the development of technology in the West, the material advantages from external contacts are now greater than ever before. The suggestion that these relations are detrimental is not only unfounded but also damaging. For instance, it has often served as a specious but plausible justification for official restrictions on the volume or diversity of these relations.

The basic realities of the results of external contacts have been obfuscated by the practice, rife both in public discussion and in the contemporary development literature, of confusing governments or elites with the population at large.[19] Many Third World governments and their local allies do indeed often benefit from state economic controls, and in particular from the restrictions on external commerce. Such restrictions enable governments to control their subjects more closely, a situation from which the rulers benefit politically and materially. Other articulate and influential local groups also benefit politically and financially from organizing or administering economic controls. These realities are concealed in allegations that the West had forced imports on Third World countries. It is, of course, the rulers who object to the imports desired by their subjects.

The allegations that external trade, and especially imports from the West, are damaging to the populations of the Third World reveal a barely disguised condescension towards the ordinary people there, and even contempt for them. The people, of course, want the imports. If they did not, the imported goods could not be sold. Similarly, the people are prepared to produce for export to pay for these imported goods. To say that these processes are damaging is to argue that people's preferences are of no account in organizing their own lives.

The disparagement of external contacts is relatively recent. Before the Second World War the role of these contacts as instruments of economic advance was widely recognized in academic and public discussion. Their role in providing both external markets and incentive goods, as well as transforming people's attitudes, was a conspicuous theme of the classical economists, including writers as different in their outlook as Adam Smith, John Stuart Mill, and Marx.

7

Apart from the damage allegedly caused to the Third World by external trade, it is frequently said nowadays that the mere existence and day-to-day activities of the peoples of the West also harm the Third World.

Cheap consumer goods developed and used in the West and available also in the Third World are said to obstruct development there because these goods supposedly encourage spending at the expense of saving. The mainstream development literature calls this the international demonstration effect. This contention disregards the level of consumption and the extension of choice as criteria of development. Yet these matters are what economic development is about. The notion of a damaging international demonstration effect also ignores the role of external contacts as an instrument of development. It overlooks the fact that the new consumer goods have to be paid for, which usually requires improved economic performance including such things as more work, additional saving and investment, and readiness to produce for sale instead of for subsistence. Thus this accusation neglects the obvious consideration that a higher and more varied level of consumption is both the principal justification for material progress and an inducement to further economic advance.[20]

An updated version of the international demonstration effect proposes that the eager acceptance of Western consumer goods in the Third World is a form of cultural dependence engendered by Western business. The implication here is that the peoples of the Third World lack the ability to decide for themselves how best to spend their incomes. They are looked on as children, or even as mere puppets manipulated by foreigners at will. In fact, however, Western goods have been accepted selectively and not indiscriminately in the Third World where they have been of massive benefit to millions of people. This charge of cultural dependence is often accompanied by the accusation that the West also damages the Third World through its patent laws. Thus, both the provision of Western goods and also the alleged withholding of them are said to be damaging.

As is not surprising, allegedly lavish consumption habits and the pollution and plunder of the environment in the West have also been pressed into ideological service. A standard formulation is that per capita consumption of food and energy in the United States is many times that in India, so that the American consumer despoils his Indian opposite number on a large scale. Professor Tibor Mende is an influential and widely-quoted writer on development. A few years ago he wrote: "According to one estimate, each American has twenty-five times the impact on the environment—as a consumer and polluter—as an Indian" (*Newsweek*, October 23, 1972). Note the reference to each American as consumer and polluter, but not as a producer.

Even babies are drafted into the campaign to promote Western guilt, notably in the familiar pictures of babies with distended bellies. An article entitled "The Greed of the Super Rich" in the London *Sunday Times*, August 20, 1978, opens as follows:

> One American baby consumes fifty times more of the world's resources than an Indian baby. . . . The wheat need of the people in Africa's Sahel region could have been met by a twentieth of the wheat European countries use each year to feed cattle.

The West has even come to be accused of mass cannibalism. According to Professor René Dumont, the widely-known French agronomist and consultant to international organizations: ". . . in over-consuming meat, which wasted the cereals which could have saved them, we ate the little children of Sahel, of Ethiopia, and of Bangladesh."[21] This grotesque allegation has come to be widely echoed in the West. According to Miss Jill Tweedie of *The Guardian* (London): "A quarter of the world's population lives, quite literally, by killing the other three-quarters" (*The Guardian*, January 3, 1977). And another article prominently featured in *The Guardian*, June 11, 1979 referred to the

> social cannibalism which has reduced over three-quarters of mankind to beggary, poverty and death, not because they don't work, but because their wealth goes to feed, clothe, and shelter a few idle classes in America, Europe,

and Japan . . . moneymongers in London and New York
and in other Western seats of barons living on profit
snatched from the peasants and workers of the world.[22]

Such ridiculous statements could be multiplied many times over.
Their expression by prominent academics and by journalists in
the so-called quality press tells much about the contemporary
intellectual scene.

The West has not caused the famines in the Third World.
These have occurred in backward regions with practically no
external commerce. The absence of external trading links is often
one aspect of the backwardness of these regions. At times it
reflects the policies of the rulers who are hostile to traders, especially to nonindigenous traders, and often even to private property. As a matter of interest, it has proved difficult to get emergency
supplies to some of the Sahelian areas because of poor communications and official apathy or hostility. Attempts permanently to
support the populations of such backward areas with Western
official donations would inhibit the development of viable agriculture there.

Contrary to the various allegations and accusations noted
in this section, the higher level of consumption in the West is not
achieved by depriving others of what they have produced. Western consumption is more than paid for by Western production.
This production not only finances domestic consumption, but
also provides the capital for domestic and foreign investment as
well as foreign aid. Thus the gap between production in the West
and in the Third World is even greater than the gap in consumption.

8

The West has indeed contributed to Third World poverty, in two
senses. These, however, differ radically from the familiar assertions.

First, Western activities since the Second World War have
done much to politicize economic life in the Third World. In the
terminal years of British colonial rule, the traditional policy of
relatively limited government was abandoned in favor of close
official economic controls. As a result of this change in policy in
most British colonies outside the Far East and Southeast Asia, a
ready-made framework for state-controlled economies or even
for totalitarian states was presented to the incoming independent

governments. The operation of official Western aid to Third World governments, reinforced by certain strands in its advocacy and by the criteria of its allocation, has also served to politicize life in the Third World.[23] These controls have wasted resources, restricted social and economic mobility and also external contacts. They have also provoked fierce political and social strife. These consequences in turn have brought about poverty and even large-scale suffering.

Many independent Third World governments would presumably have attempted in any case to politicize their economies extensively, because this greatly enhances the power of the rulers. But they are unlikely to have gone so far as they have in recent years, or to have succeeded in their attempts, without Western influence and assistance. But all this does not validate the position of the exponents of Western guilt. The most vocal and influential critics both of colonial rule and of Western contacts with the Third World have emphatically urged large-scale economic controls and other forms of politicization of life in the Third World. Indeed, they have blamed colonial governments and Western influence for not promoting such policies sooner and more vigorously.

Second, Western contacts with the Third World have helped bring about the sharp decline in mortality in the Third World which is behind the recent rapid population growth there. These Western contacts have therefore enabled many more poor people to survive and have thus increased apparent poverty. But this outcome represents an improvement in the condition of people, and is not the result of deprivation.

9

The allegations that external contacts damage the Third World are plainly condescending. They clearly imply that Third World people do not know what is good for them, nor even what they want. The image of the Third World as a uniform stagnant mass devoid of distinctive character is another aspect of this condescension. It reflects a stereotype which denies identity, character, personality, and responsibility to the individuals and societies of the Third World. Because the Third World is defined as the whole world with the exception of the West and a handful of Westernized societies (such as Japan and South Africa), it is regarded as if it were all much of a muchness. Time and again the guilt merchants envisage the Third World as an undifferentiated, passive entity, helplessly at the mercy of its environment and of the powerful West.

The exponents of Western guilt further patronize the Third World by suggesting that its economic fortunes, past, present, and prospective, are determined by the West; that past exploitation by the West explains Third World backwardness; that manipulation of international trade by the West and other forms of Western misconduct account for persistent poverty; that the economic future of the Third World depends largely on Western donations. According to this set of ideas, whatever happens to the Third World is largely our doing. Such ideas make us feel superior even while we beat our breasts.

A curious mixture of guilt and condescension is also discernible behind the toleration or even support of inhuman policies of many Third World governments. The brutalities of the rulers are often excused on the ostensible ground that they are only following examples set by the West. For instance, when Asian or African governments massively persecute ethnic minorities, they are excused by their Western sympathizers as doing no more than adopting a local variant of ethnic discrimination by Europeans. Similarly, the most offensive and baseless utterances of Third World spokesmen need not be taken seriously because they are only Third World statements, a license which has been extended to their supporters in the West. In this general scheme of things, neither Third World rulers nor their peoples have minds or wills of their own: they are envisaged as creatures molded by the West or, at best, as being at the mercy of their own environment. Moreover, like children, they are not altogether responsible for what they do. In any case, we must support them to atone for alleged wrongs which our supposed ancestors may have perpetrated on their supposed ancestors.[24] And economic aid is also necessary to help these children grow up.

Insistence on Western foreign aid is a major theme of the recent literature of Western guilt. But whether or not linked to patronization (and it usually is so linked), the idea of Western guilt is not only unfounded, but is also a singularly inappropriate basis for aid. It leads to a disregard of the effects of aid in the recipient countries and of the conduct of the recipient governments. It discourages even cursory examination of the likely political, social, and economic results of Western alms. The prime concern is with divesting the West of resources, not with the effects of its donations.

A feeling of guilt has nothing to do with a sense of responsibility or a sense of compassion. Exponents of guilt are concerned with their own emotional state and that of their fellow citizens, and not with the results of the policies inspired by such sentiments. These policies damage the West. They damage the ordinary people in the Third World even more.

NOTES

1. In current usage the Third World means most of Asia except Japan and Israel, most of Africa except white southern Africa, and Latin America. Classification of the oil-producing countries is often vague. Sometimes they are included in the Third World, sometimes not.
2. Throughout this chapter, Western responsibility refers to the accusation that the West has inflicted backwardness or poverty on the Third World. This usage again accords with the standard practice.
3. Paul A. Baran, *The Political Economy of Growth* (New York: Monthly Review Press, 1957), p. 177.
4. Peter Townsend, *The Concept of Poverty* (London: Heinemann, 1970), pp. 41, 42.
5. Kwame Nkrumah, *Towards Colonial Freedom,* (London: Heinemann, 1962). Cf. also P. T. Bauer, *Dissent on Development,* chapters 3 and 4.
6. An adulatory profile in *The Observer* (23 November 1975) cosily referred to Nyerere as "St. Julius." An article in the *Financial Times* (11 August 1975) described him as "Africa's senior statesman and a man of formidable intellect."
7. I. Potekhin, *Problems of Economic Independence of African Countries* (Moscow: Academy of Sciences, 1962), pp. 14, 15.
8. A list of such warnings and objections will be found in *Dissent on Development, op. cit.*
9. In fact, the areas most involved in the Atlantic slave trade, particularly West Africa, have become the economically most advanced areas in Black Africa. A recent study of precolonial Southeastern Nigeria examines the economic development promoted by the slave trade which ". . . led to sufficient economic development of the region" to enable the profitable trade in palm-oil to burgeon in the early nineteenth century. David Northrup, *Trade Without Rulers: Pre-colonial Economic Development in South-Eastern Nigeria* (Oxford: Clarendon Press, 1978), p. 176.
10. This extension of Marxist-Leninist ideology is reflected, for instance, in the passage from the Soviet academician Potekhin, section 2 above. Marxist-Leninist statements are apt to be designed for political purposes. Thus, in Potekhin's booklet, the passage I have quoted is followed immediately by the injunction that Western enterprises in Africa should be expropriated and economic activity collectivized. This injunction is now accepted by a number of African states.
11. This relationship was noted in Chapter 1.
12. Underprivileged is a nonsense expression akin to under- or overfed. Privilege connotes special advantages concerred on some people and denied to others.
13. See Chapter 10.

14. A convenient recent example is a statement by the Ayatollah Khomeini in January 1979: "Our people are weary of it (colonial domination). Following their example other countries will free themselves from the colonial grip." *Daily Telegraph*, 10 January 1979. In its long history Iran never was a Western colony. Further examples of this usage are noted in *Dissent on Development*, Chapter 3, "The Economics of Resentment."

15. These allegations and the demand for a New International Economic Order are discussed at some length in several essays in Karl Brunner (ed.), *The First World and the Third World* (University of Rochester, N.Y.: 1978). See especially essays by Karl Brunner, Harry G. Johnson, Peter T. Bauer, and Basil S. Yamey.

16. When some ostensible evidence is produced in support of these allegations, it usually turns out to involve shifts in base periods or in the aggregates under discussion. I have examined these matters in some detail in *Dissent on Development*, Chapter 6, "A Critique of UNCTAD."

17. Even if the West had the market power implied in many of these discussions, this would not account for a deterioration of the terms of trade, unless the effectiveness of this power increased persistently. Any such idea would be quite unrelated to reality.

18. An article in *The Observer* (22 July 1979) was entitled "The boat people's 'brain drain' punishes Vietnam." The article suggested that the refugees from Vietnam were selfish and unpatriotic people who left because they could earn more elsewhere, and because they would not accept the new socialist order. It suggested further that this brain drain deprived the country of much-needed skills, especially medical skills. The article used the terms *brain drain, exodus* and *loss* to describe what was in fact a well-documented example of a huge mass expulsion—a revealing misuse of language.

19. The distinction which applies in many contexts is pertinent also to an assessment of changes in a country's terms of trade. As noted earlier in this section, changes in the terms of trade do not necessarily correspond to the ability of people to buy imports.

20. At the official level, a damaging international demonstration effect may indeed operate by encouraging show projects and unsuitable technologies financed with public funds. But this is not usually what the exponents of the international demonstration effect have in mind. Nor is it appropriate to blame the West for the policies of Third World governments in their adoption of unsuitable external models.

21. Quoted by Daniel P. Moynihan, "The United States in Opposition," *Commentary*, March 1975.

22. The article, written by Ngugi wa Thiang'O, opened a special survey of Kenya.

23. These implications and results of official foreign aid are examined at greater length in the next chapter.

24. Cf. Chapter 5, Section 13.

SIX

The Two Kinds
of Memory

JEAN-FRANÇOIS REVEL

Henri Bergson distinguished between two types of memory, habit-memory and recall-memory. In the former, the past is preserved but blended into the present so that we can use it automatically in daily life. The latter preserves the past as such, the past delimited in time, the memory of a unique and original experience that happened at a specific moment of our lives, with its emotional tone, happy or painful. Habit-memory enables us to circulate unerringly in a familiar city while thinking of something else. Recall-memory brings back our beginnings in that city, when it was new to us and we were getting to know it. I think this psychological distinction can be applied to politics: in the democratic countries' historical consciousness, communism's past is part of habit-memory, capitalism's of recall-memory.

As things are now, it seems that only the West's failures, crimes, and weaknesses deserve to be recorded by history. Even the West accepts that rule. The ordeal of capitalism's Great Depression of the 1930s still haunts historians, journalists, politicians, and Western schoolbooks like an indelible stain on the capitalistic system despite the prodigies the system later accomplished in surmounting the added disaster of World War II to bring about a society of abundance. But the deaths of tens of millions of people as a result of a direct, deliberate policy of Communist leaders in the Soviet Union during the forced collectivization of the Society economy in those very years, from 1929

JEAN-FRANÇOIS REVEL is a distinguished French political commentator. Once a confirmed leftist, he has in recent years come to a conservative position. He is the author of *Without Marx or Jesus* and *The Totalitarian Temptation*. The following essay is taken from his recent book *How Democracies Perish* (Doubleday, 1983).

to 1934, have only a vaporous reality in the West's historical memory, as objects of scholarly curiosity.

Reality to us is what Soviet leaders are preparing to do *now* and, especially, in the future to stimulate the country's agriculture. By "now" we can mean 1945 or 1953 or 1964 or 1982 or any other date when the Western press revives the classic vaudeville show entitled *A Great Reformer Prepares to Spur Soviet Agricultural Productivity.* The production has also been dubbed into Chinese, Cuban, Vietnamese, Tanzanian, Algerian, Romanian, etc. The show's plot revolves around the very much overworked idea of Hungary's "new economic mechanism," which is nothing but a camouflaged and clumsy approximation of capitalism. We will *never* learn that socialism does not begin to work until it is jettisoned.

Thus communism's past loses its reality, melting into the eternal present of a reform the bureaucracy claims it is always about to unveil. Communism's past is always a *stage* en route to a future that, when it comes, is invariably as dismal as the past, but which is in turn promoted to the rank of a *stage*, etc.

Capitalist slumps, however, do not rank as "stages" even when they are followed by brilliant recoveries. Nor are the economic breakthroughs of capitalist countries in the Third World— Taiwan, South Korea, Singapore, even Indonesia—given any standing in the West's memory. All we remember is these countries' authoritarian politics. But the authoritarianism, to use a mild term, of the Algerian political system, for example, is not remembered, any more than the penury that Algerian socialism has inevitably caused, as state socialism always does. When Algerian citizens are permitted to leave their country, which is rare, they stock up on staples bought from their "reactionary" neighbors, Tunisia and, especially, Morocco, where a still traditional farming system still floods world markets with produce. These are countries of poverty but not penury, for only a socialist bureaucracy can arrange for permanent shortages in fertile countries.

The distinction between the two types of memory is useful not only in conditioning the West to accept fundamentally inequitable differences in the two worlds' attitudes toward living standards, political systems and human rights. It also serves to blur socialism's misdeeds while keeping those of capitalism fresh in people's minds. The Vietnamese War is still an open wound, the guilt it produced still vivid in America's consciousness and in the free world's image of the United States. But habit-memory effaced the bloodbath in Ethiopia and the Cambodians' martyrdom almost as soon as they happened. How many Westerners have even an inkling of the number of Cambodian refugees who were parked just inside the Thai border at the end of 1982?

The Soviet suppression of the 1956 Hungarian uprising, a rebellion the West did *not* provoke, was quickly legitimized by the world's indifference, as Albert Camus angrily lamented in 1958,[1] then legitimized formally in 1975 by the Helsinki agreement. But the CIA's destabilization in 1954 of the Arbenz government in Guatemala, which was definitely linked to the Soviet Union, will live on for posterity as a crime of American imperialism.

General Jacobo Arbenz Guzmán, who was elected President of Guatemala in 1951 and overthrown in 1954 at the instigation of the United Fruit Company, is one of the heroic martyrs in the progressives' calendar of saints. As recently as 1982, a historical pamphlet appeared on the subject in the United States. It was coauthored by Stephen Schlesinger, the son of Kennedy adviser Arthur Schlesinger, and Stephen Kinzer, and it carries a preface by former *New York Times* correspondent Harrison Salisbury. Its title, *Bitter Fruit*, refers to United Fruit, which once dominated Guatemala economically and politically and which, as I said, prompted the *coup d'état* against Arbenz. The line the piece takes is pure Marxism: private capital summoning its lackey, the pseudodemocratic and imperialist state, to its rescue. There is some truth in it. The relations between the United States and Guatemala were semicolonial. But it ignores what was probably the decisive element: the international aspect of the *coup d'état's* cause, its imbrication into East-West relations.

It was Rómulo Betancourt, the former President of Venezuela and the father of democracy in his country, who made me most sharply aware of that aspect. That was in Caracas in 1978, during a conference in which the senior Schlesinger, John Kenneth Galbraith, and the present Spanish Socialist Prime Minister, Flipe González, also took part. Betancourt, who, as head of the Democratic Action Party (a member of the Socialist International) had prepared the way for nationalization of Venezuela's oil industry and had resisted terrorist subversion, was obliged that day to reply to an American writer, Richard Goodwin. Attacking America's good faith in Latin America, Goodwin had cited as examples the deplorable fates of Arbenz in Guatemala and of the Dominican Republic's Juan Bosch in 1963. Betancourt spoke from firsthand knowledge because during the period of Arbenz's ouster he was a political exile living mainly in Central America.

"Richard Goodwin got the impression from my remarks

this morning," he said, "that in connection with the overthrow of certain democratic governments, I attributed the blame exclusively to errors committed by the heads of these governments, who were brought to power by popular suffrage, and that I neglected to give sufficient importance to [other] external and internal forces, especially the external forces, particularly the multi-tentacular CIA and the embassies of the United States in Latin America.

"There is no doubt that the very mysterious and shadowy CIA has contributed to the overthrow of a number of governments in Latin America, including governments elected through popular suffrage, and that its operations were sometimes carried out directly by the United States embassies. This was established and illustrated in the detailed report to the Senate by the Church Committee in the United States. But what emerges as most dangerous for the stability of democratic governments in Latin America is that every time a government is overthrown, we can say the CIA overthrew it, the State Department overthrew it. Carlos Rangel wrote a book[2] with which I basically agree and which aroused broad international debate, since it was not only a best seller in Spanish, but was also translated into English and French. He warns us against the convenient tendency of Latin American governments, when they are overthrown because they were incompetent, because they were corrupt, because they did not show a sense of responsibility toward the obligation the electorate placed in their hands, to explain these difficulties and falls as being due uniquely to external maneuvers.

"Goodwin cited to us the case of General Arbenz, who was overthrown in 1954 by an insurrectional movement wholly fabricated by the CIA. But General Arbenz, who had been placed in power by a popular vote, surrounded himself with a communist staff as soon as he took over the government.[3] Guatemala became a rallying point for communists of various origins, European and Asian as well as Latin America. Arbenz bought arms from Czechoslovakia. When Stalin died, he asked the Guatemalan Parliament to stand in silence for two minutes to show its grief.[4] When Lombardo Toledano, the Mexican communist labor leader, went to Guatemala, General Arbenz, surrounded by his *entire* cabinet, went in person to the airport to greet him. Yet all this was combined with extraordinary corruption on the part of the team in power. These defenders of the proletariat were unbridled in enriching themselves while in office. I have precise information on all that and when we Venezuelan socialists learned of the situation in Guatemala, we sent an emissary to President José

Figueres of Costa Rica with a letter explaining what was happening. Arbenz was overthrown and Arbenz left for the Eastern countries. Then he went to Cuba. I do not wish to be cruel, because he is dead, but I must be frank: since he was not a very useful imbecile, the communists dropped him and [he] disappeared.

"In the case of Juan Bosch, to which Goodwin also referred, there is usually some confusion. President Bosch was really overthrown by a military movement that he saw coming and did nothing to oppose. Throughout his term in office, he did not once call a meeting of his government. One fine day he suddenly decided to dissolve his own party, the party that had brought him to power, the Dominican Revolutionary Party. He distanced himself widely and aggressively from his democratic companions, took it on himself to tighten relations with Fidel Castro's Cuba, and was overthrown by the military. It was really not until a year later that the United States intervened, when the Caamano movement arose, which does not alter the fact that the United States' intervention in the Dominican Republic was one of the gravest and most reprehensible mistakes that government ever made. But there would have been no occasion for making that mistake if Juan Bosch had not begun by totally denaturing the mandate entrusted to him by the Dominican people."[5]

The West really accepts the idea that the Soviet Union "could not" give in over Poland or Czechoslovakia or Hungary, that it "could not" let those countries slip out of the Warsaw Pact, that its "lines of defense" and its "vital strategic interests" were at stake in these upheavals, and that, as Chancellor Schmidt declared in 1981, challenging its right to intervene in those countries meant "revising Yalta" and thus "endangering the peace."

The democracies therefore agreed to recognize communism's right to political realism, to maintain the primacy of reasons of state, especially in its so-called sphere of influence, which is really an occupation zone. But the United States is denied these natural rights in protecting its vital interests in Central America, among its nearest neighbors. It is expected to consent unreacting to open Communist subversion in the Caribbean, to Arbenz's obvious manipulation by Moscow. Yet the Soviet Union defends its presence in Afghanistan with the argument that "it cannot tolerate a hostile regime in a country with which it has a common border." This is a principle the West and the UN accepted when "signals" were transmitted concerning a "political solution" in Afghanistan at the end of 1982. For "political solution" read "an arrangement recognizing the Soviet Union's 'special position' in the country and enabling it to maintain its political domination there without having to fight for it." The democracies are the first to admit that Communist might makes right.

Fuzzy perception, murky recollection, anger that dies aborning or evaporates within a matter of days—these are the mechanics of our awareness of totalitarian activity. No one better understands our forgetfulness than the Communist leaders; we may not know them very well, but they know us. They coined the monstrous euphemism of "normalization" to describe redoubled totalitarian ferocity toward peoples who dare rebel, even fleetingly, against their masters. The term is equally precise in describing Western public opinion and leadership. We too are normalized as our indignation deflates, and it is notably short-winded. We soon find that the abnormal is normal. It's not our patience that is limited, it's our impatience. It runs out in a few months. The Soviet government and Western Communist Party bosses know from experience that after a year of martial law in Poland nothing of our indignation remained afloat but the memory of half a dozen demonstrations, a few million *Solidarnośc* buttons, and a wound in the West's side from the most bitter economic conflict between Europe and the United States that has occurred in a very long time.

So the phrase "lumping together" is not altogether adequate. Or, if you prefer, reciprocal absolution really works, feloniously, in one direction only, almost always in favor of totalitarianism and its allies. Some people say that "as long as we have Pinochet, Marcos, South Africa, and the Argentine *desaparecidos* we will not have a moral right to pillory the suffocation of Poland." Nobody ever says "as long as they have Poland and Afghanistan, we do not have a moral right to denounce apartheid and Pinochet." The most ecumenical among us talk about "the same fight," but this is wrong: it is not the same fight, and there is no real equivalence between reaction to Communist dictatorships and reaction to other dictatorships.

The last time Franco had a Basque resistance fighter[6] executed was in 1975, and the protest demonstration in Paris was so large and so angry that the neighborhood in which the Spanish embassy stood was devastated for half a mile around. Who ever heard of a demonstration, even a silent, nonviolent one, against the murder of some three thousand Ethiopians summarily executed by Lieutenant Colonel Mengistu in Addis Ababa alone? No one, and we know why. And we remain discreet despite, or because of, the presence in Ethiopia of a massive contingent of Soviet "advisers," whose prominence in the revolutionary purges there we would be unfair to deny. Until his last moment in power, another African dictator was surrounded by Soviet advisers: Francisco Macías Nguema, who could not have immolated up to a third of his fellow countrymen in tiny Equatorial Guinea without the consent or at least the silent complicity of his Russian friends. Yet when Macias in turn perished by the sword, his Soviet entourage scuttled back to Moscow, *zitti zitti, piano piano,* without anyone, as far as I know, having criticized the Soviet Union for failing to curb its protégé's little excesses.

On the other hand, a butcher on a less industrial scale, the Central African Republic's Bokassa, had his "capitalist" allegiance to thank for making headlines the world over as a murderer and alleged cannibal of schoolchildren. He put his allies in so awkward a position that his French protectors themselves had to unseat him. During the Korean War, an unfounded charge that the Americans were using bacteriological weapons, one of history's great examples of mass disinformation, launched a worldwide wave of protest that was not entirely calmed by subsequent refutation of the lie, as often happens in such cases.

In 1982, a number of eyewitnesses and several investigative committees, including one from the UN—and we can imagine how languid and cowardly its curiosity was—established beyond a reasonable doubt that the Soviets were using biochemical weapons (the mysterious yellow rain) in Afghanistan and had supplied them to Vietnam for its campaigns in Laos and Cambodia. Were consciences stirred or politicians aroused in the West and the Third World? The only campaign I can remember in this connection was not waged to force Moscow to halt this abominable practice—heaven forfend that trade be interrupted!—but against the *New York Times,* which scrupulously insisted that the accusation had not been conclusively proved by the *Wall Street Journal,* which charged its rival with refusing to face the facts. It was the *Journal* that came off best in the row, and it had plenty of time to enjoy its victory, since the Soviets went right on dropping their yellow rain on Asia with stony indifference to the timid Western yawping they knew was, as usual, totally innocuous.

The radar screens of Western perception lost sight of the Vietnamese boat people only a year or so after their mass exodus began, allowing Castro's friend Gabriel García Márquez to castigate them as "currency smugglers" and "exporters of capital" and still receive a Nobel prize. The flight of hundreds of thousands of Cuban boat people showed that communism is decidedly the same at any latitude. Yet none of these lessons helped Western seers to view, say, the Sandinista revolution in Nicaragua in its true light.

When the Sandinistas took over the government, the few

commentators who ventured to predict that they would run out every other political grouping and establish a one-party police state were accused in all good faith of being Somoza sympathizers. And when it became impossible to deny that Nicaragua was becoming a Castroist state, attention shifted to the issue of how non-Communist the rebels in El Salvador are. While they doubtless receive Cuban—thus Soviet—aid, it was affirmed, the revolution's basic causes were social injustice and poverty.

And so they were. But communism has never eliminated social injustice or poverty; it has always and everywhere accentuated scarcity and privilege. Descriptions of Nicaragua since 1982 attest that the process is holding to form there too, so much so that Nicaraguans are being to murmur that food shortages and corruption are "worse than under Somoza." It is all very classic, very wearying. The penury is acute in Poland and Romania too, but no one seriously advocates those countries' deserting the Communists for the capitalists or pleads the social injustice there would justify a guerrilla uprising backed by NATO. Yet the United States is expected to consent to the Sovietization of countries on its doorstep, even if this would not bring these neighbors either freedom or well-being, but would eliminate what little they have and effectively block any chance for them to acquire more.

I by no means contend that all Good is on one side and all Evil on the other. I am simply describing the "two-memory" syndrome, the amnesia that afflicts Westerners who applaud the guerrillas in El Salvador while completely forgetting the lesson administered by those in Nicaragua. For example, most of the media assumed, before the March 1982 elections in El Salvador, that the guerrilla boycott of the vote would be massively supported. In other words, they overestimated the Farabundi Marti Front's popularity. As late as noon on election day, ABC television newscasters were incautiously predicting a low voter turnout when, in fact, word was beginning to filter in that the peasants were defying the guerrillas' call for a boycott despite the risk of rebel reprisals. In the end, the turnout was 80 percent (versus 50 percent in 1972) with only minor voting irregularities. Indeed, confidential surveys made beginning in December 1981 had indicated that between 70 and 85 percent of the population planned to vote. But American reporters simply refused to take the surveys seriously because they contradicted their convictions. Many commentators, observers and politicians have great difficulty in understanding such complex situations as those described above by Betancourt, in which it is true that social injustice has brought a country to crisis point, false that communism can remedy that injustice, but true again that it is skilled at exploiting such situations to achieve its political and strategic objectives.

When it comes to mass extermination, communism has to polevault to prodigious heights to reach the threshold of Western perception. And even that threshold merely represents an average. Papandreou's threshold of perception, or Palme's, for example, is higher than any Communist vaulter could ever reach. The Nicaraguan Sandinistas would have been wrong to forego their minigenocide, the slaughter of several thousand Meskito Indians, reportedly under conditions of savagery the West will be arguing about for a long time to come. When in doubt, hold your tongue.

The finest display of reluctant perception and swift forgetfulness, however, is still the West's awareness and dismissal of genocide in Cambodia.

Reading catalogues can be interesting. I am in a position to provide this pleasure for those of you who enjoy lists. For I went to the trouble of combing my files to record a long list of articles about the Cambodian Khmer Rouge that appeared in publications in the United States, Britain, and France in 1975-76. Here are the headlines, in chronological order:

1975

March 25-26	*Le Monde*	"Government Reshuffle May Signal Ouster of Marshal Lon Nol"
April 25	*Le Monde*	"Three-Day Celebration Organized for Khmer Rouge Victory"
Arpil 28	*Le Point*	"A Village Under the Khmer Rouge"
May 5	*Newsweek*	"We Beat the Americans"
May 5	*Time*	"A Khmer Curtain Descends"
May 6	*International Herald Tribune*	"Ford Says Reds Slay Lon Nol Aides, Wives"
May 8	*Le Monde*	"Travel Log from Phnom Penh to the Thai Frontier"
May 9	*Le Monde*	"The Khmer Enigma" (editorial)
May 10	*Int. Her. Trib.*	"Phnom Penh: Victory of Peasants; Eyewitness Report"

May 10	*Le Monde*	"Who's Governing Cambodia?"
May 10	*Le Monde*	"Tens of Thousands of Refugees on the Roads"
May 11	*Sunday Times* (London)	"Diary of a Doomed City"
May 12	*Le Point*	"Phnom Penh: Two Million Deportees"
May 12	*Le Nouvel Observateur*	"The Fall of Phnom Penh"
May 12	*Int. Her. Trib.*	"The Last Days in Phnom Penh: Sorrow, Selfishness"
May 15	*Int. Her. Trib.*	"A Famous Victory (A Bleak View of Cambodia)"
May 19	*Newsweek*	"Cambodia's 'Purification' "
May 19	*Time*	"Long March from Phnom Penh"
May 26	*Nouv. Obs.*	"A Frenchman, Bernard Hazebrouk, with the Khmer Rouge"
May 26	*Le Figaro*	"Doum Uch's 25th Hour (The Story of a Man 'Liberated' by the Khmer Rouge)"
June 22	*Sunday Times*	"Cambodia Refugees Tell of Deaths and Famine"
July 18	*Le Monde*	"A Touchy Yen for Independence Guides Revolutionary Leaders"
July 20	*The Observer*	"Cambodia Opens a Swop-Shop"
July 27	*Sunday Times*	"What About the Executions? Only Traitors Have Been Killed"
August 18	*Le Monde*	"Cambodia, China and Indochina" (editorial)
August 19	*Newsweek*	" 'Organization' Men: a Report from Refugees"
August 23	*The Economist*	"News from No-Man's Land"
August 25	*Nouv. Obs.*	"The Return of Sihanouk"

Sept. 2	*Le Monde*	"Daily Life in the Country: Khmers May Not Own Money or Travel Between Provinces"
Sept. 8	*Newsweek*	Interview with Ieng Sary at nonaligned congress in Peru
Sept. 9	*Le Figaro*	"The Prince's Revenge (Sihanouk's Return to Phnom Penh)"
Sept. 10	*Le Monde*	"Sihanouk's Return to Phnom Penh"
Sept. 14	*Int. Her. Trib.*	"A Proposal to Overrun Cambodia"
Sept. 17	*Le Monde*	"Ieng Sary's Private Visit to Paris"
Oct. ?	*Le Point*	"Sihanouk: Chief of a State Without People"
Oct. 4	*Le Monde*	"Portrait of Prince Sihanouk During Press Conference"
Oct. 11	*Le Monde*	"Sihanouk: 'We Want to Be Neutral, Like Austria, Switzerland and Sweden'"
Oct. 12	*Sunday Times*	"My Visit to the Revolution" (by Prince Sihanouk)
Oct. 12	*Le Monde*	"Disappointed by the New Regime, Some Fifty Khmers in Peking Refuse to Return to Their Country"
Oct. 15	*Le Figaro*	"Cambodia: A People's Calvary"
Oct. 19	*Le Monde*	"Cambodia's New Leaders (Government Formed)"
Oct. 24-25	*La Croix*	"A Revolution Born in Terrible Pain" (series)
Nov. 3	*Le Point*	"Peking: Sihanouk in the Red Circle"
Nov. 8	*Le Monde*	"The Critical Difficulties in Supplying Food May be Remedied in 1976"

1976

Jan. ?	*France-Soir*	"Resistance Being Organized in the Tropical Forest" (series)
Jan. 18	*Sunday Times*	"A Peep into Cambodia Through the Eyes of Those Who Fled"
Feb. 11	*La Croix*	"The Productivist Revolution"
Feb. 17	*Le Monde*	"Cambodia Nine Months After" (series)
March 8	*Le Point*	"The Helots of the New Regime"
April 5	*Nouv. Obs.*	"A Door Ajar into Cambodia"
April 6	*Le Figaro*	"Sihanouk Leaves the Political Scene"
April 6	*Le Monde*	"Sihanouk 'Retires' "
April 11	*The Observer*	"Thousands Flee Land of Genuine Happiness"
April 16	*Le Monde*	"Cambodia and Its Revolution"
April 16	*Le Point*	"Sihanouk: 'It Was Untenable' "
April 17	*Le Figaro*	"The Smile of Angkor"
April 17-18	*Le Figaro*	"Cambodia Under the Khmer Rouge"
April 17-19	*Libération*	"The Secret Revolution" (series)
April 18	*Sunday Times*	"Cambodia Is Convulsed as Khmer Rouge Wipe Out a Civilization"
April 18-19	*Le Monde*	"Tiev Chin-leng Reports: 'A People Controls Its Destiny' "
April 18-19	*Le Monde*	"The Story of Yen Savannary" (a refugee under the Khmer regime for two hundred days)

April 23	*Times* (London)	"A Nation in Chains"
April 24	*Paris-Match*	"Terror in Cambodia"
April 26	*Time*	"Why Are the Khmer Killing the Khmer?"
April 29	*Le Monde*	"Selective Indignation"
May 17	*Newsweek*	"Two Views from Inside"
May 17	*Nouv. Obs.*	"Cambodia as Seen from Hanoi"
May 21	*Le Monde*	"Report from a Former Resident of Païlin"
May 26	*Le Croix*	"Refugees Report on Life in Cambodia"
May 31	*Le Figaro*	"Cambodia: A Mad Experiment with a New Order"
June 7	*Le Point*	"They Returned from the 'Land of the Dead'"
Sept. 18	*Le Monde*	"In a Camp Near the Khmer-Thai Border, Refugees Tell of the Lack of Freedom and the Difficulties That Forced Them to Leave"
Sept. 28	*Le Monde*	"No Victories for the Anticommunist Resistance"
Oct. 29	*Far Eastern Economic Review*	"When the Killing Had to Stop"

You will notice, to start with, that a historian five hundred years from now who has nothing but this list of headlines from which to draw an idea of what happened in Kampuchea in this crucial period (and even this is a lot more than the documents we have concerning some periods of antiquity and of the Middle Ages) could in no way guess that methodical genocide had taken place there that exterminated between a fourth and a third of the population. Translated into statistics closer to home, this would represent twelve million to twenty million people in France, West Germany, Britain or Italy, sixty million to eighty million in the United States.

In only three or four of the seventy-four headlines do the words "death" or "executions" or "land of the dead" or "two million deportees" appear to guide us through that cemetery. Our historian would probably conclude that a new regime might have executed a few dozen people from the old order. How could he guess that millions of human beings in Cambodia in the late twentieth century had their brains beat out with clubs and picks like the baby seals in Greenland? I agree that many of the articles under those headlines supplied full details about this orgy of exploding skulls. It is nevertheless odd that so many headlines were so moderate as to provide only the merest glimpse of the nature and extent of what really happened.

Some of them were deliberately easy on the Khmer Rouge. At worst, they mention "critical difficulties in supplying food," but these, of course, are on their way to being "remedied," as they have been in all Communist countries since 1917.[7] Even the accusatory articles or those testifying to the horror in Cambodia were given fairly neutral headlines. When we read that Sihanouk wanted to turn his country into another Switzerland or Austria, we figure that, in that case, things can't be too bad there. The expression "disappointed by the new regime" might well be used by French voters disillusioned with Mitterrand's perfectly constitutional and democratic socialist administration. And "it was untenable" could just as well describe one of Italy's revolving-door cabinet crises. Understatement is really the order of the day in references to refugees' complaints of "lack of freedom" and "difficulties." Do we say the Jews were "disappointed in naziism" or that they ran into "difficulties" in 1942 because of some undefinable impression of "lack of freedom"? In the headlines given, the words "killing," "killed," "slay" seldom appear, and even then "slay" refers only to ex-Premier Lon Nol's followers, which gives us no hint of mass slaughter.

Remember, too, that we are dealing here solely with reports received while the events were happening. Since then, the tides have swept the beaches of memory clean. Habit, indifference, and time have completed this task of purification.

In my list of sample headlines I did not include any from Communist publications because they obey other laws than those of perception and memory. They observe the laws of Soviet foreign policy. This is particularly true of the French Communists, and it is worth glancing rapidly at how the party newspaper L'Humanité covered the Cambodian genocide.

As long as the Cambodia liberated by the Khmer Rouge did not ally itself with China—for Moscow's peace overtures to Peking were still well in the future—the Cambodian revolution rated L'Humanité's dithyrambs. On April 23, 1975, it headlined, "Phnom Penh: Peace and Prosperity Are Independent Cambodia's Top Priorities." A farsighted prophecy if ever there was one! The paper's staff was plainly devoting itself to defending newly Communist Cambodia against the "campaign of intoxication" being waged by the bourgeois Western press, which carried early stories of the horrible conditions under which Phnom Penh's population was being forced out of the capital. When President Ford called for UN intervention "to avoid a bloodbath in Phnom Penh," *L'Humanité's* managing editor, René Andrieu, violently counterattacked on April 18, ridiculing these imperialist alarums as odious and hypocritical.

It is striking that three years later, on January 9, 1978, the same newspaper would lambaste the "frightful spectacle" in Cambodia, reporting a "gigantic attempt at authoritarian regimentation, massive deportation, families separated, summary executions, unfortunately probably wholesale." On January 29, 1979, *L'Humanité's* correspondent with the invading Vietnamese troops found prisoners of the Khmer Rouge "with slashed throats, crushed skulls, arms severed, traces of shovel blows all over the bodies. Phnom Penh . . . A soulless city. A nightmare city. A city over which constantly floats the obsessive smell of death." In other words, the bloodbath predicted in 1975 by President Ford, whose foresight Andrieu was careful not to recognize.

As a matter of fact, the atrocities reported in the Communist newspaper in 1978-79 were not exactly new. The Communist press does not go in much for scoops. What is interesting here is why, in hurling its anathema at Cambodia, it overtook and passed the worst excesses of language the bourgeois press had been guilty of in its "campaign of intoxication." There are two main reasons for this: first, the Cambodians' chose China as their protector rather than accept Soviet satellite status; second, and more important, was the invasion and occupation of Cambodia beginning in October 1977 by the forces of unfailingly pro-Soviet Vietnam. From that moment on, the Communist press geared its propaganda machine to an all-out defense of the invasion and its benefits for the Cambodian people. This meant coming down hard on earlier Khmer Rouge atrocities so as to depict the Vietnamese troops as liberators.

Some spokesmen for the non-Communist left invested even more time and ill will than the Communists in refusing to recognize genocide in Cambodia. But they had very different reasons for finally resigning themselves to it. The Communists no longer believed in the Khmer Rouge revolution. They now believed only in conquest. The non-Communist left still believed in the revolution; at first it had seen the change in Cambodia as a pure "cultural" revolution, the sort of total change of society it had dreamed of so long. So for more than a year it had remained aloof from the indigestible reports coming out of regenerated Kampuchea. Then, when the effort to ignore them became superhuman, it adopted another attitude: preening itself for being the first to condemn the genocide before the court of world opinion when, in fact, it had been the last, even behind the Stalinists.

This sort of trumpery is a refined form of cliquishness: if the left itself damns monstrous leftist deviations, they remain the left's business, become mere mishaps in its historical advance, symbols of its capacity for self-criticism and self-purification. In that case, the overall socialist explanatory system is not ruined by genocide, by the Vietnamese reeducation camps, by the boat people, by Castro, by Nicaragua, or by the annihilation of *Solidarność*. Denunciation of these crimes and errors is merely the constantly repaired springboard to the left's eternal ascension, its growing lucidity. This is why it is so important to erase criticism and even news from "the right," to bury them in the rubble of forgetfulness, for they attack the system's roots, its fundamental cause, which, wherever it is planted, produces its inevitable and always identical fruit.

I am not questioning the unusual scale of the Cambodian massacre. But wasn't its prototype Stalin's mass extermination of the millions condemned as "kulaks" in the early thirties? Then why should the West have been "surprised" again by the "unexpected" and "unforeseeable" Cambodian bloodbath? For one reason only: the delicate care with which it had wiped its memory clean of the Stalinist precedent, refusing to analyze or explain it and so becoming incapable of foreseeing a repetition, much less forestalling one.

THE DEMOCRACIES VERSUS DEMOCRACY

In most cases, then, the democracies take the attitudes and decisions Communist leaders want them to take. This acquiescence is both ideological and functional. Broad sectors of public opinion and of the West's political and cultural elite see the democracies as more reactionary, more damaging to the Third World, more aggressive militarily, especially as regards nuclear warfare, than the Soviet Union and its satellites. Westerners who favor an effective nuclear deterrent and a verifiable balance of forces are still viewed as "conservatives," "right-wingers," "warmongers," or, at best, as "cold warriors." Those advocating unilateral disarmament or, at any rate, prior and increasingly juicier concessions to the Soviet Union without reciprocal guarantees are considered "leftists," generous souls who love peace.

In practice, what these "liberals" are really promoting is an imbalance that would enable the Soviet Union to force its economic and political will on a growing number of countries without going to war, thus enlarging an already spacious orbit. Yet history teaches us that never, anywhere, have concessions coaxed the Soviet Union into making concessions. From this unhappy truth, for which they are in no way responsible, the democracies do not conclude that they must change their diplomatic approach but that they must concede still more. Apparent Soviet concessions, Moscow's flashiest sucker bait, find plenty of takers in the West; the few Western political observers competent enough to see these maneuvers as no more than deceitful propaganda cannot swim against so many currents of opinion, which will not forgive them for neglecting any "windfall opportunity" magnanimously offered by the Kremlin.

Anyone with his ear to the political ground might think the only danger to the West is Western arms and Western diplomacy. For example, the *New York Times* of April 2, 1982, worried that "An Adverse Impact Among Allies Is Feared After Reagan Remark on Soviet Superiority." That is, the real danger to America's European allies is not seen as possible Soviet military superiority, but in America's plans to counter it by reinforcing our defenses. Any President of the United States visiting Western Europe is treated to demonstrations so hostile that an unsuspecting spectator would think he were the worse enemy Europe ever had.

True, people often show better judgment than their elites and their activists. In 1982, a survey[8] showed that all the peoples of Western Europe except the Spanish thought the growth of the Soviet military potential was more important in explaining international tension than the growth of America's military potential. This had its clownish side, however: by a margin of 45 percent to 21 percent, the French people believe that American interest rates and the dollar's role in international finance are much more serious causes of tension than Russia's bulging arsenal. Let us note in passing that the people of every Western country made the mistake of blaming the arms race as a cause of tension when it is really a consequence of tension.

Despite an improved and, by 1981, clearer perception of Soviet power or perhaps because of the realism of that perception, most Europeans, and not just militant pacifists, say that if their countries were invaded, they would rather submit than resist. Asking in another poll, "If the Soviet Army entered French territory, do you think the President of France should immediately open peace talks with the Soviet Union?" 63 percent of the French answered yes, 7 percent favored the use of nuclear weapons, and 21 percent thought France should fight, but without using its nuclear missiles.[9]

Now, one may very well prefer servitude to death. But we can also avoid putting ourselves in a situation in which this grim choice is all that is open to us. Yet the will to avoid such a situation is precisely what we seem to lack. The relentless Soviet "peace offensive," therefore, has every chance of succeeding, that is, of persuading the West and the rest of the world to accept permanent military inferiority by portraying this as an absolute guarantee against war.

Any normal person naturally hates the idea of war, and, of course, this antagonism interferes with proper public information about strategy, as though the information itself were dangerous. But let's face the fact that the Soviet "peace" we are accepting is synonymous with subjugation, for which we are already being psychologically conditioned, and that its continued pursuit will lead us by imperceptible stages to a state of undeclared but total satellization. Even economic weapons, not to mention military deterrence, have been forbidden to us, or rather we've forbidden ourselves to use them. Our refusal to apply stern economic sanctions against the Soviet Union must have vastly reassured the men in the Kremlin. And if the West can no longer resort to a credible strategic deterrent or to economic weapons, what is there to prevent the Soviet Union from continuing to trample the sovereignty of other countries, other continents, of the whole world?

What practical conclusion must we expect Communist leaders to draw from our military and economic passiveness? That they can go right on doing what they have been doing. In their place, isn't that what we would think? Former Giscard d'Estaing cabinet minister Jean-François Deniau quotes a high Soviet official as having told him, "We took Angola and you did not protest. We even saw that you could have beaten us in Angola— the government was on our side, but it was within an ace of giving up—and that you did nothing to win, on the contrary. And when, to save others, we sent in thirty thousand Cuban soldiers, Ambassador Young, a member of the American cabinet,* said it was a positive step and an element of stability. All right, we noted the fact and included it in our analyses. Then we took Mozambique. Forget it, you don't even know where it is. Then we took Ethiopia, a key move. There again we noted that you could have

---

*Andrew Young was then American ambassador to the UN.

replied via Somalia or Eritrea or both. No reply. We noted that and put it into our analyses. Then we took Aden and set up a powerful Soviet base there. Aden! On the Arabian Peninsula! In the heart of your supply center! No response. So we noted: we can take Aden."[10]

Still more favorable to Communist imperialism than our diplomatic inertia is a powerful ally of that very inertia: the West's assent to the Communists' condemnation of our civilization. Not even they believe what they say about us; they know full well what sort of human values they have cultivated in their civilization, but they go on condemning us because, after all, we love to be insulted. While claiming to have learned the truth once and for all about Stalinism, about totalitarian communism, many people in the democracies still cling to the old standards of classification, even in their jargon, as though they had never learned the truth at all, which casts doubt on how much they really have learned. Anticommunism is still thought of as reactionary. What a mockery is this so-called awakening to the vices of Stalinism when the "right wing" still rejects anti-Stalinists, even accusing them of behaving like Stalinists. Capitalism and free enterprise are flayed with one voice from the academic chair and from the pulpit; cult and culture unite to preach the wildest whims as axioms that discredit the industrialized democracies, blaming them for the Third World's poverty. On what bases, with what motivation, can freedom be defended when so many opinion molders, educators, thinkers have always, openly or secretly, maintained that our civilization is "fundamentally bad"?

Maybe they're right, but where will children who are taught that their society incarnates evil find the determination to defend it later on? Many schoolbooks throughout the West are indictments of capitalism, as violently caricatural as they are contemptible scientifically. But defenseless schoolchildren lack the information they would need to read these books critically.

The Lutheran Church in West Germany is fat with tax money if poor in churchgoers. To recruit an audience, it espouses pacifism, just as the Roman Catholic clergy in Latin America offers revolution to the masses it cannot hold with theology alone. The Archbishop of Paris, Cardinal Lustiger, has written, "A rich nation that loses its soul is a nation of the dead. A sumptuous culture that loses its soul is a culture of the dead. And a nation whose soul is dead, a culture that has lost its reasons for living, economic and social systems that, in practice, contradict the goals they profess, can only give birth to nothingness and destruction."[11]

We can say in all modesty that it's us he was writing about, and no one could be rash enough to doubt for a moment that the society that is giving "birth to nothingness and destruction" is the capitalist society. Without going so far as to suggest that the Communist society is giving birth to a surfeit of Being and Creation, the archbishop is nevertheless helping to drive home the notion that democratic capitalism unquestionably, necessarily, is reactionary, selfish, destructive. Which implies with compelling logic that its opposite is leftist, altruistic, progressive.

I am not going here into why industrial capitalism, the first and only system of production that has wrested people from penury and that could perform the same service for those still experiencing penury, is the most decried. Nor will I waste time arguing at length that since the eighteenth century the nations where industrial capitalism has developed also happen to be those where modern democracy took root. This does not mean that these countries have kept consistent faith with democracy or that democracy is found wherever capitalism goes. But it does mean that two centuries of history are witness to a general concomitance between capitalism and democracy. I will only note that this monumental file of evidence has been filched and that the democracies themselves have adopted the Communists' image of the world and their perspective on history.

The falsest and most pernicious characteristic of this image and this perspective lies probably in the antithesis between socialism and capitalism, between totalitarianism and democracy. This functions in most minds as an interpretative grid, even for those opposed to socialism. Its imposition is not the least of disinformation's victories, for this disinformation no longer bears on events, but on ideas; it is philosophical disinformation, a sort of ideological mole that has burrowed into the understanding most of us have of these forces.

Adopting this grid means accepting the principle that any regime that is less than perfectly democratic may be likened to totalitarianism and so loses its right to defend itself against communism. Since the world is full of governments that are neither totalitarian nor democratic, their futures are sealed. For one thing, because no democracy, even those recognized as such, is perfect, and since there are oppressive features to any society, which regime can claim a genuine right to defend itself against communism? None. And, following the same line of reasoning, if all that need be done to legitimize communism is to show that capitalism has its faults, its vices and crises, then let's turn world power over to the Communists at once on the principle that the best way to correct a limp is to cut off both legs.

The real antithesis is not that of totalitarianism to democracy or communism to capitalism, but of totalitarian communism to all the rest. Communism is a necrosis of economics, totalitarianism a necrosis of politics, of the body civic and of culture. As a dead society, totalitarianism can be contrasted with countless social forms now and in the past that cannot be called democratic as the term is now understood in a few societies today, but which were not and are not dead either. Medieval Europe, Ming China, African, Polynesian, and American societies before their contact with Europeans, the France of Louis XV and Napoleon III, Elizabethan England, the Spain of Philip IV, India under the Gupta dynasty, and the Germany of Kant's day were neither democratic nor totalitarian, but they were all living societies that, each in its own way, created valuable civilizations.

The existence of injustice, persecution, oppression in a group is one thing; for a group to be a negation of human nature in *every* aspect of its structure and ideology is something else again. This is the group to which totalitarianism belongs. True, today we believe that to fulfill themselves all societies should aspire to democracy, progress toward it and finally achieve it. I certainly do. Nevertheless, thousands of social organizations down through history, while not comparable to modern democracies, were not negations of humanity or freedom and did contribute elements of civilization to our present patchwork culture.

I am not talking about the political scientists' classic distinction between authoritarian and totalitarian regimes. Unlike the latter, authoritarian regimes are, so to speak, biodegradable; from time to time we see Latin American-type dictatorships grow more moderate, cross back over the frontier toward an approximation of democracy, take on a pluralist structure, and open out. But communism, like a ship, cannot open without sinking.

These are rudimentary notions. I have in mind a very different, more profound, more radical distinction. It separates a body of political systems advancing in stages from autocracy to democracy, deserving of severe criticism but compatible with more or less normal civic life, with a *custom* from the totalitarian system whose mission is to destroy all social, cultural and individual autonomy.

The contrast between capitalism and socialism is more apparent than real. To begin with, capitalism was never conceived as a unified ideological system to be clamped violently and arbitrarily over societies that did not want it. It is a fusion or juxtaposition of a myriad individual behavioral fragments that have come down to us from the dawn of time, that are unified only in our minds, and that we have finally assembled into a general, erratic, and imperfect concept. Capitalism is a bundle of modes of economic behavior. Communism, however, is not an economic system; it is a political system that must necessarily asphyxiate an economy. We should therefore refuse to lump communism in with other authoritarian systems or them with it. Totalitarianism endangers not democracy alone, but life itself. Communism is not simply one despotic political system among many or one inefficient and unjust economic system among others. In normal life, despotism and inefficiency are among the rare qualities that can be corrected, as is shown by all of history—except the history of communism. To survive, communism seeks to destroy not just existing democracy but every possibility of democracy.

Any society of any type in the world today can accede to democracy, with a single exception: communist society, which cannot go democratic without destroying itself. Understandably, then, totalitarian strategists try to reverse or block this tendency in the still malleable world around them. What is less easy to understand is that they can recruit some of their most assiduous disciples from among democracy's guides and thinkers.

NOTES

1. In his preface to *L'Affaire Nagy* (Paris: Plon, 1958), Camus wrote, "In October 1956 the world rose up in indignation. Now the world is sated . . . In October '56, the UN lost its temper . . . Now the Kádár government's representative sits [in the General Assembly] in New York, where he regularly defends peoples oppressed by the West." It must be conceded that the decay of Western energy described by Camus has repeatedly and identically recurred in connection with other issues. His protest can be reused indefinitely simply by changing the names of the places and people involved.
2. *Del Buen Salvaje al Buen Revolucionairio*, Caracas, 1976.
3. In the interests of clarity, note that the popular vote could in no way have authorized domination of the Guatemalan Government by a more than negligible Communist Party of which the vast majority of voters knew nothing. In addressing a Latin American audience, Bentancourt saw no need to specify that Arbenz had been elected on a social-democratic, reformist, and nationalistic platform.
4. To put the Guatemalan Parliament's gesture in perspective, we ought to note something Betancourt seems not to have known: that the entire French National Assembly, except for one Socialist Deputy, stood to hear a memorial eulogy for Stalin.
5. I have reconstituted Betancourt's statement from notes I took during the session and from another transcript shown by his widow.
6. I am deliberately using the term "resistance fighter" here because the Spanish government then was not democratic. With Spain now a democ-

racy, the expression is inappropriate, unless we are talking about resistance to democracy.

7. "Within a maximum of ten years we should cover the distance separating us from the most advanced capitalist countries." Joseph Stalin, *Pravda*, February 5, 1931, and Nikita S. Khrushchev, *Pravda*, 1961.
8. Louis Harris poll conducted in September 1982 for the Atlantic Institute of International Relations and the *International Herald Tribune.*
9. Survey by the French Research Corp. published in the magazine *Actuel* in January 1981.
10. Jean-François Deniau, "La Détente Froide," *L'Express*, September 3, 1982.
11. *Le Monde*, February 12, 1982.

SEVEN

Central American Policies—What the Marxists Are Really Up to in South America

HUMBERTO BELLI

My thoughts on revolutions inspired by Marxist-Leninist ideology are born out of my experiences as a Nicaraguan who participated in the making of the Sandanista revolution. I was a Marxist myself for some years, and a collaborator of the Sandinista movment. I later bccame the editorial page editor of the newspaper *La Prensa*, Nicaragua's only independent newspaper, which is now under strict censorship.

I remember the day when the Sandinista revolution defeated the forty-two-year-old Somoza dictatorship in July 1979, and all my neighbors ran jubilantly to welcome the guerrilla leaders marching triumphantly through the streets of Managua. The mood was one of optimism. An uninspiring, corrupt, and decadent dictatorship had been overthrown by a band of courageous young men and women who promised to construct a new Nicaragua. The poor would be first, democracy would shape the future, and human rights would be respected.

The fact that many of the guerrilla leaders were Marxists-Leninists was the cause of some concern, but it did not dampen

HUMBERTO BELLI, once active as a Marxist within the Sandinista movement in Nicaragua, changed his alliance and joined the loyal but doomed opposition. He formerly edited the editorial page of *La Prensa* in Managua, Nicaragua, and has lived in exile since 1982. From his home in Michigan he continues to write and speak out on issues in revolution-torn Central America. The following essay is reprinted from *Imprimis* (journal of Hillsdale College), June 1984.

the prevailing optimism. Many observers, not fully aware of the dynamics of Marxism, pointed to several factors that seemed to counterbalance the presence of ideological radicalism which appeared to offer sound hopes.

One was the fact that many democratic domestic forces had supported the Sandinistas and were actively present in the overall effort to reshape Nicaragua's future. The revolution had been fought with the intense participation of the Nicaraguan business community, which staged three crippling general strikes against the Somocista regime after January 1978.

A host of non-Marxist political parties, ranging from the Conservatives to the Christian and Social Democrats, and most influential democratic labor organizations, such as the Confederación de Trabajadores de Nicaragua and the Central de Unificación Sindical, had reformed a broad opposition alliance that challenged Somoza in the political realm, and they were now present in the newly formed revolutionary congress, or State Council.

Likewise, the influential Roman Catholic Church, led by Managua's charismatic Archbishop Miguel Obando, had issued pastoral letters denouncing the government's violations of human rights and, in a latter stage, had spoken about the people's right to rebel in the face of prolonged, unbearable tyranny. Furthermore, many Christians, including some priests, had participated in the struggle.

In the international field, likewise, the Sandinista revolution enjoyed the active support of democratic countries like Venezuela—one of the main sources of funds and guns for the rebels—Costa Rica, Panama, and Mexico. Many other Western nations, including West Germany and the United States, extended their hand to the Sandinistas in spite of some reservations. During the first two years of Sandinista rule they became the greatest providers of financial support for the new Nicaraguan government.

So, in its opening stage, the Nicaraguan revolution had the support of the overwhelming majority of the Nicaraguan middle class, of unionized labor, of the Catholic Church, of several other sectors, and of Western nations. Never before in Nicaraguan history had a regime launched out with such political capital. Never before, perhaps, in the history of Latin America revolutions had there been such near-ideal conditions for creating a new kind of society.

The Nicaraguan revolution, it was widely hoped, was to be neither Communist nor capitalist, but a true third way between the inequalities and miseries of the Third World capitalism and stagnation and repression of Communist regimes. The mingling of Marxist and non-Marxist tendencies in the government, the presence in the government of Christians, and its sponsorship by non-Marxist countries seemed to warrant a favorable outcome. At the very least, the experiment seemed to deserve a chance.

Personally, I was very skeptical. As a former Marxist myself, I knew who the Sandinistas were and what were their goals. Yet the fact that a Communist regime was not very suited to our region, where anti-Communist factors were strong, made me still hope that somehow the Sandinistas could be forced to take a different path, one perhaps halfway between the not-so-closed Yugoslavian socialism and the Mexican case, where one party prevails but allows a good measure of public dissent.

Almost from the beginning, however, actual developments challenged all early expectations. Cubans arrived by the thousands as teachers and good-will advisors. Freedom of the press began to be curtailed, on a variety of pretexts, while inflammatory Marxist rhetoric of class struggle and anti-U.S. propaganda began to be broadcast from the powerful state media. The army, unlike the National Guard, which had been focused on personal loyalty to Somoza, was supposed to become a national army; but it became the Sandinista army and, as such, a branch of the Sandinista party. The Sandinistas began talking about the establishment of one single labor union. They said that since all workers had a single enemy—"the bourgeoisie"—they had to unite themselves into a single confederation: the government-sponsored Sandinista labor union. When many workers balked at such a demand, they were harassed and vilified.

In March 1980, the Council of State, equivalent to a national congress, where the Sandinistas had in the beginning roughly one-third of the seats, was changed by government decree to give the Sandinistas two-thirds of the seats. The Sandinistas also forgot their promises of early elections and, when pressured, they declared that their elections would be to select the best among the "vanguard of the people"—a clear reference to themselves.

Now, some five years after the revolution's victory, these kinds of developments have produced a deeply divided society on the brink of civil war—a far cry from the broad alliance that cheerfully celebrated the ousting of Somoza in 1979. A system increasingly similar to Castro's Soviet type of regime has come into being, instead of the original, new model of society.

What went wrong? Why did the Nicaraguan revolution, against all political prudence, travel the worn-out path of Com-

munist revolutions instead of creating a new model for developing nations?

A common answer that I have found in many circles in the
United States is that the Sandinista regime was driven to extreme
policies in good measure by the hostile policies of the U.S. government. In support of this view, North Americans often argue
that the Sandinistas have suppressed dissent and enforced censorship out of the need to defend their revolution. A statement one
frequently finds is that "the U.S. is pushing Nicaragua into the
Soviet orbit." This implies that, given more friendly treatment by
the U.S., the Nicaraguan revolution would likely have evolved
toward a more democratic outcome.

But these propositions are hardly new. Similar views were
expressed regarding the Cuban revolution. The contention in the
early 1960s was that Castro was pushed to the left by retaliatory
U.S. policies.

Moreover, this view is based on ignorance of recent history.
The most decisive strides of the Sandinistas toward the Soviets
and toward the suppression of dissent took place when the Carter
administration was the main international provider of funds to
the Sandinistas and when most domestic Nicaraguan sectors and
most Western democratic nations were on good terms with them.
It was less than a year after the revolution, for instance, in May
1980, that the Sandinistas signed in Moscow an agreement of
mutual support with the Communist party of the Soviet Union,
an agreement in which Nicaragua gave complete backing to the
Soviets' foreign policy, including the invasion of Afghanistan. No
hostile policies were then being launched against the Sandinistas
from without, nor were significant "contra" forces operating anywhere in Nicaragua.

Fundamentally, theories of the "push" leftward betray a
lack of understanding of the dynamics of Marxist revolutions.
Such theories harbor hopes of the feasibility of taming these revolutions' tendency toward totalitarianism. I myself partook at one
point in the same delusion, but I have since come to understand
that Marxist revolutions have a psychology or spirit that impels
them to become what, in essence, they already are.

A crucial dimension of Marxist-Leninist movements is
their messianic and millennial view of the world. They are convinced that the most basic evils in the world—injustice, oppression, wars, social and individual unhappiness—can be ended and
that they shall, in effect, end. The point of departure for this
analysis is a conception of the world in which all evils are ultimately rooted in the socioeconomic structures of society; more

concretely, in the private ownership of the means of production. From this "objective reality," the Marxists claim, all social classes originate—and with them all oppression, struggles, selfishness, and the rest. As a consequence, if revolutionaries can defeat the world which is structured around private ownership of production, that is, if they can defeat the forces which sustain that world—the burgeoisie and U.S. imperialism—then they will be defeating oppression at its very root and opening the way for utopia.

In the anthem of the Sandinista party there is one line that says, "Let us fight against the Yankee, the enemy of humankind." This line, which existed prior to the triumph of the revolution, is not born so much out of resentment against past U.S. interventions in Nicaragua as from a philosophy according to which the United States is a source of all evil in the world. In the Marxists' view the U.S. defends the very system that keeps all people oppressed, the system that makes injustice continue in the world. For the Marxists, the United States plays a similar role to that which Christians believe Satan plays.

Marxism thus offers an optimistic view of the world. Evil can be defeated through socio-political means—and only through them. Marxist-Leninist revolutionary practice attempts to provide the recipe for achieving the millennium, in which exploitation will end and peace and harmony will replace the nastiness of the premillennial present. Needless to say, this messianic view of Marxism can be very appealing and powerful, especially in regions such as Latin America where there is a yearning for anything which may deliver people, once and for all, from the everyday realities of suffering, injustice, and frustration.

However, if we follow this way of thinking to its logical consequences, we see that it has very dangerous implications. Marxist thinking leads to a sacralization of revolution and, when victorious, to a sacralization of power. The revolution and its concrete expression, the revolutionary party or vanguard, are worshiped as gods—for as gods they are the ones, the only ones, that can bring salvation. The call to absolute commitment to the party follows as the unavoidable next step. If it is only by means of a social revolution embodied in the party, and in the state's power, that utopia can be achieved, then whoever opposes revolution, whoever refrains from fully supporting it, is not merely differing on some issues, but is opposing the full deliverance of humankind from bondage. The dissenter is not merely favoring a different set of policies, but is preventing the definitive solution of all the evils in the world. He must then be an evil person or insane—deserving either the concentration camp or the psychiatric clinic.

I remember one day in Nicaragua watching the revolutionary leader Tomas Borge giving a speech on television. He was talking about the bright future that the Sandinista revolution was going to deliver for the Nicaraguan people. Children would grow up in a society where people would no longer be afraid of each other, where true love and freedom would flourish, where a new man would be born. We were just now going through birth pains of a new world of unsuspected possibilities.

It was a beautiful, even poetic, speech. But then I realized its hidden horror. Anyone convinced that he has the power—and the duty—to achieve a socio-political utopia will do whatever is possible, whatever is in his hands, to prevent a different outcome. Since he has placed his plan as an absolute, he will not be bound by a higher order or restrained by ethical considerations in pursuit of it. He will smash all those who dare to be an obstacle on the way to utopia, and this he will even do with gusto, for in his view he will merely be destroying those who prevent the kingdom of justice, love, and happiness from coming into existence.

I can tell you that if someday you find yourself listening to a newly inaugurated President saying that for the first time the United States is going to break all the chains of alienation, frustration, and sorrow and that a world of happiness is ahead—you should be afraid! No one but God can deliver full salvation, and when men usurp God's role, we are on the threshold of a living hell.

Naturally enough, when you find yourself face to face with a god, you cannot remain neutral. You have to be for him or against him—for the revolution or against the revolution. No middle ground is allowed. A declaration that Fidel Castro once made, and which became one of the leading slogans of the Cuban revolution, summarizes this attitude: "Anything inside the revolution, nothing outside the revolution."

Neither the individual's private realm, nor religion, nor anything independent can escape such a law. In Nicaragua the Sandinistas have repeatedly said that they consider the religion worthy of respect to be that which pays homage to the revolution. A religious mass should be a revolutionary mass: it should honor the revolution, its martyrs, and its goals in its prayers and homilies. No wonder the Pope was so openly disrespected when he celebrated mass in Managua: he commited a sin of omission—he did not pray for the martyrs of the revolution.

In December 1979, when I was working at La Prensa, we

discovered a secret memo prepared by the head of political propaganda of the Sandinista Front to all its regional leaders. The memo instructed them in how to approach the upcoming Christmas celebration. It said that the Sandinista leadership wanted to turn this into a special day for children, one "with a different content, *fundamentally political.*"

Turning every religious feast, every religous concept, into something new, fundamentally political, is one of the Sandinistas' main ideological thrusts. Everything inside the revolution, nothing outside of it.

Jesus himself has been revolutionized. A Sandinista poster on the cover of a book entitled *Christian Faith and Sandinista Revolution*, published by a Christian organization that is aligned with the government, shows a picture of a guerrilla fighter, rifle in hand, emerging from a drawing on the crucified Christ. The guerrilla fighter becomes, for the Sandinista, the embodiment of Christ in twentieth-century Latin America. Thus Christ is not openly denied, but changed.

Sin, likewise, undergoes a metamorphosis at the hands of the revolutionary movement and its allies. Sin becomes identified with a particular social system—capitalism; the struggle against sin then becomes a struggle against capitalism. The basic work of Christ, to overcome sin and reconcile mankind with the all-good Father, is translated into a purely human struggle to be waged by socio-political means. This viewpoint, preached by the advocates of a Marxist liberation theology and sponsored by the Sandinistas, envisions the true messiah, the true liberator of humankind, to be the revolutionary party.

Individuals who share the political messianism inherent in Marxism tend to see a world divided between those who are entirely good and others who are entirely evil. The good ones are those who sponsor Marxist revolution; the evil ones are all the others. When, at times, the revolutionaries recognize a defect such as vice or selfishness in their own ranks—as they sometimes talk about Stalin's "excesses"—they attribute such misbehavior either to actions of their enemies which forced them to overreact or to the fact that the revolutionaries are still carrying some of the seed of corruption inherited from the bourgeois past. But Marxism and the revolution are, in themselves, clean. It is their adversaries who are on the dark, dark side.

I was impressed, when I was working on *La Prensa*, with how, for the Sandinistas, we were all the embodiment of evil, the artful defenders of the bourgeoisie bent on manufacturing all kind of stories in order to discredit the revolution.

With all honesty I can tell you that we tried, particularly at the beginning, to avoid criticizing the Sandinistas in ways which might lead to confrontation or which would sound harsh. We had meeting after meeting of the editorial staff of the newspaper, trying to moderate our criticism, devising ways not to provoke the government's anger, and figuring out how we could offer positive alternatives. Nothing worked whatsoever.

The Sandinistas would interpret our behavior as hypocrisy, and soon they were referring to us as "the counterrevolutionary plotters," "the hidden hand of the CIA," "those who were selling out the fatherland." We could not be a dissenting voice in a pluralistic society; we were the enemies. And if the Sandinistas refrained from destroying *La Prensa* completely, it is only due to their awareness of the international political cost that such a move would entail.

This typecasting as enemies befell all the other sectors of Nicaraguan society unwilling to grant their full support to the Sandinistas' policies. The Catholic archbishop of Managua and leader of the Nicaraguan Catholic Church was labeled by Interior Minister Tomas Borge the "leading counterrevolutionary" in Nicaragua. Political dissidents who had once been members of the government junta, such as Alfonso Robela, were called "lackeys of imperialism" and "traitors." One after the other, labor unions and political parties that had struggled against the Somoza dictatorship in search of a democratic Nicaragua came to be vilified, mobbed, and terrorized in one way or another.

As a conclusion, I want to offer for reflection the proposition that a revolution or regime inspired by a messianic and therefore totalitarian creed—be it communism, nazism, or any other ism—has a powerful, unavoidable tendency toward the forcible establishment of a system which leaves no place for those unwilling to worship the new idols.

What is taking place in Nicaragua is not the outcome of misguided U.S. policies, regardless of how wise or unwise these policies might actually be. It is the outcome of a philosophy, of a world-view, which divinizes power.

Strategic considerations might force this kind of regime to offer some concessions, in keeping with Lenin's famous "one step back before going two steps forward." They might even tolerate, for a time, some liberties, some remnants of pluralism—which they abhor.

But in the long run, there is no hope that the totalitarian spirit will relinquish its dearest aim—the total submission of all citizens to the new gods.

PART THREE: THE SOCIALIST "SOLUTION" IN AMERICA

EIGHT

From Equal Opportunity to "Affirmative Action"

THOMAS SOWELL

The very meaning of the phrase "civil rights" has changed greatly since the *Brown* decision in 1954, or since the Civil Rights Acts of 1964. Initially, civil rights meant, quite simply, that all individuals should be treated the same under the law, regardless of their race, religion, sex, or other such social categories. For blacks, especially, this would have represented a dramatic improvement in those states where law and public policy mandated racially separate institutions and highly discriminatory treatment.

Many Americans who supported the initial thrust of civil rights, as represented by the *Brown vs. Board of Education* decisions and the Civil Rights Act of 1964, later felt betrayed as the original concept of equal individual *opportunity* evolved toward the concept of equal group *results*. The idea that statistical differences in results were weighty presumptive evidence of discriminatory processes was not initially an explicit part of civil rights law. But neither was it merely an inexplicable perversion, as many critics seem to think, for it followed logically from the civil rights *vision*.

If the causes of intergroup differences can be dichotomized into discrimination and innate ability, then nonracists and nonsexists must expect equal results from nondiscrimination. Conversely,

THOMAS SOWELL, a Senior Fellow at the Hoover Institution, Stanford University, is the author of numerous books, including *Ethnic America, Markets and Minorities, Pink and Brown People, Race and Economics* and *Economics: Analysis and Issues.* An economist with degrees from Harvard, Columbia, and the University of Chicago, he has taught at several leading universities and has also been a member of The National Academy of Education, a consultant to three administrations of both parties, a scholar-in-residence at three research institutes, and has received many awards and honors. As a black he gives an especially provocative analysis of the economics and politics of minorities in America. The following essay is reprinted from his most recent book, *Civil Rights: Rhetoric or Reality* (Morrow, 1984).

the persistence of highly disparate results must indicate that discrimination continues to be pervasive among racalcitrant employers, culturally biased tests, hypocritical educational institutions, etc.
The early leaders and supporters of the civil rights movement did
not advocate such corollaries, and many explicitly repudiated them,
especially during the congressional debates that preceded passage of
the Civil Rights Act of 1964.[1] But the corollaries were implicit in
the vision—and in the long run that proved to be more decisive
than the positions taken by the original leaders in the cause of civil
rights. In the face of crying injustices, many Americans accepted a
vision that promised to further a noble cause, without quibbling over
its assumptions or verbal formulations. But visions have a momen-
tum of their own, and those who accept their assumptions have
entailed their corollaries, however surprised they may be when
these corollaries emerge historically.

FROM RIGHTS TO QUOTAS

"Equal opportunity" laws and policies require that individuals be
judged on their qualifications as individuals, *without regard* to
race, sex, age, etc. "Affirmative action" requires that they be judged
with regard to such group membership, receiving preferential or
compensatory treatment in some cases to achieve a more propor-
tional "representation" in various institutions and occupations.

The conflict between equal opportunity and affirmative action developed almost imperceptibly at first, though it later became
a heated issue, repeatedly debated by the time the Civil Rights Act
of 1964 was being considered by Congress. The term "affirmative
action" was first used in a racial discrimination context in President
John F. Kennedy's Executive Order No. 10,925 in 1961. But, as
initially presented, affirmative action referred to various activities,
such as monitoring subordinate decision-makers to ensure the fairness of their hiring and promoting decisions, and spreading information about employment or other opportunities so as to encourage
previously excluded groups to apply—after which the actual selection could be made *without regard* to group membership. Thus, it
was both meaningful and consistent for President Kennedy's Executive Order to say that federal contractors should "take affirmative
action to ensure that the applicants are employed, and that employees are treated during employment, without regard to their race,
creed, color, or national origin."

Tendencies toward shifting the emphasis from equality of
prospective opportunity toward statistical parity of retrospective

results were already observed, at both state and federal levels, by the time the Civil Rights Act of 1964 was under consideration in Congress. Senator Hubert Humphrey, while guiding this bill through the Senate, assured his colleagues that it "does not require an employer to achieve any kind of racial balance in his work force by giving preferential treatment to any individual or group."[2] He pointed out that subsection 703(j) under Title VII of the Civil Rights Act "is added to state this point expressly."[3] That subsection declared that nothing in Title VII required an employer "to grant preferential treatment to any individual or group on account of any imbalance which may exist" with respect to the numbers of employees in such groups "in comparison with the total number or percentage of persons of such race, color, religion, sex, or national origin in any community, State, section or other area."

Virtually all the issues involved in the later controversies over affirmative action, in the specifically numerical sense, were raised in the legislative debates preceding passage of the Civil Rights Act. Under subsection 706(g) of that Act, an employer was held liable only for his own "intentional" discrimination,[4] not for societal patterns reflected in his work force. According to Senator Humphrey, the "express requirement of intent is designed to make it wholly clear that inadvertent or accidental discriminations will not violate the Title or result in the entry of court orders."[5] Vague claims of differential institutional policy impact—"institutional racism"—were not to be countenanced. For example, tests with differential impact on different groups were considered by Humphrey to be "legal unless used for the purpose of discrimination."[6] There was no burden of proof placed upon employers to "validate" such tests.

In general there was to be no burden of proof on employers; rather the Equal Employment Opportunity Commission (EEOC) created by the Act "must prove by a preponderance" that an adverse decision was based on race (or, presumably, other forbidden categories), according to Senator Joseph Clark, another leading advocate of the Civil Rights Act.[7] Senator Clark also declared that the Civil Rights Act "will not require an employer to change existing seniority lists," even though such lists might have differential impact on blacks as the last hired and first fired.[8] Still another supporter, Senator Harrison Williams, declared that an employer with an all-white work force could continue to hire "only the best qualified persons even if they were all white."[9]

In short, Congress declared itself in favor of equal opportunity and opposed to affirmative action. So has the American public. Opinion polls show a majority of blacks opposed to preferential treatment, as is an even larger majority of women.[10] Federal administrative agencies and the courts led the change from the prospective concept of individual equal opportunity to the retrospective concept of parity of group "representation" (or "correction" of "imbalances").

The key development in this process was the creation of the Office of Federal Contract Compliance in the U.S. Department of Labor by President Lyndon Johnson's Executive Order No. 11,246 in 1965. In May 1968, this office issued guidelines containing the fateful expression "goals and timetables" and "representation." But as yet these were still not quotas, for 1968 guidelines spoke of "goals and timetables for the prompt achievement of full and equal employment opportunity." By 1970, however, new guidelines referred to "results-oriented procedures," which hinted more strongly at what was to come. In December 1971, the decisive guidelines were issued, which made it clear that "goals and timetables" were meant to "increase materially the utilization of minorities and women," with "under-utilization" being spelled out as "having fewer minorities or women in a particular job classification than would reasonably be expected by their availability . . ."[11] Employers were required to confess to "deficiencies in the utilization" of minorities and women whenever this statistical parity could not be found in all job classifications, as a first step toward correcting this situation. The burden of proof—and remedy—was on the employer. "Affirmative action" was not decisively transformed into a numerical concept, whether called "goals" or "quotas."[12]

Though lacking in either legislative authorization or public support for numerical group preferences, administrative agencies of government were able to enforce such policies with the support of the federal courts in general and the U.S. Supreme Court in particular. In the landmark *Weber* case the Supreme Court simply rejected "a literal interpretation" of the words of the Civil Rights Act. Instead, it sought the "spirit" of the Act, its "primary concern" with the economic problems of blacks. According to Justice William Brennan, writing the majority opinion, these words do not bar "temporary, voluntary, affirmative action measures undertaken to eliminate manifest racial imbalance in traditionally segregated job categories."[13] This performance received the sarcastic tribute of Justice Rehnquist that it was "*a tour de force* reminiscent not of jurists such as Hale, Holmes, and Hughes but of escape artists such as Houdini."[14] Rehnquist's dissent inundated the Supreme Court with the legislative history of the Act, and Congress' repeated and emphatic rejection of the whole approach of correcting imbalances or compensating for the past.[15] The spirit of the Act was as contrary to the decision as was the letter.

EQUALITY OF RIGHTS AND RESULTS

Those who carry the civil rights vision to its ultimate conclusion see no great difference between promoting equality of opportunity and equality of results. If there are not equal results among groups presumed to have equal genetic potential, then some inequality of opportunity must have intervened somewhere, and the question of precisely where is less important than the remedy of restoring the less fortunate to their just position. The fatal flaw in this kind of thinking is that there are many reasons, besides genes and discrimination, why groups differ in their economic performances and rewards. Groups differ by large amounts demographically, culturally, and geographically—and all of these differences have profound effects on incomes and occupations.

Age differences are quite large. Black are a decade younger than the Japanese. Jews are a quarter of a century older then Puerto Ricans. Polish Americans are twice as old as American Indians.[16] These represent major differences in the quantity of work experience, in an economy where income differences between age brackets are even greater than black-white income differences.[17] Even if the various racial ethnic groups were identical in every other respect, their age differences alone would prevent their being equally represented in occupations requiring experience or higher education. Their very different age distributions likewise prevent their being equally represented in colleges, jails, homes for the elderly, the armed forces, sports, and numerous other institutions and activities that tend to have more people from one age bracket than from another.

Cultural differences add to the age differences. Half of all Mexican American wives were married in their teens, while only 10 percent of Japanese American wives married that young.[18] Such very different patterns imply not only different values, but also very different future opportunities. Those who marry and begin having children earlier face more restricted options for future education and less geographic mobility for seeking their best career opportunities. Even among those young people who go on to colleges and universities, their opportunities to prepare themselves for the better paid professions are severely limited by their previous educational choices and performances, as well as by their selections of fields of study in the colleges and universities. All of these things vary enormously from one group to another.

For example, mathematics preparation and performance differ greatly from one ethnic group to another and between men and women. A study of high school students in northern California showed that four-fifths of Asian youngsters were enrolled in the sequence of mathematics courses that culminate in calculus, while only one-fifth of black youngsters were enrolled in such courses. Moreover, even among those who began this sequence in geometry, the percentage that persisted all the way through to calculus was several times higher among the Asian students.[19] Sex differences in mathematics preparation are comparably large. Among both black and white freshmen at the University of Maryland, the men had had four years of mathematics in high school more than twice as often as the women.[20]

Mathematics is of decisive importance for many more professions than that of mathematician. Whole ranges of fields of study and work are off-limits to those without the necessary mathematical foundation. Physicists, chemists, statisticians, and engineers are only some of the more obvious occupations. In some colleges, one cannot even be an undergraduate economics major without having had calculus, and to go on to graduate school and become a professional economist requires much more mathematics, as well as statistical analysis. Even in fields where mathematics is not an absolute prerequisite, its presence or absence makes a major difference in one's ability to rise in the profession. Mathematics is becoming an important factor in the social sciences and is even beginning to invade some of the humanities. To be mathematically illiterate is to carry an increasing burden into an increasing number of occupations. Even the ability to pass a civil service examination for modest clerical jobs is helped or hindered by one's facility in mathematics.

It is hardly surprising that test scores reflect these group differences in mathematics preparation. Nationwide results on the Scholastic Aptitude Test (SAT) for college applicants show Asians and whites consistently scoring higher on the quantitative test than Hispanics or blacks, and men scoring higher than women.[21] Nor are these differences merely the result of socioeconomic "disadvantage" caused by "society." Black, Mexican American, and American Indian youngsters from families with incomes of $50,000 and up score lower than Asians from families whose incomes are just $6,000 and under.[22] Moreover, Asians as a group score higher than whites as a group on the quantitative portion of the SAT, and the Japanese in Japan specialize in mathematics, science and engineering to a far greater extent than do American students in the United States.[23] Cultural differences are real, and cannot be talked away by using pejorative terms such as "stereotypes" or "racism."

The racial, ethnic, and sex differences in mathematics that begin in high school (or earlier) continue on through to the Ph.D. level, affecting career choices and economic rewards. Hispanic

Ph.D.'s outnumber Asian Ph.D.'s in the United States by three-to-one in history, but the Asians outnumber the Hispanics by ten-to-one in chemistry.[24] More than half of all Asian Ph.D.'s are in mathematics, science, or engineering, and more than half the Asians who teach college teach in those fields. By contrast, more than half of all black doctorates are in the field of education, a notoriously undemanding and less remunerative field. So are half the doctorates received by American Indians, not one of whom received a Ph.D. in either mathematics or physics in 1980.[25] Female Ph.D.'s are in quantitatively-based fields only half as frequently as male Ph.D.'s.[26]

Important as mathematics is in itself, it is also a symptom of broader and deeper disparities in educational choices and performances in general. Those groups with smaller quantities of education tend also to have lower qualities of education, and these disparities follow them all the way through their educational careers and into the job market. The children of lower income racial and ethnic groups typically score lower on tests all through school and attend lower quality colleges when they go to college at all, as well as majoring in the easier courses in fields with the least economic promise. How much of this is due to the home environment and how much to the deficiencies of the public schools in their neighborhoods is a large question that cannot be answered here. But what is clear is that what is called the "same" education, measured in years of schooling, is not even remotely the same in reality.

The civil rights vision relies heavily on statistical "disparities" in income and employment between members of different groups to support its sweeping claims of rampant discrimination. The U.S. Civil Rights Commission, for example, considers itself to be "controlling for those factors"[27] when it examines people of the same age with the same number of years of schooling—resolutely ignoring the substance of that schooling.

Age and education do not begin to exhaust the differences between groups. They are simply more readily quantifiable than some other differences. The geographic distributions of groups also vary greatly, with Mexican Americans being concentrated in the southwest, Puerto Ricans in the northeast, half of blacks in the South, and most Asians in California and Hawaii. Differences in income between the states are also larger than black-white income differences, so that these distributional differences affect national income differences. A number of past studies, for example, have shown black and Puerto Rican incomes to be very similar nationally, but blacks generally earn higher incomes than Puerto Ricans in New York and other places where Puerto Ricans are concentrated.[28] Their incomes nationally have shown up in these studies as similar, because there are very few Puerto Ricans living in low-income southern states.

One of the most important causes of differences in income and employment is the way people work—some diligently, carefully, persistently, cooperatively, and without requiring much supervision or warnings about absenteeism, tardiness, or drinking, and others requiring much concern over such matters. Not only are such things inherently difficult to quantify; any suggestion that such differences even exist is sure to bring forth a storm of condemnation. In short, the civil rights vision has been hermetically sealed off from any such evidence. Both historical and contemporary observations on intergroup differences in work habits, discipline, reliability, sobriety, cleanliness, or cooperative attitude—anywhere in the world—are automatically dismissed as evidence only of the bias or bigotry of the observers. "Stereotypes" is the magic word that makes thinking about such things unnecessary. Yet despite this closed circle of reasoning that surrounds the civil rights vision, there is some evidence that cannot be disposed of in that way.

Self-employed farmers, for example, do not depend for their rewards on the biases of employers or the stereotypes of observers. Yet self-employed farmers of different ethnicity have fared very differently on the same land, even in earlier premechanization times, when the principal input was the farmer's own labor. German farmers, for example, had more prosperous farms than other farmers in colonial America[29]—and were more prosperous than Irish farmers in eighteenth-century Ireland,[30] as well as more prosperous than Brazilian farmers in Brazil,[31] Mexican farmers in Mexico,[32] Russian farmers in Russia,[33] and Chilean farmers in Chile.[34] We may ignore the forbidden testimony from all these countries as to how hard the German farmers worked, how frugally they lived, or how sober they were. Still, the results speak for themselves.

That Jews earn far higher incomes than Hispanics in the United States might be taken as evidence that anti-Hispanic bias is stronger than anti-Semitism—if one followed the logic of the civil rights vision. But this explanation is considerably weakened by the greater prosperity of Jews than Hispanics *in Hispanic countries* throughout Latin America.[35] Again, even if one dismisses out of hand all the observers who see great differences in the way these two groups work, study, or save, major tangible differences in economic performance remain that cannot be explained in terms of the civil rights vision.

One of the commonly used indices of intergroup economic differences is family income. Yet families are of different sizes from group to group, reflecting differences in the incidence of broken homes. Female-headed households are several times more common among blacks than among whites, and in both groups these are the lowest income families. Moreover, the proportion of people working differs greatly from group to group. More than three-fifths of all Japanese American families have multiple income earners, while only about a third of Puerto Rican families do. Nor is this a purely socioeconomic phenomenon, as distinguished from a cultural phenomenon. Blacks have similar incomes to Puerto Ricans, but the proportion of black families with a woman working is nearly three times that among Puerto Ricans.[36]

None of this disproves the existence of discrimination, nor is that its purpose. What is at issue is whether statistical differences mean discrimination, or whether there are innumerable demographic, cultural, and geographic differences that make this crucial automatic inference highly questionable.

EFFECTS VERSUS HOPES

Thus far, we have not even considered the actual effects of the incentives and constraints created by affirmative action policies—as distinguished from the rationales, hopes, or claims made for these policies. Because these policies are invoked on behalf of the most disadvantaged groups, and the most disadvantaged classes within these groups, it is especially important to scrutinize the factual record of what has happened to the economic position of such people under both equal opportunity and affirmative policies.

Before crediting either political policy with economic gains, it is worth considering what trends were already under way before they were instituted. Much has been made of the number of blacks in high-level occupations before and after the Civil Rights Act of 1964. What has been almost totally ignored is the historical trend of black representation in such occupations before the Act was passed. In the period from 1954 to 1964, for example, the number of blacks in professional, technical, and similar high-level positions more than doubled.[37] In other kinds of occupations, the advance of blacks was even greater during the 1940s—when there was little or no civil rights policy—than during the 1950s when the civil rights revolution was in its heyday.[38]

The rise in the number of blacks in professional and technical occupations in the two years from 1964 to 1966 (after the Civil Rights Act) was in fact less than in the one year from 1961 to 1962 (before the Civil Rights Act).[39] If one takes into account the growing black population by looking at percentages instead of absolute numbers, it becomes even clearer that the Civil Rights Act of 1964 represented no acceleration in trends that had been going on for many years. The percentage of employed blacks who were professional and technical workers rose less in the five years following the Civil Rights Act of 1964 than in the five years preceding it. The percentage of employed blacks who were managers and administrators was the same in 1967 as in 1964—and in 1960. Nor did the institution of "goals and timetables" at the end of 1971 mark any acceleration in the long trend of rising black representation in these occupations. True, there was an appreciable increase in the percentage of blacks in professional and technical fields from 1971 to 1972, but almost entirely offset by a reduction in the percentage of blacks who were managers and administrators.[40]

The history of Asians and Hispanics likewise shows long-term upward trends that began years before the Civil Rights Act of 1964 and were not noticeably accelerated by the Act or by later "affirmative action" policies. The income of Mexican Americans rose relative to that of non-Hispanic whites between 1959 and 1969 (after the Civil Rights Act), but no more so than from 1949 to 1959 (before the Act).[41] Chinese and Japanese Americans overtook other Americans in income by 1959—five years before the Civil Rights Act.

Ignoring trends already in progress for years makes before-and-after comparisons completely misleading. Yet that is precisely the approach of supporters of the civil rights vision, who proceed as if "before" was a static situation. Yet the notion that the Civil Rights Act and "affirmative action" have had a dramatic impact on the economic progress of minorities has become part of the folklore of the land, established primarily through repetition and vehemence, rather than evidence.

The evidence of the *political* impact of civil rights changes in the 1960s is far more clear-cut. The number of black elected officials, especially in the South, increased many-fold in a relatively few years, including blacks elected to public office in some places for the first time since the Reconstruction era after the Civil War. Perhaps even more important, white elected officials in the South had to change both their policies and their rhetoric to accommodate the new political reality that blacks could vote.

What is truly surprising—and relatively ignored—is the economic impact of affirmative action on the disadvantaged, for whom it is more insistently invoked. The relative position of disadvantaged individuals within the groups singled out for preferential treatment has generally *declined* under affirmative action. This is particularly clear in data for individuals, as distinguished from families.

Family income data have too many pitfalls to be taken at face value. There are, for example, significant variations in what constitutes a family, both from time to time and from group to group. But since many people insist on using such data, these statistics cannot be passed over in silence. In 1969, *before* the federal imposition of numerical "goals and timetables," Puerto Rican family income was 63 percent of the national average. By 1977, it was down to 50 percent. In 1969, Mexican American family income was 76 percent of the national average. By 1977 it was down to 73 percent. Black family income fell from 62 percent of the national average to 60 percent over the same span.[42]

There are many complex factors behind these numbers. The point here is simply that they do not support the civil rights vision. A finer breakdown of the data for blacks shows the most disadvantaged families—the female-headed, with no husband present—to be not only the poorest and with the slowest increase in money income during the 1970s (a decline in *real* income), but also with money incomes increasing even more slowly than among white, female-headed families. By contrast, black husband-wife families had money incomes that were rising faster than that of their white counterparts.[43] It is part of a more general pattern of the most disadvantaged falling farther behind the affirmative action era, while the already advantaged forged ahead.

Individual data tell the same story, even more clearly. Those blacks with less education and less job experience—the truly disadvantaged—have been falling farther and farther behind their white counterparts under affirmative action, during the very same years when blacks with more education and more job experience have been advancing economically, both absolutely and relative to their white counterparts. First, the disadvantaged: Black male high school dropouts with less than six years of work experience earned 79 percent of the income of white male high school dropouts with less than six years of work experience in 1967 (before affirmative action quotas), and this *fell* to 69 percent by 1978 (after affirmative action quotas). Over these very same years, the income of black males who had completed college and had more than six years of work experience *rose* from 75 percent of the income of their white counterparts to 98 percent.[44] Some economic trends can be explained in terms of general conditions in the economy, but such diametrically opposite trends during the very same span of years obviously cannot.

There is additional evidence that the advantaged have benefited under affirmative action while the disadvantaged have fallen behind. Black faculty members with numerous publications and Ph.D.'s from top-rated institutions earned more than white faculty members with the same high qualifications, but black faculty members who lacked a doctorate or publications earned less than whites with the same low qualifications.[45] The pattern of diametrically opposite trends in economic well-being among advantaged and disadvantaged blacks is also shown by the general internal distribution of income among blacks. The top fifth of blacks have absorbed a growing proportion of all income received by blacks, while each of the bottom three fifths has received declining shares.[46] Black college-educated couples with husband and wife working had by 1980 achieved incomes higher than white couples of the same description.[47] Meanwhile, at the other end of the spectrum, the black female-headed household was receiving only 62 percent of the income of white, female-headed households—down from 70 percent in 1970.[48]

None of this is easily reconcilable with the civil rights vision's all-purpose explanation, racism and discrimination. To explain such diametrically opposite trends within the black community on the basis of whites' behavior would require us to believe that racism and discrimination were growing and declining at the same time. It is much more reconcilable with ordinary economic analysis.

Affirmative action hiring pressures make it costly to have no minority employees, but continuing affirmative action pressures at the promotion and discharge phases also make it costly to have minority employees who do not work out well. The net effect is to increase the demand for highly qualified minority employees while decreasing the demand for less qualified minority employees or for those without a sufficient track record to reassure employers.

Those who are most vocal about the need of affirmative action are of course the more articulate minority members—the advantaged who speak in the name of the disadvantaged. Their position on the issue may accord with their own personal experience, as well as their own self-interest. But that cannot dismiss the growing evidence that it is precisely the disadvantaged who suffer from affirmative action.

BY THE NUMBERS

Averages versus Variance.
One of the remarkable aspects of affirmative action is that, while numbers—and *assumptions* about numbers—abound, proponents of the program are almost never challenged to produce positive numerical evidence for its effectiveness or to support their statistical presuppositions. The mere fact that some group is x percent of the population but only y percent of the employees is taken as

weighty presumption of employer discrimination. There are serious statistical problems with this approach, quite aside from substantial group differences in age, education, and cultural values.

Even in a random world of identical things, to say that something happens a certain way *on the average* is not to say that it happens that way *every time*. But affirmative action deals with averages almost as if there were no variance. If Hispanics are 8 percent of the carpenters in a given town, it does not follow that *every* employer of carpenters in that town would have 8 percent Hispanics if there were no discrimination. Even if carpenters were assigned to employers by drawing lots (or by some other random process), there would be *variance* in the proportion of Hispanic carpenters from one employer to another. To convict those employers with fewer Hispanics of discrimination in hiring would be to make statistical variance a federal offense.

To illustrate the point, we can consider some process where racial, sexual, or ideological factors do not enter, such as the flipping of a coin. There is no reason to expect a persistent preponderance of heads over tails (or vice versa) on the *average*, but there is also no reason to expect exactly half heads and half tails every time we flip a coin a few times. That is, *variance* will exist.

To illustrate the effect of statistical variance, a coin was flipped ten times and then this experiment was repeated ten times. Here are the results:

HEADS	3	4	3	4	6	7	2	4	5	3
TAILS	7	6	7	6	4	3	8	6	5	7

At one extreme, there were seven heads and three tails, and at the other extreme eight tails and two heads. Statistics not only have averages, they have variance.

Translate this into employment decisions. Imagine that you are the employer who ends up with eight employees from one group and two from another, even though both groups are the same size and no different in qualifications, and even though you have been unbiased in selecting. Try explaining to EEOC and the courts that you ended up with four times as many employees from one group by random chance! You may be convicted of discrimination, even if you have only been guilty of statistical variance.

Of course some employers are biased, just as some coins are biased because of the way their weight is distributed on the design. This particular coin might have been biased; overall, it came up heads 41 percent of the time and tails 59 percent. But even if the coin was biased toward tails, it still came up heads seven times out of ten in one set of flips. If an employer were similarly biased in *favor* of a particular group, he could still be convicted of discrimination *against* that very group, if they ended up with less than half the "representation" of some other group.

No one needs to assume that this particular coin was unbiased or even that the results were accurately reported. Anyone can collect ten people and have them flip a coin ten times to see the statistical variance for himself. Frivolous as this might seem, the results have deadly serious implications for the way people are convicted of violating federal laws, regulations, and guidelines. It might be especially instructive if this little experiment were performed by editorial writers for publications that fervently support affirmation action, or by clerks of the Supreme Court.

Even when conclusions are based only on differences that statisticians call "statistically significant," this by no means eliminates the basic problem. What is statistically significant depends upon the probability that such a result would have happened by random chance. A common litmus test used by statisticians is whether the event would occur more than five times out of a hundred by random chance. Applying this common test of statistical significance to affirmative action means that even in the most extreme case imaginable—zero discrimination and zero difference among racial, ethnic, and other groups—the EEOC could still run ten thousand employers' records through a computer and come up with about five hundred "discriminators."

The illustration chosen is in fact too favorable to the proponents of affirmative action, because it shows the probability of incorrectly calling an employer a discriminator when there is only *one* group in question that might be discriminated against. Affirmative action has a number of groups whose statistical employment patterns can lead to charges of discrimination. To escape a false charge of discrimination, an employer must avoid being in the fatal 5 percent for *all* the groups in question simultaneously. That becomes progressively harder when there are more groups.

While there is a 95 percent chance for a nondiscriminatory employer to escape when there is only one group, this falls to 86 percent when there are three separate groups and to 73 percent when there are six.[49] That is, even in a world of zero discrimination and zero differences among groups, more than one-fourth of all employers would be called "discriminators" by this common test of statistical significance when there are six separate groups in question.

What this means is that the courts have sanctioned a procedure which insures that large-scale statistical "discrimination" will exist forever, regardless of what the actual facts may be. They have made statistical variance a federal offense.[50]

SHOPPING FOR DISCRIMINATION

Often the very same raw data point to different conclusions at different levels of aggregation. For example, statistics have shown that black faculty members earn less than white faculty members, but as these data are broken down by field of specialization, by number of publications, by possession (or nonpossession) of a Ph.D., and by the ranking of the institution that issued it, then the black-white income difference not only shrinks but disappears, and in some fields reverses—with black faculty earning more than white faculty with the same characteristics.[51] For those who accept statistics as proof of discrimination, how much discrimination there is and in what direction depends upon how finely these data are broken down.

There is no "objective" or "scientific" way to decide at what level of aggregation to stop breaking the data down into finer categories. Nor have the laws or the courts specified in advance what will and will not be the accepted way to break down the statistics. Any individual or organization contemplating a lawsuit against an employer can arrange that employer's statistics in any number of possible ways and then go shopping among the possibilities for the one that will present the employment pattern in the worst light. This is a very effective strategy in a society in which groups differ enormously in their characteristics and choices, while the prevailing vision makes deviations from a random distribution evidence against the employer.

A discrimination case can depend entirely on what level of statistical breakdown the judge accepts, for different groups will be represented—or "under-represented"—differently according to how precisely occupations and qualifications are defined. While there were more black than Asian American "social scientists" receiving a Ph.D. in 1980, when social scientists were broken down further, there were nearly three times as many Asian as black *economists*.[52] While male recipients of Ph.D.'s in the social sciences outnumbered female recipients of Ph.D.'s by slightly less than two-to-one in 1980, men outnumbered women by more than four-to-one among doctorates in economics and by ten-to-one among doctorates in econometrics.[53] What is the employer hiring: social scientists, economists, or econometricians? He may in fact be looking for an econometrician specializing in international trade—and there may be no statistics available on that. Nor can anyone infer the proportion of women or minority members available in that specialty for their distribution in broader categories, for the distribution changes at every level of aggregation.

The same principle applies in other fields as well. A computer manufacturer who is looking for an engineer is not looking for the same kind of engineer as a company that builds bridges. Nor is there the slightest reason to expect all groups to be distributed the same in these subspecialties as they are among engineers in general. Even within a narrow occupational range such as mathematical specialists, blacks outnumber Asian Americans in gross numbers, but Asian Americans outnumber blacks more than two-to-one among statisticians.[54]

When comparing any employer's work force with the available labor pool to determine "under-representation," everything depends on how that labor pool is defined—at what level of aggregation. Those who wish to argue for discrimination generally prefer broad, loose, heterogeneous categories. The concept of a "qualified" worker aids that approach. When the barely qualified is treated as being the same as the most highly skilled and experienced, it is the same as staying at a very general level of aggregation. Anything that creates or widens the disparity between what the job requires and how the categories are defined increases the potential for statistical "discrimination."

An employer may be guilty or innocent according to what level of statistical aggregation a judge accepts, after the plaintiffs have shopped around among the many possibilities. But that is only part of the problem. A more fundamental problem is that *the burden of proof is on the accused* to prove his innocence, once suspicious numbers have been found. Shopping around for suspicious numbers is by no means difficult, especially for a federal agency, given statistical variance, multiple groups, multiple occupations, and wide-ranging differences in the characteristics and choices of the groups themselves.

Statistical aggregation is a major factor not only in courts of law, but also in the court of public opinion. Many statistics from a very general level of aggregation are repeatedly presented in the media as demonstrating pervasive discrimination. The finer breakdowns are more likely to appear in specialized scholarly journals, read by a relative handful of people. Yet these finer breakdowns of statistics often tell a drastically different story, not only for black-white differences and male-female differences but for other groups as well.

For example, American Indian males earn significantly less than white males, and Asian males earn significantly more. Yet, as one holds a wide range of variables constant, these income differences shrink to the vanishing point. Asian Americans, for example, are distributed geographically in a very different pattern from whites. Asians are concentrated in higher income states, in more urban areas, and have more education. When all of this is held constant, their income advantage vanishes.[55] By the same token, when various demographic and cultural variables—notably proficiency in the English language—are held constant, the income disadvantages of Hispanic and American Indian males also disappear.[56]

It can hardly be expected that discrimination lawsuits and discrimination as a political issue will be correspondingly reduced any time soon. The methods by which it is measured in the courts and in politics insures that it will be a continuing source of controversy.

Poverty and huge intergroup differences in income are serious matters, whether or not discrimination is the cause—and whether or not affirmative action is the cure. Yet any attempt to deal with these very real disadvantages must first cut through the fog generated by a vision more powerful than its evidence—and, in fact, a vision shaping what courts will accept as evidence.

NOTES

1. U.S. Equal Employment Opportunity Commission, *Legislative History of Titles VII and XI of Civil Rights Act of 1964* (Washington, D.C.: U.S. Government Printing Office, no date) pp. 1007, 1008, 1014, 3005, 3006, 3013, 3160, and *passim*.
2. *Ibid.*, p. 3005.
3. *Ibid.*
4. *Ibid.*, p. 1014.
5. *Ibid.*, p. 3006.
6. *Ibid.*, p. 3160.
7. *Ibid.*, p. 3015.
8. *Ibid.*, p. 3013.
9. Quoted in Nathan Glazer, *Affirmative Discrimination* (New York: Basic Books, 1975), p. 45.
10. For example, *Gallup Opinion Index*, Report 143 (June 1977), p. 23.
11. Glazer, *op. cit.*, p. 49.
12. Much semantic effort has gone into claiming that quotas are rigid requirements while "goals" under "affirmative action" are flexible. Historically, however, quotas have existed in sales, immigration, production, and many other areas, sometimes referring to minima, sometimes to maxima, and with varying degrees of flexibility. The idea that "quota" implies rigidity is a recent redefinition. The objection to quotas is that they are quantitative

rather than qualitative criteria, not that they are rigidly rather than flexibly quantitative.

13. *United Steelworkers of America v. Weber,* 443 U.S. 193 (1979), p. 207, note 7.
14. *Ibid.,* p. 222.
15. *Ibid.,* pp. 226-252.
16. Thomas Sowell, *Markets and Minorities* (New York: Basic Books, 1981), p. 11.
17. U.S. Bureau of the Census, *Social Indicators, 1976* (Washington, D.C.: U.S. Government Printing Office, 1977), pp. 454-456.
18. Peter Uhlenberg, "Demographic Correlates of Group Achievement: Contrasting Patterns of Mexican-Americans and Japanese-Americans," *Race, Creed, Color, or National Origin,* ed. Robert K. Yin (Itasca, Ill.: F. E. Peacock Publishers, 1973), p. 91.
19. Lucy W. Sells, "Leverage for Equal Opportunity Through Mastery of Mathematics," *Women and Minorities in Science,* ed. Sheila M. Humphreys (Boulder, Col.: Westview Press, 1982), pp. 12, 16.
20. *Ibid.,* p. 11.
21. College Entrance Examination Board, *Profiles, College-Bound Seniors, 1981* (New York: College Entrance Examination Board, 1982), pp. 12, 22, 41, 51, 60, 65.
22. *Ibid.,* pp. 27, 36, 46, 55.
23. *Ibid.,* pp. 60, 79; Alexander Randall, "East Meets West," *Science,* November 1981, p. 72.
24. National Research Council, *Science, Engineering, and Humanities Doctorates in the United States* (Washington, D.C.: National Academy of Sciences, 1980), pp. 13, 39.
25. National Research Council, *Summary Report: 1980 Doctorate Recipients from United States Universities* (Washington, D.C.: National Academy Press, 1981), pp. 26, 29.
26. Sue E. Berryman, "Trends in and Causes of Minority and Female Representation Among Science and Mathematics Doctorates," mimeographed, The Rand Corporation, 1983, p. 13.
27. U.S. Commission on Civil Rights, *Unemployment and Underemployment Among Blacks, Hispanics, and Women* (Washington, D.C.: U.S. Commission on Civil Rights, 1982), p. 58.
28. Thomas Sowell, *Ethnic America* (New York: Basic Books, 1981), p. 222.
29. J. C. Furnas, *The Americans* (New York: G. P. Putnam's Sons, 1969), p. 86; Daniel Boorstin, *The Americans* (New York: Random House, 1958), Vol. I, p. 225.
30. Arthur Young, *A Tour in Ireland* (Shannon, Ireland: Irish University Press, 1970), Vol. I, pp. 377-379.
31. Thomas H. Holloway, *Immigrants on the Land* (Chapel Hill, N.C.: University of North Carolina Press, 1980), p. 151.
32. Harry Leonard Sawatzky, *They Sought a Country* (Berkeley: University of California Press, 1971), pp. 129, 244. Apparently Germans prospered in Honduras as well. *Ibid.,* pp. 361, 365.
33. Hattie Plum Wiliams, *The Czar's Germans* (Lincoln, Nebraska: American Historical Society of Germans from Russia, 1975), pp. 135, 159.
34. Carl Solberg, *Immigration and Nationalism* (Austin: University of Texas Press, 1970), pp. 27, 40.
35. Judith Laikin Elkin, *Jews of the Latin American Republics* (Chapel Hill, N.C.: University of North Carolina Press, 1980), pp. 241-237. See also

Robert Weisbrot, *The Jews of Argentina* (Philadelphia: The Jewish Publication Society of America, 1979), pp. 175-184.

36. Thomas Sowell, *Ethnic America*, p. 238.
37. Daniel P. Moynihan, "Employment, Income, and the Ordeal of the Negro Family," *Daedalus*, Fall 1965, p. 752.
38. Daniel O. Price, *Changing Characteristics of the Negro Population* (Washington, D.C.: U.S. Government Printing Office, 1969), pp. 117, 118.
39. *Employment and Training Report of the President, 1981* (Washington, D.C.: U.S. Government Printing Office, 1981), p. 150.
40. *Ibid.*, p. 151.
41. Thomas Sowell, *Ethnic America*, p. 260.
42. Thomas Sowell, *The Economics and Politics of Race* (New York: William Morrow, 1983), p. 187.
43. U.S. Bureau of the Census, *Social Indicators III* (Washington, D.C.: U.S. Government Printing Office, 1980), p. 485.
44. Finis Welch, "Affirmative Action and Its Enforcement," *American Economic Review*, May 1981, p. 132.
45. Thomas Sowell, *Affirmative Action Reconsidered* (Washington, D.C.: American Enterprise Institute, 1975), pp. 16-22.
46. Martin Kilson, "Black Social Classes and Integenerational Policy," *The Public Interest*, Summer 1981, p. 63.
47. U.S. Bureau of the Census, *Current Population Reports*, Series P-20, No. 366 (Washington, D.C.: U.S. Government Printing Office, 1981), pp. 182, 184.
48. U.S. Bureau of the Census, *Current Population Reports*, Series P-60, No. 80, p. 37; *Ibid.*, Series P-60, No. 132, pp. 41-42.
49. The probability that a nondiscriminatory employer will escape a false charge of discrimination is 95 percent, when the standard of "statistical significance" is that his employment pattern would not occur more than five times out of one hundred by random chance. But the probability of escaping the same false charge for three separate groups simultaneously is $(.95)^3$ or about 86 percent. When there are six separate groups, the probability is $(.95)^6$ or about 73 percent. Not all groups are separate; women and the aged, for example, overlap racial and ethnic groups. This complicates the calculation without changing the basic principle.
50. The greater ease of "proving" discrimination statistically, when there are multiple groups, multiple jobs, and substantial demographic, cultural, and other differences between groups, may either take the form of finding more "discriminators" at a given level of statistical significance (5 percent, for example) or using a more stringent standard of statistical significance (1 percent, for example) to produce a more impressive-looking case against a smaller number of "discriminators."
51. Thomas Sowell, *Affirmative Action Reconsidered* (Washington, D.C.: American Enterprise Institute, 1975), pp. 16-22.
52. Commission on Human Resources, National Research Council, *Summary Report: 1980 Doctorate Recipients from United States Universities* (National Academy Press, 1981), p. 27.
53. *Ibid.*, p. 25.
54. U.S. Bureau of the Census, *Current Population Reports*, Series P-23, No. 120 (Washington, D.C.: U.S. Government Printing Office, 1982), p. 5.
55. Barry R. Chiswick, "An Analysis of the Earnings and Employment of Asian-American Men," *Journal of Labor Economics*, April 1983, pp. 197-214.

56. Walter McManus, William Gould and Finis Welch, "Earnings of Hispanic Men: The Role of English Language Performance," *ibid.*, pp. 101-130; Gary D. Sandefur, "Minority Group Status and the Wages of White, Black, and Indian Males," *Social Science Research*, March 1983, pp. 44-68.

NINE

Comparable Worth: The Feminist Road to Socialism

MICHAEL LEVIN

In December 1983, Federal Judge Jack Tanner accorded the fullest legal recognition it has so far received to the novel economic doctrine of "comparable worth." This doctrine holds that women in the work force are paid less than they are really "worth" in terms of the "value" of what they do. The recognition came in Judge Tanner's decision, in *American Federation of State, County, and Municipal Employees [AFSCME] v. Washington State*, that Washington owes 15,500 female state employees over four years' back pay and raises. Estimates of the cost of this judgment vary from $500 million to $1 billion. Whatever the eventual tally, Washington taxpayers will have to come up with it soon, as Judge Tanner has denied various motions by the state for time to accommodate its new burden. The case is currently under appeal to the Supreme Court, with the Reagan administration reluctant to side with Washington "against women" in an election year.

The history of *AFSCME v. Washington* reflects the development of the comparable-worth doctrine over the last decade, and illustrates as well the tactics on which comparable-worth advocates have come increasingly to rely. The idea itself has lately become the main item on the feminist agenda and has, moreover, been enshrined in the 1984 platform of the Democratic Party. It is generally introduced with a statistic and a few examples intended

---

MICHAEL LEVIN is Professor of Philosophy at City College, New York, and the author of *Methaphysics and the Mind-Body Problem*. He has written numerous essays and articles and had just completed a new book, *Feminism and Freedom*. The following essay was originally printed in *Commentary* magazine, September 1984.

to shock. One learns, first, that the average full-time working woman makes about sixty cents for every dollar earned by her full-time working male counterpart. To vivify the point, one may then be told that tree surgeons outearn librarians by several thousand dollars a year. As a sort of climax of unfairness, the advocacy literature of the National Organization of Office Workers (NOOW) stresses the case of a firm offering $745-1,090 per month for general clerks, who must analyze invoices and have "good telephone etiquette" and who are usually female, while offering $1,030-1,100 per month for shipping clerks, who need only write legibly and be able to "lift equipment in excess of 100 lbs." but who are usually male. It is presumed to be self-evident that the ability to talk on the telephone entitles one to more money than a strong back.

The big question is why women earn so little if the "human capital" they embody is so valuable and the jobs they do so important. The answers given by comparable-worth advocates may be ranked by the degree of conscious malevolence they attribute to employers. At one extreme stands the accusation that (male) employers actually conspire against women in order to reduce labor costs ("to maximize profits" is the preferred formulation). Thus, in 1980, the program director of NOOW assured the Equal Employment Opportunity Commission that banks "colluded to hold down wages"; her evidence was that (a) bank presidents regularly met for lunch, and (b) men use "cultural stereotypes" when arguing with female union organizers. Such charges, however, are not taken very seriously even within comparable-worth circles, for wage-fixing cartels, quite apart from being illegal, would be vulnerable to raids by independent firms willing to pay more for talented females. Nor is it clear why employers willing and able to rig substandard wages for women would not also rig equally substandard wages for men.

The case for conspiracy being so flimsy, comparable-worth advocates prefer two other explanations of the wage gap. The first is the "herding" of women into a "pink-collar ghetto" of typically female jobs, which floods the market and depresses wages for these jobs. According to a study done for the Michigan Department of Labor:

> The reason for sex-related pay differentials [is] the traditional sex-segregation of most jobs. Under this hypothesis, the result of "crowding" of females into the clerical and service occupations is an oversupply of labor in these occupations, with resulting lower wages.

But this "hypothesis" rests most uneasily with charges of sexual discrimination, for it concedes that at bottom female wages are determined by the market forces of supply and demand. The more would-be secretaries there are, the less an employer must offer to get secretarial help—just as, conversely, the recent scarity of nurses has driven up nursing salaries. Secretarial wages may be considered "discriminatory" and the supply of secretaries an oversupply only if "crowding" is not a metaphor but a literal description of employers forcing women into some jobs and barring them from others. The supposition that such practices exist is entirely implausible in light of the Equal Employment Opportunity Act and Title VII of the Civil Rights Act, which explicitly forbid them; nor has any comparable-worth advocate produced a single instance of such activities occurring in the last decade. But as this citation from the Michigan Department of Labor suggests, one of the more ominous themes in the comparable-worth campaign is its implicit claim that the spontaneous social factors which affect women's vocational choices are themselves forms of discrimination calling for government correction.

Since the notion of "ghettoization" is so dangerously ambiguous, comparable-worth advocates add a final factor to explain the wage gap: the systematic undervaluing of women's work as part of society's overall disregard for women. Whereas classical economics says that in a free market the wages of all workers reflect their "marginal productivity," no matter what prejudices their employers may harbor, the comparable-worth case holds that market mechanisms "don't work" for women. In the words of *Women, Work, and Wages*, a report prepared in 1981 by the National Academy of Sciences (NAS):

> In many instances . . . jobs held mainly by women and minorities pay less at least in part *because* they are held mainly by women and minorities . . . the differentials in average pay for jobs held mainly by women and those held mainly by men persist when the characteristics of jobs thought to affect their value and the characteristics of workers thought to affect their productivity are held constant. [Emphasis added]

In a remarkable display of pseudo-rigor, the NAS even produced a mathematical "coefficient of discrimination" for calculating by how much the proportion of females in a job lowers its wages.

The tricky part, of course, is being sure one has identified *all* the "characteristics" that affect the wages for any particular job. In practice, this means hiring a team of "management experts," like Hays Associates or Norman Willis or the Arthur Young Co. (authors of the Michigan report), to make a determination. As one might expect, this also in practice inexorably links the question of what factors do determine wages to the quite separate question of what factors, in the opinion of management experts, *ought* to determine wages.

The experts typically resolve any given job into a few standard factors—skill, effort, responsibility, and working conditions, or some variants thereof—and then assign a score to each factor. Jobs with equal point totals, when all dimensions are combined, are regarded as equally "valuable." The heart of the procedure—the assignment of points—is entirely subjective and universally admitted to be so by the firms that specialize in the practice. Nevertheless, it was in terms of such evaluation surveys that the NAS found women to be victims of wage discrimination.

Thus we arrive at the position of the state of Washington in the early 1970s when, heeding feminist imperatives, its governor commissioned the Willis firm to run a "point-factor analysis" of wage rates. Like most public employers, Washington at the time was compensating at the rates prevailing for the nearest corresponding jobs in the private sector. But when the first Willis survey found that predominantly female jobs (those done 70 percent or more by women) paid on average 20 percent less than jobs of the same "worth" done predominantly by men, the Washington Personnel Board resolved in 1976 to use the Willis analysis in setting wages. No steps, however, were taken in this direction, in part probably because of a memorandum cautioning that doing so would cost the state almost $65 million—in retrospect, a twentyfold underestimate. Eventually, it was not the results of the Willis survey *per se*, but Washington's failure to abide by studies it had commissioned and resolved to respect, that Judge Tanner used to sustain his finding of discrimination. Washington was hoist on the petard of its own impeccably progressive intentions.

It is vital to emphasize that equal pay for the *same* work was not at issue in the *AFSCME* suit and has not been an issue since the passage of the 1963 Equal Pay Act. Moreover, there is not a single sentence in the U.S. Code or anywhere else to give comparable worth any statutory basis whatever. What enabled AFSCME to bring its suit in the first place was the Supreme Court's 1981 ruling in *Gunther v. Washington* that litigants have a right to test the comparable-worth concept in federal court under the rubric of Title VII of the 1964 Civil Rights Act. (*Gun-*

ther concerned female prison guards of female prisoners, who claimed that their work was as valuable as that done by better-paid male guards of male prisoners in higher security prisons.) *AFSCME* was simply the first droplet in the flood of litigation released by *Gunther*.

It is true that neither of these two key comparable-worth decisions directly endorses comparable worth, nor is either a bolt from the federal blue into the wage policies of localities or industry. At the same time, however, it would be naive not to expect *AFSCME* to be replayed in the near future. Over a dozen states have undertaken comparable-worth studies of their own work forces, and there is agitation for such studies in virtually every other state and in hundreds of municipalities. These studies are invariably accompanied by disclaimers of legislative intent— "Let's simply see if our state is perpetuating discrimination"— but *AFSCME* is an obvious basis for legal action once these studies uncover wage discrimination, as they always seem to do.

To this commotion may be added the 1982 endorsement by the leadership of the Democratic party of "equal pay for work of comparable social value,"[1] a doctrine even more radical than "equal pay for work of comparable economic value." Walter Mondale is on record as supporting "equal pay for comparable *effort*," more radical still. Congress has held hearings on the issue. Comparable-worth advocates are predictably eager to impose it on the private sector, such is the stated position of the *New York Times*. An advocate of comparable worth has argued that women who occupy "traditionally segregated jobs" have a prima-facie case for wage discrimination, with the burden of disproof falling on the employer[2]—an impossible burden to discharge since "wage discrimination" was unheard of until recently, and so no employer could have acted affirmatively to prevent it. Clearly, comparable worth has followed some other notable ideas from the feminist agenda onto the national agenda.

Is it true that discrimination explains why women earn less than men? The National Academy of Sciences concluded from its survey of the statistical literature that "differences in education, labor-force experience, labor-force commitment, or other human-capital factors believed to contribute to productivity" could explain, at most, half the wage gap. It would seem evident that the failure to explain the wage gap by a given set of variables is consistent with the operation of undiscovered variables having nothing to do with discrimination. Yet comparable-worth advocates have managed to obscure this point by expeditious word-play. In the jargon of the moment, they conceive discrimination as a "residual." This means that certain variables are selected *a priori* as relevant to wages, and discrimination is then defined as what these variables cannot explain.

In the last two decades the traditional test for discrimination—"intent"—has yielded to the much more dubious test of "effects," but the "residue" test goes beyond even "effects." Stigmatizing a practice as "discriminatory in effect" requires at least that one identify some specific human activity and show that it has some definite effect on the sexes. The "residue" test is uncontrolled, conflating as discriminatory all situations in which gender differences are observed, possibly including those caused by subtle innate biological sex differences.

The NAS states:

> The burden should rest on the designer of the job-evaluation system to identify and explicitly incorporate all factors regarded as legitimate components of pay differences between men and women, not merely to assert the possibility that including unspecified and unmeasured factors or improving the measurement of existing factors could reduce the "discrimination" coefficient.

In English, this means identifying discrimination with the wage gap itself, since in practice all "unmeasured factors" are assumed irrelevant. By fiat, then, the NAS is able to dismiss such factors as differences in drive and family sex roles as imaginary.

Thus, none of the studies surveyed by the NAS properly controlled for so obvious a variable as marital status: the wages of *never-married* women with full-time, continuous labor-force participation are virtually the same as those of the average married full-time working male. Women earn less than men, it seems, because they want jobs permitting easy exit from and reentry into the labor force, preferences which flow in turn from the average married woman's perception of her family as being her primary responsibility, especially when her children are young. Men, on the other hand, see themselves as breadwinners, whose obligation to make money increases as children come along. Perhaps a further factor will prove to be the male's amply-documented greater innate competitiveness, his tendency to do whatever is necessary to ascend hierarchies, including the hierarchies of modern business organizations.

Would it exonerate all concerned of the charge of wage discrimination if the wage gap turned out to be due to differences in family sex roles? Not at all; these basic differences between men and women simply become further injustices:

> Criticizing women for "lower labor force participation rates than men, moving in and out of the labor force more frequently than men, and being more likely than men to be seeking part-time work only" fails to take certain fundamental facts into account. For instance, among *Fortune 500* executives, who is taking care of the children? Whose responsibility is it to juggle career demands with child-bearing and child-caring? Did it ever occur to you that the reason women seem less committed to careers is that they don't have the luxury of a wife to take care of home and children while they blaze their career paths?[3]

This rage at all difference in the basic social role of the sexes underlies the campaign for comparable worth.

Critics of comparable worth understandably concentrate on the biases inherent in any list of factors "deserving" compensation. For instance, all job-evaluation systems I have seen assume that a college degree enhances a worker's "intrinsic value," a bit of snobbery which shows only that the people who design evaluation systems have all been to college. Yet this is not what is fundamentally wrong with comparable worth. For while the range of objective judgments about "training" or "responsibility" is far too narrow to support sweeping doctrines like comparable worth, such judgments can nonetheless be made. Planning shuttle missions in space plainly carries greater responsibility in terms of lives and hardware than does teaching philosphy. And planning space missions is plainly harder than adding up columns of figures, if only because the latter skill is just one part of the former.

For the sake of argument, then, let us assume a skill which is objectively difficult and reflects much objectively measurable training on the part of its practitioner; but let us also suppose it is a skill no one is interested in. Consider a person who is adept at throwing arrows into the air and catching them with his teeth. This is extremely difficult to do, and takes endless practice. Basketball players earning six-figure salaries do nothing so demanding. Unhappily, nobody wants to hire our man to catch arrows. He must eke out a living as a street entertainer. Is he somehow being denied his intrinsic worth by passersby who flip him quarters? Does a circus scout who offers him a pittance for his act understood what the knack entitles him to? The answers would seem to be no. Intrinsic moral and aesthetic merit aside, the skill is economically worthless—unable to command other goods and services—if no one will pay for it. Only someone willing to trade something for the service in question can confer economic worth on it.

Money itself is merely the conventional measure of the capacity of a thing to prompt people to exchange their own goods for it. A thing's price summarizes the ebb and flow of its performance in exchange, and has no independent meaning. And here is the intellectual black hole at the center of comparable worth: there is no such thing as intrinsic economic value. It is a chimera. Conversely, the willingness to supplant the market price of labor or anything else means the willingness to override the liberty of exchange, association, and contract expressed by market prices. In each particular comparable-worth proposal, the question is only one of determining where freedom is to be suppressed.

This crucial point is easy enough to see in connection with material objects. It would be absurd to maintain that copper deserves to cost more than gold because it conducts electricity better; gold and copper, absent people's actual desires for them, would just be stuff in the ground. The point is also reasonably clear where the "just price" of money—i.e., permissible interest rates—is concerned. But the market determination of wages meets much greater resistance, perhaps because it puts our value so squarely in the eyes of our beholders.

The example of the arrow-catcher may be dismissed as a contrivance. Contrived it is, which proves its point. The skill seems freakish, worthless, precisely because no one has ever valued it or is ever likely to do so. Our very perception of skillfulness, in other words, is determined by the market. The ability to draw, or set bones, or fix automobiles seems "naturally" compensable because we are used to there being a market for such skills. But the once "naturally" compensable ability to make buggy whips does not seem so today, when people no longer want buggy whips.

A long line of thinkers, extending back through Marx to Ricardo, has attempted, and failed, to devise nonmarket criteria of economic value for labor; almost every proposal in this tradition can be found in the comparable-worth literature. The straight Marxist appeal to the "social value" of work founders on the need to specify "social value." If something is "socially valuable" just because a great many people are willing to pay top dollar for it, we are back to the market; and there is no other way to tell that society wants something than its willingness to try hard to get it.

A more frequent proposal equates the value of a job with its contribution to the employer's profit. We may overlook the obvious difficulty: that this would make wages fluctuate wildly with exogenous factors—think of proofreaders becoming superfluous when a publisher's profits are due to a single best seller. Let us, instead, consider wage rates. Classical economics holds that each employee tends to get his marginal return on his product as he bargains omnisciently with his employers: If Jones's labor is worth $20 to Smith, Jones can return Smith's wage offer of $15 with a counterdemand for $16, which is still attractive to Smith. But then Jones can hold out for $17, $19, $19.50 . . . until Smith must agree to pay the full $20. But in this case the market itself already bestows a contribution to profit. In reality, of course, the employer must retain some portion of his employee's product if he is to have any reason for hiring him. But then, the contribution criterion means deciding what portion of a businessman's profit he "deserves" to keep, an entirely arbitrary decision.

Now, if one assumes that males get the "right" return on their product while females don't, it might seem fairer and simpler to give each worker in a firm the *same* return on his product, without having to decide on a proper rate of return. A secretary, say, would be entitled to 90 percent of her product if holders of benchmark jobs like engineers got 90 percent of theirs. But benchmark figures must be determined independently, which means by the market. A firm finds that to secure the labor of scarce engineers, it must pay what amounts to 90 percent of what they earn for the firm. But if so, what fairness requires is not that the return for secretaries be proportionate to that for engineers, but that it be determined *in the same way*—which is to say, by the market. Making the availability of engineers a factor in compensating secretaries is neither equitable nor rational.

What lends an air of unreality to every version of the "contribution to profit" theory is the fact that each of several jobs may be necessary for a firm's profitability. Since it is logically impossible to give all the profits to each of several job categories, what does and must happen in the real world, in which a firm would be paralyzed both without secretaries and without engineers, is recruitment of secretaries and engineers at market wages, the wages they all agree to accept. As the English economist Thomas Hodgskin wrote, there is no "principle or rule . . . for dividing the produce of joint labor among different individuals who concur in the producing, but the judgment of individuals themselves."

A cognate difficulty undermines the related test of basing a job's wages on its contribution to the "organization's objectives," to quote the Michigan comparable-worth study. This is a measure often suggested for nonmarket organizations like universities, governments, and foundations. Yet the achievement of nonmonetary goals also requires the cooperation of many people whose contributions cannot be isolated *a priori*. Furthermore, to compete with profit-seeking organizations in attracting a sufficiently talented work force, nonprofit organizations must in any case heed market decrees about wages. Moreover, determining some government post's contribution to the "overall objectives" of government presupposes clarity about what the "overall objectives" of government are, a goal that has eluded political philosophers for some centuries. If government has accommodated comparable worth more readily than private organizations, this is not because governments have found comparable worth easier to construe; governments can finance their follies by taxation, with no worries about buyer loyalty.

Finally, comparable-worth criteria that stress job characteristics like working conditions face all the problems that beset the use of traits like skill. Collecting refuse may be "unpleasant," but it is pleasant enough to attract applicants at the going rate. We do not need elaborate analysis to see that the market wage adequately compensates refuse collectors for the unpleasantness they endure. And, again, our very perception of this circumstance is a response to the market. Most American farm workers would find intolerable the backbreaking chores that constituted farming a millennium ago.

Skill, effort, and training do play a role in determining pay. Someone who has invested much time preparing for a hard job will drive a hard bargain. More importantly, the harder a job and the training for it, the fewer candidates there will be, driving up wages still further. This naturally high correlation among difficulty, training, and salary explains the feeling that demanding jobs "deserve" higher pay. In the end, however, these factors raise wages only by influencing the choices of bargainers.

Appeal to the free market may appear slightly musty in these days of the minimum wage, banking regulation, the National Labor Relations Act, and cancer warnings on cigarettes. Yet these familiar measures are modifications of laissez faire, while the rationale and scope of comparable worth make it a frontal assault on *any* form of economic liberty.

To begin with, none of the extant labor laws is based on a nonmarket notion of value. The minimum wage was intended to insure everyone a "decent" wage, without pretense that every worker's output is "really" worth $3.35 an hour. The National Labor Relations Act banned "anti-union animus" on the part of management not because collectively negotiated wages were thought to reflect value more accurately, but to secure "labor peace." And while the minimum wage truncates the range of possible bargains, and the National Labor Relations Act affects a wide range of negotiations, both measures still permit very extensive play to market forces. Unionized plumbers may not get strict market wages, but their wages approximate market value.

Overall, the many regulations that control banking, trucking, the airlines, mergers, work-place safety, and the like are (a) industry-specific or activity-specific, and (b) intended, rightly or wrongly, to preserve the free market against its own excesses. Wage and price controls, when imposed, are usually justified as "temporary measures" to curb inflation. Even socialism itself was originally conceived as a way of harnessing in a more efficient way the productive capacity generated by capitalism. Because "New Deal"-type regulations thus purport to secure specific results, they imply built-in tests to which they can be held. A ceiling on bank interest rates is supposed to help Savings and Loan Associations, so if S & L's keep failing at the same rate after the ceiling is in place, the ceiling has not worked.

Comparable worth, by contrast, contains none of these self-limitations. Its scope includes every job in the work force; and since most jobs are "sex-segregated," most pay scales would be open to challenge. Nor does comparable worth pretend to facilitate the best tendencies of the free market; rather, it is explicit about seeking to flout the market. It does this, moreover, without a clear specification of what positive goal is to be achieved beyond "justice"; under this mantle, the pursuit of comparable worth can discount any economic havoc it wreaks as irrelevant to its "success." (A similar criterion now governs assessment of affirmative action, deemed "successful" if it increases the number of women and minorities in well-paying positions, no matter the cost in fairness or efficiency of putting them there.) Penn Kemble has called comparable worth "a feminist road to socialism";[4] if so, it is socialism without a plan.

It is instructive to reflect that comparable worth can never come about through voluntary agreement. If a firm can get secretaries at a market-clearing wage, so can its competitors. Were it to raise its secretarial wages for ethical reasons, its labor costs would rise without any gain in productivity, its products would cost more than those of its competitors, and it would slide into failure. Comparable worth presents what economists call a "coordination problem": it must be introduced all at once, or not at all. Needless to say, the favored agency for solving coordination problems is the government.

The central point is this: whether or not the marketplace offers an appropriate ideal of justice, wages will in fact tend to be set at their market value so long as people retain anything like their accustomed economic liberty. The only alternative to the market is systematic state control. Comparable worth can be implemented only by endless government intervention, in the words of a pre-*Gunther* federal court, "pregnant with the possibility of disrupting the entire economic system of America."

For if "wage discrimination" is the wage gap itself, whatever its causes, nothing less than the elimination of the gap will be allowed to count as ending discrimination. To grasp what this would mean, consider that in 1983 there were forty-nine million full-time working men whose median income was $20,683, and thirty-one million full-time working women, median income $12,172. To close the wage gap, employers would have had to pay each woman $8,500 more, or about $250 billion, or—in still other terms—about 15 percent of total wages paid in 1983. These costs would no doubt have been passed on to consumers as higher prices, and as higher taxes to finance government services.

One might think the gap could be closed more slowly by freezing or slowing the growth of men's salaries until women's salaries grew to parity. This is now the policy in San Jose, California, where the city government worked out a comparable worth agreement with AFSCME. It seems unlikely, however, that men or their unions would tolerate this arrangement on a wide scale. A man who, thanks to comparable worth, gets a smaller raise than he would have otherwise gotten has, so far as he is concerned, suffered a pay cut. Comparable worth is advertised as a boon for working women struggling to help their families with a second income, but it does not help a family to hold down the husband's wages so the wife's can be artificially boosted. On balance, the likeliest short-term effect of comparable worth would be to boost everyone's wages, thereby flooding the market with new money in the absence of new goods—the standard recipe for inflation. And this might be the occasion for the government to begin coordinating wage policy to assure the proper closure of the wage gap.

The longer-run consequence of inflating female salaries and holding down male salaries in defiance of the market would be a massive disincentive to work. Women would already be getting more without having to work harder, and men would not be permitted to get more even if they did work harder. Why, then, should anyone work harder? Nor would the work force become more "integrated," since women would have no incentive to leave "women's work" once it paid as much as less pleasant "masculine" work. If anything, men would try to invade the newly well-paid female sphere. And at the same time men were queuing up for the typing pool, there would be no reason for a man to undertake an unpleasant job like collecting refuse if high wages for it were no longer available as an inducement—so we would almost certainly see critical job shortages. Add to this the undoubted persistence of a quota system which would prevent management from firing women to make room for (possibly more desirable) men, and a crisis of extreme proportions would be upon us. If recent history teaches us anything, it is that governments meet crises of their own making with more of the coercive rules that created the crisis in the first place.

It is not surprising that a society which has absorbed busing, quotas, *Miranda*, and publicly funded abortion should look on comparable worth with numb bemusement. One can almost sympathize with a businessman happy to reach the end of a profitable quarter without some new horror from the Federal Register landing on him. It is disheartening nonetheless that the American Compensation Association should summarize the attitude of the business community toward comparable worth in these words: "Planning for the inevitable appears to be the appropriate response."[5] Like such otherwise perceptive commentators as John Bunzel (who sees comparable worth as part of the "revolution of rising entitlements"), the ACA has missed the distinctive element in the comparable-worth campaign.

Feminists realize at some level that men and women view work differently—but they believe that this should not be, and, as do all those who wish people were other than they are, feminists want the government to correct the situation. Inverting cause and effect, they ask the government to curb one manifestation of sex differentiation. The real enemy feminism has targeted, however, is not some isolable inequity in the wage system, but the family and the rest of the malign "social conditioning" which make men and women act differently, in the economy and elsewhere.

That is why one must view with mixed feelings those critics of the comparable-worth idea who fall in with the "social-conditioning" theory. Lee Smith writes that "in large part, the [wage] disparity stems from traditions and prejudices that have channeled women into low-paying jobs." Bunzel conjectures that "greater interests and responsibilities in the home" may explain the number of women in low-paying jobs, but that this may "reflect socialization toward traditional roles that, for many women, begins in childhood." Cotton Mather Lindsay, the least compromising critic of comparable worth, cites as the most important factor limiting women's access to high-paying occupations "the subtle socialization process beginning in childhood, which orients women toward domestic careers." Even John Warehman, who bluntly asserts that "women lack the necessary emotional strength to achieve executive success," says "women's 'emotional deficiencies' spring from patterns of dependency established during their childhood." These writers treat the origin of this socialization itself as a mystery.

Economists may be forgiven for not knowing that research on sex differences shows these different social roles to be innate, or so close to innate as to be unelimitable features of every human society—but when they reject comparable worth only because it penalizes employers who "had nothing to do with producing . . . female inhibitions" (in the words of Carl Hoffman, who has conducted much research on male and female motivation in the business world), they abet the most irresponsible feminist tendencies. If an adolescent girl's "socialization" really forced her to choose low-paying nursing over high-paying surgery, she may not have been cheated by her employer, but she has certainly been deprived. Wouldn't it be well to change custom and tradition so that little girls were raised to be prepared emotionally for becoming surgeons? And isn't the state allowed to do a little of the altering for the general good? Thus is the state given a blank check for the sort of intrusion of which comparable worth is an extreme instance.

Prophesying the end of the free market is a sure way to be labeled a crank. On the other hand, I am not encouraged by confident assurances that the free market can survive anything. Howard Ruff, in one of his cheerfully apocalyptic guides to the future, compares the free market to Rasputin. Rasputin was poisoned, and he was shot, and still he survived. So, writes Ruff, the regulators have done everything to American capitalism, and still it survives. Unfortunately, Ruff overlooks a final detail. Eventually, Rasputin's tormentors threw him in the river. That killed him.

NOTES

1. *Rebuilding the Road to Opportunity,* Report of the Democratic Caucus, U.S. House of Representatives, September 1982.
2. Sheila Blumrosen, "Wage Discrimination, Job Segregation, and Title VII of the Civil Rights Acts of 1964," *University of Michigan Journal of Law Reform,* 1979.
3. Letter from Susan Sharp of Sharp and Co. to *Fortune,* September 6, 1982.
4. "A New Direction for the Democrats?," *Commentary,* October 1982.
5. "Comparable Worth . . . A Few Thoughts on the Issue," *ACA News,* February 1984.

TEN

The Media—Shield of the Utopians

RAEL AND ERICH ISAAC

The movements—if not the specific organizations—that have been described in this book for the most part are familiar to the reader, for they are the daily fare of press and television. Yet much of what we have written may be surprising, even shocking, to the general reader. The reason for this is that the media have acted as a filter, screening out most of the information that could damage the utopians in the public view.

There are a number of factors that explain why the media, instead of providing the public with some perspective on the utopians, have made themselves a sounding board for them, absorbing and transmitting their perspective on crucial issues as objective "truth." The most important is that journalists have a broadly similar perspective on the major issues the utopians address. Journalist Robert Novak (of the Evans and Novak column) has called the media the setting where journalists, regardless of background, are welded into one homogeneous ideological mold.[1] Thomas Shepard, the publisher of Look magazine until it folded in 1971, noted that with only a handful of exceptions the men

RAEL ISAAC is an established professional writer whose articles have appeared in Reader's Digest, The American Spectator, Atlantic, Midstream, New Republic, and Politique Internationale. Two previously published books are Israel Divided (Johns Hopkins University Press) and Parties and Politics of Israel (Longman). A graduate of Barnard, with advanced degrees from Johns Hopkins (M.A.) and City University of New York (Ph.D.), Rael is always busy with writing assignments, travel, and an active household.

ERICH ISAAC is Professor of Geography at City University of New York. He writes prolifically and has been published in Commentary, The American Spectator, and Politique Internationale. His book Geography of Domestication was published by Prentice-Hall. Rael and Erich Issac have recently coauthored The Coercive Utopians: Social Deception by America's Power Players (Regnery Gateway, 1983), from which this chapter is taken.

and women who produced *Look* "detested big business" and "worshipped the ecological and consumerism reformers."[2]

While these observations are impressionistic, they are confirmed by surveys of the media elite. Two political scientists, S. Robert Lichter and Stanley Rothman, in 1979 and 1980, interviewed two hundred and forty journalists and broadcasters of the most influential media outlets. The survey found the media elite were markedly to the left of the American electorate as a whole. Over a sixteen-year period, less than 20 percent of the media elite had supported any Republican Presidential candidate. Their views on issues were in striking agreement with utopian articles of faith. For example, 56 percent of the media elite agreed that the U.S. exploits the Third World and is the cause of its poverty.[3]

A particularly significant indication of the media elite's sympathy for the utopians came in response to questions Lichter and Rothman addressed to both the media elite and a comparative sample of the business elite. Both elites had a very similar perception of the power of different groups in society, seeing the media, business, and unions as those with the greatest influence. But asked how they would *prefer* to see power distributed, the media elite put themselves at the top, followed by consumer groups, intellectuals, and blacks.[4]

In part, the media elite sympathize with the utopians because they define their role in much the same way. Walter Cronkite is said to have declared that journalists identify with humanity rather than with authority.[5] Similarly Julius Duscha, a reporter who became director of the Washington Journalism Center, said, "Reporters are frustrated reformers . . . they look upon themselves almost with reverence, like they are protecting the world against the forces of evil."[6]

Moreover, for all their cynicism, the media elite readily succumb to hero worship. Ralph Nader was irresistible for the role. He began as a David who bested Goliath incarnated as the biggest company of them all, General Motors. The image lived on as Nader conducted his youthful, almost children's crusades, against the great regulatory bureaucracies and major companies and banks. Nader's few ill-hanging suits, his spare single room lodgings, his avoidance of material goods and pleasures, even women, all made him a figure larger than life, totally devoted to a cause, incorruptible. To journalists, Nader was a tribune of the people, the man who assumed the role they themselves would dearly love to have played. A Nader leaflet quoted a passage from *Time:* "If there is a man in Washington who provokes pure awe and respect here and beyond the Potomac, it is Ralph Nader . . . he lives his religion, devoid of greed, filled with candor, beyond influence." Morton Mintz, the *Washington Post's* Nader-stalker, was inspired by his beat to write books whose titles could as readily have adorned Nader's covers: *America Inc.* followed by *Power Inc.* While no other single figure has captured the imagination of journalists in the same way, the utopians as a whole benefit from being viewed by journalists as people like themselves, representatives of all the people.

In the case of some of the media elite more than sympathy is involved. Some *are* utopians, sharing fully their perspective on events. Larry Stern, in a key position as national news editor of the country's second most influential paper, the *Washington Post*, was one of them. This emerged, surprisingly, at his funeral, following his sudden death in 1980, at the age of fifty, of a heart attack. He was eulogized by left-wing journalist I. F. Stone, who praised Stern as a friend of Palestine and Nicaragua (i.e., the PLO and the Sandanistas) and for hating "those huge mindless institutions that devour our substance and corrupt our fundamental ideals, like the Pentagon and the CIA."[7] (More remarkably, Stern was also eulogized by Teofilo Acosta, head of the Cuban interests section in Washington, identified by intelligence expert Robert Moss as station chief of the DGI, the Cuban intelligence service. Stern was apparently a friend of Castro's Cuba as well.) Journalist Les Whitten, who worked with Jack Anderson on the popular column, seems to have derived his political philosophy directly from Ralph Nader. He warned a high school graduating class in Maryland of the "great pirate-like corporations that swallow up the blood of the people" and informed the class that if you lined up the presidents of thirty big banks and thirty bank robbers you would have fifty-eight criminals and the only difference was that one kind did it with a gun quickly while the bank presidents did it "at 18% a year without a gun."[8]

Many in the media—including some of the elite—actually learned their craft in utopian training-grounds. A huge "underground," later called "alternative" press, burgeoned in the late 1960s, its theme that America (often spelled with a "k" wrapped in a swastika) was a fascist country. A number of journalists from these papers subsequently moved into the straight press. The best-selling novel *The Spike* described the odyssey of a reporter for *Barricades* (an obvious takeoff on the "alternative" journal *Ramparts*) whose sensational scoop exposing the CIA earns him a place on the *New York World* (clearly the *New York Times*). *The Spike's* hero Robert Hockney was presumably modelled on *New York Times* star reporter Seymour Hersh, who wrote for *Ram-*

212 / IS CAPITALISM CHRISTIAN?

parts before coming to the *New York Times* and made his name exposing the CIA. To be sure, only the first part of Hersh's career paralleled that of the fictional Hockney, for while Hockney woke up to the role he was playing on behalf of Soviet disinformation efforts, there is no evidence that Hersh's utopian perspective has changed.

Even journalists who do not start out as utopians may be drawn to them because their concerns make good copy. Utopians are endless sources of the kind of stories that sell papers. Our tuna is poisoned; the nuclear plant near our city is in danger of meltdown; nuclear bombs will destroy all life from ground zero, which is in our backyard. In addition to the inherent drama of scare stories, they have, as the utopians present them, an appealing clarity. There are good guys and bad guys, victimizers and victims. This is much more dramatic stuff than cost-benefit analyses, probability studies and theories of deterrence that are the stuff of refutation. Moreover, the utopians have solutions: shut down nuclear power plants, eliminate all pesticides, rely on the sun, endorse a nuclear freeze.

If stories told according to utopian formula make good copy for the press, they are even better suited for documentaries, television's method of exploring issues in-depth. Why this is so can be seen from a candid look into the documentary producer's world offered in 1978 by Martin Carr, a veteran in producing documentaries for all three networks. Carr noted that the producer's first step was to "arrive at a point of view." His goal was then to make the viewer feel as he felt: "If you walk away feeling differently, I failed somehow." Carr noted the obligation to provide "balance," but explained that this had to be done carefully, so as not to disturb the documentary's emotional impact. He described a documentary he had made on migrant workers in which, for balance, he had interviewed the biggest grower in Florida. But he was a charming man who could have tipped the emotional balance of the documentary in favor of his position. So Carr found another grower whose point of view was the same, but whose personality would alienate the viewer and put him on instead. As a result, Carr reports: "One could only feel a particular way at the end of the film . . . the way I felt about it."[9] The utopian point of view on most stories shapes visually striking, emotionally compelling documentaries: the good farmworker against the bad grower; the victims of disease versus the large corporation; the peasant guerrilla against government-backed exploiters, etc.

On major topics such as the environment, defense, intelligence, and foreign policy, the media serve as a vast sounding board for the utopians, while at the same time suppressing sounds the utopians prefer not to hear. The latter is especially important, for while there is dispute on how effective the media is in making the public think the way journalists do (after all, the public does not vote like the media elite), there is little dispute that the media determine what it is that the public thinks *about*. As an article in *The Journalism Quarterly* points out: "If newsmen share a pattern of preference as to what is newsworthy, and that pattern does not represent reality, they will present a distorted image of the world which may contribute to inappropriate decisions and policies."[10]

Nowhere are distortions in coverage more evident than in coverage of environmental issues, particularly nuclear energy, the issue on which the utopians have expended their greatest efforts. The impact of the utopian campaign against nuclear energy on the media is apparent from two systematic studies, one by the Battelle Center and one by the Media Center. The Battelle Center study covered four national periodicals, including the *New York Times*, from 1972 to 1976, and found that while in 1972 there were more positive than negative statements on nuclear energy, by 1976 negative outnumbered positive statements by 2-1.[11] (This, it must be remembered, was three years prior to Three Mile Island.) The Media Institute study focused on ten years of television evening news coverage, from August 4, 1968 to March 27, 1979 (just prior to Three Mile Island). Its most telling finding concerned the "experts" used by the networks on nuclear energy. Of the top ten sources used over the years, seven were opposed to nuclear power. The source most frequently used was the antinuclear Union of Concerned Scientists, while the second most consulted source was Ralph Nader.[12] After Three Mile Island, earlier tendencies became even more marked. Psychiatrist Robert DuPont examined thirteen hours of videotapes of news coverage on nuclear energy and found that fear was the leitmotif of the stories. Reporters continually examined what DuPont called "what if, worst case" scenarios. He found almost no mention of the risks posed by other energy sources or the need to balance risks.[13]

By 1982, the pattern of media coverage had produced serious misconceptions in the American public concerning the balance of opinion among scientists on nuclear energy. A Roper poll found that almost one in four Americans believed that a majority of scientists, "who are energy experts," opposed the further development of nuclear energy, and one in three members of the public believed that solar energy could make a large contribution to meeting energy needs within the next twenty years.[14] Yet, an actual survey of energy experts showed that only 5 percent wanted to halt further development of nuclear energy (among those with specific expertise in the nuclear area 0 percent wanted to halt further development). No more than 2 percent of energy experts saw any form of solar energy making a substantial contribution to energy needs in the next twenty years.[15]

The distortions in perception can be explained by the views of science journalists, who are far more skeptical of nuclear energy than scientists. A survey of science journalists at major national media outlets undertaken by Lichter and Rothman found there was a fascinating, though scarcely surprising, connection between attitudes toward nuclear energy and political ideology. The more liberal the journalist, the more he was likely to oppose nuclear energy. Rothman and Lichter found they could define the issue more precisely. "We asked them a large number of social and political questions. The best predictor of opposition to nuclear energy is the belief that American society is unjust."[16] Moreover, Lichter and Rothman found that television reporters and producers were even more hostile to nuclear energy than print journalists.

The extensive use, especially by television, of the Union of Concerned Scientists was presumably a major factor in explaining the discrepancy between what scientists think and what the public thinks they think. The public, because of its name, perceived this as an organization of scientists. But as Samuel McCracken points out in The War Against the Atom, its membership is obtained through direct mail solicitation of the public, and the only qualification for belonging is a contribution of $15. Its executive directors in recent years have not been scientists.[17] Lichter and Rothman's random sample of 7,741 scientists turned up only one who was affiliated with the Union of Concerned Scientists. On that basis Lichter and Rothman estimate that fewer than two hundred scientists among the one hundred and thirty thousand listed in American Men and Women of Science are affiliated with the Union of Concerned Scientists.[18] Little wonder, under these circumstances, that the organization refused Lichter and Rothman information needed to poll its membership!

McCracken observes that anyone would see the fraud if a general membership organization composed almost entirely of laymen and concerned principally with supporting bans on prayer in the schools were to call itself the Union of Concerned Clergymen.[19] Yet the media persist in using this organization of utopians as its chief authority on nuclear energy. The media rarely call upon Scientists and Engineers for Secure Energy, although this is an organization whose members are genuine experts on nuclear energy and includes seven nobel laureates in physics. Presumably, this is because it does not spread the utopian's message, endorsed by so many in the media, that nuclear power is immensely dangerous and the authorities are deceiving the public.

Another interesting insight into the weight of sentiment against nuclear power in the media comes from a Public Broadcasting Corporation spokesman who was castigated for the uniform imbalance of the PBC's programs. He explained that it would be difficult even to find a producer prepared to do a pronuclear film.[20]

On questions of defense, the media elite have also been supportive of utopian assumptions. Walter Cronkite summed up the media perspective in the 1970s when he said in 1974: "There are always groups in Washington expressing views of alarm over the state of our defenses. We don't carry those stories. The story is that there are those who want to cut defense spending."[21] The American Security Council, which during the 1970s issued reports and ran a series of conferences and seminars featuring defense experts who warned of the disrepair of the American military and the massive Soviet military buildup then going on, became convinced that there was some unwritten rule in the media that their activities would not be covered. But for the media, as a group advocating increased defense expenditures, the American Security Council was simply not defined as "news."

Survey results indicate how pervasively media coverage reflected utopian attitudes. Ernest Lefever, before starting his own Ethics and Public Policy Center, led a study team for the Institute for American Strategy which examined CBS News coverage of national defense for 1972 and 1973. The study showed that during that two-year period the viewer saw only one minute on the "CBS Evening News" dealing with the comparative military strength of the U.S. and U.S.S.R.[22] The study found that fourteen hundred presentations on the subject of national defense tended to support the view that threats to our security were less serious than the government thought, while only seventy-nine contradicted that position.

With Reagan's victory, the views of those who argued more defense spending was needed could not be ignored any longer, for those views represented administration policy. CBS therefore entered the debate with a massive documentary designed to counter the administration position. Called by its anchorman Dan Rather "the most important documentary project of the decade," the five-hour series in June 1981, "The Defense of the United States," was hailed by the *Washington Post* as the "first documentary epic in TV history." Its theme, as Joshua Muravchik and John E. Haynes pointed out in their analysis of the series, "CBS vs. Defense," was that "the United States is not threatened by any external enemy, but rather by the tragic propensity of the two superpowers each to see in the other a mirror reflection of its own fears and hostilities." Muravchik and Haynes noted that in the five hours devoted to examining plans for a U.S. military buildup "there was no mention—*none*—of the Soviet buildup which precipitated it."[23]

Although the public had no way of knowing it, the program's arguments, experts, even its vocabulary were derived from the utopian organizations. To testify that current defense spending was already excessive, the program used "experts" Jack Geiger and Kosta Tsipis. Tsipis is a member of the board of directors of SANE, and Geiger is a leader of both Physicians for Social Responsibility and International Physicians for the Prevention of Nuclear War (in which Soviet physicians join with American physicians to emphasize the need for the U.S. to disarm). The viewer was not informed that they were peace movement activists, however. Geiger was identified only as professor of medicine at the City University of New York and Tsipis as professor of physics at MIT.[24]

To show that Soviet influence was already on the decline (presumably making increased defense expenditures superfluous), CBS drew on the Center for Defense Information, whose report purported to show that Soviet influence in the world had reached an all-time low. After Defense Secretary Weinberger spoke of the need for a strong defense, Walter Cronkite undercut his statement: "Since 1960, the Soviet influence around the world actually has declined. Their so-called gains like Afghanistan and Angola take on a different perspective, particularly when measured against losses, like Egypt and China." CBS then offered a closeup of two lists of twelve nations, one showing Soviet gains and the other Soviet losses since 1960. The lists were erroneous, but repeated the errors in the lists published by the Center for Defense Information.[25] The voice of the Center for Defense Information had been transformed into the voice of CBS. (In a fund-raising letter the Center boasted that all three networks had used it in a total of five major documentaries in 1981.)

The utopian campaign against the intelligence agencies depended heavily on the media for its success. The campaign began in the late 1960s, when a series of books and articles on them began to appear, many of them financed by the Fund for Investigative Journalism. The Fund was established by Philip M. Stern. The Stern Fund, on whose board he serves, is a major funder of utopian projects. But it scored its first major success when the *New York Times* ran a series of articles in December 1974 by Seymour Hersh exposing CIA involvement in illegal domestic surveillance of the antiwar movement. This precipitated a series of investigations by the specially appointed Rockefeller Commission and the Senate, which resulted in "reforms" that went far beyond correction of abuses. The CIA's ability to function in crucial areas was imperiled. At one point, eight committees of Congress, the armed services, foreign relations, appropriations and intelligence committees of both houses had to be informed of every major CIA operation, which, given the all-but-certainty of leaks by staff, meant there could be no such operations.

While U.S. intelligence agencies were a legitimate subject of media interest, the problem was that in true utopian fashion the media were interested *only* in stories that revealed intelligence activities as illegal or immoral. Reports that the intelligence services were failing to perform their task of protecting U.S. citizens were not news. When the Coalition for Peace through Strength held a conference in March 1979, entitled "Our Domestic Intelligence Crisis," it was ignored by the major media. Yet revelations that the public might have thought dramatic were made, including the fact that the Secret Service only received one fourth of the intelligence it did before the media-assisted "reforms" of intelligence agencies discouraged informants who feared their identities would be exposed in response to Freedom of Information requests. It, thus, had to recommend that the President not visit certain cities in the United States. The conference also disclosed that the Federal Employment Security program had been nullified, with members of the Communist Party or even of the Weather Underground no longer barred from federal employment, even in sensitive positions.[26] The media showed no interest in informing the public about the necessary services intelligence agencies provide to the public or about the consequences of dismantling security protections.

With all the popularity of documentaries about the malfeasances of the CIA and FBI, the networks produced nothing comparable on the KGB. This was not because the topic could not be handled. A Canadian team did an absorbing documentary called "The KGB Connections," based largely on the testimony of KGB defectors. A great critical success in Canada and Europe, it was turned down by all three networks, including ABC which had

218/ IS CAPITALISM CHRISTIAN?

invested in its production. Challenged for its failure to show the documentary, ABC countered that it would shortly be showing its own documentary on the KGB, but at this writing, over a year later, ABC had not done so. The failure to examine KGB activities by both TV and print media meant, as James Tyson points out in *Target America*, that the CIA seemed to shadowbox against a nonexistent enemy. The utopian contention that covert intelligence activities were the product of deviant psychological needs of those who manned corrupt American institutions was reinforced.

Foreign policy, particularly as it touches on human rights, is yet another area in which the media almost uniformly present the utopian perspective. The reason is not simply that journalists share that perspective, although doubtless many do. Covering human rights violations in totalitarian "socialist" countries is difficult, if not impossible, for journalists. Such countries, when they do not bar journalists altogether, control their movements. This means that a major information source has to be people outside the country. Information was available on the Cambodian genocide very early, but it came from people who had escaped over the border. By 1977, *Reader's Digest* editors John Barron and Anthony Paul had produced a book, *Murder of a Gentle Land*, which, based on the eyewitness accounts of hundreds of escapees, estimated that between April 17, 1975 and the end of 1976, at least 1.2 million people had died as a result of the policies of the Cambodian government.

Yet the press coverage of events, unprecedented in horror since the Nazi destruction of six million Jews, was minimal. In 1976, the year in which Barron and Paul conducted their interviews, what was happening in Cambodia was mentioned on television network evening news programs only three times, with NBC never mentioning it at all. The country's two most influential papers, the *Times* and the *Washington Post*, together mentioned the subject a total of thirteen times in the year.[27] In 1977, when what was happening was even clearer, the three networks had a combined total of two stories. That contrasted with one hundred and fifty-nine human rights related stories on the networks on South Africa.[28] While the *New York Times* did better in 1977, referring to the Cambodian genocide thirty-four times, this still contrasted sharply with two hundred and ninety-one stories on human rights violations in South Africa. The *Washington Post* ran ten items on Cambodia; it had thirty items just on the death of Steve Biko, the black leader who died under suspicious circumstances in a South African jail.[29] In 1978, the American Security

Council made things convenient for the press corps by arranging a press conference in Washington D.C., addressed by Pin Yathay, a civil engineer who had escaped after twenty-six months in Communist Cambodia. Yathay reported losing eighteen members of his family and provided an eyewitness account of desperation and cruelty.

> And there were many macabre incidents . . . the starving people who ate the flesh of dead bodies during this acute famine. I will now tell you a story that I lived myself . . . a teacher who ate the flesh of her own sister. She was later caught, she was beaten from morning to night until she died, under the rain, in front of the whole village as an example, and her child was crying beside her, and the mother died at the evening.[30]

A dramatic story. But not one of the networks sent a representative, and while the *Washington Post* sent a reporter, the paper never carried a story.

Hedrick Smith, one-time Moscow correspondent of the *New York Times*, and then chief correspondent of the Washington Bureau, has cast light on the reasons why the coverage was so poor. He noted that the *Times*—which, as one news executive asserted, is the "bible" of the other media—is not inclined to do stories on foreign countries written outside those countries.[31] This meant, for example, that while Soviet dissidents were the subject of many stories while they were in the Soviet Union, once the same people, having found refuge in the U.S., sought to draw attention to human rights violations in the Soviet Union, they found the press uninterested. When leading figures in the Soviet human rights movement like Vladimir Bukovsky and Alexander Ginzburg participated in two days of International Sakharov Hearings in 1979, that brought sixty witnesses to Washington to testify, their efforts were virtually ignored by the press. The *Washington Post* ran a story in the "Style" section called, "Remembering Russia." That was scarcely the point of the hearings. Similarly, when testimony on conditions in Vietnam was given before a House subcommittee in June 1977, including eyewitness reports of a Vietnamese imprisoned in a series of "reeducation camps," the major newspapers carried nothing.[32]

The end result is gross distortion in coverage of human rights problems; in 1977 the *New York Times* carried forty-eight items on human rights violations in South Korea and none on North Korea.[33] More than that, as Reed Irvine, head of the media watchdog group Accuracy in Media has pointed out, what emerges is a form of collaboration between the U.S. media and the countries that most systematically violate human rights.[34]

There may have been an additional reason for the reluctance of the media to report more fully on Cambodia and Southeast Asia. In the last years of the Vietnam War, the press was an adversary of the war, and the fact that the American departure did not lead to an improved life for the people of that area was something they were, at first, unwilling to believe, later to acknowledge. For example, *New York Times* columnist Anthony Lewis, urging a cutoff of American aid on March 17, 1975, wrote: "What future possibility could be more terrible than the reality of what is happening to Cambodia now?" The possibilities were beyond anything of which Anthony Lewis dreamed. While *New York Times* columnist Tom Wicker, in the immediate aftermath of the Vietnam War, was glad to give the press credit for forcing the U.S. out of the region, once there were boat people and millions of murdered victims in Cambodia, the press did not want to be reminded of its role. The violent reaction of CBS newsman Morley Safer to an article by Robert Elegant in the English journal *Encounter* in August 1981 is revealing. Elegant was himself a journalist in Vietnam, and in the article laid bare the shabbiness of the reporting, not exempting himself from the criticism. Safer devoted a radio segment to denouncing Elegant, whose article almost none of his listeners could have seen, as worthy of the mantle of Joseph Goebbels.[35] The entire subject obviously irritated media nerves.

Coverage of human rights adhered to the utopian perspective, according to which, the world's worst human rights violator was the Republic of South Africa, followed by Third World lands friendly to the United States, especially those in Latin America. As countries came under attack from internal subversion backed directly or indirectly by the Soviet Union, media focus, in true utopian fashion, was on the injustices that lead people to revolt rather than the predictable consequences of these "wars of liberation" in inaugurating much more repressive regimes. Karen de Young, now foreign editor of the *Washington Post*, who from Nicaragua provided warm coverage of the Sandanistas in Somoza's last period, admitted: "Most journalists now, most Western journalists at least, are very eager to seek out guerrilla groups, leftist groups, because you assume they must be the good guys."[36] Walter Cronkite, speaking in Portland, said the U.S. should help countries such as El Salvador "achieve their goals even if it means interim steps of socialism and communism."[37] (As Reed Irvine retorted in *AIM Report*, communism has yet to serve as an "interim step.")

With rare exceptions—NBC, in the fall of 1982, produced a film "What Ever Happened to El Salvador" that accompanied a Salvadoran army unit on patrol rather than the guerrillas—network documentaries have been hostile to the government of El Salvador. Guatemala was the subject of a September 1982 CBS documentary that focused on the theme that revolution is inevitable there as the response to tyranny backed by the United States on behalf of our exploitative business interests. On the other hand, television journalists bend over backwards in their efforts to understand the difficulties of the Nicaraguan government. A segment of ABC's "20/20," aired in June 1980, had David Marash make the patently false declaration: "Nicaragua's revolutionary justice system has been given near unanimous international praise."

The utopian influence on public television is even greater than on the networks: here they often write and produce the documentaries. For example, Philip Agee was co-producer of an anti-CIA three-hour documentary, "On Company Business" broadcast in May 1980. The fund-raising prospectus sent out by the producers prior to the actual filming promised that the documentary would "show the broken lives, hatred, cruelty, cynicism and despair which result from U.S.-CIA policy" and would record "the story of 30 years of CIA subversion, murder, bribery and torture as told by an insider and documented with newsreel film of actual events."[38]

The "insider" who served as the documentary's central figure and moral hero was Agee, identified for the viewer only as someone who had worked for the CIA between 1959 and 1969. There was no mention of Agee's role in exposing the identities of U.S. agents worldwide or of his expulsion from the Netherlands, France, and England. Intelligence expert Robert Moss has revealed Agee was found to have met with the Cuban intelligence station chief in London at least thirty times before he was expelled from England. If the viewer had known of Agee's record and avowed identification with communism, he might have discounted everything Agee said. The documentary's solution was to keep silent. Despite this, Public Broadcasting's director of current affairs programming, Barry Chase, described the program in a memo to all public broadcasting stations as "a highly responsible overview of the CIA's history."[39] (Chase clearly did not feel inhibited by the law establishing the Corporation for Public Broadcasting that stipulates programs funded by it must be objective and balanced if they deal with controversial issues.)

The Institute for Policy Studies' Saul Landau has written films for public television of a similar calibre. "Paul Jacobs and the Nuclear Gang" (with part of its seed money from the Samuel Rubin Foundation and Obie Benz, one of the wealthy young creators of the Robin Hood Was Right species of foundations[40]) was a polemic against nuclear energy and nuclear weapons, relying primarily on emotionally charged interviews with cancer victims who believed their disease had been caused by radiation and with the members of their families. Landau also wrote "From the Ashes . . . Nicaragua," directed by Helena Solberg Ladd, who had been a lecturer at IPS. William Bennett, head of the National Endowment for the Humanities which had channeled funds for the film's production under its previous head, on seeing the film, remarked that he was "shocked, appalled, disgusted" by what he called an example of "unbashed socialist-realism propaganda."[41] Author Midge Decter, executive director of the Committee for a Free World, found even this description too mild. She noted that "we almost no longer have a working vocabulary to cover phenomena like Ms. Ladd's film."[42]

Many of the documentaries that appear on public television endorse utopian themes far more overtly than would be possible on the networks. Public Broadcasting presented, for example, a film on North Korea that could have received the imprimatur of its dictator Kim Il Sung; a hymn to Cuba called "Cuba: Sports and Revolution;" two films on China, "The Children of China," which was such good propaganda that the Chinese Central Broadcasting Administration praised it for helping American people "understand the New China," and "China Memoir" produced by Shirley MacLaine, which even Ralph Rogers, then chairman of the Public Broadcasting Corporation, admitted was "pure propaganda."[43] Boston Public Television's WGBH funded a film called "Blacks Britannica" on British racism, which won the prize at the Leipzig Film Festival in East Germany. It was too much even for the producer at WGBH, and he complained of the film's "endorsement of a Marxist point of view."[44] When he sought to edit out some of the most blatant segments, the maker of the film brought suit and the U.S. Communist Party front, the National Alliance Against Racist and Political Repression, petitioned to join the suit.[45] In the end, four minutes of the film were removed, but its Marxist message remained unmistakable.

Another utopian theme—hostility against corporations—is

also reflected in the media. A Louis Harris poll in the fall of 1982 found that an "overwhelming 73%" of high level executives believed business and financial coverage on TV news was prejudiced against business.[46] The hostility is most pervasive in a surprising area—entertainment programming. A Media Institute study, "Crooks, Conmen and Clowns," found that the image of businessmen on TV series was overwhelmingly negative, with two out of three businessmen on two hundred prime-time episodes shown as foolish, greedy, or criminal. While on occasion a small businessman was shown in a favorable light, those running big businesses were for the most part depicted as actual criminals.[47]

While it might be argued that the businessman simply offers a convenient "heavy" in plot development, Ben Stein, in *The View from Sunset Boulevard*, shows that there is an excellent fit between the opinions of TV writers and producers and the shows they create. Stein interviewed forty writers and producers of the major adventure shows and stituation-comedies and found that even those worth millions of dollars considered themselves workers opposed to an "exploiting class." A typical flippant-serious comment was made by Bob Schiller, who wrote for Lucille Ball for thirteen years and produced "Maud." He said of businessmen: "I don't judge. I think there are good lepers and bad lepers."[48] Producer Stanley Kramer could have led off a Naderite conference. He told Stein: "Everything that has to do with our lives is contaminated. The air, the streams, the food—everything is ruined."[49] It was self-evident to most TV writers that big business was responsible.

To the media, the utopians are inherently more *believable* than those who oppose them. Cynical about human motives, journalists seem unable to conceive that "public interest" spokesmen act from anything but selfless devotion to the public good. Yet Abbie Hoffman could enlighten them. He noted: "There is absolutely no greater high than challenging the power structure as a nobody, giving it your all, and winning."[50] Peter Metzger has pointed out another motivation that also has to do with heightening the individual's sense of power and self-worth. He observes that with only a few exceptions the experts cited by the utopians never made genuine scientific contributions and thus were denied the reward of recognition by their peers.[51] They have achieved the fame and status their scientific work could not gain for them through serving the needs of the utopians for men with credentials.

Journalists are ready to believe the most improbable

charges against the institutions they distrust. In January 1982, the *New York Times* featured a lengthy story by Raymond Bonner concerning events alleged to have taken place a year earlier: American military advisers in El Salvador had observed a torture training session for the El Salvadoran military in which a seventeen-year-old boy and a thirteen-year-old girl had their bones broken prior to being killed. Bonner's sole source for the story was a deserter from the Salvadoran army. The narrative, which in its original form claimed that the American advisers were *teaching* the torture session, had appeared in a leftist Mexican paper, but was such obvious Communist atrocity propaganda that it took eight months after the original publication before a taker was found among American journalists, in the form of Mr. Bonner, who offered a "sanitized" version in the *Times*.[52]

Such credulity leaves the media open to being taken in by the grossest "disinformation" forgeries. Floral Lewis, at the top of her profession as a columnist for the *New York Times*, accepted uncritically a supposed State Department "dissent document" which was distributed to newsmen. While the State Department does indeed have a "dissent channel" permitting members in disagreement with policy to have their objections heard at the highest level of the department, the document Flora Lewis accepted as authentic was marked as the product of a nonexistent State Department task force. Lewis devoted her column of March 6, 1981 to the document, which attacked U.S. government policy in El Salvador. Asserting it had been "drawn up by people from the National Security Council, the State and Defense Departments and the CIA," she went on to praise the report's "solid facts and cool analysis" and closed by telling the Reagan administration that it would "do well to listen to the paper's authors before the chance for talks is lost." At this point the State Department came out with a detailed report on the forgery which the *Times* carried as a news story, and Flora Lewis, her face plentifully covered with egg, wrote an apology in her March 9 column.

The attitude of the media elite to government assertions that contradict utopian views with which they identify is instant distrust. A storm broke over the *Washington Post* and the *Wall Street Journal* when it became known that the journalists of both had relied upon Philip Agee as a source for articles they wrote attacking a February 1981 U.S. White Paper, "Communist Interference in El Salvador." The White Paper summarized findings from captured documents of the El Salvador guerrillas, showing the extent of clandestine military support given by the Soviet Union and Cuba to the guerrillas beginning in 1979. As a result of the furor, even how the articles came to be written became public knowledge. The *Wall Street Journal's* Jonathan Kwitny told his editor of his immediate "skepticism over news accounts of the white paper."[53] The *Washington Post's* Robert Kaiser said that he had immediately been eager to explore possible deficiencies in the White Paper, and so was pleased when the *Post's* national editor, Peter Osnos, asked him to look into the matter. And Peter Osnos revealed that he had assigned Kaiser after a call from free-lance writer Jeffrey Stein who said: "Look, I can't understand how you all have let that White Paper hang out there without a look."[54] (Stein was a former fellow of the Institute for Policy Studies, suggesting that the utopian grapevine operates quickly to encourage attacks on anything the utopians consider damaging to them.) For the utopians, it was crucial to discredit the White Paper, since if the American public recognized the Soviet-Cuban role in El Salvador, the carefully fostered image of the guerrillas as indigenous liberal reformers might be undermined.

Philip Agee, according to Arnaud de Borchgrave, helped by his "Cuban friends," provided a forty-six page attack on the White Paper which was distributed in April by the *Covert Action Information Bulletin.* This publication, it will be remembered, was started after an internal factional split at *CounterSpy,* with Agee becoming associated with the new magazine. Both the *Post's* Kaiser and the *Journal's* Kwitny obtained copies. Kaiser subsequently claimed that in an early draft of his article he had mentioned Agee as a source, but that his editor at the *Post* suggested dropping the reference as "unnecessary."[55] Kwitny was taken aback when confronted with his failure to credit Agee's paper as a source in his *Wall Street Journal* story: "I was totally unaware that it had any distribution, except to a few of his friends here."[56] He insisted that while he had read Agee's paper: "There was nothing I was drawing from him or anyone else . . . I can't really remember what was in the Agee piece." Yet in a line by line comparison, *Human Events* reporter Cliff Kincaid showed that not only did Kwitny's criticisms closely parallel those of Agee, but Kwitny even repeated a specific Agee error, referring to "labor unions" (Agree said "trade unions") when the document being analyzed was talking about the Communist Party.[57]

Perhaps the most interesting revelations concerned the wide use by journalists of the Agee apparatus and the ignorance of those in executive positions on major papers of the web of utopian organizations. Frederick Taylor, Executive Editor of the *Wall Street Journal*, came to the defense of his reporter in a long article on the editorial page entitled, "The El Salvador 'White

Paper.' " Taylor declared that the *Wall Street Journal* had been accused "at the least of being the dupe of Soviet disinformation, and at the worst of taking the work of a discredited left-winger and passing it off as its own." Taylor said: "It isn't so." As proof he cited what Kwitny had told him:

> The article originated in my own skepticism over news accounts of the white paper in February. It sprouted because of two events in April. First, having been asked to sort the files of my recently deceased Journal colleague, Jerry Landauer, I called someone who had been a longstanding source of Jerry's on intelligence matters . . . This source, John Kelly, edits a magazine, *Counterspy*, which also printed a critique of the white paper. Kelly supplied me with some leads and documents.[58]

To defend the *Journal* from charges of being a dupe of disinformation and of passing off the charges of a discredited left-winger as its own by transferring responsibility from Agee to *CounterSpy* and to inform the *Wall Street Journal's* readers that they had all along been kept informed on intelligence matters by *CounterSpy* was, to say the least, a remarkable editorial defense. (A member of *CounterSpy's* board boasted it had been behind at least fifteen stories in the *Journal* on the CIA, Indonesia, South Korea, and the Phillipines.)[59]

Apparently there was a similar gap between editors and reporters at the *Washington Post.* When a *Washington Post* editorial condemned *CounterSpy's* clone, the *Covert Action Information Bulletin*, as "contemptible" and suggested its editors were less than honorable journalists, they lashed back:

> Your diatribe only highlights the gap between the editorial offices and the reporters, for your people are among the large number of working journalists from virtually all the major printed and electronic media in the country who call upon us daily for help, research, and of all things, names of intelligence operatives in connection with articles they are writing.[60]

Occasionally it is possible to trace a "disinformation" story through an elaborate international circuit. For example, a story alleging a CIA conspiracy behind a financial scandal involving the Nugan Hand bank in Australia was originally aired in *The Tribune*, the paper of the Communist Party of Australia. It was subsequently picked up by *CounterSpy* and then by the *Wall*

Street Journal's Jonathan Kwitny, who ran a front-page, three-part series in August 1982 on what was by this time a two-year-old story. Dismissed in Australia when it originally appeared because of its source and the paucity of evidence, the story was now— despite the fact that Kwitny offered no new evidence—given major coverage by the Australian Broadcasting Commission as well as by mainstream Australian newspapers. Thus a story, tainted by its source when originally aired, gathers credibility as it is picked up by mainstream media and in the end serves effectively its original purpose—to sow distrust of the United States in Australia.[61]

The difficulty journalists have in believing anything the government says, that interferes with their prejudices, has become obvious to government officials. Admiral Bobby Inman, on retiring as deputy director of the CIA, spoke of his frustration at trying to convince the public of the peril of the Soviet military buildup when the press would not even believe U.S. intelligence reports that included spy satellite pictures. Inman described an intelligence briefing for the press on the Soviet and Cuban-backed military buildup in Nicaragua in which reporters were shown photos of Soviet-type military garrison arrangements, deployed Soviet T-55 tanks, etc. Newspaper accounts the following day used the word "alleged" to describe the intelligence findings, suggesting that the reporters did not believe them.[62]

The media does more than *believe* the utopians: it protects them. News that could prove embarrassing to the utopians is often simply not reported. Reed Irvine has christened this "the Pinsky Principle," after North Carolina journalist Walter Pinsky, who described his approach in the *Columbia Journalism Review* in 1976. "If my research and journalistic instincts tell me one thing, my political instincts another . . . I won't fudge it, I won't bend it, but I won't write it."[63] Pinsky gave as an example what he called the great untold story of the trial of Joan Little in his home state. Joan Little was an imprisoned black woman who killed her guard and defended herself on the grounds that he had tried to assault her sexually. Her story was widely reported nationally. Pinsky explained that what he meant when he said it was unreported was that reporters never described the role of the Communist Party, working through its front, the National Alliance Against Racist and Political Repression, in controlling the entire political movement surrounding the case. Pinsky says that journalists kept silent "out of concern that the information might be used in red-baiting any associated with the case who did not belong to the [Communist] party."[64]

ABC newsman Geraldo Rivera, in an interview with *Playboy*, confessed to practicing the Pinsky Principle in his reporting from Panama. When the Panamanian National Guard was guilty of violence at the time of the Senate vote on the Canal treaties, "We downplayed the whole incident. That was the day I decided that I had to be very careful about what was said, because I could defeat the very thing [passage of the Treaty] that I wanted to achieve."[65]

An interesting example of the Pinsky Principle was the failure of CBS in its two-part drama "Guyana Tragedy: The Story of Jim Jones," to say a word concerning Jones as a Communist. Jones had broken with the U.S. Communist Party, according to his own account, because it had turned against Stalin and "I loved Stalin." Nonetheless his feelings toward the party had clearly mellowed, for his will provided that in the absence of immediate surviving family, his estate should go to the U.S. Communist Party. Jones had also ordered that $7 million belonging to the People's Temple be transferred to the Soviet Union. When the script's author, Ernest Tidyman, was asked about the omission, he said he did not believe Jones was a Communist. Asked what Jones' political views were, Tidyman replied: "None, particularly. He was very liberal, very progressive, very community conscious."[66] Presumably, for Tidyman, giving the facts about Jones' Communism would interfere with the image he wanted to convey of Jones as an idealistic community-builder gone awry.

More recently the Pinsky Principle has been at work in the refusal of the media to examine the utopian roots of the peace movement and its links to the international Soviet front, the World Peace Council. With rare exceptions, notably the *Wall Street Journal* and the *Reader's Digest*, the mass media have portrayed the freeze as a spontaneous outgrowth of grass-roots Middle America. Even when the organizations that created and promoted the freeze are credited, as in a *Newsweek* article of April 26, 1982, the identifications are superficial, giving no hint of the agenda of these organizations. For example, although Clergy and Laity Concerned is described as "a powerful force in the disarmament movement," it is identified only as a group "begun in 1965 to mobilize the religious community against the Vietnam War." There is an element of laziness in this: it is easier to ask a group about itself over the phone than to acquire its literature which would explain that CALC sees its task to be joining together those who "hate the corporate power which the United States presently represents . . ."

But more important, there is unwillingness to transmit

facts that might put the utopians in an unfavorable light. Eileen Shanahan, assistant managing editor of the *Pittsburgh Post-Gazette*, observed: "I saw it at the *Washington Star* and I'm seeing it here. The present 28-35 newsroom set is antiwar to a significant degree and also antinuke."[67] When President Reagan or members of Congress made any reference to the credentials of the groups behind the freeze, the prestige media lashed out. A *New York Times* editorial, on October 6, 1982, labeled all reference to such matters an "indecent debate" and a *Washington Post* editorial, on the same date, said that to bring up such topics was a "smear."

Probably the most widespread application of the Pinsky Principle is the failure to identify utopian sources. Identification is a crucial service the media offer the viewer or reader, for without it he has no way of evaluating the information offered to him. For example, the *New York Times* reported that a National Lawyers Guild delegation to the Middle East "came away convinced that the Israeli government implements a policy of torture for the annexation of the occupied areas." Since the National Lawyers Guild was identified only as "a group of American lawyers," the reader was not helped to be properly skeptical of this information.[68] Similarly the *New York Times*, which between 1979 and 1981 carried essays by Fellows of the Institute for Policy Studies on its Op-Ed page with more than twice the frequency of any other think tank, including much bigger and better known ones, identified the Institute in each case only as "an independent research organization in Washington D.C." The suggestion was that the reader was being exposed to "independent" thought, not the radical left perspective invariably provided by Institute Fellows.

A particularly dramatic example of misrepresentation through failure of identification is the media's treatment of Wilfred Burchett. Burchett was an Australian journalist. As far back as 1967, *The Reporter*, a liberal magazine of the period, published an article by fellow Australian Denis Warner which summed up Burchett's history up to that point:

> Stripped of his Australian passport by Canberra in 1955 and denied Australian citizenship for his three children by a second marriage—one born in Hanoi, one in Peking, and one in Moscow—Burchett is regarded by those reponsible for Australian security as a communist and a traitor who ought to stand trial for his role in the Korean war . . .[69]

American POWs returning from Korea had described Burchett's involvement in obtaining phony confessions from them about America's alleged use of germ warfare, some of which he had himself written and rewritten. Burchett showed up again during the Vietnam war. Senator Jeremiah Denton described being interviewed by Burchett while he was a prisoner in North Vietnam and in his book *When Hell Was in Session* says that Burchett lost his cool "when I implied that he was a cheap traitor who knew in his heart that he was prostituting his talents for money in a cause that he knew was false."[70]

In these years, Burchett's articles occasionally appeared in U.S. papers, but he was properly identified. The *Chicago Tribune* carried an essay on June 5, 1966, with the following description of Burchett: "An Australian Communist writer, Wilfred Burchett has travelled frequently to North Vietnam. He wrote this article after returning to his Cambodian home from his latest trip. It gives a communist view of the war and its effects and it should be read as such."

But starting in the late 1970s, Burchett's essays began to be printed without any identification that could alert the reader. The *New York Times* published his essays on the Op-Ed page, identifying him only as "a left-wing journalist living in Paris." After Reed Irvine complained to *Times* publisher Arthur Sulzberger that this was an inadequate identification—and Sulzberger agreed—the *Times* Op-Ed page, in the following year, identified him as "a journalist living in Paris." *Harper's* published a review by Burchett of a book attacking the CIA, identifying him only as "a left-wing journalist" and "a personal friend of Ho Chi Minh." The same *Chicago Tribune* that had fully identified Burchett in 1966 introduced him to its readers quite differently on August 6, 1982: "A man whose business is informing the world is an Australian expatriate journalist, Wilfred Burchett, now living in Paris."

What is involved here is more than "failure to identify." Implicit is a rewriting of political history. This is a major utopian target which the media abet. Communists are transformed into "liberals." Joseph Barnes, foreign editor of the former *New York Herald Tribune*, who was exposed as a Communist by a series of his former colleagues who broke with the party, started to be referred to in the press as a "liberal" in the late 1970s. The Rosenberg case has been transmogrified. In 1978, on the twenty-fifth anniversary of the execution of the Rosenbergs for treason, Public Television served up a four-year-old documentary with a new introduction and epilogue, "The Rosenberg-Sobell Case Revisited." Atom spies Julius and Ethel Rosenberg were portrayed as individuals singled out for their political beliefs by a malignant government. When Accuracy in Media wrote to the President of the Public Broadcasting Sytem to complain about the film's gross distortion of history, the reply came from the program's producer. Ignoring the long list of factual criticisms AIM had submitted, he announced loftily that the suggestion the program embodied Communist propaganda reflected discredit on AIM.[71]

In 1982, Telefrance USA, which says that its programs reach ten million U.S. homes, broadcast a four-part French-made documentary on the Rosenberg case with the emotional title, "The Rosenbergs Must Not Die." They were portrayed as innocents railroaded by a corrupt government. Dorothy Rabinowitz, in a *Wall Street Journal* essay, noted that "no more malevolent band of fascists, scoundrels, cynics and thugs" had ever appeared on a screen than the "assortment of characters supposedly representing an American Supreme Court, an American judge and prosecutor and members of the FBI."[72] While the *New York Times* reviewer at least dismissed the program, *Cablevision Magazine* allowed that there was the "recurring paradox of how a foreigner—an outsider—may have a fuller perspective on a situation, political or otherwise, than someone more directly involved."[73]

Misidentification and the rewriting of political history produce reporting that inhibits, rather than helps, public understanding of political developments. Press coverage of Kathy Boudin, the Weather Underground leader captured during the Brink's robbery in Nyack, depicted her—to quote from a typical account in the *Boston Globe*—as a "child of privilege," "a brainy, popular tomboy who graduated with honors from the 'right' schools, the type of girl that people once described as all-American." But Kathy Boudin was a red diaper baby, the child of radical lawyer Leonard Boudin. The circle of her father's friends included many Communists and individuals sympathetic to Communism. Kathy Boudin's political development would have become considerably less mysterious if the media had not concealed relevant information.

Journalistic practices like the Pinsky Principle have grown common as journalists have changed their view of their proper role. "Advocacy," "participatory," and "activist" journalism have created new models. To some extent the "new journalism," as it is sometimes called, has developed because its literary techniques produce more dramatic copy at a time of intense competition from television, with its strong visual imagery. A "composite" prostitute (and why confuse the reader by identifying her as such) can offer a more interesting biography than any single individual. Similarly a report that suggests the writer is directly privy to the thoughts and beliefs of his subject has more impact than an article with tiresome inserts like "A neighbor said that" or "The defendant's lawyer claims that . . ."

The new journalism is also a reflection of the changing aspirations of journalists. Journalists are now in a position to set the policies of papers which they could not in an earlier era, when conservative owners set their stamp upon their property. With many more years of education than they used to have, with higher status in society, journalists are dissatisfied with a role that limits them simply to chronicling what happens. As lawyer Max Kampelman noted in a 1978 essay in *Policy Review:*

> It is understandable that a significant segment of the media has become impatient with its limited information dissemination role. It is not easy and frequently not exciting for an intelligent person simply to report events. The tendency, therefore, has been for imaginative and socially dedicated journalists to go beyond normal reporting in order to seek fuller expression of their talents or social values.[74]

Veteran journalist Joseph Kraft notes: "Not only have we traded objectivity for bias, but we have also abandoned a place on the sidelines for a piece of the action."[75] Jim Bormann, a pioneer in broadcast news, offered a vivid illustration: he described listening to journalist Alex Kendrick telling a CBS news affiliate session that a good reporter should not be afraid, while covering a riot, to throw a few bricks himself. Kendrick urged the contemporary newsman to get involved and then report what he "felt inside."[76]

"Facts" are seen in a fresh light by the new journalism. As writer Naomi Munson pointed out in *Commentary*, while reporters had seen their job as sniffing out facts "more and more these days they have come to regard themselves, instead, in a grander light, as bloodhounds of the 'truth.' "[77] The problem with this is that facts then become, at best, a tool for revealing the truth. At worst, facts become an impediment to the "truth" which must be sloughed off, ignored, buried, so as not to interfere with the public's ability to perceive what in a "higher sense" is true. Gay Talese, a writer who was godfather to the new journalism, said its techniques allowed the presentation of "a larger truth than is possible through rigid adherence" to normal newspaper standards.[78]

One result of the new journalism was to make a scandal

like the one that erupted over Janet Cooke and the nonexistent eight-year-old heroin addict "Jimmy" inevitable. After the *Washington Post* was forced to return the Pulitzer Prize which the story had won, it tried to pass off what had happened as the victimization of a newspaper by one of its reporters. According to the *Post's* published account, no editor anywhere was safe from the machinations of a determined liar.

It was not so simple. Newspapers, the *Post* among them, had developed a pattern of shutting their eyes to the fictional aspects of the new journalism. When the *Daily News* accepted the resignation of its prize-winning journalist Michael Daley a month after the Cooke scandal—he was accused of manufacturing material for an article on British army brutality in Northern Ireland—Daley remarked that he had used pseudonyms and reconstructions on many of his three hundred columns and "no one has ever said anything."[79] In the case of Janet Cooke, Vivian Aplin-Brownlee, Cooke's editor on the *District Weekly*, to which she had been assigned in her first year at the *Post*, claimed that she did not believe the story from the beginning and said so to the city editor.

> I knew her so well and the depth of her. In her eagerness to make a name she would write farther than the truth would allow. When challenged on facts in other stories, Janet would reverse herself, but without dismay or consternation with herself.[80]

What this meant was that Janet Cooke was repeatedly caught in misstatements of fact while she worked for the *Post*, but the editors, instead of firing, had promoted her.

Despite what the *Post's* ombudsman Bill Green later admitted were "rumblings" in the newsroom, the *Post* made no attempt to check the story or even to ask to see Janet Cooke's tapes or notes. A few days after the story was published *Post* reporter Courtland Milloy drove Janet Cooke through the neighborhood where she claimed Jimmy lived and he could see she did not know the area. He reported his doubts to the city editor, but the editor, as he later confessed, thought Milloy was motivated by jealousy.[81] The mayor and police officials asked the *Post* to disclose the identity of the child so he could be helped. Presumably the life of an eight-year-old boy hung in the balance, but the *Post* merely launched into high-flown rhetoric on confidentiality, leaving the police to launch an intensive, expensive, and naturally vain search.

Since the police search was finally abandoned, Janet Cooke would have been safe, had she not lied about her academic credentials. The *Post* released biographical data on their prize-winning reporter, and Cooke's claim to a Vassar B.A. she did not have, led to the unraveling of the whole fabric of invention.

The media's reaction to charges of bias is one of genuine outrage. Irving Kristol has pointed out that "the television networks and national newspapers are sincerely convinced that a liberal bias is proof of journalistic integrity."[82] CBS News President Richard Salant retorted indignantly to suggestions of bias: "Our reporters do not cover stories from *their* point of view. They are presenting them from *nobody's* point of view."[83]

Yet in the spring of 1972, a "counter-convention" of American journalists, sponsored by the journalism review *More*, was being attended by over two thousand journalists, including such media "stars" as Dan Rather, Tom Wicker, David Halberstam, and Murray Kempton. In an article describing the purpose of the meeting, *More* explained: "A growing number of people who put out the nation's newspapers and magazines and splice together the nightly news are no longer going to accept the old ways of doing things." The "new" journalists, said *More*, were "sensitive" people who turned "their attention to the kind of journalism that might help improve the quality of life rather than objectively recording its decline."[84]

How do journalists manage to believe they maintain the professional journalistic creed of objectivity at the same time they transmit, as we have seen, the utopian world view? Many journalists seem to mistake a sense of superiority for objectivity. In the fifth and final segment of CBS's series on defense, President Reagan and Chairman Brezhnev were shown making speeches denouncing each other. Cronkite then appeared, like the patient parent of quarreling children, to lament that from both the Kremlin and the White House came "angry words." Presenting the United States and the Soviet Union as mirror-image societies seems to constitute self-evident proof of objectivity to Cronkite and the media elite.

Convinced of their own objectivity, the media are arrogant and dismissive when criticized. Reed Irvine notes that when he and a group of friends who belonged to the McDowell luncheon group decided, in 1969, to start Accuracy in Media, they were convinced that if they did research on cases of media inaccuracy, those responsible would have no choice but to admit they were wrong, issue corrections, and be more careful in the future. Irvine laughs ruefully as he recalls: "We soon found out it really did work that way."[85]

The arrogance is sometimes breathtaking, as the media unhesitatingly ignore, in their own case, the demands they make of others. For example, CBS has been the most aggressive of the networks in claiming for television cameras the right to cover any event open to the print media. Yet when CBS held its annual meeting in April 1980, while the press was admitted, television cameras were barred. William Paley, long-time chairman of CBS, declared they would be disruptive to the audience. Reed Irvine asked if he would recommend that Congress adopt the same policy and the following colloquy ensued:

> Paley: I would not.
> Irvine: Just CBS.
> Paley: We have adopted the policy, for the time being anyway, which has been clearly enunciated today. That's all I can say about it.[86]

One journalist remarked that it was like distillers holding a meeting and barring booze.

The reaction to criticism is sometimes vituperative. Responding to an issue of *AIM Report* that clearly touched a nerve, the *Post's* editor Benjamin Bradlee wrote to Irvine: "You have revealed yourself as a miserable, carping, retromingent vigilante, and I for one am sick of wasting my time in communicating with you."[87] After looking up "retromingent," which means "urinating backward," Irvine framed the letter and hung it in the office.

All the sins of advocacy journalism, the fictions supporting a "higher truth," the selective coverage, the attacks on what are perceived as "the bad guys" and whitewashing of the "good guys," came together in a media crusade against Israel during its war against the PLO in Lebanon in 1982. In a major study for *Policy Review*, Joshua Muravchik has provided the fullest account of media distortion on a single topic since Peter Braestrup's two-volume analysis of the media's coverage of the Tet offensive in Vietnam. Muravchik found variations in culpability: the *Washington Post* was much worse than the *New York Times*: NBC was worse than ABC, which was worse than CBS; *Time* and *Newsweek*, on the other hand, turned in equally abysmal performances.[88] *All* the media were involved in tendentious and inaccurate reporting with one target—to make Israel look bad.

Muravchik piles high the examples of media misstatement of fact. For example, wildly exaggerated casualty reports falsely attributed to the internationally respected Red Cross (in fact they came from the nonrelated Red Crescent, an arm of the PLO run by Arafat's brother) continued to be cited repeatedly after the Red

Cross had formally repudiated them. These were soon accompanied by equally inflated portraits of destruction from supposed eyewitness journalists in Beirut. While all the media were guilty of this, the prize may well have belonged to ABC which in June, before the Israelis had launched any serious bombing of the city, described Beirut as a result of Israeli shelling as resembling "some ancient ruin."

Symptomatic of the pervasive dishonesty was a photo distributed by United Press International with a caption which said it showed a seven-month-old baby who had lost both arms in an Israeli raid. Secretary of State George Shultz, in a statement meant to be critical of Israel, said, "the symbol of this war is a baby with its arms shot off." It was a symbol not of the war, but of the media's coverage of it. Subsequent investigation showed that the baby had not been badly hurt—both its arms were intact. And while civilians, including children, were obviously hit by Israeli bombs, it so happened that in this case the time, place, and direction of bombing made it clear that the baby had been hit by PLO shelling, which the media rarely mentioned, but was also a feature of the war.

Perhaps the media bias was best revealed by the television networks' attacks on Israel for censorship. (The PLO's censorship, exercised by guns directed against unwelcome TV cameras, was never mentioned.) When ABC broke Israel's censorship by broadcasting an interview with Arafat that had been disallowed by the censor, Israel punished the network by temporarily refusing it access to Israeli television facilities. ABC accused Israel, on the air, of "an intolerable act of political censorship." Israel explained that while it exercised only military censorship on reports from Israel's side of the battle line, its extension of its facilities for reports from the enemy's side was a favor to journalists which it would not allow to be used for the PLO's political advantage. ABC had agreed to the rules and then broken them. But as Muravchik notes, while Israel's position was one with which the public might or might not have sympathized, they never heard Israel's side of the story because the networks would not report it.

Yet Israel's censorship—in wartime—was far less restrictive than that of most other countries at any time and compared very favorably with that of other Middle Eastern countries. Moreover, while despatches from other Middle Eastern countries were censored, the networks only flashed on the screen references to Israeli censorship. Eventually NBC began to flash on the screen "Cleared by Syrian censors," and CBS several weeks later followed suit. But by the end of August ABC, although it often broadcast from Syria, still made no reference to Syrian censorship while routinely using "Cleared by Israeli censors." (Ironically if Israel had kept out all foreign journalists, she would presumably have fared much better at their hands. This is what the British did during their war with Argentina over the Falklands that was going on simultaneously, and the media kept silent about "censorship.")

Given the extraordinary depths to which the media sank in the reporting on Lebanon, the analysis of the *Columbia Journalism Review* on media reporting of the war is interesting. It concluded that American journalism

> reported what it saw for the most part fairly and accurately and sometimes brilliantly, provided balanced comment, and provoked and absorbed controversy. For performance under fire, readers and viewers could have asked for little more.[89]

Except for the remark that the coverage "provoked and absorbed controversy," which was certainly true, this could scarcely have been further from the mark. But it does underscore the extent to which the major journalism reviews, of which Columbia's is probably the most influential, have themselves become exponents of advocacy journalism. If the press is going to change its ways, it will not be because of monitoring by the major journalism reviews.

Media needs and attitudes and utopian goals dovetail nicely. From the point of view of the utopians, stories that the media may like because of their inherent drama break down faith in authority. When ABC launched "20/20" to compete with CBS's highly successful "60 Minutes," the program was known around the studio as the "cancer scare of the week." While ABC may have pursued ratings, for the utopians the programs reveal the wickedness or incapacity of government and corporations, which deny the reality of the dangers or fail to meet them. The media rarely report human rights violations in totalitarian societies, because they cannot gain access to them. For the utopians, these are stories that *should* be ignored, for they might interfere with their effort to mobilize public opinion against non-Communist countries threatened by those whose aim is to establish regimes of the sort that already exist in Cuba and North Vietnam.

While in theory the fondness for scare stories could make reports on the Soviet military buildup and Soviet intelligence agencies appealing, here pervasive liberal orthodoxy among journalists comes into play. It leads them to downgrade the notion that there is such a thing as a genuine Soviet threat. It also leads them to automatic sympathy with proposals that come from disarmament groups, which they become extremely reluctant to report on fully, for fear the effect would be to "unmask" them. This prevents the public from developing skepticism about the programs of these groups. The media's portrait enforces the utopian view of the world and makes the calls of the utopians for "deindustrialization," "decentralization of industry," solar roof collectors instead of central power stations, seem safer to try than they otherwise would. The utopian agenda becomes more plausible and attractive as our familiar world is seen to be threatened only by the callousness and rapacity of our own institutions.

NOTES

1. Quoted in *TV and National Defense: An Analysis of CBS News 1972-1973*, ed. Ernest W. Lefever (Boston, Va.: Institute for American Strategy Press, 1974), p. 14.
2. Melvin G. Grayson and Thomas R Shepard, *The Disaster Lobby* (Chicago: Follett Publishing Co., 1973), p. 266.
3. S. Robert Lichter and Stanley Rothman, "Media and Business Elites," *Public Opinion*, Oct./Nov. 1981, pp. 42-44.
4. *Ibid.*, pp. 59, 60.
5. Robert Loewenberg, "Journalism and Free Speech as Political Power," *Scholastic*, December 1982, p. 12.
6. Quoted by Joseph Kraft, "The Imperial Media," *Commentary*, May 1981, p. 38.
7. *AIM Report*, September 1, 1979.
8. *Ibid.*, June 1977.
9. *Ibid.*, Oct. 1, 1979.
10. Sophie Pederson, "Foreign News Gatekeepers and Criteria of Newsworthiness," *Journalism Quarterly*, Spring 1979, p. 116.
11. Stanley Rothman and S. Robert Lichter, "The Nuclear Energy Debate: Scientists, the Media and the Public," *Public Opinion*, August/September 1982, p. 51.
12. *Ibid.*, p. 52.
13. Robert DuPont, *Nuclear Phobia*, The Media Institute.
14. Rothman and Lichter, "The Nuclear Energy Debate," *op. cit.*, p. 47.
15. *Ibid.*, p. 49.
16. *Ibid.*, p. 51.
17. Samuel McCracken, *The War Against the Atom* (New York: Basic Books, 1982), p. 108.
18. Rothman and Lichter, "The Nuclear Energy Debate," *op. cit.*, p. 52.
19. Samuel McCracken, *op. cit.*, p. 108.
20. *AIM Report*, March 11, 1979.
21. Interview with Walter Cronkite, *Utica (N.Y.) Press*, Nov. 13, 1974, quoted in *TV and National Defense, op. cit.*, frontispiece.

22. *Ibid.*, p. 37.
23. Joshua Muravchik and John E. Haynes, "CBS vs. Defense," *Commentary,* September 1981, p. 46.
24. *Ibid.*, p. 45.
25. *Ibid.*, pp. 48, 49.
26. *AIM Report*, April I, 1979.
27. *Ibid.*, May II 1978.
28. *Ibid.*, February I 1979.
29. *Ibid.*
30. *Ibid.*, March II 1978.
31. *Ibid.*, October II 1979.
32. *Ibid.*, July I 1977.
33. *Ibid.*, Feb. I 1979.
34. *Ibid.*, October II 1979.
35. *Contentions*, newsletter of the Committee for the Free World, December 1981.
36. *AIM Report*, May II 1980.
37. *Ibid.*, June I 1982.
38. *Ibid.*, June II 1980.
39. *Ibid.*
40. *Ibid.*, March I 1979.
41. *Human Events*, April 24, 1982; *New York Times*, April 9, 1982.
42. *Contentions*, Committee for the Free World, April-May, 1982.
43. *AIM Report*, Sept. I 1977.
44. *Guild Notes*, publication of the National Lawyers Guild, April 1980.
45. *Ibid.*
46. *Business Week*, October 18, 1982.
47. *Crooks, Conmen and Clowns,* (Washington D.C.: Media Institute, 1981), pp. ix, x.
48. Ben Stein, *The View from Sunset Boulevard* (New York: Basic Books, 1979), p. 20.
49. *Ibid.*, p. 33.
50. *AIM Report*, September II 1980.
51. Interview with Peter Metzger, January 29, 1982.
52. *AIM Report*, July 11, 1982.
53. *Wall Street Journal*, August 21, 1981.
54. *Human Events*, July 11, 1981.
55. *Ibid.*
56. *Ibid.*
57. *Ibid.*
58. *Wall Street Journal*, August 21, 1981.
59. *Human Events*, April 9, 1983.
60. *Human Events*, Sept. 26, 1981.
61. Letter from Michael Danby, editor *Australia Israel Review*, February 28, 1983; also *AIM Report*, November II 1982.
62. *Daily News*, May 12, 1982.
63. *AIM Report*, April 1, 1982.
64. *Ibid.*
65. *Ibid.*, July I 1979.
66. *Ibid.*, May I 1980.
67. Bob Schulman, *The Bulletin*, American Society of Newspaper Editors, October 1982.
68. *New York Times*, August 2, 1977.

69. Quoted in *Review of the News*, September 8, 1982, p. 37.
70. Jeremiah A. Denton Jr., *When Hell Was in Session*, (So. Carolina: Robert E. Hopper & Assoc., 1982), Chapter 11.
71. *AIM Report*, September I 1978.
72. *Wall Street Journal*, November 16, 1982.
73. *Cablevision Magazine*, October 25, 1982.
74. Max Kampelman, "The Power of the Press," *Policy Review*, Fall 1978, p. 18.
75. Joseph Kraft, "The Imperial Media," *Commentary*, May 1981, p. 43.
76. Jim Bormann, "Honesty, Fairness and Real Objectivity—Keys to Journalistic Credibility," keynote address to Radio and Film News Directors Association, September 29, 1971.
77. Naomi Munson, "The Case of Janet Cooke," *Commentary*, August 1981, p. 49.
78. *New York Times*, May 25, 1981.
79. *Ibid.*
80. *AIM Report*, May I 1981.
81. *Ibid.*
82. *Wall Street Journal*, October 14, 1982.
83. *TV and National Defense op. cit.*, p. 11.
84. Grayson and Shepard, *op cit.*, pp. 255, 256.
85. Interview with Reed Irvine, October 24, 1982.
86. *AIM Report*, May I 1980.
87. *Ibid.*, June II 1978.
88. Joshua Muravchik, "Misreporting Lebanon," *Policy Review*, Winter 1982/83, pp. 18, 32, 41, 43, 46, 53.
89. Roger Morris, "Beirut—and the Press—Under Siege," *Columbia Journalism Review*, November/December 1982, p. 33.

PART FOUR:
THE
UNINFORMED
HYSTERIA
OF THE
DOOMSAYERS

ELEVEN

The Dismal Science

CHARLES MAURICE AND CHARLES W. SMITHSON

Based on the trends in consumption and production that prevailed in the earlier part of the 1970s, many writers went so far as to predict the collapse of the developed economies due to resource shortages. We heard people talking about the day "when the pumps run dry." Over and over, the physical scientists pointed to entropy—the second law of thermodynamics—as clear and definitive proof that we were going to run out of oil. (In the context of the energy crisis, the entropy law would say something like "deposits of petroleum are finite and you can't burn the same barrel of petroleum twice.") The shortcoming of their analysis was that they presupposed that the trends in consumption and production that prevailed in the early 1970s would continue into the future. They neglected the impact that prices have on consumers and producers. While these merchants of doom agreed that the shortage would raise the price of gasoline and other petroleum products, they did not recognize that changes in price will change the behavior of participants in a marketplace.

In fact, the rapid increases in the price of energy altered prevailing trends. With rising energy prices the rate of increase in the consumption of petroleum products declined, while the rate of growth in production increased. The net result was, of course, a surplus (or, as the press call it, a glut) at existing prices rather than a shortage in the energy market by the early 1980s. The energy crisis

---

CHARLES MAURICE and CHARLES W. SMITHSON are members of the economics faculty at Texas A & M University. They coauthored *Economics of Natural Resources* (Praeger, 1980) and *Managerial Economics* (Irwin, 1980), as well as other publications. Both have contributed numerous articles to professional publications including the *Journal of Political Economy*, the *Journal of Economics*, the *Southern Economic Journal*, the *Journal of Law and Economics*, and *Resources and Energy*. They recently coauthored *The Doomsday Myth* (Hoover Institute Press, 1984), from which this chapter is taken.

was ended, not through repeal of the second law of thermodynamics, but rather as a result of the laws of demand and supply: as prices rise, consumers will use less and producers will bring more to the market.

This experience with energy in the 1970s provides what we feel is a very optimistic view of the future for market economies. Specifically, it implies that when an economy is faced with a shortage, price will rise, leading to reduced consumption and increased production, thereby eliminating the shortage. Doomsday will be averted. We feel that such a prediction would earn economics the label of "the optimistic science." Instead, economics is (we feel inappropriately) labeled as "the dismal science." Let us begin by taking a moment to see how this label came about.

THOMAS MALTHUS'S PREDICTIONS OF DOOM

In the latter part of the eighteenth century, a British economist, Thomas Malthus, proposed a dismal view of the future for the world that was in marked contrast to the prevailing optimism of the time. On the basis of his observations of historical trends, he argued that population grows at a geometric rate (e.g., 1, 2, 4, 8, 16, 32, . . .) while food production increases at an arithmetic rate (e.g., 1, 2, 3, 4, 5, 6, . . .). We provide a graphical interpretation of Malthus's assertion in Figure 1. As is clear from the figure, such a view implies that given prevailing rates of growth, there will come a time at which the increase in population overtakes the increase in food production; so famine is inevitable. Indeed, Malthus forecasted recurring periods of starvation, with the long-run level of consumption at only the minimum subsistence level—certainly a dismal projection. (You might be interested to know what Malthus proposed as a solution. In keeping with his beliefs as an Anglican clergyman, he opposed both contraception and abortion. Instead, he supported "moral restraint"—later marriages, cold baths, and so forth. It is also interesting to note that Malthus opposed any relief to the poor. In his view, the poor had brought the problem [excess population] on themselves; any relief measures would simply aggravate the problem.)

It is this dismal prediction (and equally dismal solution) that led to economics being labeled "the dismal science." This kind of prediction, which asserts that the growth rate in consumption will swamp the growth rate in production, is normally referred to as Malthusian. In view of such dire predictions, it is not surprising that the word "Malthusian" has taken on dreary connotations. (We find it interesting that the current doom merchants refer to themselves—or each other—as neo-Malthusians.)

FIGURE 1 MALTHUS'S PREDICTION OF DOOM

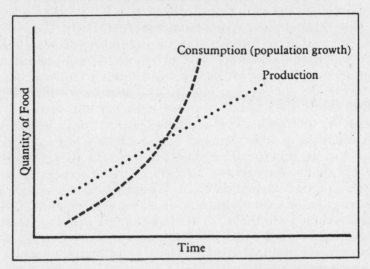

However, the most important fact is that Malthus's predictions of doom did not come true. Malthus's predictions were wrong. The reason he was wrong is that the prevailing rates of growth did not continue into the future. The growth trends in population and food production changed, with the most significant change coming in the growth rate of food production. One has only to compare the methods employed in agriculture today with those of the eighteenth century to see this. Malthus's dismal predictions were negated by technological change. The market responded to the increased demand for food (i.e., the increase in population) and the corresponding increase in price with technological improvements in food production. (To be fair, we must note that in later years Malthus himself became more optimistic. His subsequent publications recognized the importance of technological change and opened the possibility that the prevailing trends could change. Indeed, we might say that in his later years Malthus was not a "Malthusian.")

Some one hundred and fifty years after the population doomsdayers of the Malthus era, many economists were guilty of forecasting, again incorrectly as it turned out, a population problem of another sort. This time the predicted crisis was underpopulation rather than too rapid growth; but once again the doomsday prophets made the same mistake of extrapolating from past trends.

During the great depression of the 1930s, the birth rate fell dramatically in the United States and other Western countries. The reason for the decline was, of course, the massive depression. After World War II, many economists predicted continued depression. So sure were the prophets that the slump would continue indefinitely that they coined the term "secular stagnation."

The reason for expecting secular stagnation was the projected decline in population predicted from continued decreases in the birth rate. These predictions were extrapolated from the birth figures prior to and during World War II. A lower population meant a lower demand for consumer goods, and, because of the lower demand for goods, the low rate of investment and employment would continue. As soldiers became civilians again and defense industries were closed, the lack of demand would cause a huge increase in unemployment. And the unemployment would continue indefinitely. Hence, secular stagnation—a return to the depression.

But it didn't happen that way. What happened was one of the biggest population explosions ever—the postwar baby boom. Accumulated savings from the war period when incomes were high and many consumer goods were unavailable became new buying power. Newly formed families demanded houses, automobiles, appliances. All of these industries and many others needed labor. Europe had to be rebuilt. The result was high employment and investment. The forecasted secular stagnation didn't come. What came was the boom of the late 1940s and 1950s. As was the case with the earlier (over) population crisis, the underpopulation crisis just did not happen. Like Malthus, these later prophets of doom were wrong, because they based their dire predictions on previous trends. The trends simply didn't continue.

MALTHUS AND THE CURRENT DOOM MERCHANTS

When we look back on Malthus's dire forecast from the viewpoint of the late twentieth century, we often think it is simply silly to predict that trends existing at that time would continue into the future. How could Malthus have been so naive? However, the problem is that nothing has changed; people are still predicting Malthusian crises.

A clear example is found in the forecasts of doom based on energy and other natural resources. Think about it for a moment. How did Meadows and the other merchants of doom come up with their predictions? They assumed that prevailing trends in consumption and production would continue in the future and that, given these trends, there will come a time when the consumption of energy (or tin, or copper, or other resources) will overtake production and a famine becomes inevitable. Doesn't that sound familiar? It is exactly the same kind of prediction that Malthus made in 1798.

Malthus was wrong. Price-induced technological change negated his dismal forecast. And we see no evidence that there is an energy famine in our future. The market responded to the oil shortage and resulting increase in price with both technological improvements and substitution, eliminating the shortage. In both of these instances—Malthus's food crisis and our own recent energy crisis—the trends in consumption and production changed; they did not remain at their historical growth rates. Why did they change? The answer is found in price, the variable that is neglected in these trend extrapolations. If a shortage of a particular product occurs, its price goes up. As the price goes up, consumers try to use less of it; so the rate of growth in consumption declines. Conversely, with rising prices, producers try to bring more to the market to sell, and the rate of growth in production increases. Furthermore, the higher price of the product induces people to search for substitutes. Technological change is induced. Putting all these forces together, we argue that if the marketplace is permitted to function, the famine (or collapse) will never come about.

To this point, we have concentrated on the forecasts of collapse in the energy market that were made in the 1970s. As you might expect, the merchants of doom looked at other markets as well. Let us give you an example. As Julian Simon pointed out, in 1969 Paul Ehrlich predicted that "the end of the ocean came in the late summer of 1979." More specifically, Ehrlich predicted that the world fish catch would decline to thirty million metric tones in 1977—in turn leading to the starvation of fifty million people per year. Instead, according to Simon, the world fish catch in 1977 was seventy-three million tons—more than twice what Ehrlich had predicted. Another doomsday averted.

Given that so many of their dismal predictions have been proved false, you might think the doom merchants would quit the field. Such is simply not the case. There is no shortage of those predicting doom. For example, in 1981 a program was produced for the Public Broadcasting System (PBS) by KUED (Salt Lake City) entitled "The Doomsayers." The tone of this program was set in the opening by the narrator:

Now there are those who say that Western civilization has run its course. That our efforts to create a society of peace and prosperity have nearly failed. That ahead of us waits the prospect of a new dark age. Around us rise the voices of the doomsayers.

In this program, the doomsayers who were interviewed painted a picture of gloom and doom to gladden the hearts of the neo-Malthusians. In contrast to the optimism we want to convey to you, these doom merchants pointed to "the spectre of economic collapse." And, like many of their colleagues during the 1970s, they based much of the case for economic collapse on the prediction that we are going to run out of resources. As made explicit by David Brower, the chairman of Friends of the Earth, this prediction was again based on the idea of finite resources being consumed at an exponentially increasing rate. The impact of price on the behavior of consumers and producers was still not considered. The doom merchants continued to predict the future on the basis of trends that had existed in the past.

Another example of the current dismal predictions made by the doom merchants is found in *One Hundred Pages for the Future*, which was published in the United States in 1982, a report by Aurelio Peccei, president of the Club of Rome. (*Limits to Growth* was the first report published by the Club of Rome.) In the first paragraph of the foreword to the U.S. edition, Peccei sets the tone of his predictions: "There is no doubt in my mind that the human race is hurtling toward disaster." Although he attempts to divorce himself from extrapolative forecasting, much of the book is based upon trend forecasting (for example, his predictions for population and resource consumption). Once again, predictions are made without any consideration of the impact of price on the behavior of consumers and producers. However, Peccei clearly states why he gives no credence to the marketplace. In his opinion: "Neither the producer nor the consumer, not even society itself can any longer trust the 'invisible hand' of classical economics . . . Instead, they often find themselves kicked along by a 'mysterious boot.' " So in 1982, even after our experience with decontrol of the energy market, we find that the Club of Rome—the philosophical home of so many of the doom merchants—continues to assert that there exist "dangers that threaten our very survival" and that the marketplace has somehow stopped functioning. In order to survive, "everything must be invented anew."

It is precisely this attitude that we oppose. We hope to be able to show you that the marketplace is and can remain vital. In contrast to the opinion forwarded by the Club of Rome, the marketplace is not dead. As in the case of our recent energy crisis, it can be relied upon to eliminate shortages—crises—and thereby avert the doomsday that some assert is upon us. But before we go on, permit us to take a moment to say one or two things more about the extrapolative forecasting technique that has formed the basis for most of the predictions of gloom and doom.

THE SHOE ON THE OTHER FOOT

As is probably clear by now, we are not at all convinced by forecasts based on prevailing trend, regardless of the assertion by Meadows *et al.*, that "extrapolation is a time-honored way of looking into the future." Experience has shown us that shortages or surpluses will change the price of the commodity, which in turn will alter the prevailing rates of growth of consumption and production. Price changes alter the trends.

To illustrate more clearly the shortcomings of trend extrapolation, let us turn it on itself. For purposes of illustration, we will call *The Limits to Growth* (1972) the first of the (modern) doomsday books; so in 1972 a library would contain only one such book. However, the publication of *The Limits to Growth* brought many similar books to the market. In 1973, we found that six such books were published, including titles like *The Failure of Success.* Hence, in 1973, our doomsday shelf would contain seven books. The actual publication of doomsday books over the period 1972-1977 is summarized in Figure 2. Note that in 1977 the doomsday shelf in our library would have contained twenty-six books.

From Figure 2, we calculated the prevailing rate of growth of doomsday books over this period. This gave us an annual growth rate of 75 percent. Now let's forecast the number of doomsday books that will exist in the year 2000. Like Malthus and the modern doom merchants, we will assume that the prevailing trend is unchanged. Then, extrapolating from the prevailing trend, we would forecast that in the year 2000 there will exist over fourteen million doomsday books! In 1983, the total holdings of the Library of Congress—books and pamphlets—was something less than twenty million items. Let us give you another way to put this number in some perspective. Visualize the library shelf holding the doomsday books. If each book were two inches thick, the shelf would be four hundred and fifty miles long.

Obviously, our forecast is silly. The point is, however, that we admit it, while the doom merchants argue that theirs are somehow reliable. Theirs and ours are based on the same invalid assumption that prevailing trends will continue in the future.

We hope you have seen our point; but we simply can not resist telling you one more story to illustrate the dangers inherent in extrapolative forecasting. On one of the late-night TV programs we heard a guest provide a tongue-in-cheek forecast that went something like this: if George Steinbrenner continues to behave as he has in the past, by the year 2004, 70 percent of the male population of New York will have managed the Yankees. (Here we might suggest the alternative prediction that Billy Martin will have managed the

FIGURE 2 DOOMSDAY BOOKS PUBLISHED, 1972-1977

	Published	Cumulative Total
1972	1	1
1973	6	7
1974	2	9
1975	4	13
1976	6	19
1977	7	26

Yankees six thousand times.) While such a forecast is clearly far-fetched, it does rest on the same assumption that is present in all extrapolative forecasts; if prevailing trends continue, then . . .

Our point is simple. We have never seen an instance where prevailing trends have continued far into the future. Conditions always change. While we are not sure what might alter George Steinbrenner's behavior in the future, we do know how prevailing trends in consumption and production have been altered in the past and will be altered in the future—the trends are altered by changes in the price of the resource.

THE MARKET WORKS

Let us take a moment to see where we stand. In the eighteenth century, Malthus predicted that a food famine was inevitable, given the prevailing trends in production and consumption. This prediction was negated because those trends changed. Specifically, technological progress in agriculture substantially increased the rate of growth of food production. In the twentieth century, many writers predicted a famine in energy and a resultant collapse of the developed economies, again given the prevailing trends in production and consumption. By the 1980s, the forecasted shortage turned into a glut of petroleum. The crisis was averted because the trends changed. As the price of energy rose, consumers used less energy. By and large, this energy saving was the result of technical improvements and the substitution of more energy efficient cars and appliances for the gas guzzlers. Also, as the price of energy rose, producers delivered more energy. Formerly expensive technology for extracting more oil became economically practical at the higher energy prices.

In both of these instances, the fact that crisis and collapse were avoided was due not to any altruistic motives on the part of consumers or producers, nor to the intervention of a forward-looking and benevolent government, but rather to the actions of a freely functioning marketplace. The working of the market is simplicity itself. If something becomes more scarce, its price rises. As the price rises, consumers try to use less of it. How do they do so? They can either rely on technological change that makes the scarce good less essential or substitute some other commodity for the scarce good. As the price of the scarce commodity rises, producers try to provide more of it to the market. How can this be accomplished? Producers can either use new technology to provide more of the commodity in question or they can begin supplying a substitute for the scarce commodity. The end result is that, with reduced consumption and increased production, the shortage is eliminated and the price of the commodity will begin to fall.

Our thesis is very simple—we argue that markets work to eliminate shortages: so forecasts of doom or collapse based on shortages are groundless. The "invisible hand" (as first described by Adam Smith in *The Wealth of Nations*) is not palsied, as the president of the Club of Rome asserted. To paraphrase Mark Twain's famous cable to the Associated Press, we believe that the reports of the death of the marketplace are greatly exaggerated. If a shortage occurs, price will increase, and the price increase will adjust consumption and production so as to eliminate the shortage. We feel that there are two major mechanisms by which this adjustment is accomplished—substitution and price-induced technological change. As price rises, consumers substitute some other commodity for the scarce commodity. During the energy crisis, didn't you or your acquaintances substitute some insulation for the scarce—and more expensive—fuel oil? As prices rise, individuals are induced to undertake technological innovation that will reduce consumption of the scarce commodity or replace it entirely.

SOURCES

Ekelund, Robert B., and Herbert, Robert F., *A History of Economic Theory and Method* (New York: McGraw-Hill, 1975).

KUED, Salt Lake City. "The Doomsayers," produced for the Public Broadcasting System, 1981.

Peccei, Aurelio, *One Hundred Pages for the Future* (New York: New American Library, 1982).

Roll, Eric, *A History of Economic Thought* (Englewood Cliffs, N.J.: Prentice-Hall, 1953).

Simon, Julian, "Should We Heed the Prophets of Doom?" *Science Digest,* October 1983.

Smith, Adam, *An Inquiry into the Nature and Cause of the Wealth of Nations,* edited by C. J. Bullock, The Harvard Classics, Vol. 10 (New York: Collier, 1937, 1961).

TWELVE

Standing Room Only?
The Demographic Facts

JULIAN L. SIMON

Every schoolchild seems to "know" that the world's environment and food situation have been getting worse. And the children's books leave no doubt that population size and growth are the villains. As the *Golden Stamp Book of Earth and Ecology* says, "Can the earth survive this many people? . . . If the population continues to explode, many people will starve. About half of the world's population is underfed now, with many approaching starvation. . . . All of the major environmental problems can be traced to people—more specifically, to too many people."[1] This text distills into simplest form the popular adults' books and articles about population and resources.

But there is a fly in this ointment. These propositions that are given to children with so much assurance are either unproven or wrong. This essay deals instead with the demographic facts, and the dynamics of the birthrate and of population growth.

POPULATION GROWTH RATES

The demographic facts, to the extent that they are known scientifically, can indeed seem frightening—at first glance. Figure 1 is the kind of diagram that, back in 1965, impressed and scared me enough to convince me that helping stop population growth should be my life's work. What we seem to see here is runaway population growth; the human population seems to be expanding

JULIAN L. SIMON is Professor of Economics at the University of Maryland, and the author of *The Ultimate Resource* (Princeton University Press, 1981) from which this chapter is taken. Most recently he co-edited with Herman Kahn *The Resourceful Earth: A Response to Global 2000*. He has written many articles on the economics of population growth and other subjects, and is a consultant to various public and private organizations.

with self-generated natural force at an exponential rate, a juggernaut chained only by starvation and disease. This suggests that unless something unusual comes along to check this geometric growth, there will soon be "standing room only."

It may be instructive that people have long been doing arithmetic that leads to the prediction of one or another version of "standing room only." In fact, the phrase "standing room only," used so often in recent discussions of population growth, was the title of a book by Ross in 1927, and the notion is found explicitly in both Malthus and Godwin (whose conclusions differed completely, however). Just one among many such colorful calculations is that of Harrison Brown, who worried that humanity might continue increasing "until the earth is covered completely and to a considerable depth with a writhing mass of human beings, much as a dead cow is covered with a pulsating mass of maggots."[2]

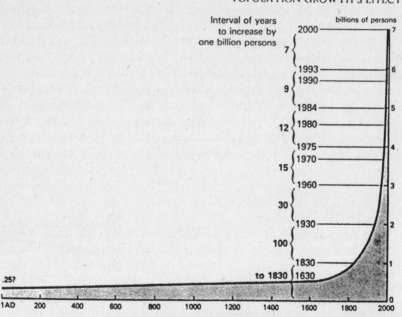

POPULATION GROWTH'S EFFECT

FIGURE 1   HOW THE U.S. STATE DEPARTMENT SAW
THE WORLD'S POPULATION GROWTH

People have worried about population growth since the beginning of recorded time. The Bible gives us this early story of population exceeding the "carrying capacity" of a particular area: "And the land was not able to carry them . . . and Abram said to Lot: . . . Is not the whole land before thee? . . . If thou will take the left hand, then I will take the right; or if thou take the right hand, then I will go to the left."[3] Euripides wrote that the Trojan War was due to "an insolent abundance of people."[4] And many classical philosophers and historians such as Polybius, Plato, and Tertullian worried about population growth, food shortages, and environmental degradation.[5] In 1802, when Java had a population of four million, a Dutch colonial official wrote that Java was "overcrowded with unemployed."[6] Now Java has most of Indonesia's one hundred and twenty-five million people, and again it is said to be overcrowded.

Just because people have worried about population growth in the past does not imply that we should not be worried now, of course. If a monster really has been on the loose for a while, the fact that it has not yet done us in is hardly reason to stop worrying. Therefore we must ask: Is population growth an unchecked monster, on the loose since the beginning of time but likely to destroy us in the foreseeable future?

Contrary to the impression given by Figure 1, population growth has not been constant or steady over the long sweep of time. Even the broadest picture of the past million years shows momentous sudden changes. Figure 2 indicates that population growth has three times taken off at "explosive" rates.

Another common misleading impression about world population is that a large proportion of all the people who have ever lived are alive now. This is very far from the truth. A well-thought-out estimate is that seventy-seven billion human beings were born from 600,000 B.C. to 1962 A.D.: twelve billion up to 6000 B.C., forty-two billion from 6000 B.C. to 1650 A.D., and twenty-three billion from 1650 A.D. to 1962 A.D..[7] Compare this to the

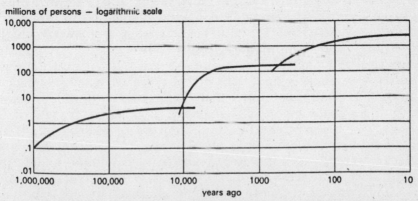

FIGURE 2 DEEVEY'S LOGARITHMIC POPULATION
CURVE

four to five billion who may be alive now. Of course many of the people born in earlier years died at young ages. But even so, the number of years of human life lived on earth in the past was large relative to the present.

It was the tool-using and tool-making revolution that kicked off the rapid rise in population around 1 million B.C. according to Edward Deevey. The aid of various tools "gave the food gatherer and hunter access to the widest range of environments."[8] But when the new power from the use of primitive tools had been exploited, the rate of population growth fell, and population size again settled down near a plateau.

The next rapid jump in population started perhaps ten thousand years ago, when men began to keep herds, and to plow and plant the earth, rather than simply foraging for the plants and game that grew naturally. Once again the rate of population growth abated after the initial productivity gains from the new technology had been exploited, and once again population size settled down to a near-plateau, as compared with the rapid growth previously experienced. It is reasonable to think that the near-plateau was reached because the known methods of making a living constituted a constraint to further population growth once the world's population reached a certain size.

These two previous episodes of a sharp rise and a subsequent fall in the rate of population growth suggest that the present rapid growth—which began perhaps three hundred or three hundred and fifty years ago, in the 1600s—may well settle down again, when, or if, the gains from the new industrial and agricultural knowledge that followed the "industrial revolution" begin to peter out. And population size may again reach a near-plateau and remain there until another "revolution" due to another breakthrough of knowledge again suddenly increases the productive capacity of mankind. Of course, the current knowledge-revolution may continue without foreseeable end, and population growth may or may not continue as long as the revolution does. Either way, in this long-term view, population size adjusts to productive conditions rather than being an uncontrolled monster.

To put the matter another way: This long-run view of demographic history suggests that, contrary to Malthus, constant geometric growth does not correctly characterize the human population. Rather, a major improvement of economic and health conditions produces a sudden increase in population, which gradually moderates as the major productive advances and concomitant health improvements are assimilated. Then, after the initial surge, the rate of growth slows down until the next big

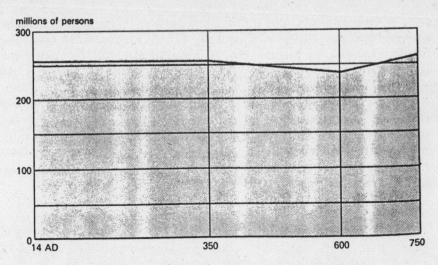

FIGURE 3 THE POPULATION OF THE WORLD,
14 A.D.-750 A.D.

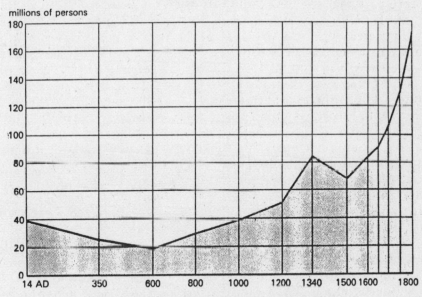

FIGURE 4 THE POPULATION OF EUROPE,
14 A.D.-1800 A.D.

surge. (It was the very large increase in life expectancy that led to the recent population growth in poor countries. Throughout history, life expectancy has hardly changed, compared with the sudden jump during the past few hundred years.) In this view, population growth represents economic success and human triumph, rather than social failure.

Deevey's picture of population history (Figure 2) still leaves us with the image of population growth as having an irresistible, self-reinforcing logic of its own, though subject to (very rare) changes in conditions. That view is so broad, however, that it can be misleading. The entire world, for example, had a stable population over the seven centuries prior to 750 A.D. as seen in Figure 3. And if we look more closely, as in Figure 4, we see that even for as large an area as Europe, where local ups and downs tend to cancel out, population growth did not proceed at a constant rate,

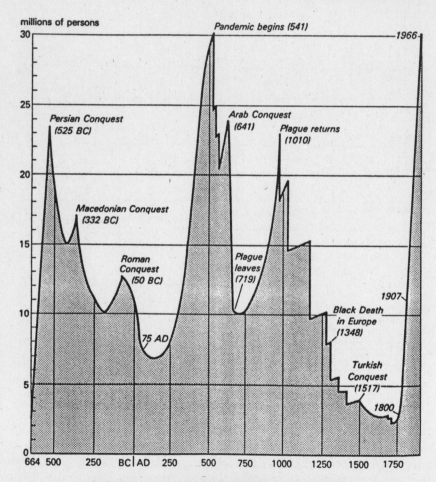

FIGURE 5   THE POPULATION OF EGYPT
664 B.C.-1966 A.D.

NOTE: McEvedy and Jones (1978, pp. 226-229) persuasively suggest that Egypt's population was nowhere near so high as Hollingsworth shows it to be.

nor was there always positive growth. Instead, there were advances and reverses. Figure 4 shows that population change is a complex phenomenon affected by a variety of forces; it is not an inexorable force checked only by famine and epidemic.

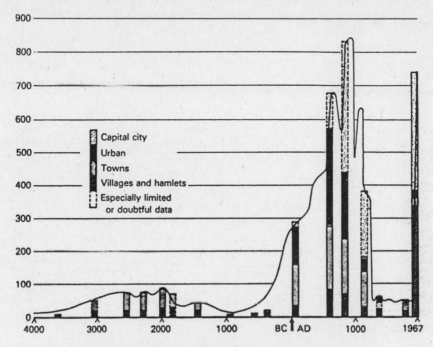

FIGURE 6 THE POPULATION OF BAGHDAD
(LOWER DIYALA, IRAQ) REGION, 4000 B.C.-1967 A.D.

Now let us move to an even greater level of detail—the individual country or region. In Figures 5, 6, and 7 we see three places where a decline in population has been more than a temporary episode. In Egypt, the breakdown of the Roman Empire led to a series of population declines due to disease and bad government, declines that ended only in the last century. In Iraq's Dyala region (around Baghdad) there were a series of political-economic perturbations that adversely affected irrigation and agriculture. It took years of population growth to overcome such setbacks—only to have another such breakdown occur. And in Mexico, it was the conquest by Cortez that set off a remarkable population decline. In the Spaniards' wake came wars, massacres, political and economic breakdowns among the indigenous civilizations, and new diseases, all of which caused death, desolation, and depopulation.

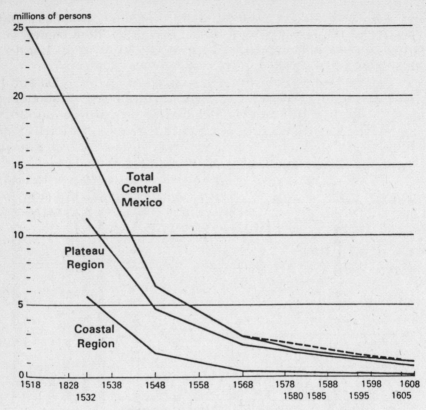

FIGURE 7   THE POPULATION OF CENTRAL MEXICO,
1518 A.D.-1608 A.D.

A shocking example close to home, for Americans, is the population decline of Native Americans in California from perhaps 310,000 in 1769 to a low of perhaps 20,000-25,000 between 1880 and 1900. "The population decline became catastrophic between 1848 and 1860. The number of Indians fell *in twenty years* from 200,000 or 250,000 to merely 25,000 or 30,000."[9]

These historical examples are strong proof that population size and growth are influenced by political and economic and cultural forces, and not only by starvation and plague. But even contemporary data show us that the rate of population growth can go down as well as up. In many poor countries—though, of course, not all—fertility has been falling. Many of the countries with the fastest-falling birthrates are small islands, which seem especially quick to respond to new conditions and currents of thought, and which may do so because they have the best communication systems, due to their high population density. But China is no island, and it supports a quarter of all humanity; yet fertility there too has apparently dropped sharply in the last decade or two.

These recent drops in fertility make it credible that countries that are now poor and have high fertility rates will sooner or later follow the pattern of the richer countries, whose mortality rate fell years ago and whose fertility rate then likewise fell. This pattern may be seen in Figure 8, which shows the well-known "demographic transition" as it actually occurred in Sweden.

In the more-developed countries, fertility is low by anyone's standard. In Figure 9 we see that the birthrate is now far below replacement—that is, below zero population growth—for many of the largest countries in Europe.

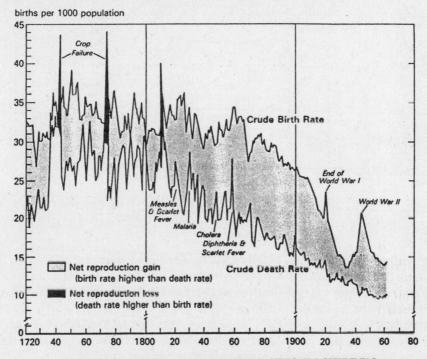

FIGURE 8   BIRTH AND DEATH RATES IN SWEDEN,
1720-1962

Let us now summarize the key facts about population growth. Population grows at various rates under various conditions. Sometimes population size shrinks for centuries due to poor political and health conditions. The doomsday myth of "standing room only" suggests a juggernaut inexorably bearing down upon the world, subject to no control. But the data suggest that economic, cultural, and political events, and not just catastrophe, control population size.

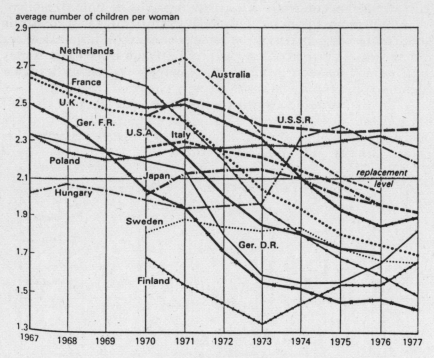

FIGURE 9   FERTILITY AND THE REPLACEMENT LEVEL
IN DEVELOPED COUNTRIES

WHAT WILL THE FUTURE GROWTH RATE BE?

When looking at the demographic facts with an eye to judging what ought to be done about population, we want to know what the future holds, how great the "pressures" of population size and growth will be. This is why population forecasts are made by governmental agencies and academic researchers.

The history of demographic predictions gives us reason, however, to feel some humility and stay cautious, and not go hogwild with fear-motivated overreactive policies. For example, in the 1930s most Western countries feared an expected decline in population growth. The most extensive investigation of the "problem" was undertaken in Sweden by some of the world's best social scientists. The dotted lines in Figure 10 show how the future looked to them then. But all of their dotted-line hypotheses about the future—intended to bracket all of the conceivable possibilities—turned out to be far below the actual course of population growth, as shown by the solid line; that is, the future turned out far better, from the point of view of those scientists, than any of them guessed it might. And had they successfully induced fertility-increasing programs, as they recommended, the results would have been contrary to what they *now* want. It may well be that we are now at an analogous point in history, except

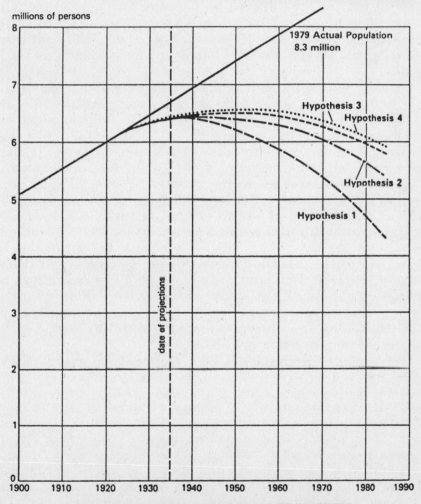

FIGURE 10   THE POPULATION OF SWEDEN
ACCORDING TO FOUR HYPOTHESES MADE IN
1935, AND THE ACTUAL POPULATION IN 1979

that now population growth is popularly thought to be too fast rather than too slow.

The Swedes were not alone in making inaccurate "pessimistic" forecasts. A U.S. Presidential Research Committee of eminent scientists reported to Herbert Hoover in 1933 that "we shall probably attain a population between 145 and 150 million during the present century."[10] Figure 11 shows a variety of forecasts made in the 1930s and 1940s by America's greatest demographic experts. For the year 2000, none of them forecast a population even as large as two hundred million people; in fact, the U.S. reached two hundred million people sometime around the year 1969, and is far beyond that already. A good many of the forecasters actually predicted a decline in population before the year 2000, which we now know is impossible unless there is a holocaust.

Even within the last eight years we have seen some astonishing flip-flops in world population forecasts. As of 1969, the *U.S. Department of State Bulletin* forecast 7.5 billion people for the year 2000, echoing the original UN source.[11] By 1974, the figure quoted in the media was 7.2 billion.[12] By 1976, Raphael Salas, the executive director of the UN Fund for Population Activities (UNFPA) was forecasting "nearly 7 billion."[13] Soon Salas was all the way down to "at least 5.8 billion."[14] And as early as 1977, Lester Brown and the Worldwatch Institute (which the UN is supporting) dropped it down again, forecasting 5.4 billion people for the year 2000. This change must be astonishing to laymen—to wit, that the forecast for a date then only twenty-three years away, when a majority of the people who will then be living were already living, could be off by two billion people, a change of more than a third of the total current forecast. Does this example of forecasting "science" give us any reason to be impressed by population predictions?

Nor is there reason to believe that contemporary forecasting methods are better than older ones. As recently as 1972, the President's Commission on Population Growth forecast that "even if the family size drops gradually—to the two-child average—there will be no year in the next two decades in which the absolute number of births will be less than in 1970."[15] How did it turn out? In 1971—the year *before* this forecast by the august President's Commission was transmitted to the President and then published—the absolute number of births (not the birthrate) was *already* less than in 1970. By 1975, the absolute number of births was barely higher than in 1920, and the number of white

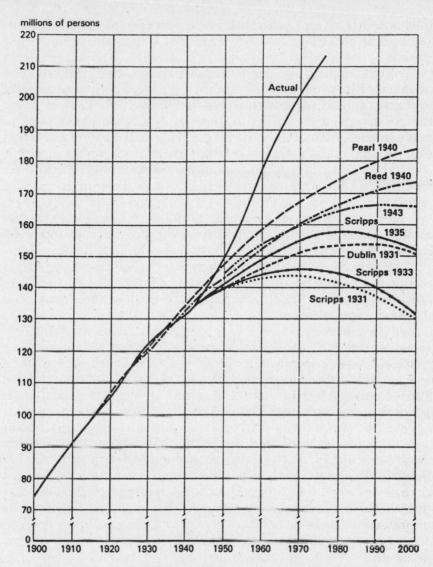

millions of persons

FIGURE 11   U.S. POPULATION FORECASTS MADE 1931-43,
AND THE ACTUAL POPULATION

births was actually lower than in most years between 1914 and
1924.

This episode shows once again how flimsy are the demographic forecasts upon which arguments about growth policy are
based. In this case the commission did not even *backcast* correctly, let alone *forecast* well. In short, the history of population

forecasts should make us think twice—or thrice—before attaching a great deal of weight to doomsday forecasts of population growth.

What population size or rate of growth does the long-run future hold in store? No one knows. One frequently hears it said that zero population growth (ZPG) "obviously" is the only viable state of affairs in the long run. But why? Why shouldn't population get *smaller* instead of staying level if it already is too large? What is sacred about the present population size, or the size that will be attained if it levels off soon? As David Wolfers puts it, the concept of ZPG is "a careless example of round number preference."[16]

Making forecasts of population size requires making assumptions about the fertility of future couples and also about the fertility of present couples who have begun but not finished bearing children. Such assumptions have proven wildly wrong in the past, as we have seen. Yet it is interesting to imagine the implications of assuming that childbearing patterns like those practiced at present will continue.

The trends shown in Figure 9 contain such an implicit forecast. For example, using a sophisticated but sensible method[17] of extrapolating the partial fertility to the total fertility of women now in the childbearing ages, Colin Clark estimated the relationship of current fertility to the number of births needed for replacement, and only replacement, of the present population (that is, for ZPG). He thereby arrived at the perhaps surprising conclusion that present fertility is far below replacement, and heading toward population decline, in the major Western countries; for example, he estimates that in 1976 the U.S. had only 81 percent of the number of births necessary for its population to remain at the present level. It must be repeated that such fertility patterns are subject to change, with a consequent change in the implied size of the future population. But this extrapolation of current fertility is at least provocative.

As to the long-run future—no one *knows* what will happen, of course. We can expect that people's incomes will rise indefinitely. But how much of that income will people feel an additional child requires? And what other activities will compete with bringing up children for parents' interest and time? These factors are likely to be the main determinants of population growth, and no one knows precisely how they will operate. We can at least say, however, that an extrapolation of the last few centuries' population growth straight upward toward infinity and doom has no warrant in the facts.

WHO WILL SUPPORT WHOM? THE DEPENDENCY BURDENS

A fast-growing population contains a large proportion of children. And children are an economic burden until they are old enough to earn their keep (just like capital investments while they are being constructed).

The difference in the child-dependency burden from one country to another can be enormous. Here are several examples: In 1955-56, 44 percent of the population of Costa Rica was younger than fifteen years old, compared with 24 percent in Sweden;[18] age-distributional differences between Mexico and Sweden in 1970 are shown in Figure 12; the proportions of the male population within the prime labor-force years of fifteen and sixty-four were 70 percent in Sweden in 1940, and 53 percent in Brazil in 1900[19] (that is, there were one hundred and thirty-two male workers in Sweden for each one hundred in Brazil, relative to the total population); as of 1970, each one hundred persons aged 20-59 in Mexico must support one hundred and twenty persons aged 0-14, whereas in Sweden each one hundred persons aged 20-59 need support only thirty-nine persons aged 0-14.[20] Clearly, the economic effect of such differences is not trivial.

The obvious conclusion one might draw from these data is that the standard of living will be higher if the birthrate is lower. For the immediate future this is undeniable; the proposition can be demonstrated by the simplest kind of arithmetic. If income per capita is our measure of economic well-being, then we have only to divide gross national production by population (GNP/population) to calculate income per person. Adding a nonproducing baby to the population immediately reduces the calculated income per capita; it is that simple.

The implications of this simple arithmetic are more complex, however. Another baby means there is less of everything to go around—for the time being. But the squeezes in schooling, feeding, and housing may bring forth additional efforts on the part of individuals and institutions to mitigate the squeezes. Also very important in assessing the impact of an additional child is the issue of who assumes which part of the burden—the parents or the public.

But the story of dependency burdens does not end here. A modern low-mortality society, with a low birthrate, supports few children. But each person in the labor force also has a great many old people to support. For example, in 1900 in the U.S., 4.1 percent of the population was over sixty-five. But extrapolations suggest that 11.7 percent of the population will be over sixty-five in 2000, and 16.1 percent in the year 2050.[21]

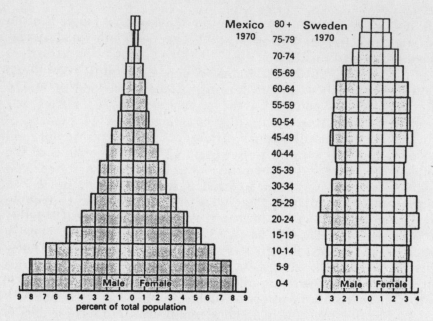

FIGURE 12   AGE DISTRIBUTIONS IN MEXICO
AND SWEDEN

The cost of supporting a retired person is much greater than the cost of suporting a child in the U.S. Least important in a society such as ours is the difference in food consumption. Consider: Old people may travel for twelve months a year in trailers on public roads, whereas children cannot. And old people need much more expensive health care than do children. Except for schooling, old people consume much more than do children in almost every category of expensive goods and services.

This pattern of old-age dependency is already causing perturbations in the U.S. Social Security program. In the future, the burden of Social Security payments will take up a much larger proportion of a U.S. worker's pay, and of the production of the economy as a whole, even without increases in the level of payments. In fact, the Social Security system is already in severe funding trouble as of 1980, and financing the payments is a serious economic and political problem for the federal government.

So we see that a reduction of birthrate means that you, the working person, have fewer people who look to you now for support. But the same reduction means that there will be fewer people to support you when you get older, and you will then be a relatively greater burden on others irrespective of the saving that you do now.

The short-run effect of a given demographic factor is often the opposite of its effect in the long run. Deciding which demographic pattern is better—faster or slower population growth—requires that you put relative values upon the long-run and short-run effects. And this, of course, requires that you decide who is to pay and who is to benefit.

"UNTRAMMELED COPULATION"

The common view of population growth—especially of population growth in poor countries—is that people breed "naturally." That is, poor people are assumed to have sexual intercourse without taking thought or doing anything about the possible consequences.

In the words of environmentalist William Vogt, whose book *Road to Survival* sold millions of copies, population growth in Asia is due to "untrammeled copulation" by Moslems, Sikhs, Hindus, and the rest of "the backward billion."[22] Biologist Karl Sax asserted that "nearly two-thirds of the world's people still rely largely on positive checks [death by starvation and disease] to control excessive growth of populations."[23] Or as Robert C. Cook, the long-time population activist and editor of *Population Bulletin*, put it more politely, "Over a billion adults in less developed countries live outside the realm of decision-making on this matter" of family size.[24] And in the words of a well-known physician in the official *Journal of the American Medical Association*, "If we breed like rabbits, in the long run we have to live and die like rabbits."[25] This idea goes hand in hand with the view that population growth will increase geometrically until starvation or famines halt it, in the ever-ascending curve shown in Figure 1.

This view of "natural breeding," "natural fertility," and "untrammeled copulation" has been buttressed by the animal-ecology experiments that some biologists offer as analogies to human population growth. Their models include John B. Calhoun's famous Norwegian rats in a pen,[26] hypothetical flies in a bottle or germs in a bucket,[27] and meadow mice or cotton rats,[28] which will indeed keep multiplying until they die for lack of sustenance. Daniel O. Price, in *The 99th Hour*, gives a typical example of this view.

Assume there are two germs in the bottom of a bucket, and they double in number every hour. (If the reader does not wish to assume that it takes two germs to reproduce, he may start with one germ, one hour earlier.) If it takes one-hundred hours for the bucket to be full of germs, at what point is the bucket one-half full of germs? A moment's thought will show that after ninety-nine hours the bucket is only half full. The title of this volume is not intended to imply that the United States is half full of people but to emphasize that it is possible to have "plenty of space left" and still be precariously near the upper limit.[29]

It is interesting that a similar analogy was suggested by Benjamin Franklin two centuries ago. In Malthus's words,

It is observed by Franklin: that there is no bound to the prolific nature of plants or animals, but what is made by their crowding and interfering with each others' means of substinence. . . . This is incontrovertibly true. . . . In plants and animals the view of the subject is simple. They are all impelled by a powerful instinct to the increase of their species; and this instinct is interrupted by no reasoning or doubts about providing for their offspring . . . the superabundant effects are repressed afterwards by want of room and nourishment . . . and among animals, by their becoming the prey of each other.[30]

Perhaps the ugliest of the biological analogies was dreamed up by Alan Gregg, the emeritus director of the Rockefeller Foundation's Medical Division: "There is an alarming parallel between the growth of a cancer in the body of an organism and the growth of human population in the earth's ecological economy."[31] Gregg then asserts that "cancerous growths demand food; but so far as I know, they have never been cured by getting it. . . . The analogies can be found in our plundered planet." And the policy implications of this analogy are quite clear. Gregg then goes on, in his paper invited by the most eminent scientific journal in the U.S., to observe "how nearly the slums of our great cities resemble the necrosis of tumors." And this "raises the whimsical query: Which is the more offensive to decency and beauty, slums or the fetid detritus of a growing tumor?"[32]

One set of demographic facts seems to confirm the view that humans will have as many children as conditions permit: After food supplies and living conditions began to improve in European countries several centuries ago, the birthrate rose. And the same effect has been observed in the poor countries in the twentieth century: "While the data are not so good as to give decisive evidence, it seems very likely that natality has risen over the past generation—certainly in the West Indies, very likely in tropical America, and probably in a number of countries of Africa and Asia."[33]

But we must recognize what Malthus came to recognize. After he published the short simplistic theory in the first edition of his *Essay on Population* and after he had the time and inclination to consider the facts as well as the theory, he concluded that human beings are very different from flies or rats. When faced with the limits of a bottlelike situation, people can alter their behavior so as to accommodate to that limit. Unlike plants and animals, people are capable of foresight and may abstain from having children from "fear of misery." That is, people can choose a level of fertility that fits the resources that will be available. And people can alter the limit—expand the "bottle"—by consciously increasing the resources available. As Malthus put it, "Impelled to the increase of his species by an equally powerful instinct, reason interrupts his career, and asks him whether he may not bring beings into the world, for whom he cannot provide the means of support."[34]

Malthus came to stress the difference between the breeding of animals and of humans, and he decisively rejected Benjamin Franklin's animal analogy: "The effects of this [preventive] check on man are more complicated. . . . The preventive check is peculiar to man, and arises from that distinctive superiority in his reasoning faculties, which enables him to calculate consequences."[35] Human beings are different from the animals in that we have much more capacity to alter our behavior—including our fertility—to meet the demands of our environment.

If people are to control their fertility in response to the conditions facing them, they must be capable of rational, self-conscious forethought that affects the course of sexual passion—the kind of planning capability that animals apparently do not possess. Therefore we must briefly ponder the extent to which reason and reasoning have guided the reproductive behavior of individual persons in various societies at different periods in their histories. To put the matter bluntly, we must inquire into the notion—often held by the well-educated—that uneducated people in poor countries tend to breed without foresight or conscious control.

For most couples in most parts of the world, marriage precedes childbearing. It is therefore relevant to a judgment about the amount of reasoning involved in "breeding" that marriages are contracted, in most "primitive" and poor societies, only after a great deal of careful thought, especially with reference to the economic effects of the marriage. How a marriage match is made in rural Ireland shows the importance of such calculations.

> The young lady's father asks the speaker what fortune do he want. He asks him the place of how many cows, sheep, and horses is it? He asks what makings of a garden are in it; is there plenty of water or spring wells? Is it far from the road, he won't take it. Backward places don't grow big fortunes. And he asks, too, is it near a chapel and the school or near town?"
>
> The Inagh countryman could pause here; he had summarized a very long and important negotiation.
>
> "Well," he went on, getting to the heart of the matter, "if it is a nice place, near the road, and the place of eight cows, they are sure to ask 350 fortune [pounds dowry]. Then the young lady's father offers 250. Then maybe the boy's father throws off 50. If the young lad's father still has 250 on it, the speaker divides the 50 between them. So now it's 275. Then the young man says he is not wiling to marry without 300—but if she's a nice girl and a good housekeeper, he'll think of it. So there's another drink by the young man, and then another by the young lady's father, and so on with every second drink till they're near drunk. The speaker gets plenty and has a good day."[36]

An astute weighing of economic conditions is also seen to affect marriage in a Southern Italian town that was "as poor as any place in the western world."[37] The young man whose account is given lived in a family of four whose totally yearly cash and computed income amounted to $482 in 1955, not much higher than the income of a peasant family in India. Edward Banfield describes the courtship and marriage decision.

> In 1935 I was old enough to marry. My sisters wanted me to take a wife because they had no time to do services for me.
>
> At that time there was a law that anyone who was 25 years old and not married had to pay a "celibacy" tax of 125 lire. That amount was much, if we recall that to earn it you had to work 25 days. I thought it over and finally decided to marry.
>
> My present wife was at that time working with relatives of my employer. Once I stopped her and asked her to

marry me, and she liked the idea too, but I had to tell it before her father. He was happy to accept me, and we talked about what she had to bring as dowry and what I had to do.

He asked me to bring my mother to call so that everything would be fine. The next time I brought my mother, and we had a nice feast. When I wanted to meet my fiancee I had to ask the boss' permission.

In 1937 I asked the girl and her family to hasten the marriage before I was 25 years old. The father told me that she was not ready with the dowry. I asked him if at least we couldn't have the civil ceremony on February 6, 1938, two months late, so that I had to pay the tax for that year.

Once my mother and I went to Addo to visit my father-in-law in order to discuss and establish definitely what they were going to give us [in the dowry]. My mother wanted everything to be conveyed through a notary. My father-in-law gave us one tomolo of land and my mother gave the little house, but she reserved for herself the right to use it. Everything was written on official taxstamp paper by the notary. As soon as my wife was ready with the dowry the church marriage was set for August 25, 1938.[38]

As to reason and self-control *after* marriage, even among the most "primitive" and "backward" of people, fertility is subject to both personal and social constraints. One example is the "primitive" (as of 1936) Polynesian island of Tikopia, where "strong social conventions enforce celibacy upon some people and cause others to limit the number of their offspring,"[39] and "the motive of a married pair is the avoidance of the extra economic liability which a child brings."[40] Another example is the effect of harvests on marriages in Sweden in the eighteenth century (a backward agricultural country then, but one that happened to keep good vital statistics). When the harvest was poor, people did not marry, as Figure 13 shows. Birthrates were also responsive to the harvest, and even unmarried procreation was affected by objective economic conditions. This is clear evidence that poor people's sexual behavior is sensibly responsive to objective circumstances.

After an extensive study of the antropological literature, A. M. Carr-Saunders concluded, "The mechanism whereby numbers may be kept near to the desirable level is everywhere present,"[41] the particular mechanisms being "prolonged abstention from intercourse, abortion, and infanticide."[42] And as a result of a study of "data on 200 societies from all over the world . . . from tropic to arctic . . . from sea level to altitudes of more than 10,000 feet," Clellan S. Ford concluded that "both abortion and infanticide are universally known. . . . It is extremely common . . . to find a taboo on sexual intercourse during the period when the mother is nursing. . . . In nearly every instance, the justification for this abstinence is the prevention of conception."[43] He also found instances of many kinds of contraceptive practices. Some are "clearly magical." Others "are relatively effective mechanical devices [for example] inserting a pad of bark cloth or a rag in the vagina . . . [and] attempts to flush out the seminal fluid with water after intercourse. . . ."[44]

Physical evidence to confirm the anthropologists' findings that customs and norms inhibit fertility comes from actual birth statistics. In virtually no observed society (except, paradoxically, the very modern Hutterites in the U.S. and Canada, and a few other such groups) does actual fertility approach women's fecundity (potential fertility). And in many "primitive" societies, fertility is quite low.[45]

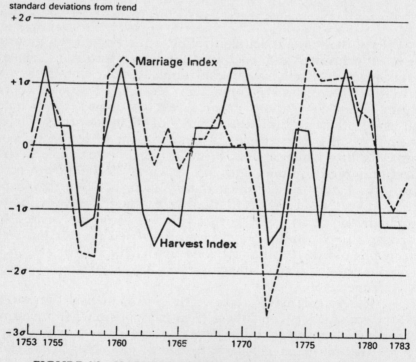

FIGURE 13   HARVEST INDEX AND MARRIAGE RATES
IN SWEDEN

Compare the facts with the vulgar error made by writers on this subject who have done no research or who use discredited anthropological accounts. Some say that poor people do not know how babies are made. For example, "not only are animals ignorant of the relation between mating and offspring, but even modern man until the last few thousand years was probably equally ignorant. In fact, there were recent reports of primitive tribes in Australia who are similarly unenlightened today."[46] More to be believed are such stories as the one about a "primitive" tribesman who said to a second: "Do you know what I told that white man? I told him I don't know how to make a baby. And—get this—he believed it!"

Clear evidence that poor people consider their incomes and economic circumstances when thinking about having children is found in their answers to questions about the disadvantages and advantages of large families. A variety of such surveys in various parts of Africa reveal that economic motivations are indeed important.

I could go on citing study after study. The central point is that poor peoples do indeed think about economic circumstances in relationship to fertility. They do not practice "untrammeled copulation" or "breed without limit."

People in developed countries also are accustomed to think about how family size fits their incomes.

GRENOBLE, France—a 29-year-old grade school teacher gave birth yesterday to quintuplets, three boys and two girls. . . . The children's grandfather, a tailor, said, "This certainly creates a lot of problems and you can't say it's really a joyous event because you've got to think about raising the little wolves."[47]

Lee Rainwater interviewed four hundred and nine Americans about "their family design." In representative interviews with three pairs of husbands and wives, all mentioned economic factors predominantly, though many other factors were also mentioned, of course.

Husband 1: Would [I] prefer two or four children? I guess two because you can give two more than four. You can send them to college. The average family could not give four very much. . . . Two is all we can support adequately.
Wife 1: Two, but if I had loads of money I would want loads of kids. . . . If I had lots of money, enough for

fulltime help, and plenty of room I would like half-a-dozen or more.

Husband 2: I think two is ideal for the average American family based on an average income of $5,000 [1950 dollars]. I don't see how they could properly provide for more children. Personally I'd take a dozen if I could afford them. I wanted four when we got married, or as many as the family income could support.

Wife 3: I think three is ideal because I feel this is all most people are equipped to raise, to give a good education and send them through college.[48]

And in another study, a sample of U.S. wives was asked why their intended family size was not bigger. The first reason given by more than half was economic.[49]

In brief, even though income in rich countries is ample to provide a bare subsistence for many more children than the average family chooses to have, people say that their incomes constrain their family size. In all societies, rich or poor, people give much thought to sex, marriage, and childbearing. Fertility is everywhere subject to some rational control, though the degree to which achieved family sizes match the desired size varies from group to group. Couples in some countries plan their family size more carefully and are better able to carry such plans to fruition than are couples in other countries because of differences in contraceptive technology, infant mortality, and communication between husband and wife. But certainly there is strong evidence that people everywhere think rationally about fertility; and hence income and other objective forces influence fertility behavior to a significant degree, everywhere and always.

The fact that large families are often found in some poor countries does not prove the absence of rational planning in matters of fertility. Behavior that is reasonable in London or Tokyo may well be unreasonable in a Tibetan or African village. The costs of rearing children are relatively less, and the economic benefits of having children are relatively greater, in poor agricultural communities than in well-off urban places. Therefore, even though the primary motive for having children—in Nigeria as in France—surely is that couples want children for the satisfactions they give, the economic conditions may differ in such a manner that the same desire for children that sensibly implies a two- or three-child family in a city may imply a five- or six-child family in a poor rural area. The economics of child rearing depend upon the amounts of time and money that people spend on children, on the one hand, and the amounts of work that children perform and the old-age support they render after they grow up, on the other hand. It costs more time and money to rear children in urban than in rural areas, and children in rural areas of poor countries perform more work than children elsewhere.[50] Hence the larger average size of rural families reflects sound economic planning. We see this vividly in the following accounts.

> BABARPUR, India, May 24, 1976—Munshi Ram, an illiterate laborer who lives in a crude mud hut in this village 60 miles north of New Delhi, has no land and very little money. But he has eight children, and he regards them as his greatest wealth.
>
> "It's good to have a big family," Mr. Ram explained as he stood in the shade of a leafy neem tree, in a hard dry courtyard crowded with children, chickens and a dozing cow.
>
> "They don't cost much, and when they get old enough to work they bring in money. And when I am old, they will take care of me. . . ."
>
> Mr. Ram, who says he is not likely to have more children, is aware that the Government is now campaigning hard with the birth-control slogan, "Stop at two." But he has no regrets.
>
> "Children are the gods' gift," he said, as several of his own clustered around him. "Who are we to say they should not be born?"[51]

Here are two more examples, this time through the eyes of an Indian writer.

> Let us take a few examples. Fakir Singh is a traditional water carrier. After he lost his job, he remained as a messenger for those Jat families which used to be his Jajmans, barely earning a subsistence living. He has eleven children, ranging in age from twenty-five to four. . . . Fakir Singh maintains that every one of his sons is an asset. The youngest one—aged five or six—collects hay for the cattle; the older ones tend to those same cattle. Between the ages of six and sixteen, they earn 150 to 200 rupees a year, plus all their meals and necessary clothing. Those sons over sixteen earn 2,000 rupees and meals every year. Fakir Singh smiles and adds: "To raise children may be difficult, but once they are older it is a sea of happiness."
>
> Another water carrier is Thaman Singh. . . . He welcomed me inside his home, gave me a cup of tea (with milk and "market" sugar, as he proudly pointed out later), and said: "You were trying to convince me in 1960 that I shouldn't have any more sons. Now, you see, I have six

sons and two daughters and I sit at home in leisure. They are grown up and they bring me money. One even works outside the village as a laborer. You told me I was a poor man and couldn't support a large family. Now, you see, because of my large family, I am a rich man."[52]

Hand in hand with the short-run reduction in fertility when times worsen in a poor country is the short-run increase in fertility that accompanies a betterment of conditions. Consider, for example, this report about an Indian village:

In the early 1950's, conditions were distinctly unfavorable. The large influx of refugees from Pakistan was accompanied by severe disruption of economic and social stability. We were repeatedly told by village leaders on the panchayat, or elected village council, that important as all of their other problems were, "the biggest problem is that there are just too many of us." By the end of the study period in 1960, a remarkable change had occurred. With the introduction of more irrigation canals and with rural electrification from the Bhakra Nangal Dam, and with better roads to transport produce to market, improved seed and other benefits of community development, and especially because there were increasing employment opportunities for Punjabi boys in the cities, a general feeling of optimism had developed. A common response of the same village leaders now was, "Why should we limit our families? India needs all the Punjabis she can get." During this transitional period an important reason for the failure of education in family planning was the favorable pace of economic development. Children were no longer a handicap.[53]

Infant mortality is another influence that uneducated villagers take into account in a very rational fashion. I asked a few men in Indian villages why they have as many or as few children as they do. A common answer came from a man with five children: "Two, maybe three, will die, and I want to have at least two that live to become adults."

Malthus's theory of population asserts that, because fertility goes up as income goes up, the extra population eats up the extra income—that is, there is a tendency for mankind to be squeezed down to a long-run equilibrium of living at bare subsistence. This is Malthus's "dismal theorem." But when we examine the facts about fertility and economic development (as Malthus himself finally did, after he dashed off his first edition) we find that the story does not end with the short-run increase in the birthrate as income begins to rise. If income continues to rise, fertility goes down.

There are two main reasons for this long-run decline in fertility. First, as income rises in poor countries, child mortality falls because of better nutrition, better sanitation, and better health care (though, in the twentieth century, mortality may decline in poor countries even without a rise in income.) As people see that fewer births are necessary to achieve a given family size, they adjust fertility downward. Evidence on the way individual families respond to the death of a child buttresses the overall historical data; several careful researchers have shown that there is a strong relationship between the death of a child and subsequent births in a family.[54] That is, couples produce additional children to "make up for" children who die. If we also consider that families decide to have additional children to allow for deaths that might occur in the future, the relationship between child mortality and fertility shows that childbearing is responsive to the family's circumstances.

The second way a rise in income reduces fertility in the long run is through a cluster of forces set in motion by increased income, including (a) increased education, which improves contraception, makes children more expensive to raise, and perhaps alters people's tastes about having children; and (b) a trend to city living, where children cost more and produce less income for the family than they do in the country.

The decline in mortality and the other forces set in motion by economic development reduce fertility in the long run. This process is the famous "demographic transition." We see it very clearly in the excellent historical data for Sweden shown in Figure 8; notice how the death rate began to fall *before* the birthrate fell. And we can see the same relationship between income and birthrate in a cross-sectional look at various countries of the world (Figure 14).

A few decades ago demographers were sure that the demographic transition would take place in developing countries in the twentieth century, just as it had earlier happened in Europe, North America, Japan, and elsewhere. But in the 1960s demographers began to worry that fertility would not fall in poor countries even after mortality fell. Then, in the 1970s, evidence showed that fertility is indeed falling in at least some developing countries. So by now we can be reasonably sure that the European pattern of demographic transition will also appear in other parts of the world as mortality falls and income rises.

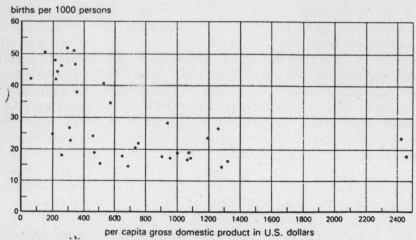

FIGURE 14   PER CAPITA GROSS DOMESTIC PRODUCT
PLOTTED AGAINST THE CRUDE BIRTHRATE FOR
SELECTED NATIONS

So the props are knocked right out from under Malthus's grand theory and his dismal theorem. At the heart of Malthus's theory—I am quoting from his last edition—is the following: "(1) Population is necessarily limited by the means of subsistence. (2) Population always increases when the means of subsistence increases."[55] The history of the demographic transition disproves the second proposition. We have seen that people respond to the two major influences on fertility—mortality and level of income—in an economically appropriate fashion. Of course, there are delays, especially in the response of society as a whole to changes in the cost to other people of a family's children. But overall, the fertility adjustment system works in such a fashion that it leads to an optimistic review rather than the "dismal" view described by Malthus in the famous first edition of his book, before he changed his view in the second edition.[56]

How many children would families have if material resources presented no constraints at all? That is, what would fertility be if child mortality were extremely low—at, say, the Swedish level—and if income were very high—say, ten times the level in the U.S. now? We have little basis for predicting whether population would tend to increase, decrease, or stabilize. It is clear, however, that where the material conditions of income and child mortality are rigorous, fertility adjusts to meet those conditions, even among poor and uneducated people.

But what about the costs that big families impose on society as a whole? Certainly this is a reasonable and important question, because any child does impose some monetary and nonmonetary costs on persons other than the parents. But we must also remember that a child produces some benefits for the people around her or him, in a variety of ways. In preview, the central question may be expressed quantitatively: Which are greater in various years following a child's birth, the costs or the benefits to others? Once we know whether these "external" effects are positive or negative in any given year, we must next ask, Are the external effects large or small compared with other costs and benefits in the social economy?

SUMMARY

At the heart of much of contemporary theorizing about population growth is the belief that, as one widely read author put it, "The Malthusian laws of population are as valid today as when they were formulated"[57] (in the first edition of his *Essay*). The core of those "laws" is that population increases faster than does the means of sustenance and continues until the standard of living has fallen to bare subsistence. This assertion is supported by analogies drawn between other forms of life and humankind. "The germs of existence contained in this earth, if they could freely develop themselves, would fill millions of worlds in the course of a few thousand years. Necessity, that imperious, all-pervading law of nature, restrains them within the prescribed bounds. The race of plants and the race of animals shrink under this great restrictive law; and man cannot by any efforts of reason escape from it."[58]

Implicit in this statement, and quite explicit in Malthus's first edition and in the writings of many writers today, is the assumption that people—or at least poor people—breed "naturally" and "without limit," due to "untrammeled copulation." But as Malthus came to accept in his subsequent editions, and as is shown with a variety of evidence in this chapter, people everywhere give much thought to marriage, sex, and procreation. The notion of "untrammeled copulation" represents either ignorance or arrogant untruth.

Income affects fertility everywhere. In poor countries, an increase in income leads in the short run to an increase in fertility. But in the longer run, in poor countries as elsewhere, a sustained increase in income leads eventually to a decrease in fertility. Decreased child mortality, increased education, and movement from country to city all contribute to this lowering of the birthrate. This process is known as the "demographic transition." Malthus's early—but still popularly accepted—theorizing does not fit the facts.

NOTES

1. George S. Fichter, *The Golden Stamp Book of Earth and Ecology* (Racine 1972), pp. 24, 25.
2. Harrison Brown, *Challenge of Man's Future* (New York 1954), p. 221, quoted in Harold J. Barnett and Chandler Morse, *Scarcity and Growth: The Economics of Natural Resources Availability* (Baltimore 1963), p. 30.
3. Genesis 13:6-9.
4. Quoted by C. L. Sulzberger, *New York Times*, December 18, 1977, p. iv-19.
5. Joseph J. Spengler, "Population Phenomena and Population Theory," in Julian L. Simon, *Research in Population Economics* (Greenwich, Conn. 1972), Vol. 1.
6. Gunnar Mydral, *Asian Drama: An Inquiry into the Poverty of Nations* (New York 1968), p. 974.
7. Annabelle Desmond, "How Many People Have Ever Lived on Earth?" *Population Bulletin* 18:1-19. Reprinted in Kenneth C. W. Kammeyer (ed.), *Population Studies*, 2nd ed. (Chicago: Rand McNally, 1975).
8. Edward S. Deevey, "The Human Population," *Scientific American* 203: 195-204, in Paul R. Ehrlich, John P. Holdren, and Richard W. Holm, eds., *Man and the Ecosphere* (San Francisco 1971), p. 49.
9. Sherburne F. Cook and Woodrow Borah, *Essays in Population History: Mexico and the Caribbean* (Berkeley 1971), p. 199.
10. *Recent Social Trends in the United States*, Vol. 1, *Report of the President's Research Committee on Social Trends*, 1933, p. xx., quoted in Daniel O. Price, *The 99th Hour* (Chapel Hill, N.C. 1967), p. 12.
11. U.S. Dept. of State, 1969, p. 2.
12. *Time*, April 1, 1974, p. 40.
13. Lester Brown, Patricia L. McGrath, and Bruce Stoker, *Twenty-two Dimensions of the Population Problem* (Washington, D.C. 1976), p. 3.
14. *New York Times*, July 28, 1978.
15. Elliot R. Morss and Ritchie H. Reed, eds., *Economic Aspects of Population Change* (Washington, D.C., 1972), p. 4, as quoted by Larry Neal, *Illinois Business Review*, March 1978, Vol. 35, No. 2.
16. David Wolfers, "The Case Against Zero Growth," *International Journal of Population Studies* Vol. 1, p. 227.
17. Gompertz curve extrapolation, in personal communication.
18. Harold F. Dorn, "World Population Growth," in Philip M. Hauser, ed., *The Population Dilemma* (Englewood Cliffs, N.J. 1963), p. 24.
19. UN, Dept. of Economic and Social Affairs, 1956, p. 15.
20. 1975 data, courtesy of Paul Handler and PLATO, University of Illinois.
21. *New York Times*, February, 1977, p. 1.
22. William Vogt, *Road to Survival* (New York 1948), p. 228.
23. Karl Sax, *Standing Room Only: The World's Exploding Population* (Boston 1960), p. 23.

24. Quoted by Howard Rusk in *New York Times*, August 4, 1968, p. 71.
25. A. J. Carlson, "Science Versus Life," *JAMA* 147:1440, quoted by Barnett and Morse, 1963, p. 31.
26. John B. Calhoun, "Population Density and Social Pathology," *Scientific American* 206, pp. 32ff.
27. Price, 1967, p. 4.
28. David V. van Vleck, "A Biologist Urges Stabilizing U.S. Population Growth," *University: A Princeton Quarterly* (Spring 1970), pp. 16-18.
29. Price, 1967, p. 4.
30. Thomas R. Malthus, *An Essay on the Principle of Population, or a View of Its Past and Present Effects on Human Happiness* (London 1803), 2nd ed., p. 203.
31. Alan Gregg, "Hidden Hunger at the Summit," *Population Bulletin*, Vol. 11, no. 5, quoted by Barnett and Morse, 1963, p. 31.
32. Alan Gregg, "A Medical Aspect of the Population Problem," *Science*, 1955:121, p. 682.
33. Dudley Kirk, "Natality in the Developing Countries: Recent Trends and Prospects," in S. J. Behrman, Leslie Corsa, and Robert Freedman, eds., *Fertility and Family Planning: A World View* (Ann Arbor, Mich. 1969), p. 79.
34. Malthus, 2nd ed., 1803, p. 3.
35. *Ibid.*, pp. 3, 9.
36. Conrad M. Arensberg, *The Irish Countryman* (New York 1968), 2nd ed., pp. 107-108.
37. Edward Banfield, *The Moral Basis of a Backward Society* (Chicago 1958), p. 45.
38. *Ibid.*, pp. 111-12.
39. Raymond W. Firth, *We, the Tikopia* (London 1936), pp. 36-37.
40. Raymond W. Firth, *Primative Polynesian Economy* (London 1939/1965), p. 491.
41. A. M. Carr-Saunders, *The Population Problem: A Study in Human Evolution* (Oxford 1922), p. 230.
42. *Ibid.*, p. 124.
43. Clellan S. Ford, "Control of Conception in Cross-Cultural Perspective," *World Population Problems and Birth Control. Annals of the New York Academy of Sciences* (New York 1952), pp. 765-766.
44. *Ibid.*, pp. 765-66.
45. Ludwik Krzywicki, *Primative Society and Its Vital Statistics* (London 1934), p. 216; Meni Nag, *Factors Affecting Fertility in Non-industrial Societies: A Cross-Cultural Study* (New Haven 1962), p. 142.
46. Alexander Stuart, *Overpopulation: Twentieth Century Nemesis* (New York 1958), p. 99.
47. *Champaign-Urbana Courier*, January 20, 1971, p. 1.
48. Lee Rainwater, *Family Design: Marital Sexuality, Family Size, and Contraception* (Chicago 1965), pp. 162-73.
49. P. K. Whelpton, A. Campbell Arthur, and J. E. Patterson, *Fertility and Family Planning in the United States* (Princeton 1966), p. 55.
50. Robert G. Repetto, "Direct Economic Costs and the Value of Children," in Ronald Ridker, *Population Resources, and the Environment*, The Commission on Population Growth and the American Future (Washington, D.C. 1976), Vol. 3; Eva Mueller, "The Economic Value of Children in Peasant Agriculture," in Ridker.
51. William Borders, "Indian Sees Benefits in His 8 Children," *New York Times*, May 30, 1976, p. 18.

52. Mahmood Mamdani, *The Myth of Population Control (Family, Caste, and Class in an Indian Village* (New York and London 1973, p. 109.
53. Carl E. Taylor, "Health and Population," *Foreign Affairs* (1965), 43, pp. 482-483.
54. Yoram Ben-Porath, "Fertility Response to Child Mortality: Microdata from Israel," *Journal of Political Economy* (1976), 84; Paul T. Schultz, "Interrelationships Between Mortality and Fertility," in Ridker; John Knodel, and Etienne Van De Walle, "Breast Feeding, Fertility, and Infant Mortality: An Analysis of Some Early German Data," *Population Studies* (1967), 21.
55. Malthus, 5th ed., 1817/1963, p. 12.
56. For me, one of the great mysteries of the intellectual world is the continued republication of Malthus's first edition—even by scholars of the first rank whose intellectual honesty is beyond question, such as Kenneth Boulding, who wrote an introduction to a republication of the first edition—though Malthus essentially repudiated his simple first-edition theorizing in later editions.
57. Sax, 1960, p. 13.
58. Malthus, quoted *ibid.*

PART FIVE: LIBERATING THE CHURCH FROM MARXISM

THIRTEEN

A Critique of Christian Marxism

DALE VREE

Aserious dialogue between Marxists and Christians has been going on in Europe for almost twenty years. This dialogue, which has frequently led to theoretical attempts to synthesize Marxism and Christianity, has certainly been intellectually innovative and stimulating. Collaborative political action between Marxists and Christians has been an important factor in the politics of Italy, France, Spain, Czechoslovakia, and Yugoslavia; but in terms of depth of commitment and readiness to resort to violence, such action has not yet been matched by what can be found in Latin America. There, important segments of the Catholic priesthood and hierarchy have been dramatically radicalized. It is not unusual to see bishops issue statements generally critical of the domestic and inter-American status quo and supportive of socialist and nationalist alternatives. Nor is it unusual to see priests—such as the late, "martyred" Camilo Torres—throw off their cassocks, pick up rifles, and run off with a band of guerrilla warriors. But in terms of political theory, the Latin Americans have been well behind the Europeans and North Americans who, having felt less urgency to act, have enjoyed more time for scholarship and reflection.

A Theology of Liberation[1], by the Peruvian theologian and

DALE VREE is the Executive Editor of the New Oxford Review. He received his B.A., M.A., and Ph.D. degrees in political science from the University of California at Berkeley. He is the author of the book On Synthesizing Marxism and Christianity. His articles have appeared in many journals, including The New Leader, American Political Science Review, National Review, and The Reformed Journal. In addition to teaching political science at Earlham College and Christian social ethics at the Anglican Theological College in Berkeley, he has been a Rockefeller Fellow at the University of California at Berkeley and an NEH Fellow at the Hoover Institute at Stanford Univerity. The essay which follows was originally printed in Liberation Theology, edited by Ronald Nash (Mott Media, 1984).

activist Gustavo Gutierrez, is an important attempt to begin to redress the imbalance in theoretical output. Although the thought of Gutierrez is not as original or complex as that of European dialogue-makers such as Jürgen Moltmann, Ernst Bloch, Johannes Metz, Roger Garaudy, and others, his book is generally recognized as a unique intellectual breakthrough; indeed, as perhaps the most sophisticated voice of Marxist-Christian dialogue in Latin America to date. Contrary to most books of this genre, its significance seems to grow with each passing year. Gutierrez has emerged as the intellectual spokesman for a new worldwide current in Christian social ethics known as "liberation theology." In the United States, liberation theology has served as the idiom for Christians anxious to promote their favorite liberation movements—particularly black and women's liberation.

More recently, liberation consciousness has been expanding to encompass the entire third world. In 1975, the Latin American Secretariat of the U.S. Catholic Conference and the Latin American Working Group of the National Council of Churches sponsored a week-long conference on liberation theology in Detroit—the significance of which was noted in *Time* magazine[2] with a full-page story. An appearance by Gustavo Gutierrez was the main attraction of the conference. Beyond the United States, the World Council of Churches—much like the United Nations—effectively functions as a forum for third world causes and interests. The World Council has already committed its prestige and its money to the liberation movements directed against the white governments of southern Africa. Indeed, the "pervasive philosophy" of the World Council has become a " 'solidarity with the oppressed' liberation theology which recognizes no challengers."[3] Israel is not much more popular with the Council than South Africa, and one wonders when Israel too will feel the lash of the Council. Because of the popularity of liberation theology in World Council circles, it would be well to have a closer look at Gutierrez's *A Theology of Liberation*, the basic guidebook of liberation theology.

Although Gutierrez borrows frequently from European thinkers, his politico-theological thought is unparalleled by Europeans because he is responding to the Latin American experience. Gutierrez is not primarily reacting to other people's ideas, but rather to his own existential condition as an inhabitant of the third world. This difference between the third world and the developed world is not only geographical: it is also psychological. For the theologian, the situation of the developed world is as Dietrich Bonhoeffer described it: the *mündige Welt* (the world come of age) where technologically competent people no longer feel a need for God. In Latin

America, on the other hand, the theologian must respond to quite another situation, a situation where people feel incompetent and helpless, and where suffering is a way of life with no end in sight. Here people *do* feel a need for God, but are at pains to understand how a loving God could have created such an unlovely world.

Inasmuch as the church is now widely regarded as the most "progressive" institution in Latin America, and insofar as much of Latin America is in a potentially revolutionary situation, we must have further reason to examine Gutierrez's *magnum opus* with some care. It is easy enough to applaud Gutierrez's book as a reflection of the Latin Catholic Church's turning from corruption and concubinage, and toward commitment and change. Be that as it may, "progressive" Latin American Catholic thought (or liberation theology, as it is now called) need no longer be patronized in that way. Liberation theology is ready to stand on its own feet, to stand up to normal intellectual scrutiny.

ESCHATOLOGY AND MARXISM

A central motif in the international Marxist-Christian dialogue is eschatology, or the doctrine of last things. The theological locution most often associated with eschatology is the "Kingdom of God." Christians have traditionally equated the fullness of the kingdom of God with the experience of heaven after death. The kingdom has also been thought to be embryonically present in the heart of the believer as a kind of foretaste of heaven. But rarely has the kingdom been thought to have any bearing on political matters. However, those Christians who have engaged in dialogue with Marxists have tried to expand the notion of the kingdom into the hope for an earthly millennial society built—in part at least—by human political action. If this notion of the kingdom is accepted, and if the full blown communism of which Marxists-Leninists speak can be understood as a secular version of millennialism, then it is obvious that Christians and Marxists have much in common and every reason to engage in dialogue.

Making eschatology a central motif allows for a much more interesting dialogue than if, say, ethics is made a central motif. A generation ago, such "First World" Christians as Hewlett Johnson (the "Red" Dean of Canterbury) and Harry F. Ward of Union Theological Seminary tended to focus on the ethics of Jesus as the basis for cooperation with Marxists (in particular, with Stalinists). The problem with that approach is twofold: First, Christianity has clearly been more than an ethical system; it has been a *theological* system which presumes to talk of God, the mystery of the kingdom, the meaning of history, and the life of the world to come. To stress ethics is to seem to be too rationalistic and too neglectful of the mystical dimensions of the faith. It is to reduce the kingdom to an ethical metaphor. Those Christians who get themselves fixated on ethics are too easily suspected of being nothing but ethical humanists—eccentric ones, to be sure. Second, Marxist-Leninists are not really interested in ethics. They are interested in the laws of history and the economy, of which ethics is only an epiphenomenon. A concern with ethics is the hallmark of utopian, not scientific, socialism. Hence, it is very difficult to achieve a sustained intellectual interchange between Christians and Marxists when attention is limited to ethics.

Because of their eschatological focus, present-day Christian dialogue-makers are in a better situation. Yes, they do talk about ethics. But they are really interested in the *dynamics* of historical, economic, and political change—just as the Marxists are. Furthermore, they do not *seem* to be ethical humanists because they are very anxious to talk about God, salvation, providence, prophecy, the Kingdom, etc.—almost all of the paraphernalia of traditional Christianity—in the same breath with which they talk of the dynamics of change. Finally, by going beyond ethics they are better able to sidestep embarrassing questions about the alleged pacificism of Jesus.

This brings us directly to Gustavo Gutierrez and his *Theology of Liberation*. Without doubt, Gutierrez is interested in salvation, and his interest in political liberation for Latin America (namely, "liberation" from American hegemony and domestic capitalism) is an integral part of his interest in salvation; indeed, liberation is part of a single salvational process. This is where matters get intriguing—and sticky. Since the Second Vatican Council, the Catholic Church has been willing to say that political action (or "liberation") has something to do with the kingdom of God, although it has refused to specify exactly what the relationship is, and has insisted that political goals cannot be identified or equated with the kingdom.

Were one to say that the kingdom is political liberation and that liberation is the product of human action, one would all too easily fall into the classical *Pelagian* heresy—that is, one would be saying that man is saved by good works, not grace. To say that is to deny the salvational significance of Christ's atoning sacrifice on the cross and his second coming. It is to deny that God in Christ is the source of salvation. Without Christ, there is no authentic Christianity. Hence, it is impossible for a *Christian* to equate liberation with salvation.

But Gutierrez is unhappy with the recent Catholic position that political action has some (unspecified) relation to the kingdom. Says he: "It is not enough to say that Christians should not 'shirk' their earthly responsibilities or that these have a 'certain relationship' to salvation."[4]

Although Gutierrez wants to relate eschatology to politics by uniting liberation and salvation into a single process, he also wants to keep liberation and salvation separate—for fear of sliding into Pelagianism. Traditionally, both Catholics and Protestants have said that salvation—or the kingdom—is an act, a gift, of God. After all, God saves man, man does not save himself: "For by grace are ye saved through faith, and that not of yourselves, it is the gift of God, not of works, lest any man should boast" (Ephesians 2:8, 9). According to official Catholic theology, the kingdom "will be the effect solely of divine intervention."[5] The problem for any *theology* of liberation is to talk of salvation as a gift without inducing passivity and indifference to politics—which is frequently what happens. So Gutierrez's problem is twofold: How can man's political liberation be seen to be a part of a salvational process which finds fulfillment in God's kingdom—without opening the door to Pelagianism? And how can one talk like a Christian out of one side of one's mouth, and like a Pelagian out of the other, without choking on the law of noncontradiction?

Let us hear what Gutierrez has to say: He sees man "assuming *conscious responsibility* for his own destiny." The result will be "the creation of a new man and a qualitatively different society."[6] And yet Gutierrez also says that, "The Bible presents liberation—salvation—in Christ as a *total gift* . . . "[7]

But how can the integral salvational process be a product of both men's "conscious responsibility" as well as a "total gift" from Christ? Is liberation-cum-salvation something humans must go out and earn for themselves or not? If so, then it cannot be a "total gift." If not, then it is something humans are not fully responsible for. Gutierrez does not seem to know whether he wants to be a Christian, a Pelagian, or both. If it is possible to grant that Gutierrez avoids complete capitulation to Pelagianism, it is not possible to grant that he escapes logical contradiction.

But perhaps what Gutierrez wants to say is that man must initiate his liberation while God will have to finish it by turning liberation into salvation. This is the most generous interpretation I can come up with. Says Gutierrez: "*Without liberating historical events, there would be no growth of the kingdom.* But the process of liberation will not have conquered the very roots of oppression and the exploitation of man by man without the coming kingdom, which is above all a gift."[8] Gutierrez is trying to protect man's autonomy and free creativity as well as God's sovereignty. But Gutierrez actually succeeds both in truncating man's autonomy (because man cannot finish what man has started) and compromising God's omnipotence (because God cannot start what God alone can finish). For Gutierrez, salvation is obviously *contingent* on man's *prior* action. Gutierrez *wants* to affirm that the coming kingdom is above all a gift, but one must conclude from what he has said that the coming kingdom (which he described as the "complete encounter with the Lord" which will "mark an end to history")[9] is first and foremost a product of human action. Enter Pelagius! Enter Thomas Müntzer and a whole host of heretical chiliasts whom Friedrich Engels correctly identified as forerunners of Marxism.

MARXISTS DOING GOD'S WORK?

At the root of Gutierrez's tortuous theologizing is his attempt to blend Marxism with Christianity. By making political liberation a necessary part of the salvational process, Gutierrez is able to bring Marxism into the drama of Christian salvation. As a result, it is obvious that Marxists are *really* doing God's work. Furthermore, by liberating man, Marxists are *quite literally* freeing God's hands so he can usher in the kingdom. Hence, Marxists are really Christians incognito.

Gutierrez says he believes in salvation for everyone—believers and nonbelievers alike. There is no doubt in Gutierrez's mind that God will grant salvation to Marxists, but curiously, there seems to be some doubt that all Christians will be saved. Lest one think Gutierrez to be a modern ethical humanist, he reminds us that he *does* believe in divine judgment: "we will be definitively judged by our love for men, by our capacity to create brotherly conditions of life."[10] And there is no doubt in Gutierrez's mind that many, perhaps most, Christians are not measuring up to that standard. So his best pastoral advice to Christians would be to join with Marxists, who are presumed to be actively creating brotherly conditions of life. This is the safest bet—Gutierrez's version of Pascal's wager! Such counsel sounds bizarre coming from a Catholic priest, but Gutierrez does not seem to be kidding. Liberation is a precondition for salvation, and, as Gutierrez repeatedly makes clear, liberation is another term for revolutionary (not social democratic) socialism. And for revolutionary socialism to be efficacious it must be a "scientific" socialism, Gutierrez tells us. Finally, he leaves no doubt in the reader's mind that he considers Marxian socialism to be scientific (although not necessarily atheistic).

Not only do the Marxists—unknowingly—hold the keys to the kingdom of God, but they are undoubtedly spiritually gifted. Since Marxists are very adept at loving mankind, and since loving mankind is the "only way" to have a "true encounter with God,"[11] and since a "knowledge of God" is actually a "necessary consequence" of loving mankind,[12] one is forced to conclude that Marxists are remarkably religious people. Never mind the fact that Marxists do not seem to be aware of their spiritual gifts; Father Gutierrez is aware of them and that seems to be what counts. The good father is empowered to turn bread and wine into Christ's body and blood. Now he presumes to turn Marxists into Christians.

But sometimes I wonder what all this has to do with helping the poor and the powerless. Priests have been notorious for sprinkling holy water on whatever political organization seemed to be the going concern at the time—or the coming concern (in the case of farsighted priests). Perhaps Marxists should allow themselves to be amused—and tickled—by this sacerdotal sprinkle. Perhaps the water is a good omen for them, signifying that Marxism holds the winning ticket in the race for power in Latin America. (Indeed, Gutierrez says again and again that he bases his thought on a reading of the "signs of the times" in Latin America.)

But Marxists would do well to bear in mind that the good *padre*, despite his frequent genuflections at the altar of scientific socialism, is no scientific socialist himself. He has *his own*—*utopian*—reasons for blessing Marxism. For him, "utopian thought" is the basis of scientific knowledge; indeed, it is the source of political action and a "driving force of history."[13] Marxists will perhaps not be surprised that behind this socialist priest there lurks a visionary dreamer. Neither perhaps will more orthodox Catholics (not to mention Protestants and Jews) be surprised that one who places Marxists at the head of God's elect is nothing but a fanciful utopian.

But let us not forget the prerogatives of priestcraft. In the old pre-Vatican Council days, priests used to stand at the altar with their backs to the people mumbling Latin words through a cloud of incense faster than the speed of sound. "Mumbo jumbo," the irreverent were wont to call it. Now the priests stand in back of the altar, face the people, and—with the help of microphones—clearly enunciate the words of the Mass in the vernacular of the people. No more mumbo jumbo. That they save for their books on politics—where Marxists are transformed into Christians by transforming Christians into Marxists.

NOTES

1. Maryknoll, N.Y.: Orbis Books, 1973.
2. Sept. 1, 1975.
3. Elliot Wright, "The Good Ship *Oikoumene*," *Worldview*, November 1975, p. 18.
4. Gutierrez, *op. cit.*, p. 46.
5. M. J. Cantley, "Kingdom of God," *New Catholic Encyclopedia* (New York: McGraw-Hill, 1967) Vol. 8, p. 191.
6. Gutierrez, *op. cit.*, pp. 36, 37, italics added.
7. *Ibid.*, p. x, italics added.
8. *Ibid.*, p. 177, italics added.
9. *Ibid.*, p. 168.
10. *Ibid.*, pp. 198, 199.
11. *Ibid.*, p. 202.
12. *Ibid.*, p. 206.
13. *Ibid.*, pp. 232-234.

FOURTEEN

For the World Against the World

RICHARD JOHN NEUHAUS

When did things begin to fall apart? The question is subject to many answers. The theologian's first impulse might be to refer to our original parents who thought it would be splendid to be like gods. The question itself assumes that things have fallen apart and, within the context of this essay, that the reference is to something more recent than the Garden of Eden. Paul Johnson begins his history of "modern times" with a sentence of bracing panache: "The modern world began on 29 May 1919 when photographs of a solar eclipse, taken on the island of Principe off West Africa and at Sobral in Brazil, confirmed the truth of a new theory of the universe."[1] The new theory then was Einstein's on relativity. In the minds of many cultural historians that marked the end of all certitudes. Yeats' intuition that the center cannot hold was confirmed by the knowledge that the center *does not hold.* In the world of religion, the battles over "modernism" had been associated with Darwin, evolution, and biblical authority. But among the "modernists" there was still high confidence in the happy convergence of cosmic forces making for progress, as evidenced in the Social Gospel movement. The traditionalists—some of whom identified with the innovation called fundamentalism—thought such confidence a poor substitute for Christian faith. Whether Christian faith produced that liberal confidence or was displaced by it, it was not to last very long.

RICHARD JOHN NEUHAUS is prominent as a Lutheran pastor who for many years has been active in inner city ministries, civil rights, and Christian ecumenism. He is editor of *Lutheran Forum* and the author of nine books including *Defense of People, Theology and the Kingdom of God, Christian Faith and Public Policy* and *The Naked Public Square: Religion and Democracy in America* (Eerdmans, 1984), from which this chapter is taken.

Scientific theories about the uncertainties of reality's order-
ing broke upon the world in conjunction with the massive disillusionments following World War I. It was a war that was not
supposed to happen in the first place. At the beginning of 1914
Andrew Carnegie financed the establishment of the Church Peace
Union (now the Council on Religion and International Affairs).
The purpose, he wrote the trustees in February 1914, is "the
abolition of war." He acknowledged that some people might
think this goal idealistic but, as one schooled in the real world of
finance and power, he assured the trustees the goal would be
achieved much sooner than some expected, for already, he said,
our imperial cousins in Great Britain and Germany had joined
hands with us "in the sacred bonds of commerce," making war
unthinkable. He therefore adjured the trustees that, when the
goal of abolishing war is achieved, they should give the remaining
monies to "the deserving poor." In August of that year the world
blew up, and the deserving poor are still waiting.

The dismal aftermath of "the war to end wars" had a corrosive impact also in American religion that is almost beyond mea-
surement. Some historians have contended that the period of
mainline religion from 1890 to 1920 represented another Great
Awakening. It was the period that witnessed the bold construc-
tion of a synthesis between Christian faith and the modern world,
according to this view. To the extent such a synthesis was effected, the match was of doubtful benefit to Christian faith. Seldom
has there been such quick and painful confirmation of the adage
that he who marries the spirit of his time will soon be a widower.
Rather than speaking of a marriage between mainline religion
and the American experience, we might think of it as a *ménage à
trois*. The key participants were Protestant Christianity, civilization, and America. Protestant Christianity produced civilization,
and America carried the promise of both.

The disillusionments following the Great War did not take
everyone entirely by surprise. Already by the midnineteenth century there were dissenters who raised questions about the trinity
of Protestantism, civilization, and America. They doubted that
the connections among these three were either necessary or real.
Beginning with the 1840s, the left wing of Unitarianism produced a transcendentalist movement that had little patience with
Protestant doctrine and its cultural self-assurance. Thoreau's *Wal-
den*, Hawthorne's *The Scarlet Letter*, Melville's *Moby Dick*, and
Whitman's *Leaves of Grass* all challenged the frequently smug
certitudes of established Protestantism. Writes one historian,
"They represented what may have been the first successful post-

Protestant generation in the United States. From then on, the intellectual and academic communities were increasingly divorced from Christian sources. After them, those who fashioned or controlled the symbols of community for the nation were free to ignore the Protestant context."[2] This intellectual divorce evident in the literary world had its counterpart in "the division of the one moral tradition" in politics and law.

It is perhaps too much to say that these cultural leaders could ignore the Protestant context, for it was still the context within which they thought and wrote. But now the context is no longer normative; it is less the norm than the foil for their thought. Nonetheless, "After their era, people have always been surprised to see expressions of loyalty to orthodox Christianity in the literary community. A schism was occurring in the national soul and psyche."[3] Ralph Waldo Emerson, among others, realized this change was not all to the good. As a leader of the "liberation movement" from oppressive orthodoxy, he was troubled about what came next. With some regret, he remembered "that old religion which, in the childhood of most of us, still dwelt like a sabbath morning in the country of New England, teaching privation, self-denial and sorrow! . . . What is to replace for us the piety of that race? We cannot have theirs; it glides away from us day by day. . . . A new disease has fallen on the life of man. . . . our torment is Unbelief, the Uncertainty as to what we ought to do; the distrust of the value of what we do. . . . Our religion assumes the negative form of rejection."[4] How now, and by whom, would the sacred symbols of the American experiment be fashioned and forged? More than a century later the question is still awaiting an answer.

Mainline Protestantism was catholic in the sense of inclusive. It did not exclude its children who threw into question its authority. It had lost its power or inclination to excommunicate. At the levels of intellect and high culture, it largely assimilated the doubts about its truth. By the end of the nineteenth century, mainline religious leaders were disinclined to insist upon their truths; they were eager, sometimes poignantly so, to assert their usefulness to the world, as others defined the world. Intellectually, they were inclined to accommodate; socially, they were eager to contribute. Accommodation was the fact, and contribution was the hope. Historian Robert Handy observes, "In the earlier period, the priority of the religious vision was strongly and widely maintained; it was Christianity *and* civilization, Christianity as the best part of civilization, and its hope. In the latter part of the century, however, in most cases unconsciously, much of the real focus had shifted to the civilization itself, with Christianity and the churches finding their significance in relation to it."[5]

It has been said of mainline Protestantism today that it is embarrassed to make any religious statement that does not possess redeeming social merit. If true, the cause can be traced back to that "schism in the American soul." In the world of ideas and the shaping of culture, Protestantism felt it was no longer needed or wanted. Its hope, again, was to be of some use, to make a contribution, on terms set by others. William McLoughlin is among those who contend that 1890–1920 represents "The Third Great Awakening" in American religion and culture. (The First Great Awakening was in the early eighteenth century and the Second in the early nineteenth. Some observers suggest we are now experiencing another Great Awakening, whatever number it is to be assigned.)

"The prophets of the Third Great Awakening," writes McLoughlin, "had to undertake an enormous rescue operation to sustain the culture. They had to redefine and relocate God, provide means of access to him, and sacralize a new world view."[6] Perhaps that is what had to be done in view of evolutionary and other theories that appeared to undermine old certitudes. But it is not so clear that the "prophets" of that era either understood or attempted the task. Social Gospel proponents such as Walter Rauschenbusch and Washington Gladden were for the most part content to demonstrate the moral power of the churches to "Christianize" the social order, specifically to challenge "laissez-faire capitalism" with a "social" or "fraternal" reordering of the economic system. Toward the end of this "Great Awakening" popular preachers such as Harry Emerson Fosdick and a host of religious academics were preoccupied with "reconciling" religion and science in the hope of demonstrating the intellectual respectability of Christian faith. As McLoughlin notes, the "key concepts" in this movement were relativism, pragmatism, historicism, cultural organicism, and creative intelligence. All of these concepts, be it said, were important, and some had significant explanatory power. But none of them emerged from Christian sources and some of them were, at least in origin, explicitly hostile to religion.

This eager movement to accommodate and contribute became known as Liberal Protestantism. (Its opponents, and some of its participants, called it Modernism.) Kenneth Cauthen kindly defines Liberal Protestantism as "the attempt of men who were convinced of the truth of historic Christianity to adjust this ancient faith to the demands of the modern era."[7] Sixty years ago, and still today, there were other Christians who believed it to be less a matter of adjustment than of abdication of historic Christian claims. Most secular thinkers were quite indifferent to these religious efforts; others viewed them with amusement; yet others cheered on those Christians who were trying so hard to board the ship of the modern world of which they, the secular thinkers, were clearly now in charge. Clambering aboard an already sinking ship does not, in retrospect, have the appearance of a Great Awakening.

The "prophets" of what might more accurately be called the Great Accommodation were for the most part honorable, and often courageous, men. Yet they now appear to have been less prophets than pacifiers. They were prepared to accept nature's laws as promulgated by science, and to allow no exceptions for God. Their God was reliable, he would not embarrass anybody by challenging the "realities" determined by prestige opinion. As McLoughlin admits, "Religion under Liberal Protestantism . . . was bereft of its miraculous and transcendent quality. Only the Pentecostals and Holiness people held to this faith, and for them it was purely personal; it saved them from a real world that was doomed by its materialism."[8] There were and would be other voices raised to challenge the course of accommodation—intellectually astute and socially conscious voices calling themselves evangelicals. And, from the heart of Liberal Protestantism, a counterattack would be launched by "neoorthodoxy" under the American leadership of the Brothers Niebuhr, Reinhold and H. Richard. But, these dissents aside, mainline Protestantism assumed during this period the social, cultural, and intellectual posture that continues to this day.

The mainline churches would come to view themselves as moderate, tolerant, ecumenical, more disposed to dialogue than to confrontation. Still, in the 1980s, however, they also wanted to see themselves as "prophetic" on selected social and political issues. "Consciousness raising" with respect to the "systemic victimization" of the poor would lead some to endorse revolutionary violence in liberation struggles for justice. These more "radicalized" tones emerged intermittently in the NCC during the 1960s and 1970s, as they were similarly evident in other institutions, notably the universities. In church circles they continued long after student radicalism had become the stuff of nostalgia. In part, that is no doubt because student generations are very short while the careers of church bureaucrats can be very long. Also, churches fit the category of "soft institutions," and thus are subject to becoming a haven for refugees from radicalisms past. Radicalized forms of making a contribution to the modern world have been more persistent in the World Council of Churches. The WCC, while not organically related to the NCC, shares a world of free circulation of ideas and personnel.[9] Thoughtful observers such as Thomas Derr, writing from the WCC, acknowledge the conceptual and practical problems posed when such agencies hitch their fortunes to one highly politicized version of "the future."[10]

The picture of the mainline and of its agencies such as the NCC and the WCC does not lend itself to simple categories of conservative versus liberal. In American life, writes Marty, mainline Protestantism has been marked by "a decorous worldliness with which (its) popular preachers could christen the culture."[11] Christening culture is generally thought to be a conservative course. It is the course for which today's television preachers are criticized when it is said that they christen, indeed apotheosize, the American Way of Life. But there are different definitions of American culture, and perhaps conflicting cultures, and it depends on which is being christened. From the Great Accommodation of 1890–1920 on, mainline Protestantism has read "the signs of the times" and thrown in its lot with what is deemed to be liberal, progressive, avant-garde. It is therefore not surprising that, when the secular left-of-center definition of cultural change was "radicalized," mainline Protestantism followed suit. In the 1980s, when it is widely thought that culture and politics reflect a conservative trend, the mainline may again change course. But it is probably unfair to accuse the mainline of being no more than "trendy." It may be that its leaders have learned something from the cultural captivities of the past and are now prepared to be genuinely countercultural on principle. Or it may just be that the once "radicalized" functionaries of the several denominations and ecumenical agencies are either too entrenched or too weary for such a change of direction to happen.

Reading the signs of the times is as parlous as it is imperative. Jerry Falwell declares, "I can feel the wind of God blowing across the country and across the world. You can go with the wind or you can go against it. As for me, I'm moving with the wind of the Lord!"[12] A very leftist Episcopalian bishop says that he follows the rule of thumb, "When in doubt, go with the future." Both are reading the signs of the times, but obviously they are reading different signs or reading the same signs very differently. Both are engaged in the essentially conservative enterprise of christening the culture. Both are moving with and not against what they perceive to be the trend. Neither is prophetic.

This shifting with the wind—"trendiness," as some would have it—of mainline Protestantism has not been without its critics. In the period of cultural disillusionment after World War I, a strong critique by Francis P. Miller, Wilhelm Pauck, and H. Richard Niebuhr was titled *The Church Against the World*. Miller put it quite directly: "The plain fact is that the domestication of the Protestant community in the United States within the framework of the national culture has progressed as far as in any western land." Niebuhr asserted: "The church is imperiled not only by an external worldliness but by one that has established itself within the Christian camp. . . . The crisis of the church from this point of view is not the crisis of the church in the world, but of the world in the church."[13] Forty years later, in 1975, an ecumenical group of Christian thinkers issued a book of strikingly similar title, *Against the World for the World*, containing the "Hartford Appeal for Theological Affirmation."[14] The writers took to task both Protestants and Catholics, liberals and conservatives, for their "loss of the transcendent" as evident in their succumbing to the slogan, "the world sets the agenda for the church." (The apparently slight difference between the titles of the two books may be significant. Forty years later "the world" had attained such uncritical theological status that the suggestion of being against it had immediately to be modified by "for the world.")

The "mainline" is a many-splendored thing. As we have suggested, its story line is not smooth or unbroken. For example, from the 1930s through the late 1950s it was challenged by a formidable theological movement commonly termed "neoorthodoxy." This movement was scathingly critical of the cultural accommodationism and illusions of inevitable social improvement that had marked the dominant liberalism. In league with the European "crisis theology" of Karl Barth and Emil Brunner, neoorthodoxy grew out of the post-World War I disillusionment and the later need to abandon pacifist "sentimentality" in order to confront the embodiment of the demonic in Nazism. The emphasis was on "Christian realism," and Reinhold Niebuhr's best-known title, if not his best-read book, was *Moral Man and Immoral Society*. In it he emphasized that the individual ethics of biblical piety could not be transferred easily, if at all, to the conflictual relationships between interest groups and nations. Later, during the Vietnam years, "Christian realism" fell into disrepute among some, largely because the apologists for the war claimed to have realism, if not always Christian realism, on their side. This despite the fact that Reinhold Niebuhr had by the late sixties and near the end of his life turned strongly against U.S. policy in

Indochina. (His critics quipped that Niebuhr turned out to be no Niebuhrian, but a minority strand of opposition to Vietnam was motivated by a "realistic" assessment of American interests and responsibilities.)

Almost nobody today comes right out in favor of cultural accommodation. Cultural accommodation, once expressly affirmed as the mission of mainline Protestantism, has become a term of opprobrium, just as that perfectly nice word, appeasement, came to mean something different by virtue of Neville Chamberlain's illusions about Hitler. Even the critics of cultural accommodation, however, can be co-opted to serve a different cultural mood, which is to say, to serve cultural accommodation. Thus Jacques Ellul, the French jurist and lay theologian, has seen his critique of "technological society" employed to condemn free societies, despite his own condemnation of "false signs of the kingdom" embraced by varieties of religious radicalism. Thus also Karl Barth's assertion that the preacher should preach with the Bible in one hand and the daily newspaper in the other has been turned, according to one wag, into the revolutionary doctrine that "Christianity should be preached with the daily newspaper in one hand and a gun in the other, while standing on the Bible." The late Marxist, Herbert Marcuse, complained about a society that practiced "repressive tolerance," ingeniously assimilating its revolutionary critics. So also the critics of Protestantism's cultural accommodationism are accommodated within liberalism's commodious mansions. At least that has been the pattern in the past.

It is not clear today that the mainline either can, or is inclined to, assimilate its critics. The practice of co-optation requires a degree of confidence. It may be that in more recent years an influential and "radicalized" minority that establishment leaders view as extremists who can be tolerated have come to the conclusion that the mainline is, and should be, no longer mainline. In their view, the critics of their "progressive" views are not to be co-opted but confronted. While still claiming the name "ecumenical," their disposition is toward the narrow, exclusive, and partisan. When the criticism is too strong to be confronted successfully, they assume the posture of the besieged. This reaction was evident in some mainline churches and in the NCC in face of "conservative" political victories at the end of the 1970s and mounting criticism of mainline leadership in the early 1980s. The besieged posture appears to be defensive, and it is. Yet when we hunker down, we may also be acting upon the assurance that "the future" is on our side, that it is only a question of patiently and bravely waiting out the storm.

Among its more "radicalized" leadership, then, the current defensiveness of the mainline need not betray a lack of confidence. This sector of the leadership is in the minority, however, representing one "positive" interpretation of what are manifestly hard times for mainline Protestantism. The main line of the mainline story was confidence and hope regarding the Americanizing of Christianity and the Christianizing of America. In its most ideological forms, today's "radicalized" interpretations evident in some liberation theologies are a matter of putting the best face on the collapse of that earlier confidence and hope; what cannot be transformed by cooperation must be overthrown by revolution. For the less ideological, which is the great majority of leaders and followers alike, the response is closer to what Handy describes as "religion's loss of confidence and morale."[15]

Whether one traces that loss to the cultural "schism in the American soul" or to Gladden's belief that the truth of Christianity would be proven by its social utility, or to a mix of these and other factors, in the 1980s the story of the mainline did not seem to be moving to a happy ending. Since the days of Bushnell there have been causes and crusades and revivals, but nowhere in the mainline today is there assurance that here in America would be established "the complete Christian commonwealth." Perhaps that is just as well. The need for culturally formative religion cannot be met today by a revival of mainline Protestant hegemony. We do well to remember, however, that the vision of today's moral majoritarians was in large part lifted from the mainline. Its notion of Christian America is not peculiarly fundamentalist, and it is most certainly not "un-American." The estranged cousins have come back decked out in the family wardrobe. It is always embarrassing to be confronted by the ideals of our younger and more vital days.

1890–1920, liberalism's formative period, was not, then, the Third Great Awakening. For better or for worse, it was, in Handy's phrase, "the second disestablishment." The first disestablishment of the colonial churches was completed by 1830. Afterward, even those who had virulently opposed disestablishment came to see it as a blessing that liberated the juices of what would come to be admired as American voluntarism. After this second and informal disestablishment (no laws were passed to that specific effect), there was little cause for cheering. Mainline religion was no longer in the intellectual or cultural lead; indeed it was pathetically pleased if those who shaped the culture deigned to take note of religion at all. The mainline was left to sniff around for crumbs that fell from the tables of the cultural elite. Or, like an aged and somewhat eccentric aunt who shares the house, it was thanked for occasionally helping out with tasks defined and controlled by others. The great white tower of 475 Riverside Drive turned out to be not the capitol of the Protestant empire, but a marginal service agency trying very hard to be helpful in other people's "progressive causes."

Of course there is nothing wrong in helping out with other people's progressive causes. But somebody has to decide which causes are to be helped. When causes are highly politicized, such decisions inevitably lead to political partisanship. To which it may be asked what is wrong with political partisanship. Was not the abolitionist movement against slavery politically partisan? So today many urge that the risks of partisanship must be taken in, for example, supporting revolutionary movements aimed at overthrowing apartheid in South Africa. Others (although not generally in the mainline churches) believe the risks of partisanship are mandated in defending the unborn and the handicapped from a society that ever more narrowly defines the community entitled to legal protection. Without a shared world of moral discourse that transcends the divisive issues at hand, however, partisanship slides into dehumanizing polarization.

In the nineteenth century the substantive questions behind the issue of slavery were articulated. There were shared points of reference that made moral discourse possible, even if that discourse finally failed and led to arbitrament by arms. It may be that, in view of the bloody costs, the existence of a shared world of moral discourse was small comfort. But it is no little thing that thoughtful antagonists could understand themselves to be moral actors. Whether we judge an action to be morally right or wrong, there is a gesture of respect in the judgment itself. The final obscenity is not war, but the dehumanizing of war that reduces it to an animal fight over interests, particularly over that sleaziest of interests which the modern world mistakes for a moral value, survival. It is tragically possible that moral discourse gives way to mortal conflict. It is even more tragic when we come to believe that the cure for conflict is the abandonment of moral discourse. When that step is taken, human action, which is to say morally significant action, is displaced by animal behavior. When the public square is thoroughly desacralized, political action is, in every sense of the term, thoroughly demoralized.

The public framework of moral reference cannot sustain itself; it cannot stand on its own feet, so to speak. It needs to be attended to and articulated. This is the task not just of individuals but of institutions, most particularly the institutions of religion. During most of our history it has been the task attended to by mainline Protestantism. In an earlier civil rights movement, Martin Luther King, Jr., invoked and employed that framework of moral reference. To their credit, the more consistent proponents of liberation theology in the mainline churches today recognize this need for a comprehensive and compelling moral vision. Unfortunately, the encompassing sense of purpose they propose, such as "getting America on the right side of the world revolution," brings them into alliance with forces that claim to believe that moral discourse is nothing more than an exercise in false consciousness. And unfortunately, the vision they propose implies the dismantling or destruction of the values and advantages most Americans cherish. Therefore, their surrogate for the traditional moral vision borne by mainline Protestantism is not likely to command popular support.

Most of the leadership of mainline Protestantism today, it may be safely assumed, identifies neither with the traditional vision nor with its current antitheses. There is what appears to be a middle ground. The idea is frequently touted that the whole concept of Christianity as a culture-forming force is pretentious and dangerous. The ambitions of that older Protestantism are dismissed as "triumphalism," of a piece with the cultural and political ambitions of pre-Vatican II Catholicism in, for example, Franco Spain. The alternative to triumphalism is a "servant church" which does not delude itself into thinking that it is the sole or even the chief instrument through which God is working. There is much that is attractive in this viewpoint. It refuses to equate the church with the kingdom of God, or to mistake our limitations for the limits of what Christ can do and is doing. There is also much that is attractive in the idea of cultural accommodation, despite its negative connotations. If cultural accommodation means respect for secular wisdoms and a determination to speak the gospel in a manner attuned to the particularities of a cultural moment, then cultural accommodation is of a piece with the Christian mission itself. And, as we have seen, there is much that is attractive in helping other people in their good causes, if we do not lose hold of the moral references by which we understand good and evil.

Mainline readers may think of Harvey Cox's *The Secular City* as a book from a long, long time ago. Among some moral majoritarian writers today, however, that 1965 volume is much quoted. John Whitehead and others quote it approvingly for Cox's sharp distinction between secularization and secularism. Its much greater influence in the Protestant mainline is still evident, however. Cox, being a more thoughtful soul, has since been critical of some forms of liberationism and has written about the religiously borne transcendence that challenges the disenchantment of the modern world. But his greater and continuing influence is in the gravamen of *The Secular City,* that Christians should trust and supportively engage themselves in God's secular struggles and achievements. *The Secular City* was written in the glow of John F. Kennedy's Camelot, and of the aggiornamento of Pope John XXIII; it reflected a high point of liberal confidence— before black power turned nasty, before Vietnam, before acid rock, before Charles Manson, before Watergate, in short, before the secular city (or at least the American version of it) went sour.

Yet the basic argument still has wide sway: "The world sets the agenda for the church." Christian-Marxists (or, as some would prefer, Christians who "employ Marxist analysis") believe that axiom, and they have their own reading of what the world is up to. And more moderate mainliners seem to believe that, although they are more at home in their societies, trusting the elites of secular society to provide the terms of discourse, to produce the good causes to which the church hopes to be helpful. This description of affairs might be challenged by those who could point to numerous statements and resolutions from, e.g., the NCC which are critical of this secular society. But that says nothing more than that, when selected causes are declared to be good, opposing causes are declared to be bad. In the selection itself, the mainline very seldom dissents from left-of-center conventional wisdoms. Yet those critics of the mainline miss the main point when they focus on the "leftist" orientation of church pronouncements. It would be as troublesome—although exceedingly unlikely in view of the "new class" placement of mainline church leadership—were the pronouncements typically "rightist." The main point is that in making such pronouncements we do not believably articulate the framework of public moral reference by which all positions—right, left, or unlabeled—must be evaluated. To do that would be uncomfortably close to agreeing with the moral majoritarians that there is in fact an authoritative moral tradition to which public discourse should be held accountable. Rather, facing a selection of prepackaged positions, we make our choice and because in some sense we are presuming to speak for the church, we try to remember to append a Bible passage or two. Secular opinion-leaders, if they take note at all, are at a loss to understand in what way such pronouncements are specifically religious or Christian, since they seem to do nothing more than to restate, in mode of argument and conclusion, one of several viewpoints already in public play.

The rather odd consequence is that those who do not claim any specific religious warrant for their views call upon religious leaders to be more significantly religious in advancing theirs. One of many instances is a *New York Times* editorial of June 1983. (This instance is additionally odd because the statement that occasioned the editorial was also subscribed by some moral majoritarian leaders, which is perhaps an indication of the price some of them might pay for "respectability.") Jeremy Rifkin had coordinated a statement signed by a broad range of Protestant, Catholic, and Jewish leaders calling for a ban on introducing inheritable traits into the human gene set.

The editorialist believes that the religious leaders were wrong "to utter so far-reaching a proscription on the basis of little argument." He thinks that although it is not yet technologically possible, there would be considerable merit in altering the gene set of people who are especially prone to inheritable diseases such as sickle-cell anemia. The editorial disagrees with the religious leaders who contend that "no one has a right to decide for future generations which genes should be preserved and which replaced." The editorial reflects a particular irritation that the religious leaders' statement seems to add nothing to the debate since it arbitrarily picks out one possible direction of genetic research for condemnation.

"According to the book of Genesis," the editorial says, "man is made in God's image. Does that make it sacrilege for humans to change their own genetics? Most theologians do not interpret their faith so literally. In any case the religious petitioners, surprisingly, do not rest their case on theology. . . . Those now demanding a veto have acted at the persuasion of Jeremy Rifkin, director of the Foundation on Economic Trends and author of a new book of human genetic engineering. . . . If they really want a ban, they should state it in their own terms and words rather than letting Mr. Rifkin be their only spokesman. The issue deserves more than a slogan without a rationale."[16]

The incident of the statement and the editorial reaction to it is of interest in several respects. The statement indicates what the editorialists and others view as an antiscientific or at least antitechnology bias. The mainline leaders who signed it have in this instance, it might be suggested, gone over to the fundamentalist side with its traditional suspicion of "scientific progress." (A similar suspicion, even hostility, is evident in mainline rhetoric about space exploration.) We noted earlier the ways in which the "radical" counterculture with its animus toward modern technology prepared the way for a convergence between elite opinion and a traditional fundamentalist disposition. Also of interest is the editorial complaint that the religious leaders do not make their case on the basis of theological or ethical argument. To that complaint it could be answered that the editors of the *New York Times* would not recognize a theological argument if it fell like a stone tablet on their heads. It might also be pointed out that in the months prior to this editorial the paper had given extensive coverage to the Roman Catholic bishops' pastoral on nuclear warfare and paid little attention to the theological argumentation that it contained in abundance; the *Times* was chiefly interested in how the pastoral agreed or disagreed with the defense politics of the administration in Washington.

These points made, however, the editorial response is significant in what it says about mainline Protestant penchants in the issuing of social pronouncements. Here and elsewhere, the "progressive" wing of Christianity assumes a "prophetic" posture against what the world takes to be progress. At the same time the prophecy does not invoke distinctively religious claims, since such claims were muted or abandoned as a condition for religion's marriage with the world's agenda. The marriage, however, turns out to rest upon a one-way agreement. The world did not agree to having its agenda taken on by the church. In the "big world" of secular reality the other players do not understand the basis of religion's intervention in their games. If religion intervenes with truths that are otherwise being ignored, its intervention may be welcomed or resisted, but at least the reason for the intervention would be clear. But when religion wants to intervene in the secular arena with secondhand claims that are already current there, and indeed originated there, it must not be surprised when its offer to help is declined, not always so politely, by those in charge of the world's agenda.

These then are some of the problems encountered by the idea of "the servant church." For the idea to be effective, the church must be clear about the service it has to render. It can in a modest way offer money, prestige, and some recruits for the causes that it believes signal God's work in the world. But such an approach means drawing upon declining capital. The capital was created by a community of faith gathered by distinctive truth claims; it can only be replenished by proclamation and faith's response. This means recovering the metaphor of "the church militant," a metaphor almost entirely absent from mainline religious thought today. Against the world for the world; the church's significant contribution is to significantly challenge. The challenge is not significant when the church merely endorses existing positions that challenge other existing positions. Significant challenge means throwing all positions into question.

Only the church militant can be a servant church. Today talk about the church militant seems impossibly triumphalistic. Yet it is worth asking whether the current polemic against triumphalism is not the result of the failure of a different triumphalism. No doubt mainline Protestantism with its historic belief in the trinity of Christianity, America, and civilization believed itself to be on the road to triumph. Cultural accommodation was not simply a marriage of convenience; it was a marriage through which this trinity would conquer. That hope has been disappointed most severely. The image of the church militant does not propose another triumphalism, thus setting up the church for further disappointment. Ultimately, to be sure, we believe that the church will triumph in the sense of being vindicated in the coming kingdom of God. Because it has said Yes to that hope, the church must say No to all lesser hopes of influence. Precisely in the power of that Yes and No, however, lies its influence short of the final vindication. The church militant is marked by an "againstness" that is for the world. Using H. Richard Niebuhr's terms, it is an instance of "Christ transforming culture" by pointing the culture to a transformation that is beyond its own means to attain or even imagine.

The muting of Christian distinctiveness, the rejection of the idea of the church militant, the polemic against triumphalism, all are consequences of the collapse of the synthesis attempted by the Great Awakening of 1890-1920, an "awakening" that resulted in a second and thoroughly demoralizing disestablishment of mainline Protestantism. Current talk about the servant church smells of rationalization. It betrays a yearning to play in the big arena of the secular world, to be useful to somebody, somehow. If those in control of the dominant forces of our time do not want our help, then we will seek out the opposition to those forces and find our meaning in helping them to overthrow their oppressors. Thus we have moved from christening the culture of the strong to signing up with the revolutionary opposition to that culture, but in divorcing one party and marrying another we are a servant church to neither. The church, in biblical imagery, is the bride of Christ, and its proper service is to proclaim the revolution of the coming kingdom, by which all existing establishments and revolutionary would-be establishments are brought under divine promise and judgment.

NOTES

1. Paul Johnson, *Modern Times: The World from the Twenties to the Eighties* (Harper & Row, 1983), p. 1.
2. Martin E. Marty, *Righteous Empire,* (Dial Press, 1970) p. 114.
3. *Ibid.,* p. 41.
4. *Ibid.,* p. 116.
5. Robert Handy, *Christian America: Protestant Hopes and Historical Realities* (Oxford, 1971), p. 110.
6. William G. McLoughlin, *Revivals, Awakening, and Reform* (Chicago 1976), p. 152.
7. Quoted in *ibid.,* p. 157.
8. *Ibid.,* p. 156.
9. Ernest Lefever, *From Amsterdam to Nairobi.* (Ethics and Public Policy Center, 1979). A much earlier critique of what he called the "church and society syndrome" was offered by the eminent ethicist Paul Ramsey of Princeton in *Who Speaks for the Church?* (Abingdon, 1967).
10. Thomas Sieger Derr, *Barriers to Ecumenism* (Orbis, 1983).
11. Marty, *Righteous Empire,* p. 234.
12. Jerry Falwell in an April 1981 meeting in Washington, D.C., observed by the author.
13. Quoted in *Righteous Empire,* p. 235.
14. Peter Berger and Richard John Neuhaus, eds., *Against the World for the World* (Seabury, 1976). At the time this title was chosen, the editors did not know, although Neuhaus should have known, about the earlier book of similar title.
15. Handy, *Christian America,* p. 203.
16. "Genes and Genesis," editorial in *New York Times* (June 11, 1983).

FIFTEEN

A Pilgrimage in Political Theology: A Personal Witness

CLARK PINNOCK

While evangelical Christians agree about the central doctrines of the Christian faith, their thinking about social and political issues evidences increasing division and disagreement. Evangelical reflection about social and political issues is like a turbulent river which turns this way and that, and contains several strong currents. Persons who lack strong convictions in such matters can easily find themselves tossed about with uncertainty. To some extent, this has happened to me. Since I believe that this record of my own pilgrimage may help explain how committed Christian leaders can be misled into thinking that the Bible requires a rejection of political conservatism and an acceptance of leftist convictions, I have decided to tell my story. I hope it will help others who are struggling in this difficult and confusing area.[1]

Many evangelicals in our day realize that privatism in faith is wrong. The gospel speaks to the whole of life; its social implications are inescapable. The "great reversal" of which Timothy Smith speaks has in large measure itself been reversed. Many contemporary believers are eager to apply their faith to the issues of life in society. The issue today therefore is what *kind* of in-

---

CLARK PINNOCK is presently Professor of Theology at McMaster Divinity College in Hamilton, Ontario. Prior to this he taught at Regent College, Trinity Evangelical Divinity School, New Orleans Baptist Theological Seminary, and the University of Manchester (England), from which he gained his doctorate in New Testament. He is the author of *Reason Enough*, *Biblical Revelation*, and *Set Forth Your Case* and has two new books in the press on biblical inspiration and contemporary theology. He has been contributing editor of *Christianity Today* in recent years. The essay which follows is taken from *Liberation Theology*, edited by Ronald Nash (Mott Media, 1984).

volvement and what *sort* of action is required by the Bible. We agree that God's will ought to be done on earth as it is in heaven. But what is His will? The poor ought to be helped. But what specific actions will help them? Unlike the social apathy that often existed a generation ago, we all believe now in the social implications of the gospel. But what program shall we follow, and on what platform shall we stand? To which evangelical thinker shall we turn for leadership? What policies and actions will bring liberty and justice in their wake? Finding the correct answers to these questions constitutes the agenda for the 1980s.

My own pilgrimage has been a struggle to gain a degree of clarity in this area. My path over the years has turned out to be a fairly straight line with the exception of one enormous zigzag in the middle. My own quest went through three major phases. Until I began experimenting with political radicalism in 1970, I had moved quite generally in the mainstream of North American evangelical political thinking. My theological conservatism was coupled with leanings in the direction of political conservatism. Because my eschatology during those earlier years was amillennial, I really did not place much emphasis upon political affairs. I valued democracy, our historical Christian roots, and capitalist institutions. But in 1970 my political thinking underwent a paradigm shift—a total transformation. Living in the United States at the time, I began to read the Bible from an anabaptist perspective and soon found myself looking at society through the eyes of the new left. Things formerly valued in American society became targets of my disapproval as I became more conscious of the effects of materialism, racism, injustice and the Vietnam war. The radical edge of Scripture had caught my attention, and I could not ignore the evils of democratic capitalism. It was a new political-theological world to move in and it produced a heady experience which intoxicated me and many others. It led me personally to sympathy and support for the Marxist movements of the world. By 1974, having returned to my native Canada, I even voted for communist candidates in the Vancouver civic elections. Looking back on this radical period now, it seems incredible that I could have accepted so many implausible things, and I am reminded forcefully of my human condition. It is now easier for me to understand how people can be swept along in their support of strange causes like the German people in the 1930s. The real excitement that can be created by a new ideology can sweep away a good deal of critical sense.

The third phase in my political pilgrimage began after I had spent some eight years in the radical movement. This new conversion followed much the same course as my earlier conversion to radicalism. Gradually I began to reassess my position, and my alienation from North America began to fade, replaced by a certain critical appreciation of democratic capitalism that I had had before 1970. At the same time, I was becoming more conscious of the reasonableness of Reformed hermeneutics over against the anabaptist approach. The urgency I had acquired from the radical evangelicals has, with regard to political action, been internalized and applied to my new political orientation. I have not returned to the relative indifference I felt toward politics in my first phase, but have picked up some enthusiasm for what I would term neo-Puritan politics. With this brief outline of my sojourn now drawn, let me turn to a more detailed account of my search.

PHASE ONE: IN THE MAINSTREAM, 1953-1969

I was born and raised in a middle-class southern Ontario home and a socially respectable progressive Baptist church. I was converted through the witness of evangelical believers and organizations like Youth for Christ. While for a time my theology could be described as fundamentalist, I came increasingly under the influence of the kind of mainstream evangelical theology associated with the old Princeton Seminary. During the years following my conversion, I was introduced to all the major lines of evangelical social thought. I admired Billy Graham and accepted his approach to social change through evangelism. While he taught us to love America, he also helped us recognize her sins. While spending some time at L'Abri in the early 1960s, I came under the influence of Francis Schaeffer. Through him, I learned to emphasize theological over political issues. While Schaeffer sometimes spoke in support of the Vietnam war, he also spoke out against the rise of secularism in America and showed sympathy for the flower children who needed Christ. What seeds of radicalism I may have picked up from Schaeffer came not so much because he broke with democratic capitalism (he didn't), but because he identified with alienated youth in a way that appeared to support some of their concerns. Carl Henry also influenced me (in the direction of a cautious reformism) through two books on ethics and his writings in *Christianity Today*. I also have to admit a fascination and respect for Bill Buckley and the feisty way in which he defended the capitalist way against its critics. (I still do today.)

During phase one of my sojourn, I was far more concerned with the problem of biblical inerrancy than the issue of racism. I was fairly skeptical of the effectiveness of governmental intervention in economic matters and in the case of social welfare. I viewed the "Great Society" as a bit of a farce. I thought that society's greatest need was the conversion of its people. I saw democratic capitalism in a good light and strongly disapproved of atheistic communism. As far as Vietnam was concerned, I was a Canadian who felt it was an unpleasant American duty to defend freedom in Southeast Asia; I wished them well.

In addition to the possibility that Schaeffer may have quickened the radical impulse in me, my conversion to premillennialism in the late 1960s through influences at Dallas Theological Seminary could be seen as another radical seed. Although it is true that dispensational premillennialists are notoriously passive politically, it is also true that such an eschatology puts one in radical opposition to the powers that be and makes one a potential radical.

PHASE TWO: OUT ON THE EDGES, 1970-1978

A contagion was in the air for young people in the 1960s and influenced many of our generation. It happened for me. At Trinity Evangelical Divinity School Jim Wallis gathered a small group of people deeply critical of America and supportive of radical politics and anabaptist hermeneutics. Out of this circle came first the *Post American* and then its successor, the widely influential *Sojourners.* In sympathy with these young people, I too began to be turned off by what we saw as plastic culture, the violence in Vietnam, and America's unacknowledged racism. Without my conscious awareness, I bought into a fusion or synthesis of the new left and anabaptist thought.[2] At that time I perceived the union as enjoying God's favor.

I can best explain my new standpoint by referring to three corners of a triad. First, there was a deep alienation from North American culture. Some of the mainstream evangelicals like Carl Henry, Francis Schaeffer, and Billy Graham had emphasized the point that America was corrupting herself and selling her birthright, but they had something different in mind. They did not mean that the whole system was evil or that the church had betrayed the gospel. They wanted reform of a basically good culture, not a complete overthrow. But we saw North America as the polar opposite of the gospel. We saw practically nothing to celebrate in it. Our rhetoric knew no bounds. We applauded William Stringfellow when he identified America with the great whore of Babylon of Revelation 17-19.[3] To be fair, we believed in the great American revolutionary heritage as we understood it, but saw no evidence of that tradition at work in the present. In our ideology, America was wholly given over to the Babylon pattern and was a worthy successor to Nazi Germany. Now it is also true that we viewed *all* earthly systems as evil in line with our anabaptist exegesis, and if pressed would insist that we disliked the Marxist societies just as much. But it is doubtful if this really was the case. I at least looked wistfully at those "revolutionary" societies which seemed to embody the communitarian ideal more perfectly than my own.

But our concentration was not on political solutions. We tended to be skeptical of those. As evangelicals and anabaptists we tended toward a new community where Christians would give up their privileges in the middle class, share their possessions and assets, and embody the new humanity beside the poor. That was the solution we were committed to, God's "original revolution."[4] In our minds, it was God's wise social strategy, and it mattered not if the world complained it was not enough. As radicals, we did not accept the ideals of our fellow evangelicals such as individualism, patriotism, and capitalism, but bought into the denunciation of the Western democracies as a zone of oppression and injustice. It was doomed, and we planned to sing the Hallelujah Chorus when it fell. We were convinced by the crisis mentality of the Club of Rome and found ourselves out of line with almost every policy and behavior we saw our culture pursuing. It was a revolt of the advantaged. We hated those who were successful in the system, and therefore ourselves who had tasted all of its benefits. For me, radicalism served to take away the guilt I felt for being born into an advantaged situation. I do not fully understand the dynamics at work here, and leave the matter to a psychologist.[5]

Second, about the same time there was a resurgence of anabaptist theology and it facilitated the radicalizing process by providing theological foundations. When it dawned upon us, we had the feeling of a second conversion. It was Christ-centered and biblicist and so appealed to our evangelical instincts, but it was radical and subversive of every status quo and so confirmed the cultural alienation we felt.[6] It taught us a way to go back to our conservative churches and preach the new gospel of Christian radicalism in an evangelical modality. The Bible teaches a radical message, we said, and that was that. Anabaptist theology was made to order for our situation. It told us that North America, like all cultures, was a fallen order with which the Christian could not compromise. Jesus Christ had come to smash all such systems, not by violence, but by speaking of a new order in which all systems of domination in regard to money, rank, and hierarchy will be overthrown, and those who are first in this world will be last in that one. The great mistake of the church, committed first by Constantine, was the decision to ally herself with satanic power and betray her radical identity. The call was for the faithful to come out from Babylon, including the apostate evangelical churches, and form radical communities which would take their courageous stand against the materialism and violence of our culture. Simple lifestyle, nonviolence, economic sharing, equality, communitarianism—these were the signs of the authentic church today. By this means perhaps the world could be changed through the effect of a light that cannot be hid. Anabaptist theology supported our alienation admirably. To be a Christian was to be a radical and a subversive! We exist as sojourners to call the establishment into question, and to live our lives for others. It was also a hermeneutic which interpreted the New Testament, and particularly the Sermon on the Mount in a radical way. Historically it led believers to avoid the use of oaths, personal or military force, legal justice, and at times even the possession of private property. It also tended to cause them to withdraw from political and social life and to a strict separation of church and state. As radical evangelicals, we did not withdraw from public life, but our involvement in it was always countercultural and never culture-reclaiming. There was a dualism between the pure community and the evil social order and a situation of constant tension.

Third, the political context of the radical movement of which we were a Christian segment was the new left. It was alienated from America and could say why in nontheological terms. Corporate capitalism was the root of America's degeneracy and the source of its injustice, violence, and racism. It was a system which raped the environment and ruled the world on behalf of the wealthy minority. It was a corrupt system and had to be overthrown. Without being ideologically left myself, I was in considerable agreement with what the new left said both by way of criticism and suggestion. I remember being asked if I realized the Marxist content of what we were saying in the *Post American* and being puzzled by the question. I was a babe in political thinking and was saying things based on what I thought were exegetical grounds, the importance of which I did not fully understand. I felt that the poor were poor because the rich were rich, and what was needed was state intervention and voluntary poverty on the part of Christians. It seemed reasonable to think of the rich as

oppressors, and the poor as their victims. The Bible often seemed
to do the same thing. It was obvious to me that the welfare state
needed to be extended, that wealth ought to be forcibly redistrib-
uted through taxation, that the third world deserved reparations
from us, that our defense spending was in order to protect our
privilege, and the like. I did not require proof of such propositions—they all seemed obvious and self-evident. The excitement
of the change of thinking suppressed even the small amount of
critical judgment I had acquired before 1970.

Socialist ideals also provided allurement. Was socialism not
a grand vision of a just and humane order which distributed its
resources fairly and equitably among all its people according to
their need? Was it not true democracy where decisions were made
not by the wealthy elite but by the people? Without equating the
two, it was so easy for me to associate in my mind the socialist
utopia and the promised kingdom of God. There was a high-
mindedness to the vision which made it compelling. It was this
attraction which had drawn churchmen in the ecumenical movement to the left for decades prior to our conversion. We admired
what we thought was happening in the new China under Mao,
and we hoped that the Viet Cong would win out against American forces. Our radicalism was a fusion of anabaptist hermeneutics and new-left political orientation.[7]

PHASE THREE: RETURN TO THE CENTER, 1978-1984

Late in the 1970s each of the three points of the radical triad
began to lose their power over me. First, I began to awaken out of
my radical dream, and to see once again the positive tendencies of
democratic capitalism which had been eclipsed. I began to view
such things as free speech, limited government, an independent
judiciary, genuine pluralism, and a concern for human rights to be
evidence of the promise of America in a world so largely lacking
these privileges. It now struck me as somewhat ridiculous to
overlook those positive features of North American life which
had incidentally made it possible for radicals like me to express
and live out our concerns. How could I have had such deep contempt for a culture which surely stands as a beacon of hope in
this suffering world? How ironic to call for "liberation" in the
very place there is probably more of it than anywhere else in the
world, and to be sympathetic toward those societies where neither liberty nor justice is in good supply. It began to dawn on me
that if one was looking for Babylon in this present world, one

might rather look toward the threat of totalitarian government which seeks to usurp all sovereignty in a culture. What really endangers liberty and justice in our world is not a flawed America, but that political monism, whether of the fascist right or the communist left, which declares itself to be absolute and answers to no transcendent value. How ironic that the *Reader's Digest*, which we refused to read in the 1960s, should now seem to have grasped the truth about the world, and *Ramparts*, which we read avidly, should have been so blind. But it is so. We radicals thought we loved peace and justice, but we simply did not grasp the nature of tyranny in the modern world. We thought Stalin was an aberration in the history of socialism rather than its symbol. We refused to see that communism was fascist and spelled the destruction of the human spirit—as Solzhenitsyn put it, "a levelling unto death."[8]

Once freed from the hold of the radical perspective, many of the old issues took on a different aspect. For example, I used to find discrimination everywhere, whereas now I do not. What impresses me now is the degree we have been able to overcome racism and the fact that our society in North America is remarkable for its open pluralism. On the ecological side, the old crisis mentality seems quaint. We are not running out of energy or natural resources, but are finding abundant new ones. We are not running out of land or food—production outstrips demand. Pollution is not insoluble, but decreases as soon as we take the problem seriously.[9] Even the Vietnam war looks quite different now. Although the peace movement meant well, it addressed itself to the wrong powers and as a result led to the enslavement of large parts of Southeast Asia. Solzhenitsyn does not exaggerate when he says that we radicals were accomplices in the betrayal of those nations. Christians must be peacemakers, but surely that does not mean we have to assist totalitarian powers gain still more slaves. Will we never learn the lesson of Neville Chamberlain?

In one respect, though, my politics continues to be radical. Not radical in the directions I now disavow, but in the direction of a neo-Puritan vision. Still a millennialist, I now see a greater realization of the kingdom in society before the eschaton. I anticipate Christ's enemies being put beneath his feet and his rule extending to all nations in history. He commanded us to disciple all nations, to bring them under his sway, and now I have a stronger faith this will actually be done. Like the postmillennialists of an earlier era, I look forward to the day when Jesus shall reign wherever the sun, as Watts puts it, and the knowledge of the

Lord will cover the earth. This is, of course, the old Puritan eschatology and vision, and we see it undergoing a resurgence on many sides, in the recent work of Schaeffer, in the ministry of the New Right, and in the Chalcedon movement for Christian reconstruction.

Although I do not believe the program we should follow is yet complete or beyond criticism, I do think it is a positive direction and constitutes a major new form of evangelical social theology. One of the implications is that the church need not find itself perpetually in a countercultural posture. In cultures like our own where the gospel has taken deep root and penetrated many areas, the task of the church can be to encourage the christianization of the culture and call the nation to the will of God, and to assure people that God will surely bless the nation whose God is the Lord. Christians should be busy calling for fiscal responsibility, effective law enforcement, limited government, the right to life, the stability of the family, adequate defense, the needs of the poor, the problem of pornography, and the like. I agree with the radicals that the gospel is meant to have far-reaching social implications, and look for the coming of God's kingdom and a society governed according to his law.

Second, just as the cultural alienation of the second phase required an anabaptist hermeneutic to sustain it, so this phase is in keeping with a Reformed one. To effect the shift from one to the other all one needs to do is recover the Old Testament as the foundation of New Testament politics. The anabaptist reading of the Bible pits the Old Testament against the New at many crucial points. It turns away from its emphasis on the legitimacy of earthly powers and the responsibility believers have to exercise them in a godly manner. It finds virtue instead in a repudiation of such power and delights in powerlessness as the mark of the Christian. The true believer is supposed to refuse to try to manage society even if he has the opportunity and to avoid all coercive activities. But this makes no sense in the context of the Old Testament, where blessing is pronounced upon the godly rulers. It seems to me now that it is unnatural to read the New Testament as if it rejects the Old Testament framework in these areas. We are told to pray for the governing authorities because they are ordained by God. The gospel affirms the abiding validity of God's law, including such things as the proper responsibility of civil magistrates and their duty to resist evildoers. While it is possible to read the Sermon on the Mount differently, it is not necessary to do so. I have returned to the view that evangelical political work ought to have an institutional as well as intentional component.

It is not just a question of building new community, but also of bringing society under God's law. Human societies need not be under Satan's sway and the goal of political theology ought to be to conform to God's scriptural will. In the case of our Western democracies, it seems plain to me now that the Christian heritage operating in them is profound and precious, and renders them worthy of critical support and reforming efforts. The future is open. It belongs to the Lord of history who intends to reclaim the whole creation. Therefore, we ought to be hopeful and energetic in pressing the crown rights of the Redeemer.[10]

Third, there is an ideological component in all this too. I have changed my mind about democratic capitalism. Like Peter Berger and many others, I have come to see it in a very different light. Far from being the enemy of the poor, it now seems to me to offer both liberty and prosperity in abundance and to deserve our cautious support. Socialism, on the other hand, has a dismal record of providing neither.

I am not an expert in economics, far from it, but I can now see why North America is rich and many other nations are not. It is not because we have exploited the third world and robbed them of their wealth. Quite the contrary, the world is poorest precisely where there has been no contact with the West. What prosperity there is in the third world has often been the result of contact with it.[11] No, the rapid economic growth we have experienced is largely the result of a set of factors including the rise of industrial capitalism. In Britain alone in the nineteenth century there was a 1600 percent rise in goods and wages.[12] It was as if the human race had at last hit upon an effective formula for raising whole populations from poverty to unheard of standards of wealth. The capacity of capitalism to generate wealth is unparalleled in history, and quite possibly one of the greatest single blessings bestowed on humanity. No system has been so helpful to the poor and provided such opportunity to rise out of suffering. It has done so chiefly by reason of the fact it allows wealth to be diversely controlled and be freely invested in new causes. Real wealth is not the possession of natural resources. It is human creativity and ingenuity and that is what democratic capitalism releases in good measure. Any system will prosper which gives liberty to this ultimate resource.

It is irresponsible for me as a theologian to be ignorant of what will help the poor while claiming piously to be in solidarity with them. We have to say what is needed if the standard of living of the poor is to rise; namely, a commitment to economic growth, and liberty for economic agents to undertake the kind of risks and investments which will lead to an accumulation of wealth for the people. Democratic capitalism has a proven record in the area of wealth production; if we care for the poor, we ought to promote it rather than condemn it. In addition to providing material prosperity, the system also produces liberty, since it is an economics in which individuals can operate at will and the state does not take charge. Political freedom is consonant with a free market. As Milton Friedman has said, "I know of no example in time or place of a society that has been marked by a large measure of political freedom, and that has not also used something comparable to a free market to organize the bulk of economic activity."[13]

Should we go so far as to say that the Bible supports this economic policy? I think we should be cautious in this area. If the Bible does teach this policy, it is strange why we did not discover it earlier. It is also risky to tie the Scriptures to any such system, thus repeating the radical mistake of regularly linking it to socialism. Nevertheless, the Bible offers many insights which bear upon economics and are at least consistent with market practices. It calls upon all of us to be stewards of resources and to have dominion of the earth. It implies that it is a moral activity which we choose or refuse to do. It praises diligent and honest labor. It prohibits theft of property and promises wealth to the godly. It insists upon stable currency, just weights and measures. It does not see the role of the state to be active in this area except to ensure justice. Scripture teaches us that long-term economic growth flows from obedience to God and that stubborn poverty is the result of disobedience. It defends the rights of the disadvantaged and calls upon the godly to help them get on their feet by means of the Lord's tithe. God is not on the side of the poor in some abstract general sense, but he is moved in mercy toward the oppressed and commands his people to show mercy in speaking on their behalf and extending favor to them. Often when we hear talk about Christian economics, it is actually secular economics imported into theological ethics. What we need to do is study and utilize the biblical materials on this subject more fully.

Although I do see democratic capitalism as a resource of relative good and hope in this fallen world, I do not think its future is necessarily bright. We have become secular and materialistic and risk losing all we have been given. We have succumbed to the very materialism which has produced the communist tyranny. We no longer stand tall for the great values that lie beneath our feet. There is nothing to prevent our civilization from ending up on the scrapheap of history. God's law makes it plain that while he will bless the faithful, he will not hesitate to judge the unfaithful. Consider the enormous deficits we have amassed which rob future generations, inflate the currency, and slow the engine of growth. Think of the irresponsibility of our banks which have lent out vast quantities of our resources to unworthy debtors, thus placing our own economy in jeopardy. In many ways we are drifting and deserve ruin and judgment. We have a great opportunity to exercise leadership in the world, but it is not certain that we have the ability and maturity to do so. Instead of presenting a spiritual alternative to the Soviet barrenness, we have ourselves fallen into self-centered materialism which reduces everything to a monetary value. The same God who promises to bless his faithful people and those who respect his law also threatens to curse those who refuse to follow his statutes (Deut. 28:1-68).

Aligned to this reawakened belief in the promise of democratic capitalism came a corresponding disillusionment with the socialist ideal. I have come to feel with so many others that socialism represents false prophecy and a cruel delusion. It is an enemy of the poor because it destroys prosperity. By uniting economic and political power in one center, it produces tyranny. Marxism promised to explain and then change the world, but it has done neither. It exists as an orthodoxy to justify and legitimate total power. As Kolakowski puts it, "Marxism has been the greatest fantasy of our century... (it) neither interprets the world nor changes it: it is merely a repertoire of slogans serving to organize various interests."[14] Worst of all it has led to a nightmare of oppression and totalitarian control.

Even in its democratic form, as in Sweden and North America, it threatens our liberties and bankrupts our economies.[15] Even the welfare state which seems to be such a genuine response to the plight of poor people and which as a radical I thought ought to be expanded is no solution. Its general effect on the poor is to destroy their families (because the payments are better if the husband has left the family) and lock them into their sorry condition (because its payments make the unattractive entry-level job seem even less appealing and encourage permanent joblessness). Welfare is an enemy of the poor and friend of the vast and expensive bureaucracies which it creates. It prevents poor people from taking the only road that leads out of poverty: development through hard work and accumulation. It is important to be truthful when it comes to poverty and not perpetuate myths regarding the morality of the rich and duties of the poor.[16]

Living in Canada has afforded me daily examples of how to destroy the private sector and prosperity and how to expand government so that it gains control in every possible area of life. Pierre Trudeau has led what amounts to a socialist government for a dozen years and has brought Canada to its knees economically by eating up about 40 percent of the GNP and introducing government regulation into every sector.[17] The budget is out of control. The state owns one hundred and seventy-five (at last count) "crown corporations" whose financial affairs are not under close parliamentary scrutiny. It has a national energy policy which has devastated the petroleum industry and diverted huge funds into the state treasury instead of fresh exploration and development. We have a huge bureaucracy, a million officials for only twenty-five million Canadians. Although the country is rich in space and resources, it is in pathetic shape because of socialist policies on every hand. Ironically, the Catholic bishops are calling for more government intervention and handouts. They do not explain how one can redistribute wealth not available or how one creates jobs if industry has been brought to its knees. But it is quite typical for theologians to dogmatize political matters in which they have no expertise.

IN CONCLUSION

This has been my pilgrimage to date in political theology. I hope I have been making progress. Certainly I am learning from the struggle to achieve clarity. The process has not been painless. One does not embrace and then break with a radical movement without being viewed with suspicion and resentment. I feel badly that some who appreciated my writing during the radical period now find me some distance from those ideals. I realize that our idea was to convert mainline evangelicals to the radical vision and not the other way around. But this is what happened to me and I set it forth as a possible lesson to all. The zigzag experience in and out of radicalism confirmed for me the considerable truth of the hermeneutical circle. We are deeply affected in our reading of the Bible by our circumstances. It is virtually impossible to disentangle the threads of biblical teaching and cultural experience. In particular it compels me to ask at this time in my life whether my present position is really scriptural or reflects my own class setting. At least one valuable remnant of my earlier radicalism is the fact I have to ask such questions of myself. In the late 1960s evangelical social thought jumped forward in a passionate radical expression which continues to impress itself upon an important minority of our movement. Now in the 1980s we see the rise of a liberal (people call it neo-conservative) neo-Puritan cultural vision which is sweeping large numbers into its program. Though viciously criticized from the left and often shallow in its thinking, this democratically-oriented social movement is the new liberation theology of our time, and in the days to come a great debate will take place around the issues it raises. Given my meandering, I have to wonder where it will lead.

NOTES

1. For helpful clarification of the spectrum of opinion, see Robert B. Fowler, *A New Engagement, Evangelical Political Thought 1966-1976* (Grand Rapids: Eerdmans, 1982).
2. Arthur Gish saw it in these terms and communicated that to me at least: *The New Left and Christian Radicalism* (Grand Rapids: Eerdmans, 1970).
3. William Stringfellow, *An Ethic for Christians and Other Aliens in a Strange Land* (Waco: Word, 1973).
4. John H. Yoder was the thinker behind the change in our social and political thought. See his *The Original Revolution* (Scottdale, Pa.: Herald Press, 1971).
5. Norman Podhoretz refers to this dynamic in his own biographical memoir covering this period: *Breaking Ranks* (San Francisco: Harper & Row, 1979), pp. 361-365.
6. Not all radical evangelicals bought the whole anabaptist package, however. In Toronto there was a group at the Institute for Christian Studies which shared the cultural alienation within the Reformed context. They published a *Survival (!) Handbook for Radical Christians Today* in 1971.
7. I would have agreed with Orlando Costas when he says that the poor can only receive justice "in a socialistically organized society." *Christ Outside the Gate* (Maryknoll, N.Y.: Orbis Books, 1982), p. 95. See also Rael and Erich Isaac, *Sanctifying Revolution* (Washington, D.C.: Ethics and Public Policy Center, 1981).
8. *Solzhenitsyn at Harvard*, edited by Ronald Berman (Washington: Ethics and Public Policy Center, 1980), p. 12.
9. Julian L. Simon, *The Ultimate Resource* (Oxford: Robertson, 1981).
10. Rousas J. Rushdoony, *God's Plan for Victory* (Fairfax, Va.: Thoburn Press, 1980). On the anabaptist hermeneutic, see Willem Balke, *Calvin and the Anabaptist Radicals* (Grand Rapids: Eerdmans, 1981), ch. 10, 12.
11. P. T. Bauer, *Dissent on Development* (Cambridge, Mass.: Harvard University Press, 1976) and Karl Brunner, editor, *The First World and the Third World* (Rochester: University of Rochester, 1978).
12. Paul Johnson in *Will Capitalism Survive?*, Ernest W. Lefever, editor (Washington: Ethics and Public Policy Center, 1979), p. 4.
13. Friedman, *Capitalism and Freedom* (Chicago: University of Chicago Press, 1962), p. 9.
14. Leszek Kolakowski, *Main Currents of Marxism* (Oxford: Clarendon, 1978), p. 523.

15. On Swedish socialism see Roland Huntford, *The New Totalitarians* (New York: Stein and Day, 1980).
16. George Gilder has a lot of insight in such matters in *Wealth and Poverty* (New York: Basic Books, 1981).
17. *The Economist*, August 7, 1982, "The Crumpled Maple Leaf."

SIXTEEN

Ecclesiastical Economics: Envy Legitimized

P. T. BAUER

After Pryde wol I speken of the foule sinne of Envye, which is, as by the word of the philosophre, sorwe [sorrow] of other mannes prosperitee.

Chaucer, *The Parson's Tale*

1

Envy is traditionally one of the seven deadly sins. Vocal modern clerical opinion endows it with moral legitimacy and intellectual respectability. The results of this specious legitimization of envy are the principal themes of this chapter.

2

Since the Second World War, prominent clergymen and theologians have been much preoccupied with domestic and international differences in income and wealth. A broad consensus has emerged, and its supporters range from recent popes to explicitly Marxist clerics.

The following are the central theme and its supporting arguments. Social justice requires that incomes should be substan-

---

P. T. BAUER, one of the world's leading economists, is Professor of Economics at the London School of Economics and fellow at Cambridge University. He received a peerage from the British government in 1983 in recognition of a life of impeccable scholarship in economics. The following article is taken from his most recent book *Reality and Rhetoric: Studies in the Economics of Development* (Harvard University Press, 1984).

tially equal; appreciable differences in incomes reflect exploitation, oppression, discrimination or improper privilege; and politically organized redistribution is desirable, or even a Christian duty. These opinions are particularly common, insistent and strident in discussions on economic differences between the West and the Third World, and on those within individual Third World countries.

I shall discuss these opinions primarily by examining two influential documents by Pope Paul VI: the Encyclical Letter, *Populorum Progressio* (1967), and the Pontifical Letter, *Octogesima Adveniens* (1971), referred to hereafter as the papal documents or letters. The two documents must be treated synoptically as the latter relies heavily on the former, which is also generally more explicit than its successor.[1]

3

The main theme of the papal documents is that economic differences, consistently termed inequalities, reflect injustice.

According to these papal documents, substantial economic differences reflect the perversion of that just and natural state which is to be expected from the fact that God has created the earth for all mankind and created man in his image. The differences result from the exploitation and oppression of the weak by the strong, including denial of opportunities to the former by the latter.

The Pope quotes the Second Vatican Council: "God intended the earth and all that it contains for the use of every human being and people" (*Populorum Progressio* 22). He then quotes St Ambrose: "You are not making a gift of your possessions to the poor person. You are handing over to him what is his. For what has been given in common for the use of all, you have arrogated to yourself. The world is given to all, and not only to the rich" (*Populorum Progressio* 23).

These passages are reproduced on posters and in leaflets in numerous churches in the West. Often they refer particularly to the Third World, usually in terms such as that the earth belongs to all its peoples, yet at the same time three-quarters of them do not share in it.

Subsidiary themes support the main theme, that inequality means injustice. A major problem is the question of ". . . the fairness in the exchange of goods and in the division of wealth between individuals and countries" (*Octogesima Adveniens* 7).

The economic system left to itself widens international economic differences: ". . . rich peoples enjoy rapid growth whereas the poor develop slowly. The imbalance is on the increase: some produce a surplus of foodstuffs, others cruelly lack them and see their exports made uncertain" (Populorum Progressio 8).

Again, "in trade between developed and underdeveloped economies, conditions are too disparate and the degrees of genuine freedom available too unequal" (Populorum Progressio 61). This inequality is responsible for the persistent deterioration in the terms of trade of primary producers. "The value of manufactured goods is rapidly increasing and they can always find an adequate market. On the other hand, raw materials produced by underdeveloped countries are subject to wide and sudden fluctuations in price, a state of affairs far removed from the progressively increasing value of industrial products. . . . The poor nations remain ever poor while the rich ones become still richer" (Populorum Progressio 57).

In some cases the difficulties are legacies of colonialism. The colonial rulers have sometimes "left a precarious economy bound up for instance with the production of one kind of crop whose market prices are subject to sudden and considerable variation" (Populorum Progressio 7).

The situation calls for urgent action: "We must make haste: too many are suffering and the distance is growing that separates the progress of some and the stagnation, not to say the regression, of others" (Populorum Progressio 29).

Both within countries and also on the international plane, inequalities of wealth go hand in hand with inequalities of power: "There is also the scandal of glaring inequalities not merely in the enjoyment of possessions but even more in the exercise of power. While a small restricted group enjoys a refined civilization in certain regions, the remainder of the population, poor and scattered, is deprived of nearly all possibility of personal initiative and of responsibility, and often times even its living and working conditions are unworthy of the human person" (Populorum Progressio 9).

The Pope refers also to ". . . unproductive monopolization of resources by a small number of men" (Populorum Progressio 66). All these differences lead to ". . . social conflicts which have taken on world dimensions" (Populorum Progressio 9).

Specific groups are singled out for condemnation. They include landowners whose "landed estates impede the general prosperity because they are extensive, unused or poorly used, or because they bring hardship to peoples or are detrimental to the interests of the country (so that the common good sometimes demands their expropriation)" (*Populorum Progressio* 24). There are also people who transfer part of their money ". . . abroad purely for their own advantage, without care for the manifest wrong they inflict on their country by doing this" *(ibid)*.

There are those who create superfluous wants, so that while ". . . very large numbers of people are unable to satisfy their primary needs, superfluous needs are ingeniously created" (*Octogesima Adveniens* 9). There are those who derive "inadmissible profits" through speculation in necessities (*Octogesima Adveniens* 10). Leaders of multinational enterprises are chided for returning to ". . . inhuman principles of individualism when they operate in less developed countries" (*Populorum Progressio* 70).

There are also specific categories of victims of injustice. These include people who cannot find ". . . a decent dwelling at a price they can afford" (*Octogesima Adveniens* 11); and those ". . . who are denied the right to work [at] equitable remuneration" (*Octogesima Adveniens* 14).

Suggestions or hints for action are scattered about in the two documents. The suggestions are often extremely vague, and at times implicit rather than explicit. However, the general direction is clear. It is along the following lines.

Christians must do their best in a spirit of charity to remedy the injustice of social, cultural and especially economic differences, which, according to the Pope, at times cries to heaven. Individual action is insufficient to deal with the problems. Collective action is required and to be effective has to be political. This is so partly because of the magnitude of the problems. Another even more important reason why action has to be collective and political is that, in the explicit opinion of the Pope, governments always act for the common good (*Octogesima Adveniens* 46, quoted below). The efforts should take the form primarily of concerted international actions and plans.

The proposals revolve around the theme of politically organized redistribution. The primary theme is the urgent need for official international wealth transfers to redress existing international inequality and injustice and thereby to promote development and peace.

These official transfers are necessary ". . . to further the progress of poorer peoples, to encourage social justice among nations, to offer to less developed nations the means whereby they can further their own progress" (*Populorum Progressio* 5). For this purpose "all available resources should be pooled" (*Populorum Progressio* 43).

"Advanced nations have a very heavy obligation to help the developing peoples. . . . Every nation must produce more and better quality goods to give to all its inhabitants a truly human standard of living, and also to contribute to the common development of the human race" (*Populorum Progressio* 48).

"We must repeat once more that the superfluous wealth of rich countries should be placed at the service of poor nations. The rule which up to now held good for the benefit of those nearest to us, must today be applied to all the needy of this world. Besides, the rich will be the first to benefit as a result. Otherwise their continued greed will certainly call down upon them the judgment of God and the wrath of the poor, with consequences no one can foretell" (*Populorum Progressio* 49).

"May everyone be convinced of this: the very life of poor nations, civil peace in developing countries, and world peace itself are at stake" (*Populorum Progressio* 55).

In international trade, major changes are required to rectify the inequality of bargaining power between the West and the Third World and the lack of genuine economic freedom of the latter. International agreements ". . . would establish general norms for regulating certain prices, for guaranteeing certain types of production, for supporting certain new industries" (*Populorum Progressio* 61). "Internationally organized investment, production, trade and education would help to create employment in countries where population is growing rapidly" (*Octogesima Adveniens* 18).

Other suggestions for international action include technical assistance to less developed countries, and regional agreements among weak nations for mutual support (*Populorum Progressio* 71, 77).

The Pope writes under the heading "Development Is the New Name for Peace": "Excessive economic, social and cultural inequalities among peoples arouse tensions and conflicts, and are a danger to peace. . . . To wage war on misery and to struggle against injustice is to promote, along with improved conditions, the human and spiritual progress of all men, and therefore the common good of humanity. Peace cannot be limited to a mere absence of war" (*Populorum Progressio* 76).

The United Nations has a key role "to bring not some people but all peoples to treat each other as brothers. . . . Who does not see the necessity of thus establishing progressively a world authority capable of acting effectively in the juridicial and political sectors?" (*Populorum Progressio* 78). "Some would consider such hopes Utopian. It may be . . . that they have not perceived the dynamism of the world which desires to live more fraternally" (*Populorum Progressio* 79).

The Pope also envisages far-reaching policies within countries to promote progress and to remedy injustice: "Development demands bold transformations, innovations that go deep. Urgent reforms should be undertaken without delay" (*Populorum Progressio* 32). "As we have seen, these reforms will include expropriation of the properties of at least some categories of landowners" (*Populorum Progressio* 24).

Under the heading "Programmes and Planning" the Pope writes: "It pertains to the public authorities to choose, even to lay down, the objectives to be pursued in economic development, the ends to be achieved, and the means of attaining them, and it is for them to stimulate all the forces engaged in this common activity" (*Populorum Progressio* 33). These tasks must be left to governments, to the representatives of political power, ". . . which is the natural and necessary link for ensuring the cohesion of the social body. . . . It always intervenes with careful justice and with devotion to the common good for which it holds final responsibility" (*Octogesima Adveniens* 46).

The ultimate aim is to build a world where "every man, no matter what his race, religion or nationality, can live a full human life, freed from servitude imposed upon him by other men or by natural forces over which he has not sufficient control; a world where freedom is not an empty word and where the poor man Lazarus can sit down at the same table with the rich man" (*Populorum Progressio* 47).

4

The Pope's diagnosis and proposals are remarkably commonplace. There is nothing distinctively Christian or Catholic about them. They were already in vogue when the pronouncements were issued, and they are still in vogue today.[2] They are to be found, for example, in so secular a document as the Brandt report, *North–South: A Programme for Survival.*

Third World Catholic opinions on these matters are particularly notable because by the end of the century the great majority of Catholics are likely to be in the Third World, primarily Latin America. Here are some examples, which again I shall quote without at this point examining their validity.

According to Monsenor Alfonso Lopez Trujillo, the Secretary General of the Latin American Bishops' Conference: "The

United States and Canada are rich because the peoples of Latin America are poor. They have built their wealth on top of us."[3]

Dom Helder Camara, known as Brother of the Poor or the Red Bishop, has become an international figure with speaking engagements all over the world. In an interview with the London-based magazine *South* (December 1980) headed "The Church That Refuses to Think for the Poor," he is reported as saying:

> But it [rural poverty] is not a local problem: it is a national problem, even a continental problem. You know that the prices of our raw materials have always been set in the great decision-making centres of the world. . . . And while we [the Catholic Church] supported what amounted to social disorder, the United Nations were proclaiming that two-thirds of mankind live in inhuman conditions of misery and hunger.

Dr. Julius Nyerere, President of Tanzania (and a Catholic), said in London a few years ago:

> In one world, as in one state, when I am rich because you are poor, and I am poor because you are rich, the transfer of wealth from the rich to the poor is a matter of right, it is not an appropriate matter for charity. . . . If the rich nations go on getting richer and richer at the expense of the poor, the poor of the world must demand a change in the same way as the proletariat in the rich countries demanded a change in the past.[4]

Finally, an example from an influential source which explicitly brings in the multinational companies. Peter Nichols, Rome correspondent of *The Times* (London), wrote in his much-publicized book *The Pope's Divisions* (London 1981): "Much of the economy [of Latin America] is dominated by multinationals who take out basic raw materials in return for impossible wages."[5]

5

Income differences cannot be discussed sensibly without looking at their background. Individuals, groups and societies can be poor for any number of different reasons. Thus a person may become poor because he has habitually overspent a large income; or he may be poor for circumstances entirely beyond his control such as incurable disease, confiscation of his assets, or the restriction of his opportunities. Individuals and groups may be materially unambitious. Contrast for instance the conduct and position of Malays and Chinese in Malaysia. Again, if many poor people survive longer in an ldc, this depresses *per capita* incomes and leads to what is habitually termed a worsening of income distribution, both within the particular country and relative to richer countries. Conversely, if more of the poor die or a society reverts to subsistence production, this brings about more equal incomes within a country, accompanied by a rise in *per capita* incomes in the former case and a decline in the latter case.

In egalitarian discourse, the notion that the well-off have prospered at the expense of the poor is rarely far below the surface, a notion which is useful or even necessary for the moral plausibility of politically organized redistribution. Without such an underpinning, the case for redistributive taxation (which in effect is partial confiscation) or for other forms of expropriation is not self-evident. Why should social justice mean substantially equal incomes? Why is it obviously unjust that those who contribute more to production should have higher incomes than those who contribute less?

The case for politically organized redistribution becomes yet more dubious when it is remembered that this policy is apt to aggravate the lot of the poorest as well as to aggrandize those who organize the transfers. To begin with, state-organized redistribution often benefits middle income groups at the expense both of the rich and of the poor. This is now widely recognized in the context of redistribution within a country, especially when the benefits accruing to the administrators of these policies are also taken into account. Moreover, redistribution inhibits enterprise and effort and the accumulation and productive deployment of capital, and this result retards a rise in living standards, including those of the poorest.

The adverse effects of redistribution on the living standards of the poorest are perforce ignored when income and wealth are envisaged, as they often are, as being extracted from other people, or somehow achieved at their expense by depriving them of what they had or could have had. They are regarded as fixed totals rather than as the results of productive activities and processes over time. In market economies, however, incomes are normally earned; they are not shares in a pre-existing total.

Group differences in economic performance abound in the Third World. In Malaysia, for instance, Chinese economic performance has for many years been far superior to that of Malays in spite of long-standing discrimination against them. In recent years, indeed, attempts to combat by political means the results of their superior economic performance have become the cornerstone of official economic policy. (Other examples of the relative success of groups discriminated against are commonplace in economic history.) In Latin America also, the prosperity of the landowners, industrialists and merchants has not been achieved at the expense of the poor. The economic conditions of the poorest groups, such as the Indians of Central and Southern America and the Negro descendants of slaves in Brazil, are no worse, and in many ways are far better, than were those of their ancestors. The economic conditions of Negroes in Brazil do not differ greatly from those of Africans in the more advanced parts of black Africa.

The notion that incomes of the more prosperous have somehow been achieved at the expense of the less prosperous has had a long and disastrous history. In its duration and consequences it is perhaps the most pernicious of all economic misconceptions. On the contemporary scene it has contributed to the persecution of economically productive but politically unpopular and powerless minorities in the Third World.

There are, of course, major exceptions to the general proposition that the incomes of the prosperous are earned. Perhaps the most important exceptions are incomes derived predominantly from government-conferred privileges. Such privileges are especially significant and widespread in the extremely politicized societies of the Third World. Their many forms include state subsidies, restrictions on competition, allocations of licences and privileged forms of employment. These privileged incomes are not what the Pope and other clerics have in mind in their attacks on inequality. Such privileged incomes are not relevant to international differences in income. And in the national sphere it is the papal view that governments act for the general good, so that the results of their policies cannot be the subject for redress through politically organized redistribution. Moreover, recipients of such privileged incomes are not necessarily rich. Finally, egalitarian discourse is addressed to income differences as such, not to privileged incomes *vis-à-vis* other incomes.[6]

6

Sometimes the papal documents do not ascribe the poverty of the poor to exploitation or oppression. Instead, the failure of poor people, notably poor societies, to share in contemporary prosperity is attributed to lack of natural resources, especially land.

Lack of natural resources, including land, has little or nothing to do with the poverty of individuals or of societies. Amidst abundant land and natural resources the Indians before Columbus remained wretchedly poor when much of Europe with far less land was already rich. In the less developed world today, many millions of extremely poor people have abundant cultivable land. Over much of Asia, Africa and Latin America very large numbers of extremely poor and backward people live in areas where cultivable but uncultivated land is free or extremely cheap. The small size and low productivity of farms and the presence of landless workers in such areas reflect not the shortage of land but primarily the lack of ambition, enterprise and skill.

Of course, land which has been improved by the efforts and savings of productive people is the target for demands for redistribution even where unimproved land is plentiful. Who would not welcome a free gift of valuable assets? Land on its own is unproductive, and yields nothing of value to mankind. It becomes productive as a result of ambition, perceptiveness, resourcefulness and effort. These attributes and characteristics are present very unequally among different individuals, groups and societies.

Sustained prosperity, as distinct from occasional windfalls, owes little or nothing to natural resources: witness West Germany, Switzerland, Japan, Singapore, Hong Kong and Taiwan. The wide differences in economic performance between individuals and groups in the same country with access to the same natural resources throw into relief the personal and cultural differences behind economic achievement.

The conditions of the poorest and most backward people throughout the Third World, such as tribal societies, pygmies and aborigines, cannot possibly have anything to do with lack of land, Western exploitation or the activities of ethnic minorities.

These groups have few contacts either with the West or with economically active ethnic minorities. They also have abundant land at their disposal. Much the same applies to the causes of famine and to the lack of so-called basic facilities. For instance, the famines in sparsely populated African countries such as Ethiopia, the Sahel, Tanzania, Uganda and Zaire reflect the low level of subsistence or near-subsistence activity, perpetuated or aggravated by the lack of public security and by damaging policies such as official suppression of trading activity, forced collectivization and the persecution of productive groups, notably ethnic or tribal minorities.

7

I turn now to some issues, including moral issues, raised by the Pope's general approach to income differences and to the policies appropriate to their reduction or elimination. This approach entails major spiritual and moral implications and consequences which many people may well consider even more destructive than the political and economic effects. I should perhaps recall here that the Pope's opinions expressed in *Populorum Progressio* and *Octogesima Adveniens* reflect what is virtually a consensus of opinions of contemporary churchmen on what they call social justice. Indeed, the language of the younger Catholic clergy and of Protestant churchmen is apt to be much more strident.

The persistent preoccupation with income differences and with the contrast in prosperity between the West and the Third World is much more likely to arouse envy than to elicit compassion. The allegations that prosperity reflects misconduct and therefore injustice lace envy with resentment and righteous indignation. Such notions also reflect and reinforce the contemporary tendency to play down personal responsibility by suggesting that people's economic conditions depend on external forces rather than on themselves.

The modern clerical consensus endorsed by the Pope buttresses and encourages envy and resentment by conferring apparent moral legitimacy and intellectual validity on these sentiments. Insistence on politically organized redistribution within and between countries also fuels envy and resentment. Articulate clergymen and many academics have traditionally shared an attitude of suspicion and hostility towards people actively engaged in the process of wealth creation, and also an attitude of supercilious disdain for its results.

Envy and resentment are soul-destroying sentiments liable to corrode people afflicted by them. What the Pope asserts, in common with so many other modern clergymen, serves to encourage one of the seven deadly sins.

To arouse these sentiments is to provoke tension and conflict. In this way conflicts originating in politicization or in other influences can be extended, intensified and brutalized. Moreover, the fear of being exposed to envy and to its political and social consequences inhibits economic performance and improvement. This applies notably in tribal societies.

The catch-phrase "the earth belongs to all" epitomizes the central thrust of the papal documents and is bound to provoke envy, or something stronger. This slogan has become a rallying cry in inflammatory propaganda against the West and against well-to-do people both in the Third World and in the West. The principal theme is that some three-quarters of mankind languish in poverty, excluded from their rightful heritage through misconduct of the well-to-do, and especially by the sinister domination of Western financial institutions and multinational companies.

A leaflet distributed in Chartres cathedral in 1979 is typical. Entitled (not surprisingly) "The Earth Belongs to All" ("La terre est à tous"), the leaflet quotes a resolution of thirteen Brazilian bishops—who claim to be the voice of their voiceless people—that nothing will change in their country without fundamental changes in the advanced countries where the centres of domination and private capital are located. The leaflet insists that radical changes in the West are necessary to bring about a new international economic order, meaning large-scale confiscation of wealth as restitution for supposed economic wrongs. These political demands are described as the essence of Christ's message— the only mention of Christ in the four-page document.

Such propaganda plays upon and reinforces the widespread feeling of guilt in the West towards the Third World, a feeling which does nothing to assist the ordinary people in ldcs, but is more likely to harm them.[7] Exponents of collective guilt rarely examine either the ground for their allegations or the results of the policies they propose. In the context of foreign aid, such allegations are most likely to lead to indiscriminate wealth transfers to Third World governments and to various international organizations. The emphasis on guilt precludes close examination either of conditions in the recipient countries or of the conduct of the recipient governments. These considerations are pertinent, especially because guilt so often parades as compassion and is so readily confused with it. The exponents of guilt routinely exempt themselves from their accusations; they do not speak of *mea culpa* but of *nostra culpa*, or rather *vestra culpa*. This is not accidental; allegations of collective guilt go hand in hand with a decline in personal responsibility and a sense of personal sin.

The Pope regards official transfers as a discharge of moral duty and as action substantially similar to voluntary charity. Yet there is an evident difference in moral content between voluntary sacrifice to help one's fellow men and public spending out of taxes. Taxpayers have no choice, and many may not know that they contribute for this particular purpose. The political and economic effects of the two forms of transfer also differ profoundly. The activities of voluntary agencies, especially non-politicized charities, do not politicize life as does official foreign aid, and thus they avoid the baleful results of the politicization of life promoted by official transfers. Moreover, voluntary charity is generally adjusted far more effectively to the conditions and needs of local people. In particular, voluntary agencies are much more interested in alleviating the lot of the poorest than are most rulers in the Third World.

At one point the Pope insists on liberating people from subjection to the forces of nature. But many millions of people in Asia do not share the Western outlook that nature should be harnessed to man's purposes. They think or feel that man should learn to live with nature rather than try to subordinate it to his own purposes. Generally, Western culture envisages nature as serving the purpose of man, who has the right, indeed the duty, to subordinate it to his own purposes. The indigenous cultures of South Asia envisage organic creation as a continuum which man has no special right to subject to his own purposes.

The Pope enjoins his audience to respect non-Western civilizations and cultures. The cultures of large parts of the less developed world are uncongenial to economic achievement and advance. The idea of material progress, in the sense of a steadily increasing control by man over nature, is wholly of Western origin. It is anomalous to insist that the West should respect Third World cultures and at the same time to urge that the West should pay taxes for the benefit of those who embrace cultures inimical to economic advance.

In the face of the clerical consensus on Western responsibility for Third World poverty, it was unexpected and refreshing recently to find an opinion by a Third World prelate who disagrees fundamentally with received opinion and who has the moral courage to say so. He is Monseigneur Bernard Bududira, Bishop of Bururi in Burundi in Central Africa, and an African. Part of an article by the Bishop in a French-language African journal was reproduced in German translation in the Swiss newspaper *Neue Zürcher Zeitung* of 4/5 January 1981. It is a remarkable article.

Bishop Bududira's principal theme is that the local cultures in Africa and elsewhere in the Third World obstruct material progress. The Bishop insists that economic improvement of a person depends on the person himself, notably on his mental attitudes and especially on his attitude to work. Unquestioning acceptance of nature and of its vagaries is widespread in Africa and elsewhere in the Third World. Man sees himself not as making history but as suffering it. To regard life as inexorably ordained by fate prevents a person from developing his or her potential. Under these influences people become passive rather than active, and the obligations of the extended family system stifle ambition and creative imagination. Initiative may be inhibited further by dependence upon tribal groups which suppress innovation and regard efforts for change and improvement as forms of rebellion. The Bishop concludes that the message of Christ frees people from the shackles of tribal thinking, and leads to a greater sense of personal responsibility. The required changes can best be achieved by Christian groups working with local communities.

Some of these ideas used to be familiar, but they are very rarely heard nowadays. The translator commented that only an African could now write such an article. This observation is notable recognition of the success of the pedlars of Western guilt. Were it not for this factor, it would be by no means obvious why a European should not now write along such lines.

8

According to the opening paragraph of *Populorum Progressio*, the document is to help people "to grasp their serious problems in all its dimensions . . . at this turning point in human history." This promise is not fulfilled. The papal letters are not theological, doctrinal or philosophical statements reaffirming Christian beliefs or helping people to find their bearings. They are political statements supported by bogus arguments, and as such can only confuse believers.

As will be clear from what has gone before, the Pope has lost all contact with reality, both in what he says and what he ignores. Amidst large-scale civil conflict (as in Nigeria and Vietnam at the time of *Populorum Progressio*), massacres, mass persecution and expulsions in ldcs, the Pope wrote about the solidarity and brotherhood of humanity in the less developed world, and also stated that governments always act for the common good. He ignores the relation between culture and economic achievement and the relevance of mores and beliefs to economic performance and progress. There is also a complete disregard of historical processes and of the perspective of time, as evidenced by the neglect of the fact that until very recently extreme material backwardness characterized most of the Third World. And yet applications of the time perspective used to be very much an element in Catholic thinking.

Even the eternal verities are overlooked. The responsibility of a person for the consequences of his actions and the fundamental distinction between mankind and the rest of creation are basic

Christian tenets. They are pertinent to the issues raised by the Pope; but they are ignored throughout these documents.

In common with many other modern Christian clerics, Paul VI, his predecessor John XXIII, and to some extent also John Paul II, have chosen to speak on subjects with which they have been unfamiliar. People who pronounce on matters about which they are ignorant are apt simply to absorb ideas propagated or taken up by other élite or establishment groups. Nature abhors a vacuum not only in the physical world but also in the world of politics and ideas.

The Pope's arguments and allegations reflect unthinking surrender into intellectual fashion and political nostrums. This is obvious in the major themes, particularly in the insistence on large-scale official aid. The more specific topics and proposals are also a recital of modish remedies such as land reform, debt cancellation, commodity agreements and regional co-operation among ldcs.

The spirit of these documents is contrary to the most durable and best elements in Catholic tradition. They are indeed even un-Christian. Their Utopian, chiliastic ideology, combined with an overriding preoccupation with economic differences, is an amalgam of the ideas of millenarian sects, of the extravagant claims of the early American advocates of foreign aid, and of the Messianic component of Marxism-Leninism.

There is a familiar and ominous ring in the insistence that economic advance requires "bold transformations, innovations that go deep" by political means. Such a stance has been regularly advanced to justify pervasive coercion and brutal policies. These harsh consequences are a familiar outcome of replacing conduct based on experience and reflection by ideological politics. In this sphere also it is true that those who wish to turn men into angels are more likely to turn them into beasts. The chiliasm of these documents is alien to the traditional down-to-earth attitude of the Catholic Church in worldly matters.

Populorum Progressio and *Octogesima Adveniens* are documents which are immoral on several levels. To begin with they are incompetent, and they are immoral because they are incompetent. Their lack of reflection and ideological commitment leads to proposals and promotes policies directly at variance with the declared sentiments and objectives of the papal documents. There is profound truth in Pascal's maxim that working hard to think clearly is the beginning of moral conduct. This applies with altogether special force to the head of a worldwide Church issuing major pronouncements. The documents are also immoral in that they give colour to the notion that envy can be legitimate; and they spread confusion about the meaning of charity.

It seems that many contemporary churchmen have lost their way and have moved into realms which are strange to them. They may perhaps have been seeking a new role for themselves in the face of widespread erosion or even the collapse of traditional beliefs. Their preoccupations may reflect a panic reaction to fear of the loss of their clientele. Some of the utterances of the modern clergy recall Othello's predicament when he felt that his occupation had gone, together with the attendant pomp and circumstance. It is paradoxical that the clergy are preoccupied with material conditions and progress at a time when the failure of material prosperity and advance to secure happiness, satisfaction and tranquillity is everywhere evident.

Acceptance of ideas plainly at variance with reality may, however, also reflect the ready credulity of people, clerics included, who have lost their faith. Chesterton predicted long ago that when men cease to believe in a deity, they do not believe in nothing: they then simply believe in anything.

Truth may be great and will perhaps prevail. Scholars at any rate must act as if they believed both parts of this statement. But it requires exceptional strength of belief to hope that truth will triumph in the decades ahead in egalitarian discussions, especially about the Third World. The modern clerical consensus will certainly not help it to victory. Prelates such as Bishop Bududira might do so.

NOTES

1. The numbers in parentheses in the text refer to the numbered paragraphs in these documents. The passages are quoted from the official English texts published by Polyglot Press, Vatican City, in 1967 and 1971. Unless stated otherwise, references to the Pope are to Paul VI. Some of the passages I quote incorporate statements from other prominent Catholic sources. As these statements are accepted and endorsed by the Pope, I shall usually not refer to the original sources but quote them as expressions of the Pope's views. The present Pope, John Paul II, seems to share the central opinions on economic matters of his recent predecessors. This is suggested by the encyclical *Laborem Exercens*, 1981, which is, however, less calculated to arouse envy and resentment than the encyclicals of Paul VI. I shall not on this occasion quote Protestant clergymen or theologians. Elsewhere I have examined some opinions by Professor Ronald J. Sider, a prominent evangelical churchman, on the subject of economic differences between the West and the Third World. His opinions are typical of much contemporary evangelical thought. He is quoted extensively in the chapter entitled "Western Guilt and Third World Poverty," in

P. T. Bauer, *Equality, the Third World and Economic Delusion*, London and Cambridge, Mass., 1981.
2. The modishness, one might say trendiness, of the papal documents is evident throughout. Section headings include "Women," "Environment" and "Development—A New Name for Peace." The documents also, unsurprisingly, discuss such topics as debt rescheduling, commodity agreements and rent controls—in every instance at an amateur, populist level.
3. Quoted by Malcolm Deas, "Catholics and Marxists," in *London Review of Books*, March 19, 1981.
4. Julius Nyerere, "The Economic Challenge: Dialogue or Confrontation," in *African Affairs*, London, April 1976.
5. Quoted by Malcolm Deas, "Catholics and Marxists," in *London Review of Books*, March 19, 1981.
6. Especially in the past, people have often acquired wealth not by peaceful economic contacts in commercial transactions, but by despoiling other people. Where there is no public security, the strong can despoil the weak so regularly that this is not even regarded as criminal. Such conditions may well have been widespread in the fourth century A.D. when St. Ambrose denounced the rich (cf. section 3 above), though it is doubtful whether he specifically had in mind spoliation by the rich. The acquisition of wealth in this way does not, of course, represent the generation of income as this is usually understood. Moreover, spoliation results from lack of public security. Where a government fails to perform its primary function, it is extremely improbable that it would or could organize redistribution on any basis likely to be fair.
7. Cf. Chapter 2, section 9, and Chapter 3, section 7, above.

SEVENTEEN

Compassion and the Poor

LLOYD BILLINGSLEY

The poor, say those on the religious left, are the only ones who have the right to inscribe on their belt buckles, like German soldiers in 1914, the words *Gott mit uns.* Or as it is usually phrased: God is on the side of the poor.

People are poor for various reasons, not for one only, but one would never guess this from reading radical Christian publications. For instance, people can be poor because of their own lack of discipline and initiative. A steady provider can develop an alcohol or cocaine habit and plunge himself and his family into poverty. This group gets no sympathy from the Bible at all. In fact, they earn God's judgment.

Other poor people are genuine victims, suffering from injury, disease, or catastrophes such as famine and earthquake. The people of God are commanded to help such ones, because God himself is moved with compassion for them.

Still others are poor because of economic exploitation. Slavery is a historical example of this; South African apartheid and the East Indian caste system are contemporary versions. In case of exploitation, the victims have rightful claim to biblical justice.

A final group are the voluntary poor, who willingly give up affluent careers to better serve God and their fellow human beings. With ministerial salaries what they are, pastors could almost be included in this group en masse. Missionaries are another obvious example.[1]

The radical Christians see poverty as almost exclusively the

LLOYD BILLINGSLEY is a novelist and screenplay writer and a regular contributor to *Christianity Today.* His book *The Generation That Knew Not Josef,* from which this chapter is taken, was very recently published (Multnomah Press, 1985). A novel, *A Year for Life,* is scheduled for publication by Crossway Books.

result of economic victimization. Somehow, Western structural mechanisms like an open market and universal suffrage discriminate against the poor, while a controlled economy and one-party state such as that of Cuba is seen as somehow liberating and beneficial. It is assumed that the free enterprise model is the exploiter. Large corporations receive the radical's wrath in spite of the fact that, as Louis Fischer pointed out, Marxist governments are one huge corporation that controls *everything* and from which there is no escape, as there is from Nestle or Exxon. As Djilas shows, the capitalism that Marxists rave about no longer exists, but the radical Christians do not appear to have noticed. They are living in the past, nostalgic for the days of the dark satanic mills described by Charles Dickens and Karl Marx.

The exploitation model also begs the question of why living standards are higher in free economies. People *flee* closed societies like mainland China for better conditions in free enterprise countries. When refugees leave poor countries such as Mexico or El Salvador, they most often go to the United States, not to socialist Nicaragua. Why is this, if capitalist, open-market, politically free countries are examples of exploitive structures? If socialist dictatorships are so desirable, why must they wall in their subjects? It bears repeating that even Hitler did not need such draconian measures.

The economic exploitation explanation for poverty demands a political solution. It assumes that those groups that have risen out of poverty have done so by political means. There is little if any evidence for this, as Thomas Sowell shows in *The Economics and Politics of Race.* The overseas Chinese, the Italians in Brazil, the Irish and blacks in America, and the Jews in many countries have generally kept their distance from politics. Where they have bettered themselves economically, Sowell shows, it has been the result of hard work, thrift, and personal sacrifice. These can yield results only in an open economic system. If there is a political solution, it lies in keeping the option for people to initiate their own economic activity.

The radical Christians explain poverty in the lesser developed countries by echoing the Leninist explanation first advanced to show why, contrary to what Marx predicted, capitalist workers got wealthier instead of poorer. Lenin said, in effect, that the capitalist bosses were exploiting poor countries and forestalling revolution at home by buying off their workers with high wages. Today this explanation is called the North-South Economic Dialogue. It fails to explain two things: why the lesser developed countries were poor in the first place, and why those that have had most contact with the allegedly imperialist powers have higher standards of living. This theory is popular because it advances an explanation of poverty based not on any inadequacies on the part of the lesser developed countries themselves, but only on moral deficiencies on the part of others. As Sowell writes:

> The enduring and fervent belief in imperialism as the cause of Third World poverty is difficult to understand in terms of empirical evidence. But this belief is much more readily understandable in terms of the high psychic and political cost of believing otherwise. These costs are high not only to some people in the Third World, but also to those in the West whose whole vision of the world depends upon seeing poverty as victimization and themselves as rescuers—both domestically and internationally. Many such people assume a stance of being partisans of the poor. But even to be an effective partisan of the poor, one must first be a partisan of the truth.[2]

One notices too a clear selectivity in the poor that the religious left chooses to champion. There are certain poor groups in their view worthy of love and support—and then there are others that are not. Jacques Ellul, who radical Christians readily quote when he agrees with them, points out that groups like the Kurds, the Tibetans, and the monarchist Yemenites do not attract the attention of radical Christian groups. Why is this? Are they not as poor as American blacks or the Philippine underclasses? Why do radical Christians find them uninteresting? Ellul has a theory.

> Alas, the reason is simple. The interesting poor are those whose defense is in reality an attack against Europe, against capitalism, against the U.S.A. The uninteresting poor represent forces that are considered passé. Their struggle concerns only themselves. They are fighting not to destroy a capitalist or colonialist regime, but simply to survive as individuals, as a culture, a people. And that, of course, is not at all interesting, is it? But the choice violent Christians make has nothing to do with love of the poor. They choose to support this or that group or movement because it is socialist, anti-colonialist, anti-imperialist etc.[3]

To touch on the issue of labeling here, Ellul normally uses the term "revolutionary Christians" in his book on violence. Here, he substitutes "violent Christians."

Every issue of *Sojourners* and *The Other Side* bears out this interesting/uninteresting distinction. They support, for the most part, the aristrocratic poor who have advocates in the UN and among film stars, such groups as the PLO and SWAPO. They say nothing about the others. Hence, their call to aid the poor lacks credibility.

Listening to the religious left, though, one wonders whether it is even desirable for any people to lift themselves out of poverty. The mindset of *Sojourners* and *The Other Side* reveals a tension between ameliorating conditions of the poor and exalting poverty as a virtue in itself. Theoretically, once people lift themselves out of poverty, they become part of the materialist mainstream and thus fodder for broadsides to "be more concerned about the poor."

On the one hand, they say poverty is abominable, and God's wrath is called down on us for allowing it (even though Jesus Christ himself said the poor would always be with us). On the other hand, radical Christians lead us to believe that poverty is the only acceptable lifestyle for Christians and hence desirable. One cannot have it both ways.

The radical Christian ethic exalting poverty as a virtue in itself is a new version of the thirties intellectuals' deification of the proletariat. Arthur Koestler explained how eggheads like himself would willingly eschew their background and learning and lobotomize themselves just to be like Ivan Ivanov—the prototypical poor worker. Everyone unproletarian was dismissed as bourgeois. Being proletarian can even become a question of wearing the right clothing. Muggeridge described Orwell as decked out in "proletarian fancy-dress." The call to holy poverty is the same sort of social descent.

Can it really be contended that North American and European Christians are not concerned about the poor? American Christians give billions each year in charitable donations. Groups like the Salvation Army have been on the scene at foreign and domestic disasters before anyone else. They are the ones who run missions for derelict alcoholics—a case of the uninteresting poor if there ever was one—not Greenpeace or the Socialist Workers Party or the Sierra Club. What of the clinics, the counseling, the hospitals founded by religious groups? What of the acceptance of refugees from countries as diverse as El Salvador and Vietnam?

The March 1983 issue of *The Other Side* derided groups such as the Salvation Army for being "supportive of the political status quo," even though the Army also operates in Cuba and Nicaragua. In those countries, should they denounce the revolutionary status quo?

Government programs for the poor in the West have tended to be very generous. It has been said that the only budgets in the world larger than the American allocation for the Department of Health, Education and Welfare are the entire budget of the United States and the entire budget of the Soviet Union. In any case, it cannot be seriously maintained that Western governments do nothing about the poor. They even take in the poor created by their enemies, such as the United States' acceptance of the last flotilla from Cuba, many of whom were elderly and handicapped. Theoretically, the marvelous social services of the Cuban state should draw the poor from the four corners of the world.

When there have been earthquakes and natural catastrophes in various parts of the world, many Western nations have rushed material aid, medicine, and personnel to the scene. When Mount St. Helens devastates a huge portion of a state or when a tornado destroys 90 percent of a Wisconsin town, what Third World country constantly accusing the United States of being a grasping exploiter is there lending a hand? None. Western capitalistic nations, to their great credit, have continued to feed the hand that bites them. Some Third World leaders such as Julius Nyerere, whose country of Tanzania has received more aid than any other, have used transfers of funds to consolidate their own power, persecute their enemies, and continue economic experiments which have miserably failed.

I do not suggest that Western societies and their economic systems are perfect. But as the record shows, they tend to outperform their scientific socialist counterparts when it comes to providing for the poor.

None of us, especially those like myself who see a small role for government, should rest on our laurels. We need to be constantly exhorted to do more for the poor, within the church and without. God commands us to do so. Whether the religious left holds the moral qualifications to make this exhortation— along with their occasional appeal for donations for themselves— remains to be seen.

When Jesus saw the multitudes, the Gospels tell us, he was "moved with compassion."[4] The face of the Savior must have had a way of radiating his inner feelings. In another place we are told that Jesus, beholding the rich young ruler, "loved him."[5]

Compassion is a beautiful word, but now so abased as to be barely usable. Politicians have been largely responsible for this. The late David Lewis of the Canadian New Democratic party (socialist) based his 1974 election platform on a call for a "Compassionate Canada," with the adjective in this case meaning,

"More control by a government of its citizens' resources." The American Democratic party describes itself as "the party of compassion." The word in this connection has come to mean something like "the willingness of a representative to spend other people's money." Those unwilling to spend at acceptable levels are charged with "lacking compassion."

Jim Wallis outlined the radical Christian position on compassion in a September 1979 *Sojourners* editorial about Vietnamese refugees called "Compassion Not Politics for Refugees." Wallis concedes that the suffering of these people is "real," hardly an original revelation. He understates their perils, though, by neglecting to mention marauding Thai pirates who prey on the refugees and sink entire ships. He goes on to say that it is important to "get the facts straight" and that the coverage of the boat people has been "filled with inaccuracies, myths, misconceptions, and outright lies," though he neither mentions nor refutes any of these with facts of his own. The situation, we are told, "is complex and highly politicized and does not lend itself to easy explanations."

The shift away from simple explanations represents a change for the radical Christians. During the war it was very simple indeed; if you favored the American-South Vietnamese side, you were wrong; if you favored an American pullout and the victory of the North, you were right. It was simplicity itself. You were either part of the problem or part of the solution. But now easy explanations are eschewed, though Jim Wallis goes on to advance one himself.

Did the Vietnamese government, by any chance, have anything to do with this problem? Perhaps a bit. Their policies, wrote Wallis, were "harsh." One should pause a moment here and contemplate this adjective.

When the Reagan administration, a government elected by an overwhelming majority, put forth its 1980 budget, the cover of *Sojourners* thundered, "ASSAULT ON THE POOR." Its writers readily use pejorative terms such as "militant," "oppressive," "reactionary," and "right-wing" for those who disagree with them. But when a revolutionary government strips people who merely want to leave of all their belongings, extorts outlandish "exit fees," then shoves them off to sea in rusty tubs that barely float, all this merits the description "harsh," something one might say of an overbearing high school principal. What word would they use if West Germany sent its Turkish minority packing on rafts in the North Sea? It would probably not be "harsh." But there is more.

After this scolding, Wallis says that the government "must

take more responsibility for the orderly and safe exit of those who choose to leave." One looks for terms like "right" and "wrong" here, but the government simply must take "more responsiblity," whatever that means. "In this respect," Wallis continues, "the revolution has become the regime and has begun to behave like governments everywhere." Really? Do governments everywhere do this kind of thing to potential emigrants? Does Iceland? Sweden? Belgium? Uruguay? As it happens, only socialist, revolutionary governments such as that of Vietnam have made crossing borders a tricky procedure, particularly on the way out.

It is not long before Wallis gets around to those who are, in his view, really responsible for the refugees—the United States, of course, even though this happened after the American forces left, something that Wallis urged for years.

Slipped into all this is an amazing sentence about the refugees themselves that should be read over several times, preferably aloud, and as slowly as possible. It says a great deal about radical Christian compassion.

> Many of today's refugees were inoculated with a taste for a Western lifestyle during the war and are fleeing to support their consumer habit in other lands.

Notice the sweeping generality ("many") applied to those who were inoculated with this criminal taste for Western lifestyle. And what does Western lifestyle mean? A tendency toward democracy? Mickey Mouse T-shirts? Freedom of religion? A large welfare budget? Abundance of the necessities of life? What? The imagery is that of the addict, fleeing to support his habit. The conclusion is inescapable: many of the refugees to some degree *deserve* what they are getting. Their crime was to be "inoculated with Western lifestyle." This, we are led to believe, merits banishment in leaking boats.

Imagine this scenario: You are a Vietnamese refugee, drifting on a derelict freighter in the South China Sea. Water is low, food almost nonexistent. You have no medical supplies or resources of any sort. Speedboats appear, full of heavily armed Thai pirates who rape the younger women, take some prisoner, steal everything they can find, murder some people outright, then sink the ship. You are left treading water, the cries of the drowning ringing in your ears. Wouldn't it be comforting to know that in secure, faraway America, the editor of a radical magazine, in an editorial about compassion, is announcing to the world that you are a Western junkie, fleeing to support your consumer habit in other lands?

The November 1979 *National Geographic* reports that Hong Kong officials picked up a pregnant woman and her child who were in two inner tubes being pushed through shark-invested waters by the woman's swimming husband. The consumer addiction of this group was indeed serious. Doubtless, they were after that color television set denied them under socialism.

Wallis denounces then-Vice President Walter Mondale for calling the Vietnamese government callous and arrogant and ends his editorial with, "Our response to the refugees must be one of active concern for the refugees, not out of political self-interest, but out of the compassion of Christ." All in all, quite a performance.

As it stands, this statement on the boat people is a piece of poltroonery ranking with the most bigoted and vicious I have ever read. It is similar to Anna Louise Strong dismissing the murder of kulaks on the grounds that Russia could get along without them, and explaining that Uncle Joe Stalin, after all, had only authorized what the people were already doing. The kulaks too, I suppose, in refusing collectivization, had thus inoculated themselves with Western lifestyle. Then too it has the ring of *Pravda* statements about "rootless cosmopolitans" who have the nerve to leave the Soviet Union.

One wonders what, by these standards, constitutes an attack if this editorial, as claimed, expresses compassion. *Sojourners* does give us some clues. In February 1980, Danny Collum reviewed Bob Dylan's *Slow Train Coming* album. On one of the cuts, "Gonna Change My Way of Thinking," Dylan says he is going to "stop being influenced by fools." This was too much for Collum, who called it "accusatory" and "downright mean." One would almost think that Dylan was in the process of fleeing to support a consumer habit. Has the government of Vietnam ever been "downright mean"? Or just "harsh"?

Other questions arise. What of the Central American refugees pouring into the United States? Are they, too, fleeing to support a consumer habit? Should they stay at home and be happy in poverty? It hardly need be said what the implication is for those of us who live in the West.

Compassion? When a radical Christian says this, he really means compulsion. This attack on helpless refugees betrays a tunnel vision that is almost clinical. There is an ideological fungus on the political retina of radical Christians, blinding them to the faults of the dour Stalinists who currently run Vietnam. Before they would make any negative statements about a revolutionary (good) government, they attack the moral integrity of the victims of that government. It is assumed that the Vietnamese who remain are bound to do what they are told, even forced labor, euphemistically described in other *Sojourners* articles as "participating in the building of a new society." In the meantime, for the radical Christians, it is up onto Rosinante and off at a gallop to the next crusade on behalf of the downtrodden and oppressed through whose plight the United States can be denounced.

Michael Novak was once something of a radical Christian. As an antiwar activist, he even wrote speeches for George McGovern. When asked in an interview why he had changed his stance, he answered:

> One thing that encouraged me in that direction, in fact necessitated this direction, was the destructiveness of radical politics in foreign affairs. The terrible plight of the Cambodian people, the boat people of South Vietnam, and the extraordinary suffering of the people of Vietnam today, have led me to realize that those of us who called for the end of the war in Vietnam unwittingly did something terrible. We caused even more destruction and more suffering, and we are guilty of the consequences of our actions. The least we can do is to learn from such things.[6]

Here is a man who, facing the facts, says that he was *wrong* about Vietnam. No such admission has been forthcoming from the radical Christians. This is a bit surprising.

At other junctures in recent history, *Sojourners* has been strong on apologizing. In the wake of the Iranian hostage crisis, Wallis wrote an editorial entitled "We Could Just Ask Them to Forgive Us,"[7] even though it was the Iranians, not the Americans, who took the hostages. The piece ends, "If our national pride and arrogance prevail over our reason and compassion, we will indeed reap the whirlwind." To apologize for someone else's wrongdoing, then, is to show compassion.

Perhaps the boat people deserve an apology for the things *Sojourners* has said about them; but, for now at least, being a radical Christian means never having to say you're sorry.

Barely anything that appears in publications of the religious left challenges the assumption that change is progress. In their view, the worst possible action anyone can take, particularly a Christian, is to defend the status quo in any way. The changes that are urged are of a structural, institutional variety and will, we are told, lead to social justice.

What this progressive view lacks is an historical perspective. A status quo composed of a divine-right monarch, an arrogant aristocracy, an authoritarian church, and an all-powerful police force is one thing. A status quo of a government of freely elected officials, a free press, universal suffrage, an open market economy, generous welfare programs, public education, and a police force that must read one his rights before arrest is something else. Yet the superstition of radical Christians is that to challenge the sort of institutions that exist not only in the U.S.A. but also in Canada, Lichtenstein, Belgium, and Holland is progressive; to hold that they are adequate is reactionary.

The test for anything is not whether it is progressive, but whether it is right. A preponderant government that simultaneously dominated and took care of everyone was what feudalism was all about. Free enterprise democracy constitutes an improvement on that model. To identify progress with an ever-increasing government that serves a kind of omnipresent wet nurse is to endorse a return to a modern form of feudalism. André Gide used these very words of the Soviet Union. In this system, the arrogant landowner is replaced by the arrogant bureaucrat.

Christian radicals, like mainline liberals, are slow to recognize that good intentions are not enough and that government programs set up to eliminate poverty sometimes only create dependency. Their main beneficiaries are often administrating bureaucrats. Yet it is the politician who most *talks* about poverty and social justice who attracts the support of the religious left. Curiously, many politicians of this description—Teddy Kennedy and Pierre Trudeau for instance—are independently wealthy as a result of business acumen.

But a political candidate who is for free enterprise and business does not merit the support of the religious left because his *intention* is to help people make profits, regardless of what other benefits accrue to the community as a result of the increased economic activity.

In free societies, people have certain rights: life, liberty, and property, for instance. It is the role of government to guard these rights. The religious left confuses rights and goals. Living independent of government dole, in adequate circumstances, with enough surplus to help others, is an admirable goal. But no one can demand it as a right. It is the result of hard work—even, in many cases, of making a profit.

Of course, making a simple case for basic economic realities is less rhetorically appealing than denouncing the powers that be in the name of God. The truth is not always spectacular.

When it gets down to models of the kind of progressive societies radicals would have us emulate, the term "democratic socialism" emerges and Sweden invariably is named.

Yet Sweden is really a confiscatory, welfare-capitalist state. Democratic socialism as applied to, say, East Germany (German Democratic Republic) really means undemocratic socialism. It is hard to believe that people would voluntarily assent to the continued total control of their lives—especially control that resulted in reduced living standards. Democratic socialism—"socialism with a human face"—remains an illusion.

All governments have limits. No system can avoid the foibles of life. In Sweden, Denmark, and Holland, people smell bad, die young, go insane, have car accidents, contract terminal diseases, love each other, murder each other, and commit suicide much like the citizens of Brazil or Nepal.

There are no utopias. The advocacy of increased government control, far from being progressive, leads, as F. A. Hayek wrote, down the road to serfdom. One wonders why radical Christians lean so hard on political solutions.

NOTES

1. R. C. Sproul, "Biblical Economics: Equity or Equality," *Christianity Today,* March 5, 1982, p. 94.
2. Thomas Sowell, *The Economics and Politics of Race* (New York: Morrow, 1983), p. 229.
3. Jacques Ellul, *Violence* (New York: Seabury, 1969), p. 67.
4. Matthew 14:14.
5. Mark 10:21.
6. "Interview with Michael Novak," *The Wittenburg Door,* November 1982, 24.
7. Jim Wallis, "We Could Just Ask Them to Forgive Us," *Sojourners,* January 1980, 3.

APPENDICES

ONE

Underdevelopment Revisited

PETER L. BERGER

The poverty in which large numbers of human beings live has been a stubborn and morally troubling reality for a long time. The terminology describing this reality has often changed, however. During the hopeful years of decolonization in the aftermath of World War II, "backwardness" (a term suggesting mental retardation) gave way to "underdevelopment" (implying a merely physical lag). This "underdevelopment" was to be cured by "development," in turn identified with "growth" (as a child catches up with an adult). The manifesto of this period was Walt W. Rostow's *The Stages of Economic Growth*, first published in 1960, and reminiscent of Jean Piaget's child psychology in its self-confident prescription of how a country develops from "take-off" to "maturity."

Then came the late 1960s and early 1970s, when this entire way of looking at the poorer portions of the globe was radically debunked, both in the "underdeveloped" countries themselves and in influential academic sectors of the West. Not only did the "children" throw the book at their "teachers," but many teachers recanted their earlier pedagogic doctrine. The quasimythological phrase "Third World" came into vogue, while the bureaucratic agencies concerned with the poorer regions fell back either on the relatively optimistic term "developing countries" or on the seemingly neutral term, "less developed countries" (with its official acronym, LDC's).

In the last few years, as the revolutionary redemptions of the

---

PETER L. BERGER is currently University Professor at Boston University and was previously a Professor of Sociology at the New School for Social Research. He is a sociologist and theologian and has written many books, including *A Rumor of Angels* and *The Sacred Canopy*. His most recent book is *The War Over the Family: Capturing the Middle Ground* (with Brigitte Berger). The following essay was originally printed in *Commentary* magazine, July 1984.

"Third World" have proved ever more disappointing, the favored term has become "South," as in "North/South dialogue." "South" suggests sunshine, perhaps even natural abundance, but also languid siestas in the heat of the day. The ambiguity is telling.

Changes in terminology sometimes reflect advances in knowledge; sometimes they are covers for ignorance. Which is the case here? How much have we really learned about the world's poverty and the remedies for it?

If one is in the habit of writing books, these books can sometimes serve as convenient landmarks to measure both advances in learning and perduring ignorance. It is now almost exactly ten years since the publication of my *Pyramids of Sacrifice*, which was a tentative summing-up of what I had learned about "development" since becoming involved in the topic a few years earlier. As it happens, this book (somewhat to my surprise) is still being read; more importantly, it reflects a particular phase in the intellectual and political debate over the issue of poverty and development. For this reason a look at what I said in 1974 may be a useful exercise.

I wrote *Pyramids of Sacrifice* in response to two powerful experiences. One was my first contact with Third World poverty, which shocked me morally as well as emotionally. The other was the eruption in American academia of a neo-Marxist rhetoric, which purported to understand the causes of Third World poverty and which also claimed to know the remedies. I was never convinced by this rhetoric, but I wanted to be fair to it. More than anything else, I wanted to explore, with moral engagement and skeptical rationality, an area which at that time was suffused with violent emotions and blatantly irrational opinions.

The book argued that both capitalism and socialism had generated myths that had to be debunked—the capitalist myth of growth, which mistook an increase in GNP for improvement in the condition of the poor, and the socialist myth of revolution, which provided an alibi for tyranny. In the service of demythologizing these ideas, the book advocated an open, nondoctrinaire approach; neither capitalism nor socialism, it argued, offered a panacea. Each country would have to think through, in pragmatic terms, what its most promising development strategy should be. As far as moral criteria were concerned, such a pragmatic assessment should be guided, I thought, by two calculi—a "calculus of pain," by which I meant the avoidance of human suffering, and a "calculus of meaning," which I defined as respect for the values of the putative beneficiaries of development policies.

A centerpiece of the book was a comparison of Brazil and China, important respectively as the largest capitalist and the largest socialist case. I had traveled extensively in Brazil just before writing *Pyramids;* although I had not been to China, I had read voraciously about it. I concluded that both "models" should be rejected—curiously, for the same reason. Both were willing to sacrifice a generation for an allegedly certain goal of development, Brazil through the adoption of economic policies that condoned widespread and bitter misery as the short-run price for long-run prosperity, China through terror and totalitarianism. Neither the Brazilian technocrats nor the Chinese ideologists, I wrote, could be certain about the eventual outcome of their policies. This being so, they lost any moral warrant for the sacrifices they were imposing on their peoples.

Yet neither case, the book suggested, exhausted the possibilities of the capitalist or socialist development models. Capitalism need not be practiced as brutally as in Brazil, and there could be a more humane socialism than that of Maoist China. In this connection, I said some nice things about Peru (then under Velasco's Left-leaning regime) and Tanzania; I had been briefly in both places and had been favorably impressed.

A number of readers of *Pyramids of Sacrifice* were misled by my wish to be fair to the Left (which, practically, meant that I desired to go on talking with most of my colleagues). They read the book as advocating democratic socialism. That had not been my intention at all. What did come through, however, was some vague notion of a "third way," perhaps some sort of a so-called mixed model. I had no clear conception of what this might look like; I was unsure of much, and I admitted it. I did feel sure of two things, however: that people should not be allowed to starve if the means to feed them were at hand, and that people should not be subjected to totalitarian terror under any circumstances.

Obviously, *Pyramids of Sacrifice* is today obsolete, because of the changes that have taken place in the world (more of this below). But looking back on it now, I am struck as well by the changes that have occurred in my own perspective. Not to put too fine a point on it, I am much less evenhanded today in my assessment of capitalist and socialist development models: I have become much more emphatically procapitalist. Some part of the shift I have undergone is undoubtedly due to personal experience. In 1974, except for one foray in Africa, my acquaintance with the Third World was limited to Latin America; inevitably, this made for a very specific bias. In 1977, however, I had my first experience of East Asia and since then my attention has turned very strongly to that region. East Asia is inconvenient territory for those who want to be evenhanded as between capitalist and socialist development models. Specifically, the capitalist "success stories" of East Asia and the lessons they hold must be confronted by any reflective person with a concern for world poverty.

To speak of success stories implies a definition of success. And here I would today insist that, minimally, there are three criteria to be applied.

First, successful development presupposes sustained and self-generating economic growth. To that extent, at least, Rostow and the other enthusiasts of the 1950s were perfectly right, while the late fantasists of zero growth were perfectly wrong. We have a pretty clear idea of what a zero-growth world would look like. It would either freeze the existing inequities between rich and poor, or it would see a violent struggle to divide up a pie that is no longer growing. Neither scenario holds out the slightest promise for such values as human rights or democracy. The existing inequities would have to be brutally defended or brutally altered. I daresay that this root insight of political economy is by now widely recognized, even on the Left (except, perhaps, among the remaining holdouts of romantic environmentalism).

Secondly, successful development means the large-scale and sustained movement of people from a condition of degrading poverty to a minimally decent standard of living. In insisting on this point, I continue to give credence to the critique (mostly from the Left) of the earlier development theories, which tended to see economic growth as a synonym for development rather than as its precondition. On that point, the critics were right: the most impressive growth rates can cover up massively inequitable distribution of the benefits of growth; there can be growth without development, and there can even be what André Gunder Frank has called "the development of underdevelopment." Brazil in the early 1970s was a striking example of this—staggering economic growth, so maldistributed that abject misery (measured by hunger, infant mortality, low life expectancy, and the like) not only continued unabated but, in parts of Brazil, worsened.

I would even go a step further in conceding a point to the Left. The advocates of liberation theology have contributed a phrase, "the preferential option for the poor," which sounds like a bad English translation of a bad Spanish translation of neo-Marxist German, but means simply that one is morally obligated to look at things from the viewpoint of the poor. Fair enough. After all, it was Dr. Johnson, not exactly a premature Marxist, who said that "a decent provision for the poor is the true test of civilization."

In focusing on this particular criterion for defining successful development I am invoking, of course, the ideal of equity; but I am *not* invoking "equality," a utopian category that can only obfuscate the moral issues. It is inequitable and immoral that, next door to each other, some human beings are starving while others gorge themselves. To make this situation more equitable and thus morally tolerable, the starvation must stop and the poor must become richer. This goal can be attained without the rich becoming poorer. In other words, I do not assume the need for a leveling of income distribution. Western societies (including the United States) have demonstrated that dramatic improvements are possible in the condition of the poor without great changes in income distribution; the poor can get richer even while the rich get richer too. And there are good economic grounds for thinking that income-leveling policies in the Third World inhibit growth, with the poor paying the biggest price for this inhibition. "Equality" is an abstract and empircally murky ideal; it should be avoided in assessing the success or failure of development strategies.

Third criterion: development cannot be called successful if the achievements of economic growth and equitable distribution come at the price of massive violations of human rights. This criterion applies to both of the calculi formulated in *Pyramids of Sacrifice*. In 1974 it seemed to me and to many others that China offered an illustration of the "calculus of pain." We now know that the economic and egalitarian achievements of Maoism were themselves largely fictitious. Still, I believe that I was correct to insist that, *even if* it were true that Maoism had vanquished hunger among China's poor, this achievement could not morally justify the horrors inflicted by the regime—horrors that entailed the killing of millions of human beings and the imposition of a merciless totalitarian rule on the survivors.

As for the "calculus of meaning," Iran now offers a good instance. The Shah's regime undoubtedly achieved economic growth, it ameliorated the condition of many of the poor (even if a corrupt elite greatly enriched itself in the process), and its violations of human rights, ugly though they were, did not come even close to the horrors of Maoism (not to mention the nightmare of terror of the Khomeini regime). However, as Grace Goodell has persuasively argued, the reform program of the Shah systematically trampled on the mores and values by which the largest number of Iranians gave meaning to their lives. It was a program of rapid and coercive modernization, contemptuous of tradition and of indigenous institutions. Logically enough, this alliance of technocrats, profiteers, and secret police evoked a neotraditionalist reaction. The tragic consequences following the triumph of these reactionaries, and the fact that the new regime has worsened the condition of the Iranian people, cannot provide an *ex-post-facto* justification of the Shah's policies. (By analogy, the Bolshevik Revolution was a catastrophe for the Russian people; but it does not follow from this that czarism, though in many ways morally superior to its successor regime, was a wise and humane system.)

It should be clear what I mean by "massive violations of human rights": mass killings, concentration camps, forced deportations, torture, separation of families, pervasive intimidation—in other words, the standard practices of twentieth-century totalitarianism. But I should stress at the same time that I do *not* include democracy as a necessary element in this criterion for successful development. Democracy is the best available form of government in the modern world; moreover, I consider it the only reliable protection of human rights under modern conditions.* In the long run, I also believe that democracy and development are necessarily linked realities. All the same, the case regrettably cannot be made that democracy is indispensable to successful development.

Armed with these criteria for development we may now turn to the evidence that has accumulated over the last ten years. Perhaps the most important piece of evidence is negative: the absence of even a single successful case of socialist development in the Third World.

Even in the early 1970s it should not have been news that socialism is not good for economic growth, and also that it shows a disturbing propensity toward totalitarianism (with its customary accompaniment of terror). What has become clearer is that socialism even fails to deliver on its own egalitarian promises (the second criterion of success). In country after country, socialist equality has meant a leveling down of most of the population, which is then lorded over by a highly privileged and by no means leveled elite.

Put simply, socialist equality is shared poverty by serfs, coupled with the monopolization of both privilege and power by a small (increasingly hereditary) aristocracy. That this was so of the Soviet Union had already been accepted by most Western and Third World leftists by the late 1960s and early 1970s. What is evident now is that a Soviet-style *nomenklatura* seems to spring up predictably wherever socialism extends. It has done so in China, in Vietnam, in Cuba, and in such lesser socialist experiments as Angola and Mozambique. None of these countries, not even Cuba, is directly or entirely under Soviet rule. It seems to be the intrinsic genius of socialism to produce these modern facsimiles of feudalism.

*I have explained why at some length in "Democracy for Everyone?," *Commentary*, September 1983.

The fact that there is not a single case of economically successful and nontotalitarian socialism has begun to sink in. (The social democracies of the West, of course, should not be subsumed under the category of socialism.) The monumental failures of Maoism, failures proclaimed to the world not by its old enemies but directly from Peking, have made a deep impression in Asia; so have the horrors of the triumphant socialist revolution in Indochina. In Asia more than elsewhere in the Third World, there now seems a new openness to the possibility of capitalist models, even if the word itself is avoided in favor of circumlocutions like "market mechanisms" or euphemisms like "pluralism." The radical shift from a socialist to a capitalist model in Sri Lanka illustrates this tendency, especially because it came about as the result of open debate and democratic politics.

Two cases touched upon in *Pyramids of Sacrifice*, Peru and Tanzania, are interesting in this connection. The socialist experiments of the Velasco regime ended in economic disaster, after which, prudently, the military handed the mess back to a civilian government that stopped the experiments. It is not clear, however, to what extent the brief and limited socialist policies of the Velasco regime can be blamed for economic problems that antedated it.

The case of Tanzania—an economic fiasco—is much more instructive. Here was a country that in the early 1970s had much going for it—reasonably good resources (especially in agriculture); a dubiously democratic but relatively humane government led by Julius Nyerere, an intelligent and attractive leader by most standards; and freedom from foreign domination. What is more, Tanzania had long been the darling of development-aid institutions, which poured vast amounts of money into the country. Whatever else one may say about the economic and political failures of Tanzania, these cannot be blamed on corrupt leadership, on bad Soviet influence, or on the hostility or destabilizing policies of Western capitalism. The fiasco was self-made.

Tanzania's much-vaunted Ujamaa program of socialist agriculture has come close to destroying the agricultural productivity of the country. As the program has failed economically, it has become more coercive. The government had at first tried to persuade peasants to move to Ujamaa villages by means of incentives; by the late 1970s, pressure had to be applied. As for the nonagricultural sector of the economy, small enough to begin with, the "para-statal organizations" that operate it have succeeded in running that little into the ground. This particular failure has been augmented by systematic pressures on the Indian minority, who (in Tanzania as in other East African countries) comprise much of the small entrepreneurial class. Not surprisingly, the economic failures have gone hand in hand with increasing political repressiveness; Tanzania today is even less democratic and certainly less humane than it was in 1974.

Events in China and Brazil, the two countries discussed at greatest length in *Pyramids of Sacrifice,* have been momentous. In the book, I rejected the Maoist model because of its human costs; now the model must also be rejected because of the costs brought about by economic and social mismanagement. To put it differently, where I rejected Maoism on non-Maoist grounds, now the Maoist experiment can be shown to have failed even by its own criteria of success.

Brazil is a more complicated case. Before the oil shock and the ensuing indebtedness crisis, there were some modest signs of a more equitable distribution of the benefits of growth. There has also been an impressive move from harsh military dictatorship toward democracy. It is noteworthy that Fernando Henrique Cardoso, the father of Latin American "dependency theory," is today a federal senator of the largest opposition party and speaks more in the moderate tones of Swedish social democracy than in the fiery neo-Marxist rhetoric of the early 1970s. All the same, by the criteria set forth above, Brazil cannot be cited as a case of successful development, and cannot (yet) be used as an argument for capitalism.

One other case in the Americas, that of Jamaica, is interesting because it (like Sri Lanka) abruptly veered from a socialist to a capitalist course, and did so as a result of democratic politics. Jamaica, however, is beset with manifold troubles; the capitalist experiment of the Seaga regime is still very new; and the place of the experiment remains uncertain.

A number of other cases (such as the Ivory Coast) are sometimes cited in favor of capitalism. But these aside, the most dramatic and convincing success stories today, and the ones offering the strongest brief for capitalism, are in East Asia.

There is, first of all, the astounding instance of Japan. To be sure, Japan is no longer regarded as anything but a highly advanced industrial society—in some ways a more successful one than the societies of North America and Western Europe. This very achievement, however, is what makes Japan crucial for any responsible theory of development. Here is the only non-Western society that has moved from underdevelopment to full-blown modernity within the span of a century. Moreover, whatever variables may have been in play (political, cultural, geographical, and so on), Japan is a successful *capitalist* society. How did the Japanese pull this off? And can others learn from their success? Not surprisingly, Third World politicians and intellectuals, even in countries that have reason to fear Japanese power, such as those of Southeast Asia, talk of the "Japanese model" as something to be admired and emulated.

But Japan no longer stands alone as a success story. There are the four countries of what may be called the Asian prosperity crescent—South Korea, Taiwan, Hong Kong, and Singapore. Despite important differences among them, each has employed an exuberantly capitalist strategy to move out of underdevelopment to the newly designated status of "New Industrialized Country" (or NIC). And this has happened with breathtaking speed and thoroughness, within the span of two decades. In no meaningful sense can these countries any longer be regarded as parts of the Third World (though Hong Kong, depending on China's policy toward it, may fall back into underdevelopment in the near future). There are even grounds for thinking that their prosperity is pushing into other countries, especially in Southeast Asia (Malaysia, Thailand, and possibly Indonesia).

South Korea, Taiwan, Hong Kong, and Singapore are successful by all three of the criteria listed above. Their rates of economic growth continue to be remarkable. They have completely wiped out Third-World-type misery within their borders. What is more, they (especially Taiwan and South Korea) have forcefully challenged the so-called "Kuznets curve" by combining high growth with a highly egalitarian income distribution. Their regimes, while not democratic, are authoritarian in a generally benign way (especially when compared with others in the region).

These four countries, only one of which, the Republic of Singapore, operates within the United Nations system, are increasingly attracting the attention of analysts of development and are more and more frequently cited as examples to be emulated. They constitute the most important evidence in favor of a capitalist path of development.

What, then, do we know today about development? We know, or should know, that socialism is a mirage that leads nowhere, except to economic stagnation, collective poverty, and various degrees of tyranny. We also know that capitalism has been dramatically successful, if in a limited number of underdeveloped countries. Needless to say, we also know that capitalism has failed in a much larger number of cases. What we do *not* know is why this is so.

It seems to me that the issue of socialism should be put aside for good in any serious discussion of development; it belongs, if anywhere, to the field of political pathology or *Ideologiekritik*. The question that should be of burning urgency (theoretical as well as practical) is why capitalism has succeeded in some places and failed in others. What are the variables of success and failure? That is the crucial question.

The success stories of East Asia have, very understandably, led some analysts to think that an important causal factor may be the culture of the region. A "post-Confucianist hypothesis" proposes that all the successful societies and ethnic groups (notably the overseas Chinese) share a common economic ethic derived from Confucianism, deemed to be a functional equivalent of Max Weber's famous "Protestant ethic." But Confucianism is by no means the only cultural element that may be relevant. Others may include the political traditions of East Asia, patterns of family and household, and different components of the area's religious heritage (such as Mahayana Buddhism).

One does not have to be a disciple of Weber to want these hypotheses addressed. Indeed, if one is concerned with Third World development in general, one would dearly love to see them falsified—not out of antagonism toward East Asia, but because the East Asian success stories can only become models for other parts of the world if they do not hinge on a nonexportable cultural factor. One might advise an African country to adopt the economic policies of South Korea; one can hardly advise the Africans to adopt Korean culture.

In *Pyramids of Sacrifice* I put forward a "postulate of ignorance": we are compelled to act politically even when we do not know many of the factors determining the situation in which we find ourselves. I formulated this postulate in the context of recommending a nondoctrinaire approach to development policy. I would reiterate it today. We are less ignorant than we were ten years ago, but there is still much that we do not know. Those charged with political responsibility in the matter of development, however, do not have the luxury of the social scientist who can always say that more research is needed. Science is, in principle, infinitely patient; politicians must act out of the urgencies of the moment. In such a situation the morally sensitive politician should be fully conscious of the fact that, whatever he chooses to do—and often the range of choices is narrow—he will be gambling. The evidence today strongly suggests that it is much safer to bet on capitalism.

TWO

Famine, Development and Foreign Aid

NICK EBERSTADT

In recent years, American foreign-aid policies have been shaped increasingly by the argument that the many different problems facing the poor nations are inextricably interconnected, woven together into an all-encompassing "seamless fabric." However pleasing this notion may seem to theoreticians, its practical implications are dangerously wrong. The problems facing poor nations can be distinguished from each other and treated separately—and must be. It is no act of charity to suspend the rules of policy analysis and problem-solving at the borders of the Third World.

Although current American policies often fail to distinguish among them, three separate purposes underlie our foreign-aid programs. The first is the humanitarian purpose of alleviating suffering and minimizing loss of life from the upheavals following sudden, unexpected catastrophe. The second is the developmental purpose of encouraging poor nations to find their best path to economic health, self-sustaining growth, and general prosperity. The third purpose is to promote the security of the United States and the Western order through military aid or security assistance to a foreign government.

Military aid to less developed countries is but a part of a larger, global American defense strategy. The aid the United States extends to nations which happen to be poor, moreover, is only a tiny fraction of the money it expends to preserve the

NICK EBERSTADT, a visiting fellow at the Harvard Center for Population Studies, is the author of *Poverty in China* and the editor of *Fertility Decline in the Less Developed Countries*. He has written several articles for *Commentary* magazine, including the following essay, which was originally printed in the March 1985 issue of that journal.

security of Allied nations that are already rich—such as Japan and the NATO countries. Military aid to less developed countries, then, is not in any meaningful sense a Third World policy, even though it involves transfers of money and resources to nations in the Third World.

Humanitarian aid and development aid are quite different. These address, respectively, short-term exigencies and long-term prospects of poor nations, and are governed by an attention to poverty. To understand the best use of these different forms of aid, we must appreciate the problems each must address. Let us examine them separately.

II

Much of mankind continues to live under the shadow of life-imperiling disasters and upheavals. Floods, earthquakes, and storms still endanger millions of people every year, and the human cost of famine is even greater. Since the end of World War II, it is believed that tens of millions of people have perished from famine in Asia alone.

To deal effectively with today's natural disasters, we must begin by recognizing that there is very little that is natural about them. Acts of God cannot be prevented, but the quotient of human risk and suffering they exact can be vastly and systematically reduced. Current events underline the point. The United States and Japan happen to be more subject than most regions of the earth to sudden natural disturbances. The Japanese archipelago, after all, is an earthquake zone, buffeted by tropical storms and exposed to *tsunami* (tidal waves). The U.S. land mass is threatened by earthquakes, tropical storms, and tornadoes, and the country, in addition, has more active volcanoes than any other. Nevertheless, very few people in Japan or America die from these natural perils.

The African continent, by contrast, would appear to be comparatively well protected against sudden disasters. It is exposed only slightly to tropical storms and tidal waves, has only a small earthquake belt, few active volcanoes, and it experiences tornadoes only in South Africa. Despite these natural advantages, however, sub-Saharan Africa has been stricken by perennial disaster in the decade since decolonization was effectively completed. These disasters are believed to have cost hundreds of thousands of lives.

Western peoples have not always enjoyed their present protection against adverse acts of nature. In the first ten years of the twentieth century, over eight thousand Americans died in hurricanes,[1] as opposed to the one hundred who died over the past ten years. What accounts for this almost 99 percent drop, despite a doubling of the population and a steady urbanization of the coasts where hurricanes most often strike? Affluence, as manifested in safer dwellings, explains part of the change; even more, however, is explained by those handmaidens of affluence, technical advance and government competence. Improvements in communications, transportation, weather tracking, emergency management, rescue operations, and relief capabilities have made it possible to reduce dramatically the human price exacted by even the worst hurricanes in the most populated areas. Purposeful private and governmental action can now substantially cut the toll from other natural disasters as well, even in the poorest nations.

Not all governments, however, work at minimizing the havoc which sudden disasters wreak upon their people—as the two most costly sudden disasters of the 1970s attest. In 1970 East Pakistan, as it was then known, was devastated by a typhoon. The Pakistani government—seated in and dominated by West Pakistan—responded to the extreme distress in its Bengal territory with what might at best be described as reserve. As many as one hundred thousand Bengalis are thought to have perished in the aftermath of that typhoon.

In 1976, the city of Tangshan in China was flattened by an earthquake. One of the Chinese government's first responses to the disaster was to announce it would refuse all international offers of aid for the victims. Details about the actual rescue operations which China itself undertook remain obscure to this day. One of the few accounts of the disaster permitted in the Chinese press at the time was a front-page feature in the *People's Daily* praising a peasant who let his own two children die as he rescued instead an aged party cadre; local and foreign readers came to their own conclusions about what this carefully placed article was intended to suggest. Since the rise of Deng Xiaoping, China's media have severely criticized his predecessors' handling of the Tangshan affair; they now state that almost a quarter-of-a-million people died in the disaster.

If government action can be consequential in limiting the suffering caused by sudden upheavals, it can be even more important in controlling or preventing famine. In the past, famines were typically related to regionalized crop failure. It is now possible to cushion the impact of crop failure in even the poorest regions of the earth. Concerned governments can monitor the progress of their nations' harvests by following local markets, by direct on-site inspection, and by studying the data from world-wide aerial and meteorological surveillance services.

These early-warning systems can give governments valuable months in which to prepare against food shortfalls. Food grain may be purchased from the world market, which trades and transports over two hundred million tons each year. If for some reason a government cannot finance its emergency food-grain needs, it may draw upon the seven million ton reserve of concessional food aid which Western governments set aside each year. If a government lacks the administrative capacity to manage a far-reaching relief effort, it may request free assistance from the many impartial international organizations which have proved they can both supervise and staff effective relief operations on short notice and under difficult conditions. Almost twenty years ago, concerted American-Indian cooperation after a series of harvest failures saved millions of Indians from starvation, and even seems to have prevented death rates from rising in the afflicted provinces. Since then, the capabilities of both the world food system and international relief organizations have grown steadily. They now present even the most modest and least sophisticated government with an oportunity to control famine within its borders—if it wants to do so.

The terrible truth, however, is that many governments in the world today have demonstrated that they are not interested in seeing their people fed. Some have deliberately ignored signs of incipient crisis. Others have interfered with international relief for their stricken groups. Still others have actually created famine conditions through premeditated action. In every recent instance where a potential food shortfall has developed into a mass famine, the hand of the state has been prominently involved.

Consider the great famines that have gripped the poor regions over the past quarter-century. In China, the Three Lean Years lasted from 1959 to 1962. Chinese officials now say that millions of people died during this famine, and Western demographers have recently suggested that "excess mortality" during this period may have been as much as thirty million. The Three Lean Years were a direct consequence of the Great Leap Forward, an awesomely ambitious social and economic experiment which resulted in a nationwide collapse of agriculture and a brief but virtually total destruction of the national food system. Even as their policies were causing millions of their citizens to starve,

China's leaders denied there was a crisis, refused all offers of international aid, and exported food.

In Nigeria, where perhaps a million ethnic Ibos died of famine in the late 1960s and early 1970s, the federal government deliberately encouraged starvation in that province, which had proclaimed its independence, in the hope that this would hasten its reconquest. In Ethiopia in the early 1970s, the Haile Selassie regime consciously concealed a famine which was ravaging its minority peoples; it is now said that several hundred thousand people lost their lives as a result of this deception, although the exact cost will never be known. In the mid-1970s, the Indonesian government attacked, occupied, and annexed the territory of East Timor; it used hunger as a weapon of conquest. It is believed by outside observers that over one hundred thousand Timorese starved to death before Indonesia allowed the island to be fed; in all, as much as a quarter of the Timorese population may have perished from famine. In the late 1970s as many as two million Cambodians may have died as a result of hunger; they did so only because the Khmer Rouge government made the mass extermination of whole segments of the national population its official policy.

Once again there is famine in Ethiopia. Though its ultimate toll is yet to be determined, its causes are already apparent. After seizing power in 1974, Ethiopia's Marxist-Leninist *Dergue* (Armed Forces Coordinating Committee) launched a campaign against "capitalism" in the countryside, restricting and ultimately prohibiting the private sale and marketing of farm produce and agricultural implements. At the same time, a newly formed secret police executed thousands of students and skilled workers in this predominantly illiterate nation, imprisoned tens of thousands more, and caused even greater numbers to flee their homeland. With the encouragement of Soviet and Cuban advisers, the government used its foreign aid to underwrite military buildup and war.

In a country like Ethiopia, which has always been subject to drought, such policies insured that widespread famine would be only a matter of time. When famine finally did strike, moreover, the *Dergue* gave little priority to relief efforts. Although millions of its citizens were said to be directly affected by the food shortage, the regime concentrated on commemorating its tenth anniversry in power—in a celebration which is said to have cost the equivalent of over $100 million.

Relief operations do not seem to have begun in earnest

until after an outcry in the West over the plight of the famine victims. Even then, the Ethiopian government continued to obstruct international efforts to alleviate its people's distress. Instead of helping rescue workers reach famine victims in Tigre and Wollo—stricken regions where the *Dergue* is especially unpopular—the government began a program of mass deportations; 2.4 million of those areas' most able-bodied (thus least endangered) people were scheduled for eventual removal. And in contravention of the two basic principles of humanitarian relief—impartiality and nondiscrimination—the *Dergue* forbade all relief for the territory of Eritrea. Half-a-million people were reported to be starving in Eritrea, but this did not stop the Ethiopian armed forces from attacking convoys suspected of bringing relief supplies into the afflicted region.

Ethiopia is not the only government currently contriving to foment mass starvation. The ongoing efforts of the Soviet Union in Afghanistan, for example, are often forgotten. Since the 1979 invasion, Soviet forces have carefully destroyed the food system in many resisting regions. In so doing, they have turned literally millions of Afghans into destitute refugees, no longer able to feed themselves in their own nation. Over two million of these people subsist today in refugee camps in Pakistan. They are kept alive by charity from the West.

The American architects of the postwar international order did not anticipate such problems. In 1943, as President Franklin D. Roosevelt laid the foundations for the broadest and most successful relief effort the world had ever seen, he explained that the new United Nations Relief and Rehabilitation Agency (UNRRA) would be operating only in "liberated areas." He assured "liberated peoples" that "in victory or defeat, the United Nations have never deviated from adherence to the basic principles of freedom, tolerance, independence, and security." President Roosevelt believed that preventing famine would be an eminently manageable task under governments which respected the sanctity of human life and upheld Western values, and he was right. With the spread in membership in the United Nations, moreover, it seemed that enlightened governance might eventually prevail across the entire globe. Today, however, only a handful of countries beyond the borders of the West embrace the values codified in the United Nations' Charter and its Universal Declaration of Human Rights. Many member states now disregard these codes when they prove inconvenient. Others reject them out of principle, since they are inconsistent with their regimes' totalitarian or anti-Western ideologies.

It is now almost forty years since our victory in World War II. Even so, very few of the worlds poorest and most vulnerable peoples live in what President Roosevelt would have considered "liberated areas." It is this fact and not any other which accounts for the persistence of famine in the modern world. Nations can always share the West's technical capacities to save people stricken by catastrophe, but regimes that do not share the West's values cannot be counted on to put these capacities to use.

III

According to many leaders in the Third World and to some development organizations in the West, the principal obstacle to accelerating the pace of material progress in low-income nations today is the insufficiency of concessionary aid from Western countries. It is striking, and inadvertently revealing, that such criticisms of Western giving often neglect to discuss either the quality of the aid received or the ends that it achieves. Such thinking is worse than illogical. By dissociating development aid from measurable results, it reduces Western assistance from a practical policy to an aesthetic, possibly only a symbolic, gesture. To advocate massive new aid programs irrespective of their impact on the economic health of recipient nations would be expensive for the West, but could prove far more costly to the world's poor.

Few people in the West appreciate the magnitude of current resource flows from Western societies to the Third World. Such flows are, in fact, extremely difficult to measure, not only because of the inevitable delays between commitments and disbursals, but because of the complexities of tracking and accounting for funds in a world financial system which is at once open and closed. Nevertheless, the Organization for Economic Cooperation and Development (OECD) attempts to measure these flows, and its computations are instructive.[2] In 1982, the most recent year for which OECD has made estimates, the net total for what it labels "overseas development assistance" provided directly by Western nations to Third World countries was about $18 billion.

But there was more. Multilateral development banks and multilateral development agencies, underwritten overwhelmingly by Western donations, provided an additional sum whose 1982 net OECD put at about $8 billion. And there was still more. Western nations were also providing finance capital to less developed countries under a variety of arrangements, including bank lending, government-to-government loans, export credits, and direct private investment. All told, OECD placed the total net transfer of financial resources from Western nations to Third World countries at almost $80 billion in 1982. This, it must be emphasized, is supposed to be the *net* total: the residual after financial withdrawals, profit repatriation, and loan repayments have been taken into account.

Of course, 1982 is but a single year. OECD estimates of financial flows to developing countries extend back to 1956. According to these computations, the net transfer of financial resources (both concessional and commercial) from Western nations to less developed countries between 1956 and 1982 exceeded $670 billion. This figure, however, seriously understates the true magnitude of the transfer, since it is denominated in current rather than inflation-adjusted dollars. Adjusting for intervening inflation, we find that the OECD estimate would be valued today at over $1,500 billion—that is, over $1.5 *trillion*.

Even this figure, however, understates the total postwar transfer of resources from the West to the Third World. It does not, for example, seem to measure either concessional grants or commercial loans for military matters, even though these play a prominent role in the finances of many developing countries. And it obviously cannot measure the net flow of resources in either the first half of the 1950s or the years since 1982. Taking everything into account, it seems quite possible that the total net transfer of capital from the West to the Third World since the beginning of the postwar international order may have already exceeded $2 trillion at today's prices. Although the complexities of international financial accounting and the unavoidable inexactitudes of adjusting for inflation and international fluctuations in exchange rates prevent us from arriving at a more precise figure, $2 trillion will probably do as the nearest round number to describe the magnitude of the net financial transfer from the West to the poor nations in the postwar era.

Large figures tend to seem abstract, and $2 trillion is an especially large figure. One way to appreciate its size is to consider what it could buy. Think of the entire U.S. farm system. Now think of all the industries listed on the New York Stock Exchange. At their current market values, $2 trillion would pay for *both*.

What has been the impact on the societies which have received this extraordinary transfer of Western wealth? The answer is obviously different in every case. Even so, broad and unmistakable patterns arise, some of which can be glimpsed in the composition of the transfers themselves. Less than one-quarter of the inflation-adjusted total for the years 1956 to 1982, for example, appears to have accrued from direct (and voluntary) overseas private investment. That fraction, moreover, has steadily diminished over time. Whereas in the late 1950s direct private investment accounted for almost two-fifths of the net financial flows to the less developed countries, in the last five years for which OECD has published figures, the fraction has dropped to below one-sixth.

One of the original arguments for foreign aid was that development assistance would increase the capacities of poor nations to make productive use of international-investment resources. The record seems to suggest that precisely the opposite has happened. Despite hundreds of billions of dollars of Western development assistance, and a generation of economic growth in the meantime, the less developed countries, taken as a group, obtain a far smaller fraction of their foreign resources from direct private investment today than they did a quarter of a century ago. This must mean either that Third World nations, taken as a group, have grown more hostile to direct private investments, or that they have become less capable of attracting such investment, or both.

The eclipse of direct private investment from the West was made possible in no small part by the ascension of an alternative medium of capital transfer, commercial lending. Unlike direct private investment, bank loans to less developed countries accrue principally to governments and state-owned public corporations. Such lending effectively severed the connection between the provision of capital and the right to manage it. The responsibility for determining the use of these funds, and of repaying them, fell squarely on the state. It was not long before dozens of nations in the Third World announced that they would be unable to repay their commercial obligations to their Western creditors on schedule.

The attitudes which led to this generalized debt crisis were highlighted in the subsequent rescheduling negotiations in which many Third World governments requested debt relief. Such proposals would have converted a substantal portion of their obligations into a retroactive and unintended gift from the West. This view of Western capital suggested not only that it would be appropriate to convert commercial funds into concessional bequests without warning, but, no less significantly, that there was no reason to expect concessional bequests to earn productive returns.

Within the diverse and disparate amalgam of nations that goes by the name Third World there has been a dramatic and general improvement in material living standards during the era of Western transfers. This fact should be neither ignored nor belittled. Life expectancy for the people of "developing regions," according to the World Health Organization, rose by over 50 percent between the late 1930s and the late 1960s, and has risen still further since then.[3] Although no great confidence can be placed in economic estimates for the less developed regions, the World Bank says that per-capita GNP has more than doubled between 1960 and 1980 for the billion people living in what it terms "middle-income economies."[4] According to the same source, per-capita GNP rose by over 30 percent in India during this period. Even that most troubled category of states, the "other low-income economies" of Africa and Asia, are said to have experienced a 20 percent increase in per-capita GNP during these two decades alone.

But while the peoples of the less developed countries have seen far-reaching material advances in their societies, their economies have also typically undergone strange and troublesome transformations. In a great many countries of the Third World it has proved possible to finance the ambitious and comprehensive recasting of the national economy in ways not unlike the mobilizations of societies preparing for protracted and total war. These exercises in economic conversion have left the structures of some less developed countries grotesquely distorted, unnecessarily incapable of meeting either the social needs or the commercial demands of their people. They have left many others in a curious state of economic imbalance: richer than ever before, yet less capable than ever of pursuing self-sustaining growth.

In the Western nations, agricultural development proved to be a key factor in overall economic development. In the era of Western transfer, many governments in Africa, Asia, and Latin America have attempted to bypass agricultural development in their rush to industrialize. They have pursued policies systematically prejudicial to the interests of their rural populations: overtaxing farmers, underpricing their produce, and diverting resources so that the growth of cities and factories may be sustained at a forced pace. Neglect and exploitation have left many poor nations with unnaturally small agricultural sectors in relation to their people's needs or their development potential. Imitating the style of development without capturing its substance, such efforts at development planning have, by and large, succeeded in replicating the structure of the industrialized economies while leaving the populace in poverty.

Some of the resulting distortions may be illustrated by international economic comparisons. (The estimates for poor nations, which come from the World Bank, should not necessarily be treated as reliable or even meaningful, but they are the most commonly used figures in such exercises.) For Peru and Mexico in the early 1980s, the proportion of agriculture in overall GNP was put at roughly 8 percent. This is only half the share that Germany devoted to agriculture in the 1930s, even though Germany then was much more prosperous than Peru or Mexico today by almost any economic measure. By the same token, the share of agriculture in Ecuador's GNP today is apparently smaller than Holland's was in 1950. Bolivia's ratio of agriculture to GNP is lower today than that of Greece, although by any other measure it is Greece which should be considered the more industrialized society. Present-day Nigeria and the Denmark of the early 1950s show roughly equal ratios of agriculture to GNP. Senegal, a nation affected by the Sahelian food crisis, has managed to reduce its current ratio of agriculture to national output down to the level that characterized Japan in the early 1950s. The relation of agriculture to output in Pakistan and India is about the same as in prewar Italy, and is only slightly higher in Bangladesh today than it was in Italy at the turn of the century.[5]

The same policies which produce industrialization without prosperity have created an equally paradoxical phenomenon in many less developed countries: investment without growth. By the estimates of the World Bank, in the early 1960s the ratio of gross domestic investment to GNP in Jamaica, Mauritania, Liberia, and what is now the People's Republic of the Congo was equal to or higher than that of Japan in the early 1950s, at the start of its remarkable boom. Yet over the course of the 1960s and 1970s, while Japan was quadrupling its per-capita output, Mauritania and Liberia are said to have raised theirs by less than 40 percent; the People's Republic of the Congo, by the World Bank tally, registered a rise of less than 20 percent; and Jamaica apparently increased its per-capita output by a mere 13 percent. It is worth considering the scale of economic mismanagement necessary to achieve such results. We might also wonder how a poor government could maintain such strikingly high rates of capital accumulation in the face of indisputable and continuing economic mismanagement.

Just as agricultural sectors in the Third World have been artificially restricted and diminished by national policies, so what is termed investment has been artificially swollen. According to the World Bank, the region of the world with the *lowest* overall

investment rate today is the West. In the "middle-income economies," overall rates of gross domestic investment are said to be
just short of the historically extraordinary levels Japan achieved
at the start of its growth spurt in the 1950s. For the "low-income
economies," overall rates of gross domestic investment are higher
today than they ever were in the United States or the fastest-
growing nations of Western Europe.

But these patterns of investment cannot be taken as a sign
of economic promise. In many countries, they have already
proved to be manifestly unsustainable—the "debt crisis" affecting so many poor nations is only a formal recognition *in extremis*
of this fact. To a distressing degree, the capital buildup to which
so many Third World governments have committed themselves
over the past three decades was guided not by economic logic, but
by the political imperative of maximizing the resources and power in the hands of the state. The misuse of resources, always
costly, is especially hard on the populace of poor societies. It is
poor people, after all, who can least easily forgo consumption
today, and investment is by definition forgone consumption.

The postwar transfer of resources from Western nations to
the less developed countries, as it has been conducted, appears to
have accorded with neither of the two original premises for extending "development assistance": it has not improved the climate for productive international investment, and it has not contributed generally to self-sustaining economic growth. Ironically,
financial transfer from the West may actually have made it possible for many nations to avoid participating more fully in the
world economy. Under the best of circumstances, financial aid
increases the local money supply, and thus stimulates inflation
and reduces international competitiveness unless offsetting measures are enacted. Many regimes have demonstrated that they are
not interested in enacting such measures. After all, overvaluing
the local currency makes imports cheap, and to the extent that
foreign finance is available, exports are unnecessary.

The justification for "development assistance" which has been
voiced increasingly since the early 1970s is the need to "build
human capital." There should be no mistaking the crucial importance of human capital in economic growth. Health, education,
knowledge, skills, and other immutably human factors determine
the maximum pace at which development may proceed. But returns from human capital, as from any other potentially productive resource, depend upon the environment in which they are

put to use. Where physical capital is mismanaged and depleted, it would seem unrealistic to expect human capital to be carefully preserved, augmented, and utilized.

Human capital is much more difficult to measure and evaluate than physical capital—a fact that may not have escaped advocates of new spending programs in this area. Nevertheless, it is possible to make some tentative assessments of the effectiveness of some of the human-capital programs Western aid has helped sponsor. Consider education. As a very rough rule of thumb, the literacy rate in a poor society today should be similar to its primary-school enrollment ratio twenty years earlier. The rule holds in many developing nations, but not in all. According to the World Bank, for example, 47 percent of Bangladesh children were enrolled in primary schools in 1960, but the nation's literacy rate in 1980 was only 26 percent. In Togo, the enrollment ratio was 44 percent in 1960, but literacy is put at 18 percent today. In Zaire, the enrollment ratio was 60 percent in 1960, and the literacy rate today may be as low as 15 percent.[6]

Literacy, of course, is notoriously difficult to measure. Such radical discrepancies, however, appear to speak to something more fundamental than inexact definitions. They suggest that spending in the name of human capital can be wasted, and often has been. The irony is that such wastage seems most likely to occur as governments restrict their societies' contact with the world economy—preventing them from participating in the learning process which has so demonstrably enhanced the productivity of nations at all economic levels in modern times.

In the final analysis, the economic impact of Western financial transfers on the nations of Asia, Africa, and Latin America seems to depend very largely on the attitudes and inclinations of the recipient government. Taiwan and South Korea were both major beneficiaries of foreign aid in the 1950s and early 1960s, and South Korea has been a major borrower of international capital in the 1970s and the early 1980s. Both countries have used these resources in ways that have enhanced their overall economic productivity, improved their international competitiveness, and increased their ability to take advantage of the growing opportunities afforded by world markets. But easy credit and free aid need not be put to economically constructive purposes. They may also be used for quite different goals—even to underwrite practices so injurious that they could not otherwise be afforded.

IV

If opinion surveys are correct, the American people are troubled by our present policies to relieve distress and promote prosperity in the poorer regions of the earth. They are right to be so. As they are currently conducted, American foreign-aid policies cannot be relied upon to encourage economic health or self-sustaining growth in low-income nations; indeed, they may actually subsidize practices that perpetuate or even generate poverty in certain places. Such programs betray the wish of the American people to extend their help to the world's least fortunate groups and dangerously compromise America's moral role in the world.

In the decades since they were initiated, the official development policies of the United States have undergone a progressive divorce from their original purposes and principles. To judge by the results of current foreign-aid programs, the United States government has become comfortable with the idea of conducting a special, separate foreign policy toward the world's poor—a policy whose principles and goals are distinct from, even opposite to, those by which we guide ourselves in the rest of the world. Pursued to their logical conclusion, America's current aid policies would leave poor nations ever less capable of self-sustaining growth, and increasingly dependent on foreign largesse to maintain or improve national standards of living. These same aid policies appear to be indifferent to the politically induced suffering which so many poor peoples must endure at the hands of irresponsible or actively mischievous governments. Would we ever think of guiding our relations with another Western people by such rules?

The terrible irony of this situation is that the United States created a new global order at the end of World War II precisely to eliminate the sorts of suffering we now seem to be inadvertently underwriting in different poor nations. The economic pillars of this new order were an International Monetary Fund, a World Bank, and a generalized arrangement for the promotion of international trade; the political framework for this order was to be the United Nations. The liberal international economic system which was built on those foundations has proved to be the greatest engine of material advance the world has ever known; it has demonstrated its ability to contribute to prosperity in any and all nations willing to avail themselves of its opportunities. The values we impressed upon the original documents of the United Nations not only laid down the guidelines for decent and humane governance, but suggested the approach to policy most likely to relieve suffering and promote general prosperity. These postwar arrangements, which the United States struggled to produce, have created the greatest opportunities for satisfying the wants and needs of mankind that history has yet seen.

A generation of divisive rhetoric and drift has taken its toll on the United States. What is often easy for Americans to forget is that our divisive rhetoric and drift take an even greater toll on other peoples. The fact is that the United States—as a nation, a power, and an idea—is the greatest hope that the world's poor and unprotected peoples have. It is the American people's unmistakable preference that the peoples of the poorer regions of the earth should eventually be liberated—in the true meaning of that word. The United States can do much to help these peoples in their liberation. But we will not be true to our own preferences, or the promise of our system, if we divorce our policies toward the world's poor from the values, institutions, and international economic arrangements which we cherish for ourselves.

1. Cited in Anders Wijkman and Lloyd Timberlake, *Natural Disasters: Acts of God or Acts of Man?* (London and Washington: Earthscan, 1984).
2. *Geographical Distribution of Financial Flows to Developing Nations,* Paris, OECD, 1984. The calculations here are based on this volume and its predecessor series.
3. World Health Organization, "Mortality Trends and Prospects," in *WHO Chronicle,* 1974, Vol. 28.
4. World Bank, *World Development Report,* 1982, Oxford University Press, 1982.
5. Data for "developing countries" come from various issues of the World Bank's *World Development Report.* Historical figures for Western nations are from Simon S. Kuznets, *Modern Economic Growth* (Yale University Press, 1966) and *The Economic Growth of Nations* (Harvard University Press, 1971).
6. *World Development Report,* 1982 and 1983. The World Bank did not publish literacy estimates in the 1984 edition of its report.

THREE

The Networks vs. the Recovery

PAUL H. WEAVER

In the summer of 1981, some six months after Ronald Reagan took office, the U.S. economy stopped growing and began to contract. Over the ensuing year-and-a-half the country experienced a recession of about average intensity and duration for the postwar period. Real gross national product contracted by 2.5 percent. The unemployment rate rose from 7.2 percent to 10.8 percent. In December 1982, when contraction gave way to recovery, twelve million Americans were out of work.

The recession, naturally, was covered intensively by the press, including the television networks' nightly news programs. Night after night, month after month, they reported the latest economic statistics, which generally painted a picture of growing millions out of work, sagging morale, and a still substantial (though declining) inflation rate. Having rehearsed the essential statistics, the anchormen would then switch to filmed reports from correspondents in the field showing the scenes and replaying the sounds of plants being closed and people losing jobs or looking for work. In this period, the economic news was unrelievedly discouraging. But so were the economic conditions it reflected.

In December 1982, the economy started growing again, and during the twelve months that followed, the country experienced an economic recovery and expansion whose size once again made it about average for postwar expansions. Real gross national product rose by 6.2 percent, total employment grew by 3.9 million, unemployment fell to 8.2 percent, and one measure of inflation,

PAUL H. WEAVER, who worked as an editor both at *Public Interest* and *Fortune*, is De Witt Wallace Fellow in Communications at the American Enterprise Institute in Washington, D.C. The following essay is reprinted from *Commentary* magazine, July 1984.

the producer-price index, rose by 0.6 percent—the smallest increase since 1964. Automobile sales grew smartly, rising 18 percent above the previous year's depressed level. Real per-capita after-tax income went up by 5.3 percent, and the Dow Jones Industrial Average hit record highs.

But as the economy itself began growing again, the networks' economic coverage became curiously schizophrenic, according to a study conducted by the Institute of Applied Economics, a small New York research group that videotaped and analyzed every economic news story on the three network nightly news programs from July 1 through December 31, 1983. The Institute's analysts identified two main types of economic news stories. One genre—there were from four to fifteen of these per month in the period under study—was the news item, often short, that in the typical case reported freshly released economic statistics. Of these, nearly all (about 95 percent) conveyed a positive impression: things in the economy were getting better, the data reflected the improving trend, and the stories reflected the data.

A second genre of news story identified in the study was the longer, in-depth, interpretative news analysis, typically narrated by a reporter in the field. These stories took as their point of departure some event of the day; often the "news peg" was the announcement of upward movement in an economic indicator. But having quickly noted the news peg, the stories would then turn to their real purpose—delving beneath the surface of the news to identify some larger, more meaningful economic reality or trend. According to the study, the networks ran one hundred and four of these longer, more analytic, less event-oriented news pieces during the second half of 1983. Of these stories, eighty-nine, or about 85 percent, featured bad news, emphasizing not any reassuring resurgence of economic growth or welcome increase in employment, but the recession's lingering ill effects, or the persistence of structural economic problems that demanded attention now that the recession had passed.

Their length and documentary character made this second group of stories the dominant body of network economic-news coverage—and the impression they conveyed was strongly negative. The economy, they suggested, though perhaps technically in recovery, was not really much better. Major problems of hunger, chronic unemployment, and regional and structural stagnation remained. The pains and scars of a long recession were far from forgotten. Presiding over the entire worrisome situation, these stories suggested, was an uncaring, politically manipulative administration that sought political advantage in the nation's recovery from a recession which the administration's policies had probably made worse.

Overall, then, as the study concludes: "The economic news was good in the second half of 1983. The coverage on network television was still in recession."

A typical example of this pattern was broadcast on December 2, 1983, when the Bureau of Labor Statistics announced preliminary unemployment statistics for November. On ABC, senior economics correspondent Dan Cordtz summarized the news with his customary—and, alas, among the men and women of television news, unique—precision and generosity:

> Unemployment fell significantly last month for almost every category of worker. . . . And employment went up in most of the 186 different industries on which the government collects statistics. In just two months, the total number of unemployed Americans has dropped by well over a million. That's a remarkable decline, and a sign of how surprisingly strong the economic recovery is. At the rate things are going, unemployment may not even be a political issue by the time election day rolls around next year.

Picking up on Cordtz's theme, anchorman Peter Jennings observed, "The White House called the drop in unemployment 'remarkable,' and President Reagan was obviously pleased." Film showed a beaming Ronald Reagan exulting before a White House press conference earlier that day, "We're a little ahead of schedule on the recovery." Jennings, broadcasting from Chicago, concluded the segment by noting, "Here in the Midwest, a lot of people have still been left behind, and a little later we'll have a report on them."

Soon Jennings was back: "And now those unemployment figures again. . . . Here in Illinois, once again, there are many families for whom the statistics, as good as they are, have little meaning. This week we met a couple of them." One was Jack Lauderbach, forty-eight, whom we watched jogging along the streets of his "fairly well-to-do Chicago suburb" on a cold winter day. "He'd worked hard all his life, he'd become a successful executive—the American dream, if you will, become reality. . . . Twenty months ago, the dream began to dissolve" when he was fired as a $39,000-a-year personnel director of the Brunswick Corporation during a reorganization. We also met Frank Foster, thirty-three, who was raking leaves in the front yard of his rented house in an attractive neighborhood in Rockford, Illinois. Over a decade he had worked his way up in the local Borg-Warner automobile-parts factory to an $11-an-hour job as a stock clerk. "A year and a half ago, he lost his job. His dream dissolved as well." Both men, Jennings informed us, were "among the nation's chronically unemployed. That's a word usually applied to illness. It means prolonged, and lingering. Frank and Jack *never* expected to be out of work."

Foster, a cheerful, modest, well-spoken father of two who left school early to work his way up in the company, had lost his house; the bank foreclosed when he and his wife, also unemployed, were unable to meet the mortgage payments. "Losing their own home, more than anything else, was an attack on the status they'd worked for," said Jennings. "Their faith in the American dream has been badly shaken." Mrs. Foster, now also out of work, explained: "The way America was, you could start at the bottom and go up. . . . Now there's not too much to do to start at the bottom." Jennings added that "now could be a particularly bad time for the Fosters." A Johns Hopkins University psychologist was then brought on to say of chronically unemployed people like the Fosters, "It is exactly when things seem to be getting better for other people that they find themselves isolated."

Lauderbach, we then discovered, had sent out twenty-five hundred resumés (we saw him typing on his sleek Olivetti electric); "so far, no success." With his severance pay and unemployment insurance exhausted, his wife had taken two jobs, and his mother, who lives with him, was contributing her Social Security check. "In this family, it isn't that there's no food, it's the price Jack pays in dignity," Jennings said. He showed film of Jack explaining that "if you give up, you're dead," and admitting that though "it's dumb, and I'll never do it," he has thought of suicide ("taking the pipe," he called it).

Jennings noted pointedly that the recent drop in unemployment "hasn't solved Jack Lauderbach's or Frank Foster's problem." He said that Louis Ferman, a labor-market expert at the University of Michigan, "expects new faces in the ranks of the chronically unemployed." Ferman: "It's no longer that mechanization is only being thrust into the blue-collar world. It's being thrust all over, top to bottom. Every job is in a sense vulnerable." Having delivered that gloomy assessment, Jennings gave his two chronically unemployed subjects some parting words. The former stock clerk was optimistic: "Just hope for the best," he said with his shy smile. The former personnel director was hopeful, too, but there was desperation in his words: "Sooner or later, I'm gonna get something. I mean, I gotta feel that way. If I don't, you know, I'm gonna take the pipe."

The Institute for Applied Economics sums up: "A story that began with an 0.4 percent drop in unemployment ended in complete despair and talk of suicide."

Jennings's theme was bitter irony—the illusoriness of the economy's seeming improvement, the persistence of deep and disturbing problems—and it was repeated again and again during this period. The networks ran dozens of long, interpretative stories about hunger, the burden of which was, as CBS's Lem Tucker put it in December at the end of a long report that closed with videotape of a homeless man sleeping on a subway grate in Washington, D.C.: "The nation is now in its fourteenth month of economic recovery. Unemployment is the lowest it's been in two years. *They* [the hungry] are *still* there." And it was not just the hungry whose numbers were undiminished amid declining unemployment. In November, an NBC story on unemployment stated, "One of the painful side-effects of high unemployment in many areas was a significant increase in cases of wife beating. However, the problem of battered women doesn't go away when the economy improves. . . . It is always there."

Other stories suggested that as the employment situation got better, it only got worse. On July 8, when the Labor Department announced a drop in unemployment, CBS reporter Ray Brady emphasized that there were 1,250,000 new people in the labor market seeking only three hundred and fifty thousand available jobs, and focused on worsening unemployment in certain industrial states. In November, after unemployment fell from 9.2 percent to 8.8 percent in a month, ABC stated that the drop in unemployment was the result of many jobless Americans ending their search for work. Thus, the "news is not as good as it sounds. . . ." Throughout the period, the networks reported numerous cases of reopened plants attracting far more applicants than there were new jobs. The impression created was that such events disappointed more people than they helped. As Peter Jennings put it in August: "There was another of those huge job lines today. . . . In Galesburg, Illinois, forty jobs opened up at the Admiral Appliance factory; 10,500 people lined up to fill out applications."

The ultimate irony of all was the one broached by ABC's Dan Cordtz in August at the close of a long and generally excellent exploration of recession and recovery in two very different states—West Virginia, with the nation's highest unemployment rate (19.5 percent), and Massachusetts, with one of the nation's lowest (6 percent). After explaining that the two states were so different because they had such different industries, Cordtz ended by saying: "In a number of states like Massachusetts, the outlook is pretty bright, and that's clearly good news. But it also means that the gap between the beneficiaries of the recovery and the victims of a lingering recession will grow even wider in the months ahead." In other words, just as the recession had widened the gap between rich and poor, now the recovery was about to do its part to make the rich richer and the poor poorer.

The effort to see irony and contradiction in the events of the recovery led television news in some instances to make errors of fact. In December, Ford Motor Company, in the wake of an unsuccessful effort to sell its aging Rouge steel subsidiary to the Japanese, announced it would spend $168 million to modernize the facility, the nation's eighth largest. On CBS, anchorman Dan Rather briefly sketched the Ford announcement, then dismissed it: "That kind of business investment so far hasn't played a major role in the drama of recovery." In the lengthy interpretative story that followed, reporter Ray Brady added: "It is the shadow which darkens the eleven-month-old economic recovery. While many companies once again are making huge profits, so far they've been reluctant to invest those profits in new plants and new machinery." In fact, according to Commerce Department data, "nonresidential fixed" investment of precisely the type Ford was undertaking at the Rouge plant was running about 50 percent ahead of the norm for recoveries in the postwar era. In its enthusiasm to deny the reality of the economic expansion, network news not only misrepresented an important trend, but virtually passed over an event of significance in its own right.

The fascination of the networks with the recovery's weaknesses and the economy's underlying problems was closely associated with their even more intense interest in the person and policies of Ronald Reagan. To play through the Institute's videotapes of network economic news stories is to enter a world that revolves around the White House. In this Reaganocentric view of the universe, everything is explained by a few simple equations. In one equation, Reaganomics equals the interests of the rich equals indifference to the poor. In another, the claims of the poor are associated with the press, which is arrayed against Ronald Reagan and his policies.

This way of looking at life is not limited to this particular body of news coverage. In a study of, among other things, net-work coverage of the first one hundred days of 1983, political scientists Michael Robinson and his colleagues identified the same set of identities and oppositions. Of forty-six "soft-news" stories about policy issues mentioning Ronald Reagan, twenty-seven were directly negative toward Reagan and just two were positive. As the authors pointed out, the stories were notably critical of Reagan's economic policies:

> In a feature report on Reagan's first two years, Sam Don-aldson and ABC superimposed the President's picture over a brightly colored visual that traced the phenomenal growth in unemployment during Reagan's first term. In those same frames, ABC also used audiotape in which Reagan predicted that the recession was over. The report made it perfectly clear that Reaganomics had failed. . . . "There is," concluded Donaldson, "plenty of room for dis-agreement over whether Ronald Reagan should receive a passing or failing grade for these past two years. But there is a consensus in Washington that unless he changes his game plan, economically the grade for the next two years will almost certainly be an F."*

For the networks, therefore, covering economic news con-sisted in large part of trying to demonstrate that under the influ-ence of Ronald Reagan's policies, the economy was unfair and/or was performing badly. Alternatively, on occasion it consisted of an effort to show that while the economy was doing all right, Ronald Reagan and his associates were not.

The anti-Reagan animus was vividly demonstrated by two episodes in the second half of 1983. The first occurred on July 20, when CBS ran the only substantial news account I saw on video-tape that was unqualifiedly positive about the recovery. The story was introduced by Dan Rather, sitting in front of a graphic dis-play showing a map of the U.S., bedecked with stars-and-stripes bunting, on which were superimposed the words, "Gross Nation-al Product":

> "Stunning—the figure leaves us a little breathless." That was one analyst's reaction to today's Commerce Depart-ment reports that the gross national product grew at a

---

*Michael Robinson, Maura Clancy, and Lisa Grand, "With Friends Like These. . . ," *Public Opinion*, June/July 1983.

surprising 8.7 percent annual rate in the year's second quarter. That's the fastest pace for economic growth in more than two years.

Then Rather handed the narrative over to reporter Bruce Hall, who proceeded to give a report on the strength of the economy in Atlanta, where resurgent consumer spending was helping the city lead the nation out of the recession.

The entire lengthy story consisted of an exploration of the sources and consequences of Atlanta's economic buoyancy. A viewer learned that sales at a major shopping mall were up 13 percent, that salesmen could see the increased consumer optimism that was leading people in the area to spend a higher proportion of their disposable income. We were told that consumer spending in the second quarter of the year rose at an annual rate of 10 percent, and that clothing and automobiles were selling particularly well. Hall took his audience on a visit to a dress shop, then showed a couple buying a new Cadillac (for cash). The story was unusual, and interesting, in its willingness to give specifics about the recovery in one city. It was also unusual in not hastening to seek out a dark irony, hidden contradiction, or worrisome underside of Atlanta's economic comeback. It concluded simply, "With the customers returning, much of Atlanta is beginning to enjoy life just a little bit more."

Dan Rather immediately reappeared on the screen to introduce the next story:

President Reagan hailed the Commerce Department report today. He said, quote, "Vigorous growth is the surest route to more jobs, declining deficits, and a future filled with opportunity." It's hard to quarrel with those words. The problem, Ray Brady explains, lay with some of the President's statistics.

Only in America would the story that followed be broadcast on national television. For over the next few minutes Brady, using videotape of a Ronald Reagan press conference earlier that day, showed the President making four significant factual errors in a series of extemporaneous, upbeat statements about the economy. And using official government statistics, Brady coolly refuted each error, one by one. The effect was electrifying: it isn't often that one witnesses a direct, one-on-one confrontation between a journalist and the President of the United States. In the "kicker" that concluded his story, Brady did not try to calm the charged atmosphere, but pressed the attack:

The White House press office said this afternoon the figures could have different interpretations. And an administration source told CBS News the President was obviously doing some fast figuring in his head.

It does not seem accidental that the one lengthy TV story in the period under study that did not deny or qualify the recovery appeared back-to-back with this extraordinary personal challenge to and rebuke of President Reagan by a network newsman. Together, the stories sustained the underlying equations that shaped the content of TV economic news. It seems equally uncoincidental that on the one occasion during the period in question in which a senior member of the Reagan administration stepped out of the indifferent-to-the-poor persona to which the press had become accustomed among the President's men, the networks went to extraordinary lengths to ridicule the effort and deny its reality.

The event in question occurred in August 1983, when the press and the Democrats were harping on the hunger issue and the President was about to appoint a task force to look into it. Apparently as part of the administration's response to the problem, Secretary of Agriculture John Block and his family conducted an experiment in which they lived for a week on food stamps. The effort was kicked off with a shopping visit and photo-opportunity session in a Bethesda supermarket, where the Blocks bought $54 worth of groceries (food-stamp recipients get $58 worth of stamps), and it ended a week later at a press conference in which the Blocks described their experiences. It was a symbolic gesture, but a meaningful one, since Block is responsible for administering the food-stamp program, and since it is always desirable for someone in such a position to know from experience what his "clients" go through. That it was also a good way to grab a bit of publicity for himself and his boss does not negate its intrinsic value.

CBS's Dan Rather wasted no time derogating this gesture. This was the first sentence of his introduction to the story: "Agriculture Secretary John Block is a millionaire farmer who owns a $300,000 house in the Washington suburbs." (Its hostility aside, this statement is breathtaking in its hypocrisy, considering the identity of the man making it. Does Rather mean to invite people commenting on his doings and undoings to preface their remarks with the comparable observation: "Dan Rather is a multimillionaire TV star and national celebrity who lives in a half-a-million-dollar coop on Manhattan's posh Park Avenue and who often presents himself as caring about the poor"?) Reporter Eric Engberg began his filmed report this way:

The hustle and bustle at this supermarket was the work of Agriculture Secretary John Block's staff, whose cash crop today was publicity. The Secretary and his wife Sue made a carefully staged trip through the aisles to show that the government's recommended food-stamp allotment for the poor . . . can provide a nutritious diet.

A week later, when the Blocks reported on their adventures, the people at CBS News were still on the warpath. Rather opened:

A week ago, Agriculture Secretary John Block and his family began a short experiment of living on a food-stamp budget. They did so among much well-orchestrated publicity. Critics insisted that it was all designed mainly to feed the Reagan administration public-relations mill.

This time reporter Engberg was much straighter in covering the Blocks' experiences, which were instructive. Clearly they had not found the experiment easy, particularly at the beginning, and the Secretary ordered free distribution of a government booklet they had used in planning their food buying, which, they found, was tricky on the tight budget. But Engberg nevertheless invoked the theme of the public-relations gesture again in his kicker, in which he showed videotape of Block, an avid runner, suited up and taking off from the starting line in a one-mile race: "Moving on to run a mile in a promotion of fitness, Block said he felt better qualified to oversee the $12-billion food-stamp program than he did a week ago."

In all this the networks were acting in part out of liberal political animus. It is impossible to watch these stories without concluding that the journalists writing and performing them had a low opinion of Ronald Reagan, his conservative philosophy, and his economic policies. It is hard not to conclude that their opinion of the man and his program was so low that they were determined to do everything within their legitimate discretion, and perhaps then some, to prevent their reportage from suggesting that the policies worked, or that a recovery was in full swing, or that the President might be in line for some credit for the expansion of the economy.

In part too the networks were acting out of an institutional animus. To watch these stories is to be in the presence of the acts and utterances of people who evidently believe passionately that their mission is to criticize and oppose the President—any President—as if they were members of an opposition party in a parliament. This "adversary" role, as it has been called, is relatively new for American journalism, which historically has thought of itself as politically neutral, save in those rare or anyway limited cases where it serves as a watchdog defending basic concepts of law and personal morality. What this development signifies is the institutionalization of the ideas and attitudes that infected the media in the 1960s.

Yet the strongest impression these stories leave is not of liberalism or of institutional imperialism, but of opportunism and incoherence. In December, in the wake of the flap created by presidential counselor Edwin Meese when he questioned whether all those being fed in soup kitchens were really in need, ABC ran a long and evidently lengthily prepared story by national correspondent James Wooten intended to get to the bottom of the issue and sort out what is and is not known about hunger in America.

Early on, Wooten put the issue squarely:

> By any standard and in any season, America is a generous community. Nearly $20 billion tax dollars this year alone for federal food programs, and another $50 billion at least donated to private charities. . . . So if we're spending all that much money, why do we still have hungry neighbors?

A good question to which, as it happened, Wooten had no coherent answer. At first he said, quoting food lobbyist Nancy Amadei, that "if there are more people without money, there are more people at risk of hunger." But in a dramatic conclusion, he shifted course:

> Hunger and need and poverty persist in this country, not from a lack of money, but a lack of commitment, not as a consequence of policy, but a product of politics.

The meaning of this statement was never explained. Then once again Wooten shifted course:

> And as the debate drones on and on into the presidential campaign, the problem simply grows.

It is hard to avoid the impression, finally, that this confusion, this refusal to lay troubling questions to rest where possible—which had their counterparts in virtually every story in the period under study—reflects the very essence of television journalism in its current form. This is an institution whose behavior seems to do only one thing consistently: create conflict and agitate issues, and present itself as the arbiter of the resulting maelstrom.

In other words, television denied the reality of the recovery in large part out of the institutionalized egomania that TV journalism has become. The filmed TV news story is an intensely personal and interpretative narrative form, dominated by the voice, language, image, thought, and feeling of the omniscient narrator, the reporter, who is completely in control of every element of the story. These excerpts from the networks' coverage of the recovery suggest that the people of TV news have finally internalized this stance of omniscience, that they had begun to take this formal fiction literally. They proceed in these stories as if they were superior to events, superior to the audience, superior to elected politicians, superior to everyone and everything. No one and nothing is good enough for them; all they can see about them is bad news. A recession is bad news; a recovery is also bad news. So insistent are these newsmen on interpreting reality and laying bare subsurface meanings and broader trends—as they choose to define reality, meanings, and trends—that they cannot report mere actual events, no matter how important. Neither can they sustain the discipline to form a coherent image of the trends and circumstances surrounding them. As a result, they misrepresent and falsify what is going on in the world.

In my opinion, the networks' coverage of the recent economic recovery and expansion limns one of the more unattractive and depressing episodes in the history of American journalism. At the end of a long period of growing economic disarray and decay, and in the wake of a deep and painful economic contraction—a contraction sharply criticized by TV journalists—the network news programs effectively denied the reality of the long-awaited recovery. Things were at long last getting better. A set of policies was working; even if one disagreed with their premises, they deserved to be taken seriously, rather than mindlessly derogated. These realities were blacked out on the network news.

This cannot be explained away as the perhaps unfortunate but nevertheless inevitable result of the supposed iron laws of television journalism that apologists conventionally adduce to exculpate network news and explain away poor performance. We are often told, for example, that with their meager twenty-two minutes a night in which to present the news of the world, the networks must omit or radically condense much that is important. But that was not the problem in this case, since the networks could have achieved a reasonably truthful sketch of events simply by reversing the emphasis of their coverage—spending most of the time on the recovery, and noting in introductory or parenthetical passages or in an occasional feature story the persistence of pockets of unemployment, or permanent poverty and hunger, or structural maladjustment in West Virginia and other such areas. Similarly, the old saw about television being a visual medium and needing colorful action film does not explain why people going back to work and factories reopening are not news, while people without work and shut-down factories are news. No, what the Institute of Applied Economics study reflects is misrepresentation by journalists corrupted by hubris.

In recent decades the most widespread and insistent theme of press criticism has been the denigration of the "objective" tradition in modern journalism as mindless and irrelevant and misleading. What really matters, the critics have declared, is the meaning of news events and the broader trends of our time; accordingly, the main mission of journalism should be to divine trends and meanings, not to assemble data describing the noise and random flux of the day's events.

This view, alas, is mostly wrong-headed; in fact, the truth is just the reverse. What is enduringly valuable in journalism—not to mention hard to get—is accurate information about what actually happened today or yesterday; assembling and presenting such information is the highest ambition journalism can realistically pursue. Trends and meanings are fictions that merely aggrandize the journalist and manipulate the audience, not inform it; they, not the date of actual experience, are the true noise of history. The cure for what has come to ail network news is therefore straightforward: it is to abandon the false sophistication of the thematic, interpretative television news story, and to return to the oldest tradition of American journalism—the description of daily events and the pursuit of hard fact.

FOUR

Introduction to
The Resourceful Earth:
A Response to Global 2000

JULIAN SIMON AND
HERMAN KAHN

EXECUTIVE SUMMARY

The original 1980 *Global 2000 Report to the President* (*Global 2000* hereafter) is frightening. It received extraordinarily wide circulation, and it has influenced crucial governmental policies. But it is dead wrong. Now *The Resourceful Earth*, a response to *Global 2000*, presents the relevant reliable trend evidence which mainly reassures rather than frightens.

Two paragraphs summarize the "Major Findings and Conclusions" of *Global 2000* on its page 1:

> If present trends continue, the world in 2000 will be more crowded, more polluted, less stable ecologically, and more vulnerable to disruption than the world we live in now. Serious stresses involving population, resources, and environment are clearly visible ahead. Despite greater material

---

JULIAN SIMON is Professor of Economics at the University of Maryland, and the author of *The Ultimate Resource*. He has written many articles on the economics of population growth and other subjects, and is a consultant to various public and private organizations. Until his untimely death in 1983, HERMAN KAHN was the head of the Hudson Institute in New York. Julian Simon and Herman Kahn are co-editors of *The Resourceful Earth: A Response to Global 2000* (Basil Blackwell, 1984) The Introduction to that volume, written by Simon and Kahn, is reprinted here.

output, the world's people will be poorer in many ways than they are today.

For hundreds of millions of the desperately poor, the outlook for food and other necessities of life will be no better. For many it will be worse. Barring revolutionary advances in technology, life for most people on earth will be more precarious in 2000 than it is now—unless the nations of the world act decisively to alter current trends.

To highlight our differences as vividly as possible, we re-state the above summary with our substitutions in italics:

If present trends continue, the world in 2000 will be *less crowded* (though more populated), *less polluted, more stable ecologically,* and *less vulnerable to resource-supply disruption* than the world we live in now. Stresses involving population, resources, and environment *will be less in the future than now*... The world's people will be *richer* in most ways than they are today... The outlook for food and other necessities of life will be *better*... life for most people on earth will be *less precarious* economically than it is now.

The highpoints of our findings are as follows:

(1) Life expectancy has been rising rapidly throughout the world, a sign of demographic, scientific, and economic success. This fact—at least as dramatic and heartening as any other in human history—must be fundamental in any informed discussion of pollution and nutrition.

(2) The birth rate in less developed countries has been falling substantially during the past two decades, from 2.2 percent yearly in 1964-65 to 1.75 percent in 1982-83, probably a result of modernization and of decreasing child mortality, and a sign of increased control by people over their family lives.

(3) Many people are still hungry, but the food supply has been improving since at least World War II, as measured by grain prices, production per consumer, and the famine death rate.

(4) Trends in world forests are not worrying, though in some places deforestation is troubling.

(5) There is no statistical evidence for rapid loss of species in the next two decades. An increased rate of extinction cannot be ruled out if tropical deforestation is severe, but no evidence about linkage has yet been demonstrated.

(6) The fish catch, after a pause, has resumed its long upward trend.

(7) Land availability will not increasingly constrain world agriculture in coming decades.

(8) In the U.S., the trend is toward higher-quality cropland, suffering less from erosion than in the past.

(9) The widely-published report of increasingly rapid urbanization of U.S. farmland was based on faulty data.

(10) Water does not pose a problem of physical scarcity or disappearance, although the world and U.S. situations do call for better institutional management through more rational systems of property rights.

(11) The climate does not show signs of unusual and threatening changes.

(12) Mineral resources are becoming less scarce rather than more scarce, affront to common sense though that may be.

(13) There is no persuasive reason to believe that the world oil price will rise in coming decades. The price may fall well below what it has been.

(14) Compared to coal, nuclear power is no more expensive, and is probably much cheaper, under most circumstances. It is also much cheaper than oil.

(15) Nuclear power gives every evidence of costing fewer lives per unit of energy produced than does coal or oil.

(16) Solar energy sources (including wind and wave power) are too dilute to compete economically for much of humankind's energy needs, though for specialized uses and certain climates they can make a valuable contribution.

(17) Threats of air and water pollution have been vastly overblown; these processes were not well analyzed in *Global 2000*.

We do not say that all is well everywhere, and we do not predict that all will be rosy in the future. Children are hungry and sick; people live out lives of physical or intellectual poverty, and lack of opportunity; war or some new pollution may do us in. *The Resourceful Earth* does show that for most relevant matters we have examined, aggregate global and U.S. *trends* are improving rather than deteriorating.

In addition, we do not say that a better future happens *automatically* or *without effort*. It will happen because men and women—sometimes as individuals, sometimes as enterprises working for profit, sometimes as voluntary nonprofit-making groups, and sometimes as governmental agencies—will address problems with muscle and mind, and will *probably* overcome, as has been usual throughout history.

We are confident that the nature of the physical world permits continued improvement in humankind's economic lot in the long run, indefinitely. Of course there are always newly arising local problems, shortages and pollutions, due to climate or to increased population and income. Sometimes temporary large-scale problems arise. But the nature of the world's physical conditions and the resilience in a well-functioning economic and social system enable us to overcome such problems, and the solutions usually leave us better off than if the problem had never arisen; that is the great lesson to be learned from human history.

We are less optimistic, however, about the constraints currently imposed upon material progress by political and institutional forces, in conjunction with popularly-held beliefs and attitudes about natural resources and the environment, such as those urged upon us by *Global 2000*. These constraints include the view that resource and environmental trends point towards deterioration rather than towards improvement, that there are physical limits that will increasingly act as a brake upon progress, and that nuclear energy is more dangerous than energy from other sources. These views lead to calls for subsidies and price controls, as well as government ownership and management of resource production, and government allocation of the resources that are produced. To a considerable extent the U.S. and the rest of the world already suffer from such policies (for example, on agriculture in Africa), and continuation and intensification could seriously damage resource production and choke economic progress. In particular, refusal to use nuclear power could hamper the U.S. in its economic competition with other nations, as well as cause unnecessary deaths in coal mining and other types of conventional energy production. We wish that there were grounds to believe that a shift in thinking will take place on these matters, but we do not find basis for firm hope. So in this respect we are hardly optimistic.

We also wish to emphasize that though the global situation may be reasonably satisfactory or improving in some given respect, there are likely to be areas in which there are severe difficulties which may be on the increase. Such local problems may be due to local mismanagement, or they may be due to natural catastrophe which the larger community may not yet have been able to help mitigate. Such local problems should not be glossed over in any global assessment.

BACKGROUND

More than one million copies of the original *Global 2000 Report to the President of the United States* have been distributed. It has been translated into five major languages. Other countries such as Germany have commissioned studies imitating *Global 2000.*

Global 2000 also underlies important U.S. policy pronouncements. For example, the following paragraphs, and the rest of the full speech at the Alpbach European Forum in 1980, which was an official "American perspective on the world economy in the 1980s," were founded squarely on *Global 2000:*

> Defying the generally buoyant mood, Richard Cooper, U.S. under secretary of state for economic affairs, delivered a grim message. If present trends continue, he said, the world population will swell to five billion by 1990 from four billion at present, leading to "open conflict, greater terrorism and possibly localized anarchy," as well as "congestion, famine, deforestation."
>
> The decade's population growth would equal "nearly half the total world population when I was born," he said. Even then, he added ominously, "some political leaders were calling for more lebensraum" (or living space). (*The Wall Street Journal*, 15 September, 1980, p. 32)

Before *Global 2000* was even completed, President Carter had discussed its conclusions with other world leaders at an economic summit held in Italy. Immediately upon receiving the Report, the President established a task force to ensure that *Global 2000* received priority attention. The task force included the Secretary of State, the director of the Office of Management and Budget, the President's Assistant for Domestic Affairs, and the director of the Office of Science and Technology Policy. Secretary of State Edmund Muskie used *Global 2000* as the centrepiece for an address to the UN General Assembly. The Joint Economic Committee of Congress launched a series of hearings on the Report. The President instructed the State Department to arrange an international meeting of environmental and economic experts to discuss population, natural resources, environment, and economic development, the subjects of *Global 2000.* Finally, in his farewell address to the nation, President Carter referred to the subject of *Global 2000* as one of the three most important problems facing the American people (the other two being arms control and human rights). And *Global 2000's* effect did not disappear with the change of administration. It continues to be cited as support for a wide variety of forecasts by governmental agencies.[1]

The press received *Global 2000* with great respect and enormous attention. *Time* and *Newsweek* ran full-page stories, and *Global 2000* made front-page newspaper headlines across the country as an "official" government study forecasting global disaster. Though the Report included some qualifications, it was interpreted by all as a prediction of gloom-and-doom. For example, *Science's* story title was: "Global 2000 Report: Vision of a Gloomy World."[2] *Time's* title was "Toward a Troubled 21st Century: a presidential panel finds the global outlook extremely bleak."[3] *Newsweek's* title was "A Grim Year 2000."[4] The typical local paper in central Illinois had this banner across the top of the front page: "U.S. Report Says World Faces Ecological Disaster."[5] And its story began:

> Mass povety, malnutrition and deterioration of the planet's water and atmosphere resources—that's a bleak government prediction that says civilization has perhaps 20 years to act to head off such a world-wide disaster.

A full-page advertisement for the volume in *The New York Review of Books* was headed:

> Government Report as follows: Poisoned seas, acid rain, water running out, atmosphere dying.

However—and seldom can there have been a bigger "however" in the history of such reports—the *Global 2000* is totally wrong in its specific assertions and its general conclusion. It is replete with major factual errors, not just minor blemishes.[6] Its language is vague at key points, and features many loaded terms. Many of its arguments are illogical or misleading. It paints an overall picture of global trends that is fundamentally wrong, partly because it relies on nonfacts and partly because it misinterprets the facts it does present. (In partial defense of the writers who prepared the *Global 2000* work, the summary Volume I—which was the main basis for the news stories—egregiously misstated, for reasons which we can only surmise,[7] many analyses and conclusions in the working-paper Volume II, thereby turning optimistic projections into pessimistic ones.)

Our statements about the future in *The Resourceful Earth* are intended as unconditional predictions in the absence of an unforeseeable catastrophe such as nuclear war or total social breakdown. We feel no need to qualify these predictions upon the continuation of current policies, as *Global 2000* claimed to do, and in fact we believe that such a qualification is not meaningful. Throughout history, individuals and communities have responded to actual and expected shortages of raw materials in such fashion that eventually the materials have become more readily available than if the shortages had never arisen. These responses are embodied in the observed long-run trends in supply and cost, and therefore extrapolation of such trends (together with appropriate theoretical attention) takes into account the likely future responses.

THE SPECIFIC CONCLUSIONS

"More crowded."
There surely will be more people on earth in the year 2000 than there are now, barring a calamity. But a growing population does not imply that human living on the globe will be more "crowded" in any meaningful fashion. As the world's people have increasingly higher incomes, they purchase better housing and mobility. The homes of the world's people progressively have more floorspace, which means people dwell in less-crowded space with more privacy. The United States, for which data are readily available, illustrates the trends in developed countries. In 1940, fully 20.2 percent of households had 1.01 or more persons per room, whereas in 1974 only 4.5 percent were that crowded (U.S. Department of Commerce, 1977, p. 90). (Also relevant: in 1940 44.6 percent of housing units lacked some or all plumbing facilities; but in 1974 only 3.2 percent were lacking. In 1940, 55.4 percent had all plumbing facilities, whereas in 1974, 96.8 percent had all plumbing; U.S. Department of Commerce, 1977, p. 91.) The world's peoples are getting better roads and more vehicles; therefore they can move around more freely, and have the benefits of a wider span of area. In the U.S., paved highways have increased from zero to over three million miles since the turn of the century. Natural park areas have been expanding (Figure 1). And trips to parks have increased to an extraordinary degree (Figure 2). These trends mean that people increasingly have much more space available and accessible for their use, despite the increase in total population, even in the poorer countries. All this suggests to us that the world is getting less crowded by reasonable tests relevant to human life.

"More Polluted."
Global 2000 asserts that the world is getting more polluted. But it cites no systematic data for the world or even for regions. It is certainly reasonable to *assume* that man-made industrial pollutions increase as the most backward countries begin to modernize, get somewhat less poor, and purchase pollution-creating industrial plants. The same is true of consumer pollution—junked cars, plastic bags, and pop tops of beverage cans. But it is misleading to suggest that there are *data* showing that such pollution is a major problem.

In the early stages of industrialization, countries and peo-

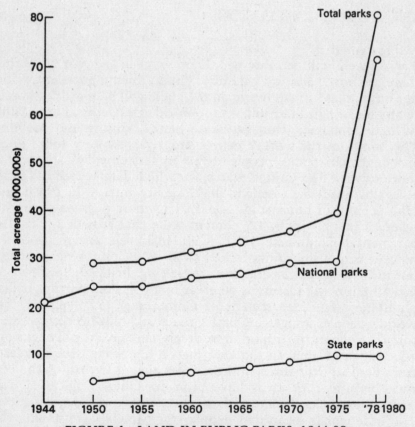

FIGURE 1   LAND IN PUBLIC PARKS, 1944-80.
Sources: *Statistical Abstract of the U.S.*, 1973, p. 202, 1980, p. 242 for 1950-79; *Information Related to the National Park System*, United States Department of the Interior, National Park Service, 30 June 1944, p. 35 for 1944.

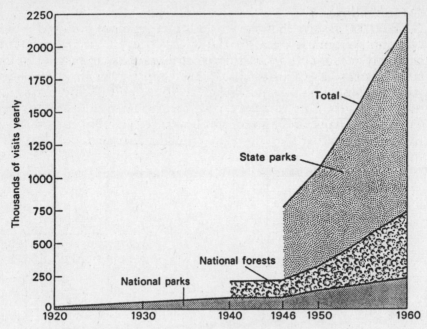

FIGURE 2   VISITS TO PUBLIC PARKS, 1920-60.
Source: see Simon, 1981, Figure 16-5.

ple are not yet ready to pay for clean-up operations. But further increases in income almost as surely will bring about pollution abatement. (At the same time, biological disease pollution has been declining, even in the poor countries, at a rate far outweighing any hazardous effect of man-made pollution, as seen in increased life expectancy.)

In the richer countries there is solid evidence that hazardous air pollution has been declining. Figure 3 shows the Council on Environmental Quality's new Pollutant Standard Index for the U.S., and Figure 4 shows one key measure of air quality for which data are available since 1960; the benign trend has been under way for quite a while, and does not stem only from the onset of the environmental movement around 1970.

Water quality, too, has improved in the richer countries. Figure 5 shows the improvements in drinkability of water in the U.S. since 1961. Such alarms of the 1960s and 1970s as the impending "death" of the Great Lakes have turned out totally in error; fishing and swimming conditions there are now excellent. (Ironically, the "death" that was warned of is really a condition of too much organic "life," and is therefore self-curing as soon as

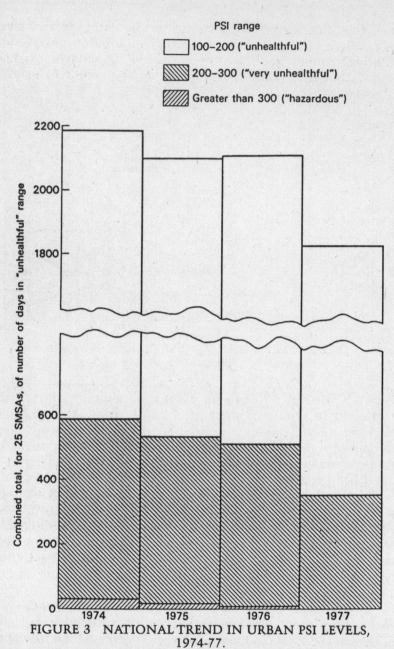

FIGURE 3   NATIONAL TREND IN URBAN PSI LEVELS,
1974-77.
Source: Based on U.S. Environmental Protection Agency data, reproduced
from the tenth annual report of the Council on Environmental Quality,
1979, p. 39.

people stop adding so much nutrient to the water.) In the developing countries the proportion of the urban population served by a safe water supply rose modestly in the 1970s, and rose markedly among the rural population (but from 14 percent to only 29 percent; Holdgate *et al.*, 1982, p. 135).

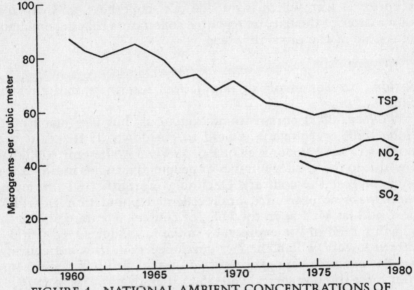

FIGURE 4   NATIONAL AMBIENT CONCENTRATIONS OF TOTAL SUSPENDED PARTICULATES, NITROGEN DIOXIDE, AND SULFUR DIOXIDE, 1960-80. DATA MAY NOT BE STRICTLY COMPARABLE.
Source: U.S. Environmental Protection Agency

The long-run historical record, to the extent that there are data, offers examples upon which one may seize to argue almost any shade of opinion about pollution. But many of the oft-cited series that purportedly show "deterioration" prove, upon inspection, to be the result of forces other than recent human activities.

"Less stable ecologically, and more vulnerable to disruption."
These concepts are so diffuse that we have no idea how one would measure them directly. *Global 2000* gives no relevant trend data.

Perhaps *Global 2000* had in mind that there is more danger of disruption as humankind's capacity to alter the ecosystem increases. In itself, this must be true. But at the same time, humankind's ability to restore imbalances in the ecosystem also increases. And the trend data on pollution, food (discussed below), and life expectancy suggest that the life-supporting capacities have been increasing faster than the malign disturbances. Of course some unprecedented catastrophe such as the Black Death may occur, but we can only look into the future as best we can, and conclude that no such catastrophe is in view. The one crucial exception is war, which is outside our scope here, and which is not a matter of the natural resource constraints that depend upon the nature of the physical world.

"Serious stresses involving population, resources, and environment . . ."
This *Global 2000* phrase sounds ominous, but like many other *Global 2000* warnings it is hard to pin down. If it means that people will have a poorer chance of survival in the year 2000 than now, due to the greater number of people, the trends in life expectancy suggest the contrary. Declining mortality and improving health have accompanied unprecedented population growth in the world (as well as in the U.S., of course). Figure 6 shows the long-run trend of life expectancy in the more-developed world, a pattern toward which the less-developed countries are converging. For example, life expectancy in less-developed regions rose from forty-three years in 1950/55 to fifty-three years in 1970/75

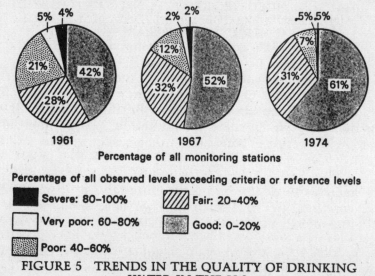

FIGURE 5   TRENDS IN THE QUALITY OF DRINKING
WATER IN THE U.S.
Source: U.S. Council on Environmental Quality, Annual Report, 1975,
p. 352.

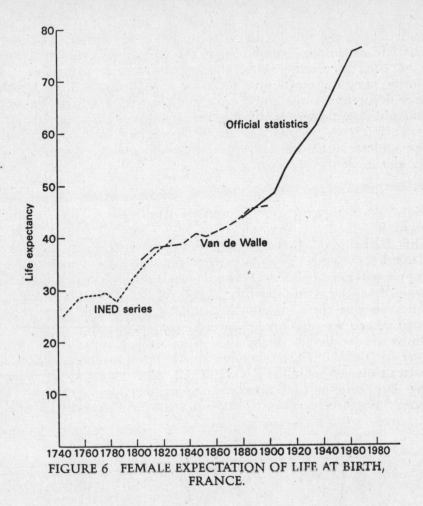

FIGURE 6   FEMALE EXPECTATION OF LIFE AT BIRTH,
FRANCE.

(the rise in Asia being even greater), a much bigger jump than the
rise from sixty-five years to seventy-one years in the more-developed regions (Gwatkin, 1980).

If the phrase "serious stresses" implies that along with
more people in the year 2000 will come more costly resources
and a deteriorated environment, the trends suggest the opposite,
as noted above for the environment, and as discussed next for
resources. If the phrase means that life expectancy, resource availability, and the quality of the environment could be even better in
the year 2000 with fewer people than are expected, Global 2000
has not even attempted to demonstrate such a complex causal
correction. The existing research on the subject does not suggest
to us that such would be the case.

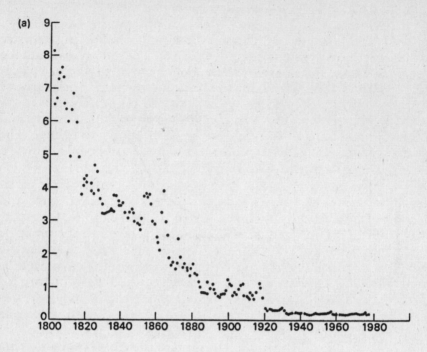

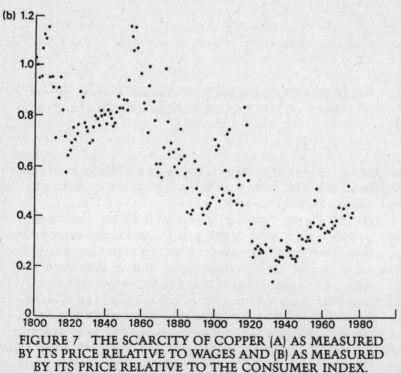

FIGURE 7   THE SCARCITY OF COPPER (A) AS MEASURED
BY ITS PRICE RELATIVE TO WAGES AND (B) AS MEASURED
BY ITS PRICE RELATIVE TO THE CONSUMER INDEX.

". . . resources . . ."
Global 2000 projected a 5 percent yearly increase in the real price of nonfuel minerals until the year 2000. There has always been "serious stress" in the sense that people have to pay a price to get the resources they want. But the relevant economic measures of "stress"—costs and prices—show that the long-run trend is toward less scarcity and lower prices rather than more scarcity and higher prices, hard as that may be for many people to believe. The cost trends of almost every natural resource have been downward over the course of recorded history.

An hour's work in the United States has bought increasingly more of copper, wheat, and oil (which are representative and important raw materials) from 1800 to the present (see, for example, Figure 7). The trend is less dramatic in the poorest countries, but the direction of the trend is unmistakable there too, because per person income has been rising in poor countries as well as rich ones. The same trend has held throughout human history for such minerals as copper and iron. Calculations of expenditures for raw materials as a falling proportion of total family budgets make the same point even more strongly.

These trends mean that raw materials have been getting increasingly available and less scarce relative to the most important and most fundamental element of economic life, human work-time. The prices of raw materials have even been falling relative to consumer goods and the Consumer Price Index. All the items in the Consumer Price Index have been produced with increasingly efficient use of labor and capital over the years, but the decrease in cost of raw materials has been even greater than that of other goods. This is a very strong demonstration of progressively decreasing scarcity and increasing availability of raw materials. The trend of raw material prices relative to consumer goods, however, has much less meaning for human welfare than does the trend of resource prices relative to the price of human time—a trend which is decidedly benign, as we have seen. Even if raw materials were rising in price relative to consumer goods, there would be no cause for alarm as long as it takes progressively less effort, and a smaller portion of our incomes, to obtain the service from raw materials that we need and want.

Moreover, the observed fall in the prices of raw materials understates the positive trend, because as consumers we are interested in the service we get from the raw materials rather than the raw materials themselves. We have learned to use less of given raw materials for given purposes, as well as to substitute cheaper materials to get the same services. Consider a copper pot used long ago for cooking. The consumer is interested in a container that can be put over heat. After iron and aluminium were discovered, quite satisfactory cooking pots—with advantages as well as disadvantages compared with pots of copper—could be made of those materials. The cost that interests us is the cost of providing the cooking service, rather than the cost of the copper.

A single communications satellite in space provides intercontinental telephone connections that would otherwise require thousands of tons of copper. Satellite and microwave transmission and the use of glass fibers in communications are dramatic examples of how a substitute process can supply a service much more cheaply than copper.

"The world's people will be poorer in many ways . . ."
The *Global 2000* qualifying phrase "in many ways" could imply that a decrease in the number of elephants, or the deaths of some elderly beloved persons, are ways in which the world's people will be poorer in the future than now; if so, the statement is logically correct. But if we consider more general and economically meaningful measures, the world's people have been getting richer rather than poorer, and may be expected to be richer in the future. Measured in conventional terms, average income for the world's population has been rising. Particularly noteworthy, and contrary to common belief, income in the poorer countries has been rising at a percentage rate as great or greater than in the richer countries since World War II (Morawetz, 1978). Another vivid proof of the rise in income in poorer countries is the decline in the proportion of the labor force devoted to agriculture—from 68 percent to 58 percent between 1965 and 1981 in the developing countries, consistent with the trend in developed countries where the agricultural labor force has plummeted to, for example, well below 3 percent in the U.S. The rising average income in poorer countries combined with the rough stability of their internal income-distribution shares suggests that the poorer classes of representative countries have been participating in this income rise along with the richer classes.

"The outlook for food . . . will be no better."
Consumption of food per person in the world is up over the last thirty years (Figure 8). And data do not show that the bottom of the income scale is faring worse, or even has failed to share in the general improvement, as the average has improved. Africa's food

production per capita is down, but no one thinks that has anything to do with physical conditions; it clearly stems from governmental and other social conditions. Famine deaths have decreased in the past century even in absolute terms, let alone relative to population. World food prices have been trending lower for decades and centuries (Figure 9), and there is strong reason to believe that this trend will continue. This evidence runs exactly counter to *Global 2000's* conclusion that "real prices for food are expected to double." If a problem exists for the U.S., it is a

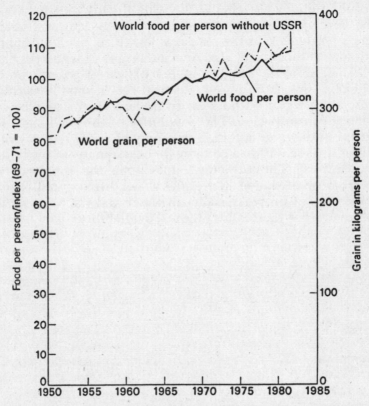

FIGURE 8   WORLD GRAIN AND FOOD PRODUCTION
PER PERSON.
Source: USDA, FAS FG-8-82 (3-15-82); USDA WASDE-133 (5-11-82);
Brown, *Building A Sustainable Society* (Norton, 1981), p. 81 (with authors'
extrapolation of 1981 and 1982 population). The Food index includes all
food commodities—including grain, pulses, oil-seeds, vegetables, and fruit;
it excludes the PRC. Source of index USDA ERS, Statistical Bulletin
No. 669, July 1981; USDA, Personal Communication,
Dr. Patrick M. O'Brien
(1980, 1981 index).

problem caused by abundance. Food production in the U.S. is now so great that farmers are suffering economically. Food stocks in the world are so high that they are causing major problems (Figure 10). Agricultural yields per hectare have continued to rise in such countries as China, France, and the U.S. These gains in production have been accomplished with a decreasing proportion of the labor force—the key input for and constraint upon the economic system.

Careful study of the quantities of actual and potential agricultural land in various countries, plus possibilities for irrigation and multicropping together with yields already routinely reached in the developed countries, suggests that agricultural land will not be a bottleneck in the foreseeable future, even without new technological breakthroughs. And the supply of water for agriculture (which is by far the largest use of water) poses even fewer problems arising from purely physical conditions. Physical measurements of water withdrawal in the world as a whole provide no relevant information. The possibility of the world as a whole running out of water is zero. The supply of water is always a local or regional issue within a country (or occasionally at the border of two countries). The key constraints upon the supply of water arise from institutional and political conditions, and especially the structure of property rights to water and the price structure for water, rather than mere physical availability.

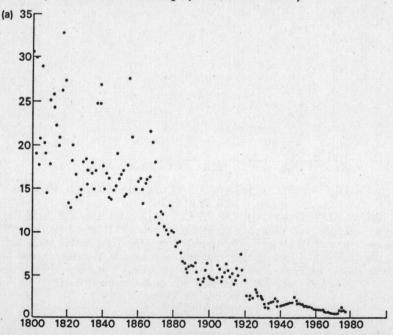

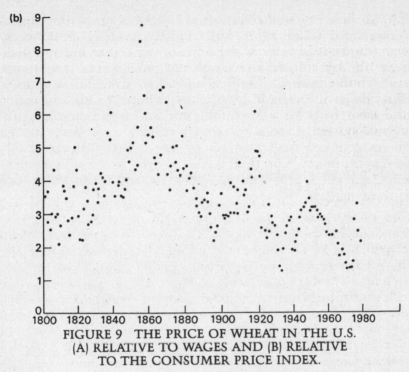

FIGURE 9   THE PRICE OF WHEAT IN THE U.S.
(A) RELATIVE TO WAGES AND (B) RELATIVE
TO THE CONSUMER PRICE INDEX.

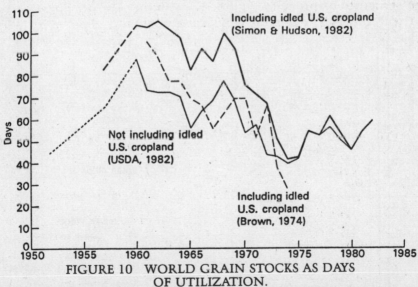

FIGURE 10   WORLD GRAIN STOCKS AS DAYS
OF UTILIZATION.

Sources: (1) USDA, FAS, FG 8-82 (3-15-82); USDA WASDE-133 (5-11-81);
(2) Brown, *By Bread Alone* (Praeger, 1974), p. 60; Brown, *Building a
Sustainable Society,* p. 96; authors' estimates for 1981, 1982. Data for
1952 and 1957 from D. Gale Johnson, *World Food Problems and Prospects;*
USDA, ERS 479, *U.S. Corn Industry,*
February 1982, Table 46.

The issue of a well-constituted system of property rights—the absence of which often leads to "the tragedy of the commons"—arises sharply with respect to water rights; but appropriate rules for private property are also of fundamental importance in many other natural resource and environmental situations. Drilling rights in oil basins, rights to pollute the air and water, and hunting rights for wild animals are but three dramatic examples. A sound set of social rules with respect to property can go far to ensure a satisfactory supply of resources and an acceptably clean environment. On this there is ever-growing agreement among naturalists, economists, geologists, and others concerned with these matters.

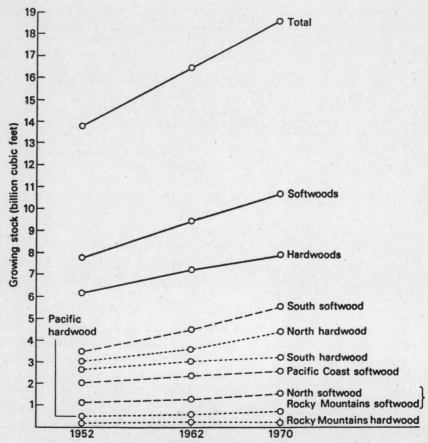

FIGURE 11   FOREST RESOURCES IN THE U.S., 1952-70.
Source: Perspectives on Prime Lands, U.S. Department of Agriculture (1975).

"Significant losses of world forests will continue over the next 20 years."

According to *Global 2000*, "by 2000 some 40 percent of the remaining forest covered in LDCs will be gone." If nonsense is a statement utterly without factual support, this is nonsense. Forests are not declining at all in the temperate regions. In the U.S., for example, the total quantity of trees has been increasing, and wood production has been increasing rapidly (Figure 11). The rate of deforestation in tropical areas has been far slower than suggested by *Global 2000*. The prospects for world wood production to meet demand without grave deforestation are excellent, especially because plantations which require only small land areas have just begun to make the major contribution to total world production of which they are capable.

"Arable land will increase only 4 percent by 2000. . . . Serious deterioration of agricultural soils will occur worldwide, due to erosion."

Arable land has been increasing at a rate very much faster in recent decades than the rate *Global 2000* projected for coming decades—an increase which we can approximate at fully 16 percent over the twenty-year period from 1950 to 1975 for which there are good data (Table 1). There is no apparent reason why in the next decades the increase should fall anywhere nearly as low as the 4 percent *Global 2000* suggests. A comprehensive assessment of the earth's land resources for agriculture by an authoritative President's Science Advisory Committee suggested that arable land will not be a key constraint upon food production in the world, and our findings agree. Rather, social and economic conditions are the key constraints on the amount of land brought into production.

In the United States, the conversion of farmland to urbanized land is proceeding at about the same rate as in recent decades, rather than at three times that rate, as was widely reported recently by a now-discredited agency of the U.S. Department of Agriculture (the National Agricultural Lands Study), the source of the *Global 2000* statement on the subject. Furthermore, each year more (and better) new land is being brought into cultivation by irrigation and drainage than is being urbanized and built upon.

Concern about the "loss" of cropland to new housing, and the resulting governmental regulations that have constrained housing starts and raised the price of new homes, especially in California, does not square with contemporary federal policies for reducing planted acreage to meet the problem of "overproduction" of grain. In 1983 perhaps 39 percent of U.S. crop acreage was kept idle by federal subsidy programs, at an unprecedented high cost to U.S. taxpayers of $18.3 billion (compared to an original estimate of $1.8 billion for the year; *New York Times*, January 31, 1983, p. 5). The argument is sometimes made that governments must act to save cropland for future generations, but this argument lacks support from either economic analysis or technological considerations. The driving motive behind urging government action to "preserve" farmland seems to be more aesthetics than economics.

TABLE 1(a) CHANGES IN LAND USE, 1950-60

	Arable land as a percentage of total area		Percentage of arable land that is cultivated		Cultivated land as a percentage of total land (1 × 3) and (2 × 4)		Agricultural land (arable and pasture) as a percentage of total area	
	(1)	*(2)*	*(3)*	*(4)*				
	1950	*1960*	*1950*	*1960*	*1950*	*1960*	*1950*	*1960*
Africa	14.27	15.30	36.21	42.72	5.2	6.5	46.50	49.02
Middle East	12.87	13.91	52.11	57.88	6.7	8.1	13.06	17.34
Asia	19.03	20.78	82.06	86.17	15.6	17.9	46.35	49.60
No. and So. America, U.S.S.R., Australia, New Zealand	6.88	7.75	82.75	82.96	5.7	6.4	34.27	38.59
Europe	30.79	30.98	89.02	90.06	27.4	27.9	45.63	46.10
All regions	10.73	11.73	82.74	83.99	8.9	9.9	37.35	41.07

Source: Kumar, 1973, p. 107.

TABLE 1(b) CHANGES IN LAND USE, 1961-5 TO 1975

	Arable land as a percentage of total area				Agricultural land (arable and pasture) as a percentage of total area			
	1961-65	*1966*	*1970*	*1975*	*1961-65*	*1966*	*1970*	*1975*
Africa	6.28	6.50	6.76	6.96	32.88	32.96	33.13	33.29
Middle East	6.25	6.38	6.54	6.79	21.91	22.12	22.32	22.62
Far East	28.87	29.37	29.88	30.73	33.08	33.62	33.80	34.56
North America	11.50	11.43	12.17	13.08	26.10	25.85	25.88	25.50
U.S.S.R.	10.24	10.24	10.39	10.37	26.83	27.34	27.09	26.97
Latin America	5.64	5.97	6.43	6.82	29.56	30.29	31.29	32.41
Western Europe	27.21	26.55	25.97	25.04	46.35	45.08	44.83	43.72
All regions	10.41	10.58	10.93	11.25	33.13	33.38	33.71	33.99

Source: UN, Food and Agriculture Organization, 1976.

Soil erosion is not occurring at a dangerous pace in most parts of the United States, contrary to much recent publicity. In most areas topsoil is not being lost at a rate that makes broad changes in farming practices economical from either the private or public standpoint, though recent advances in tillage may change the picture somewhat. Regulating or subsidizing particular tillage practices portends greater social cost than benefit in the long run. The largest social cost of soil erosion is not the loss of topsoil, but rather the silting-up of drainage ditches in some places, with consequent maintenance expenses. In the aggregate, just the opposite of land ruination has been taking place, as the soil of American farms has been improving rather than deteriorating, and as fewer rather than more crop acres suffer from severe erosion over the decades since the 1930s. The continuing advance in agricultural productivity per acre is consistent with the improvement in the quality of farmland.

"Extinctions of plant and animal species will increase dramatically. Hundreds of thousands of species—perhaps as many as 20 percent of all species on earth—will be irretrievably lost as their habitats vanish, especially in tropical forests."
This assertion by *Global 2000* is remarkably unsupported by statistical evidence. The only scientific observations cited in support of a numerical estimate of future species extinction are (a) between 1600 and 1900 perhaps one species every four years was extinguished, and (b) between 1900 and 1980 perhaps one species every year was extinguished. The leap to *Global 2000's* estimate of 40,000 species extinguished each year by the year 2000 is based on pure guesswork by the *Global 2000* writers and the source upon which they draw (Myers, 1979). We do not neglect the die-off of the passenger pigeon and other species that may be valuable to us. But we note that extinction of species— billions of them, according to Mayr (1982)—has been a biological fact of life throughout the ages, just as has been the development of new species, some or many of which may be more valuable to humans than extinguished species whose niches they fill.

"Atmospheric concentrations of carbon dioxide and ozone-depleting chemicals are expected to increase at rates that could alter the world's climate and upper atmosphere significantly by 2050."

The longest available records of climatic variations reveal very wide temperature swings, much or all of which may be thought of as random. In that context, recent changes in temperature may reasonably be viewed as normal oscillation rather than as a structural change induced by man's activity, including changes in CO_2.

The CO_2 question is subject to major controversy and uncertainty—about the extent of the buildup, about its causes, and especially about its effects. It would not seem prudent to undertake expensive policy alterations at this time because of this lack of knowledge, and because problems that changes in CO_2 concentration might cause would occur far in the future (well beyond the year 2000). Changes in the CO_2 situation may reasonably be seen, however, as an argument for increased use of nuclear power rather than fossil fuel. Continued research and monitoring of the CO_2 situation certainly is called for.

If it is considered desirable to reduce the amount of CO_2 released into the atmosphere by human activity, on the grounds that atmospheric change with unknown effects carries undesired risks, only two possibilities are feasible: reduce total energy consumption, or increase energy production from nuclear power plants. Reduction in total world energy consumption below the level determined by prices reflecting the production cost of energy is clearly unacceptable to most nations of the world because of the negative effects on economic growth, nutrition and health, and consumer satisfaction. This implies an inverse tradeoff relationship between CO_2 and nonfossil (especially nuclear) power.

"Acid rain . . ."
There is trend evidence that the pollution of acid rain has been getting more intense, and that it has some ill effects on freshwater lakes and their fish, upon perhaps forests, and hence upon people's ability to enjoy nature. Emissions from combustion of fossil fuels are undoubtedly a partial cause, although natural sources also contribute. There is some evidence of limited local ecological damage, but no proven threat to agriculture or human life. The trend deserves careful monitoring. The consensus of recent official committee reports (with which we agree) questions the use of high-sulfur coal for power production. This squares with our general advocacy of nuclear electricity generation. Whether any tighter pollution controls are warranted, economically or otherwise, has not been established. Fighting acid-rain effects on fish by liming lakes does not generally seem economically feasible. The acid-rain issue increases the comparative advantage of nuclear power plants relative to coal-burning plants.

As with CO_2, then, there is an inverse tradeoff relationship between nuclear power and acid rain.

"Regional water shortages will become more severe."
In the previous decade or so, water experts have concluded that the "likelihood of the world running out of water is zero." The recent UN Report of the World Environment, for example, tells us not to focus upon the ratio between physical water supply and use, as *Global 2000* does nevertheless, and emphasizes making appropriate social and economic as well as technological choices. From this flows "cautious hope from improved methods of management." That is, an appropriate structure of property rights, institutions, and pricing systems, together with some modicum of wisdom in choosing among the technological options open to us, can provide water for our growing needs at reasonable cost indefinitely.

Moreover, *Global 2000's* statements about the world's future water situation are completely inconsistent with—in fact, are completely opposed to—*Global 2000's* own analysis of what can reasonably be said about the world's water resources. It develops a sound analysis that finds that no reasonable or useful forecasts can be made about the world's water supply, but then proceeds to offer frightening forecasts totally inconsistent with its analysis. This inconsistency should be more than sufficient grounds to reject *Global 2000's* gloomy conclusions out of hand.

"Energy . . ."
The prospect of running out of energy is purely a bogeyman. The availability of energy has been increasing, and the meaningful cost has been decreasing, over the entire span of humankind's history. We expect this benign trend to continue at least until our sun ceases to shine in perhaps seven billion years, and until exhaustion of the supply of elemental inputs for fission (and perhaps for fusion).

Barring extraordinary political problems, we expect the price of oil to go down. Even with respect to oil, there is no basis to conclude that the price will rise until the year 2000 and beyond, or that humankind will ever face a greater shortage of oil in economic terms than it does now; rather, decreasing shortage is the more likely, in our view. For the next decade or two, politics—especially the fortunes of the OPEC cartel, and the prevalence of war instability—are likely to be the largest element in influencing oil prices. But no matter what the conditions, the market for oil substitutes probably constitutes a middle-run ceiling price for oil not much above what it is now; there could be a short-run panic run-up, but the world is better protected from that now than in the 1970s. And if free competition prevails, the price will be far below its present level.

Electrical power from nuclear fission plants is available at costs as low or much lower than from coal, depending upon the location, and at lower costs than from oil or gas. Even in the U.S., where the price of coal is unusually low, existing nuclear plants produce power more cheaply than from coal. Nuclear energy is available in unlimited quantity beyond any conceivable meaningful human horizon. And nuclear power gives every evidence of costing fewer lives per unit of energy produced than does coal or oil. The main constraints are various political interests, public misinformation, and cost-raising counterproductive systems of safety regulation. Nuclear waste disposal with remarkably high levels of safeguards presents no scientific difficulties.

Energy from sources other than fossil fuel and nuclear power, aside from hydropower where it is available, do not hold much promise for supplying the bulk of human energy elements, though solar power can be the cheapest source of power for heating buildings and water in certain geographic locations. The key defect of solar power, as well as with its relatives such as power from waves, is that it is too dilute, requiring very large areas and much capital to collect the energy.

"Rapid growth in world population will hardly have altered by 2000 . . . The rate of growth will slow only marginally from 1.8 percent a year to 1.7 percent."
Population forecasting involving fertility is notoriously unreliable. The birth rate can go down very rapidly, as numerous countries have demonstrated in the past few decades, including a country as large as China. (The rate can also go up rapidly, as the baby boom in the U.S. following World War II demonstrated.) Therefore, confidence in any such forecast for a matter of decades would be misplaced. The passage of only a handful of years already seems to have knocked the props out from under *Global 2000's* forecast quoted above. The world's annual growth rate, which was 2.2 percent less than two decades ago in 1964-65, is down to 1.75 percent (*U.S. Department of Commerce News*, August 31, 1983), a broad decline over the bulk of all the poorer and faster-growth nations. Though the growth rate may have stabilized in the last few years, these data alone seem inconsistent

with the *Global 2000* forecast. The author of that forecast acknowledges that we have already moved from their "medium" forecast to their "low" forecast.

Even the apparently surefire *Global 2000* forecast that "in terms of sheer numbers, population will be growing faster in 2000 than it is today" might very well turn out to be wrong. Because the total population will be larger in 2000 than now, the fertility rate would have to be considerably smaller than it is now to falsify that forecast. But the drop would have to be only of the magnitude of the drop during the past two decades for that to come about, which would not seem beyond possibility.

More generally, the *Global 2000* forecasts of a larger population are written in language that conveys apprehension. But viewing the long sweep of human history, larger population size has been a clear-cut sign of economic success and has accompanied improvement in the human lot. The growth in numbers over the millennia, from a few thousands or millions living at subsistence to billions living well above subsistence, is proof positive that the problem of sustenance has eased rather than intensified. And the increase in life expectancy, which is the main cause of the increase in population size, is not only a sign of success in agriculture and public health, but also is the fundamental human good.

In the long run, human beings are the only possible source of human progress. Therefore, we consider *Global 2000's* choice of language to describe population developments to be inappropriate and misleading.

Our positive statements about the recession of the physical constraints upon human progress are based primarily upon presently known progress, not taking into account possible or even likely advancements in technology. If we were to take into account such possibilities as the resources available to us in space and other such advances—even those possibilities which are already solidly worked out scientifically—our assessment would be much more "optimistic" than it is.

WHY THE EXTRAORDINARY DIFFERENCES BETWEEN GLOBAL 2000 AND THE RESOURCEFUL EARTH?

The stark differences between *Global 2000* and *The Resourceful Earth* cry out for explanation. There are several causes:

(1) *The Resourceful Earth* relies heavily on trend data, which we present in abundance. *Global 2000* said that

trend data are the proper basis for such an analysis, but
nevertheless presented few such data. (It is ironic that
we follow this recommendation of *Global 2000*, whereas the original did not follow its own advice.) Our projections of agriculture and natural resource availability
exemplify the fundamental role of such trend data.

(2) Even in the rare cases in which *Global 2000* did present
trend series, it heavily weighted a few recent observations, rather than looking at the long-run trends. The
fish catch may serve as an example. *Global 2000* presented a data series ending in 1975, and it extrapolated
continued stagnation from the last few years' data leading up to 1975. Data for the years since 1975, which we
show, indicate that in spite of the extraordinary rise and
fall of the Peruvian anchovy fishery in the 1960s and
1970s, the long-run trend toward a larger catch has resumed, as we would have expected based on the overall
trend in the series (see Figure 12), though the rate of
increase may have been decreasing.

(3) *Global 2000* drew far-reaching conclusions about many
issues in the almost total absence of data. The rate of
deforestation, and of species loss, are two examples.
Reinspection of the skimpy data used to "demonstrate"
species loss reveals that *Global 2000's* extrapolation
from those scraps of evidence is quite unsupported by
the evidence. Our further investigation of deforestation
time-series provides much firmer ground for our un-
worried assessments than the one-time survey data provide for *Global 2000's* alarming projections.

(4) *Global 2000* relied on inappropriate assumptions for its
projections. For example, it projected that food prices
would double, in large part because it assumed that
energy prices would go up. This assumption about energy prices was unsound in several demonstrable ways.
First, there was no sound reason simply to assume without evidence that energy prices would rise, especially in
the face of the long-run trend of falling energy prices.
Second, *Global 2000* focused on the price of energy
rather than the price of fertilizer, the production of
which accounts for much of the use of petroleum in
agriculture. The price of fertilizer has been falling in
the 1970s, due to technological improvements, even despite energy price rises. Perhaps most important, *Global
2000* implicitly assumed that private farmers do not

respond to economic incentives to produce more food,
which is as wrong as any assumption possibly could be.

(5) There are glaring inconsistencies between *Global 2000's*
statements about particular matters in its various chapters.[8] The very pessimistic assertions in the summary
(Volume I) conflict sharply with statements in the
working papers (Volume II).

THE FORECASTING CAPACITY OF GOVERNMENT

The Resourceful Earth is not "the U.S. Government's projections," as *Global 2000* said about itself, or the projections of any
other organization. Rather, *The Resourceful Earth* is a compendi-
um of work by independent U.S. scientists who are employed
outside the government, and who are considered authorities by
their scientific peers. The work has not passed through any bureaucratic editing. Other authorities probably would disagree
with some of our emphases and evaluations, but few (if any)
would disagree with the trend facts adduced here.

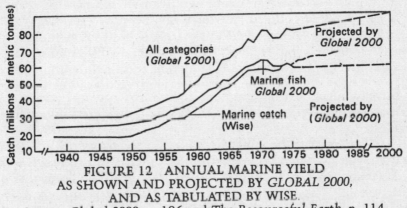

FIGURE 12   ANNUAL MARINE YIELD
AS SHOWN AND PROJECTED BY *GLOBAL 2000*,
AND AS TABULATED BY WISE.
Source: *Global 2000*, p. 106 and *The Resourceful Earth*, p. 114.

The fact that the writers of *The Resourceful Earth* are outside government is crucial, in our view, because we believe that
government agencies are not well-equipped to produce sound
assessments of long-run future trends concerning resources. Too
often the agency making the assessment has an axe to grind that
derives from its perceived mission and which biases its forecasts.
Furthermore, staff-produced government reports must pass
through reviews at various stages up the chain of command, and
the final conclusions of the staff report, therefore, are likely to

emphasize conventional views and to reduce the range of opinion expressed. The resulting work cannot then be attributed to individuals, and no individuals need take full responsibility. In contrast, individuals take full responsibility in *The Resourceful Earth*, and our reputations hang on the quality of the work. Our aim here is not to denigrate the efforts of capable, hard-working, and dedicated civil servants, or to suggest that all (or even most) bureaucratic review is bad. Rather, our aim is to point out that internally prepared assessments can and do suffer scientifically because of the organizational forces that prevail in government no matter what the administration. (If all this sounds a bit holier-than-thou, please forgive us. We admit we are proud of *The Resourceful Earth's* independence as well as convinced of the importance of this fact.)

By its own admission, *Global 2000* did indeed present the public with views distorted by such bureaucratic procedures. Gerald Barney, director of *Global 2000*, has written, for example, that much "misunderstanding" was caused by the first four words on page 1 of Volume I in the "Major Findings and Conclusions" section, "If present trends continue." He notes that

> the statement "If present trends continue . . ." was that of an editor at CEQ, and although I objected to the statement as incorrect, it was not possible to have it corrected. (Barney, 1982, p. 9)

If bureaucratic editing can have that much effect, little in such an"official" report as *Global 2000* can be considered scientifically reliable.

Still another disability of internal "government" analyses is that they are often a hodgepodge of elements of unknown origin and nature. Barney says that *Global 2000* suffered from this disability, too. "The technological assumptions were left entirely to the professionals in the government's agencies," (Barney, 1982, p. 9), and were not necessarily the assumptions that the director or staff would have chosen. Independent outside studies of the sort that underlie *The Resourceful Earth* are less vulnerable to this danger. Again, the individual authors of *The Resourceful Earth* take full responsibility for the assumptions they make.

After completion of *Global 2000*, Barney made clear how troublesome these institutional circumstances are for carrying out a study such as that one:

> As they have evolved, the Government's agencies now have a hidden layer of decision makers—computer pro-

grammers and modelers. These decision makers are, by and large, very skilled professionals, but they are often working in institutional circumstances which prevent them taking into account all the factors they know should be taken into account. Furthermore, the assumptions that they make have a profound influence on the range of policy options considered by senior government officials, and their assumptions are not well documented, are not understood by senior government officials, and are not available for peer review and commment. (Barney, 1982, p. 3)

The inability of government agencies to predict resource trends, and the ill effects of such "official" but badly-made forecasts, would be amusing if not so sad. After a sharp price rise in the late 1970s, timber prices in 1983 fell about three-quarters, causing agony for lumber companies that contracted for government timber at the high prices.

Industry trade groups argue that the government owes the industry help because its policies led to the bidding disaster. In the late 1970s, [an industry spokesman] says, government economists predicted timber shortages and helped to fan the bidding. *(Wall Street Journal,* 1 April 1983, p. 13)

The Department of Energy caused havoc for airplane manufacturers, airlines, for a host of other industries, and for foreign governments by its forecasts that the price of oil would continue to rise after 1979. And that was the forecast in *Global 2000*, in contrast to the editors of this volume and of the authors of the chapters on oil, who are all on record as predicting that the price would *not* continue to rise. The same story describes the recent histories of the other raw materials, too. (Being right does not endear one to others, or make one's opinions more sought, as a rule.) Does this history constitute the basis for increasing the role of government in these matters, or of decreasing it?

We suggest that it would be sensible to compare systematically the record of long-run government forecasts against the record of a reasonable sample of forecasts made outside the government, before making any decision in favor of further centralization. The only available data, those of Ascher (1978), suggest no advantage to government forecasts over private forecasts. To proceed without evidence of a governmental advantage in the activity would not seem responsible legislation.

We know of no body of scientific evidence assessing the effects of ill-founded pessimistic forecasts about resources and the environment upon public morale, innovation, and economic progress. We are agreed, however, that we adjudge the effects, past and future, to be severe and costly.

POLITICAL FRUITS OF GLOBAL 2000

Enter now the Global Tomorrow Coalition, an umbrella organization consisting (as of October 1982) of forty-nine environmentalist and population organizations[9] with total membership of five million persons; it represents the Global 2000 movement that has evolved since the publication of Global 2000. In response to the circumstances mentioned in the quotation from Gerald Barney above, Barney and the Global Tomorrow Coalition are calling for more government computer modeling in the form of a "government global model," and for more centralized control of that modeling. "[I]ncreased coordination of models development and documentation (sic) is needed by the Executive Office of the President" (Barney, 1982, p. 3). Barney sees the matter as follows:

> Some of the problems of using computer-based models are illustrated by the difficulties encountered in using the government's models to conduct the Global 2000 study. The Global 2000 analysis was initiated with an eight-page memorandum listing all of the projections which would be needed for the study. This memorandum was circulated to the participating agencies along with an indication of which of the projections the agencies would be responsible for. The agencies were all visited and the most professional personnel, the best models, most current and complete data were located. The professionals were then asked to produce a first draft within six weeks.
>
> At the time the first drafts were due, a weekend-long retreat was held at the Belmont House in Maryland. The primary discovery at that meeting was that none of the professionals directly responsible for the long-term global analysis in each of the participating agencies had ever met. They were total strangers. The energy expert had never met the water expert. The food expert had never met the population expert, etc. As a result, our first priority was to make acquaintance and begin the process of seeing that the assumptions being used by the various departments were as internally consistent as we could make them.
>
> At that time we also began the analysis of the content of the models. We knew in advance that the Govern-

ment does not have what is normally thought of as a "global model," i.e., a single model containing separate interacting sectors dealing with the population, resources, and environment. We discovered, however, the Government does have a "global model." In the Government's global model, the population sector is located in a computer at the Bureau of the Census. The energy sector is located in a different computer at the Department of Energy. The food sector is located in a different computer at the Department of Agriculture, etc.

In analyzing these sectoral models, we discovered that they are in fact an interacting set of global sectoral models that collectively constitute the Government's global model. Each of the sectors needs information from the others. The energy sector, for example, needs economic and demographic and water projections for input. The population projections require information on the social and economic conditions that influence fertility and mortality rates as inputs. The food model needs information on fertilizer and energy prices, on water availability, economic conditions, and demographic trends.

In analyzing these models, we found that information was flowing from one sectoral model to another even though the persons responsible for the models did not know each other. The medium of communication was the Government Printing Office. Studies were prepared with one sector of the Government's global model, sent off to the Government Printing Office, printed, purchased by another government agency, and the results entered into another sector of the Government's global model. In the process of conducting the *Global 2000* study, we introduced all the Government's professionals to each other, expediting interaction among the models by a factor of perhaps as much as a million simply by bypassing the normal mode of communication through the Government Printing Office. (Barney, 1982, pp. 16-18)

At the behest of the Global Tomorrow Coalition and its member organizations, legislation concerning "foresight capability" with respect to population and resource is now (August 1983) before the Congress. Integrating the various models used in government into a single grand "global model" is one of the objectives of these bills. Another aim is to establish an "Office of Research and Policy Analysis on Global Population, Resources, Energy and the Environment" (Willson memo, September 17, 1982, p. iii).

We do not share the belief that such integration of models

will advance "global foresight capability." One of the outcomes of our preparation of *The Resourceful Earth* is that we believe even more strongly than ever that creating one big "government global model" by hooking up the various sectoral models used by various government agencies will *not* improve long-run predictions concerning the topics to which *Global 2000* is addressed. We have great respect for some computer models; almost all of the authors of *The Resourceful Earth* are heavy users of such models in our own work. But we are wary of the call for a governmental "global model" of the sort envisaged by the Global 2000 movement for these reasons:

(1) Models that are developed for one purpose often are fatally flawed for other purposes; using them for such other purposes is likely to produce fallacious results. For example, a model intended to estimate the price and usage of oil in the U.S. in the short run of, say, the next month or year, will probably give worse results than no model at all for predicting price and usage in the long run of five or ten years. Some of the key factors that operate in the long run—such as the substitution of other fuels in response to increased prices of oil—are not likely to be included in the short run model.

(2) We do not agree that data on all (or even on most, or some) of the various elements discussed in *Global 2000* are crucial inputs for predicting the other elements. For example, the future price of energy is not a key input for estimating the future price and quality of food; actions by governments concerning agricultural price controls and subsidies, and the amount of agricultural research done, among other forces, are likely to be far more important in the long run of twenty and more years. Population growth may even not be a central variable if viewed in the conventional fashion of more people implying a higher price of food; in the long run the effect may be the opposite, as greater population density leads to better farm-to-market transportation, and to a host of institutional and technological developments, as has been the history of humanity until now. Ignoring most or all of the interdependencies among the sectors touched on by *Global 2000* may not be disastrous, as *Global 2000* suggests it is and necessarily will be. It may even be a prudent scientific strategy to ignore them. (This assertion may seem proposterous until

you examine the track records of predictions about resources and environment made without extensive consideration of such interdependencies, and compare
them with predictions of the global modelers who insist—at least in principle—on including such interdependencies in models.)

(3) The strength of computer simulation models for prediction is dealing with the following type of problem:
(a) each of the relevant interacting forces is understood
rather well, and (b) there is relatively little uncertainty
about the underlying conditions, but (c) there are too
many such forces for an analyst to be able to sort them
out with paper and pencil alone. Properly programmed
for the behavior of each of the forces, and for their
interactions and feedbacks, the great calculating power
of the computer can work through the large number of
necessary computations to arrive at a better answer
than can an analyst without the aid of such computing
power.

The analytic problems confronted by *Global 2000*
have quite different characteristics, however, not only
because the interaction of the individual elements is not
well understood as yet—a drawback that has properly
been emphasized by *Global 2000* and by its director
after the completion of the Report—but even more because the key assumptions cannot be made with confidence. In the illustrative case of energy again, *Global
2000* believed it necessary to feed energy price forecasts
into the agricultural and the resource models. But what
forecast of energy prices should be used? The forecast
must depend on such factors as whether OPEC will
collapse, the state of future public opinion toward nuclear power from fission, and whether nuclear fusion
will become economical (which would affect the present price of oil even if fusion were not commercially
available for decades). These are the kinds of considerations for which simple paper-and-pencil analyses are
likely to prove best (perhaps with the help of the computer for parts of the analysis).

A major advantage of paper-and-pencil analyses is
that they clearly reveal the extent of the uncertainties,
and thereby reduce the likelihood of carrying faulty
partial analyses from one part of an overall global assessment to another. The writers of *Global 2000* and the

Global Tomorrow Coalition believe that more intensive and more integrated modeling is the answer; we believe that such reliance on complex modeling was responsible for the misleading statement made by *Global 2000* about the future course of energy prices, and also was responsible for the confusion caused in *Global 2000's* agricultural analysis by the introduction into that analysis of the computer-generated forecast of energy prices.

Nobel prizewinner Gunnar Myrdal commented as follows on complex modeling, in the context of the Club of Rome's "Report," *The Limits to Growth*, of which *Global 2000* is a direct lineal descent both in its personnel and its approach to modeling:

> [T]he use of mathematical equations and a huge computer, which registers the alternatives of abstractly conceived policies by a "world simulation model," may impress the innocent general public but has little, if any, scientific validity. That this "sort of model is actually a new tool for mankind" is unfortunately not true. It represents quasi-learnedness of a type that we have, for a long time, had too much of, not least in economics, when we try to deal with problems simply in "economic terms."
>
> In the end, those conclusions from the *[Limits to Growth]* Report's analysis that are at all sensible are not different and definitely not more certain than could have been reached without the elaborate apparatus by what Alfred Marshall called "hard simple thinking aware of the limitations of what we know." (Myrdal, 1975, pp. 204-5).

Great difficulties were caused for *Global 2000* by reliance upon the outputs of various computer models, which were inconsistent with each other and with judgments derived from other sources. This is starkly revealed in the section called "Closing the Loops," which deals with the environmental consequences of various projections of population and resources given elsewhere in *Global 2000*. As a reviewer noted:

> Whereas the report up to this point has emphasized the environmental impacts of the projections, now the direction of the analysis is reversed and the authors explore the effect of environmental consider-

ations on the realism of the projections. This is a commendable undertaking for it reveals inconsistencies among the projections. But it is virtually a total repudiation of the projections made by the agencies and as modified by the *Global 2000* staff. Time and time again, the earlier projections are characterized as inadequate, incomplete, inconsistent, or inaccurate. Originally, the federal agencies' assistance had been sought because of their expertise, but here the study staff substitutes its judgments for those of the agencies.

Why was such a curious and circuitous process followed? Once the projections were considered unreliable, why were they then published, only to be refuted? One is left to guess at the reasons, but whatever they may be, their effect is confusing at best. At worst, the abrupt turnabout raises questions about the credibility of the entire project. (Clawson, 1981), p. 20)

(4) Another perspective on the matter of "centralized foresight": a larger place for government activity in this field implies a smaller place for outside assessments— that is, fewer assessments such as we are now offering in *The Resourceful Earth*. More reliance upon a "government global computer model" implies less reliance on assessments built upon the entire armamentarium of scientific tools, including wide-ranging experience and historical perspective, such as is the approach of *The Resourceful Earth*. In considering the desirability of our approach compared with "centralized foresight" and a "government global model," it would seem prudent to compare track records. Many of the authors represented in *The Resourceful Earth* are on record with forecasts made more than a decade ago which ran exactly counter to the forecasts of the gloom-and-doom modelers in *The Limits to Growth* tradition, in the middle of which squarely stands *Global 2000*. And *The Resourceful Earth* authors were correct—especially on such topics as nutrition and famine; climate; pollution in the U.S.; and prices and supplies of agricultural products, mineral resources, and oil. In contrast, the global modelers were dead wrong. Such a comparison does not build confidence or lend support for placing more rather than less reliance upon global modelers in *The Limits-to-Growth-cum-Global 2000* tradition. Comparison

of predictive success would seem to recommend more reliance upon wide-ranging and independent outside studies such as we offer here, and less reliance upon global computer-simulation modeling in the vein of *The Limits to Growth* and *Global 2000*.

(5) Staff-performed government studies such as *Global 2000* have a built-in tendency toward self-perpetuating error in their chosen method of modeling by compilation of other government studies. (Barney said that *Global 2000* "should be thought of as an image of the future as seen by government agencies, rather than as an independent study of the subject." This is in stark contrast with *The Resourceful Earth*, which stands on its own, and can duck no responsibility for error by pinning the blame upon other studies which served as our base.) The self-perpetuating nature of the process may already be seen in the many government reports since *Global 2000* that base *their* conclusion upon *Global 2000* as a source of authoritative information.

(6) Studies performed inside government are more subject to manipulation by political pressure groups than are studies by independent scholars. For example, governments usually do not like to say that a report which they urged upon the world was out-and-out wrong. Diplomats worry about "credibility." Such a disavowal seems "unstatesmanlike," especially when a report is labeled "the U.S. government projection" as is *Global 2000*. Therefore, governments usually try to do an about-face without showing the movement—now you see it, now you don't. *The Resourceful Earth* was originally conceived out of an initiative by the Environmental Protection Agency to the editors. When the environmental movement learned of this, our views about *Global 2000* and our analyses of resources and environment being on record, there began a campaign to prevent the project from being funded. The campaign included such public ventures as a leaked story in the *New York Times*, protest letters from congressmen to EPA, and a press release from Stanford University; the private politicking cannot be so well documented, but was widespread; and EPA never came through with funding.

The reader may wonder whether this account is sour grapes. We think not. We initiated the project in May 1982, before it was clear that EPA would not fund it, because we found low-budget backup support from Heritage and because we were too impatient to wait for the EPA funding battle to come to an end. Along the way we offered to sell the product to any major government agency or responsible individual for just one dollar ($1). Our aim in making that offer was to obtain an "official" label for the volume. We adjudged that it was its "official" label that obtained such wide circulation for *Global 2000*. The fact that *The Resourceful Earth* received considerable attention early on was a pleasant surprise to us, but if a tenth or even a twentieth of the number of copies of *The Resourceful Earth* are sold as of *Global 2000*, one of us will eat a copy of this introduction—with an appropriate sauce, of course.

(7) Once a model is entrenched inside a government agency, it is likely to remain in use long after it is no longer credible, due to lack of channels for independent criticism. A frightening example of this tendency has recently surfaced right smack in the middle of the context of Club of Rome *Limits to Growth* models (as are also *Global 2000* and the Global 2000 movement's recommendation for further work). The Department of Defense—or more specifically, the Strategic Plans and Policy Branch of the Military Studies and Anslysis Division of the Command and Control Technical Center (CCTC/C313) uses as its "major analytic tool" what it calls the "World Integrated Model" ("WIM"), which is an outgrowth of the Mesarovic-Pestel model, which in turn was the Club of Rome's first successor to its *Limits to Growth* model. This DOD adaptation dates from 1974, and continues on its merry way regardless of the fact that the Mesarovic-Pestel and *Limits to Growth* models have been damned as foolishness or fraud by every serious economic critic; for example, Myrdal's assessment. No scientific support or even scientific publication—where criticism is possible—is cited for DOD's WIM model, and though its operators talk about comparing the output with actual data from 1975 to 1980, apparently no such comparison has been made. Its operators refer to it as "the finest global forecasting model available today" (Hamilton memo, p. 6). But the only basis given for belief in its usefulness is the following laudatory remark from an "Executive Office of the President memorandum":

> Basically the Mesarovic-Pestel (WIM) is in a class to itself. There appear to be no detailed dynamic feedback models of similar quality that take a world perspective. The model incorporates a great deal of knowledge and has a strong systems perspective. (Hamilton memo, p. 5)

The WIM is run at great cost to the taxpayer; two to three person-years are required just to *update* the WIM model every two years; far more than the cost of the entire *The Resourceful Earth* enterprise. Worse, the WIM output is used for "strategic" purposes, on the assumption that there is a connection between impending violence, and the WIM model's forecasts about raw material and population forecasts.

In brief, WIM is a model using an economic framework and publicly available economic data, built and operated without roots in the community of professional economists and without publication for examination in the economic literature (none is cited in its list of references), and using a basic model (*Limits to Growth* type) universally condemned by economists who have looked into it. Yet so seductive is this kind of work that it continues to help shape the nation's fortunes.

In short, we must not be seduced by the magic that computer modeling promises but cannot deliver. Centralization of such modeling, as is called for by the Global Tomorrow Coalition, is particularly dangerous because it reduces the opportunity for independent checks upon erroneous programming and inappropriate assumptions. Difficult and unpleasant as it is for many people to accept, it is crucial to understand that governments are not repositories of wisdom, and can be as mistaken on crucial matters—including scientific issues—as the least-educated layman. Such understanding is especially important because of the Global Tomorrow Coalition's current push toward "centralized foresight."

RECOMMENDATIONS

The Resourceful Earth aims to provide sound and balanced assessments of key issues concerning resources and the environment, and thereby to correct false, gloomy impressions left by

Global 2000. Policy recommendations are not our mission, and practically no recommendations are contained in the chapters. However, we do have a few views about possible policies which we mention briefly in passing. (We have already expressed our views about a policy of centralizing the government's "foresight capability.")

The recommendations that flow from Global 2000, and which are at the core of the Global 2000 movement and the Global Tomorrow Coalition, are contained in Global Future: Time to Act (called Global Future hereafter). In the words of that document:

> The Global 2000 Report to the President identified the problems; it did not attempt to find solutions. The President then directed agencies of the government to undertake the next step—to look at present government programs related to these long-term global issues, assess their effectiveness, and recommend improvements. One of us, Gus Speth, Chairman of the Council on Environmental Quality (CEQ), chaired this effort. [The other was Edmund Muskie, Secretary of State.]
>
> The report that follows, prepared by the Council on Environmental Quality and the Department of State, responds to the President's charge. (1981, pp. iii-iv)

Global Future contains approximately one hundred recommendations which fall into three general categories: (1) mobilize interest in the general topic among foreign governments and within the U.S. public; (2) increase U.S. spending in Global 2000-related programs; (3) create governmental institutions that will centralize activities concerning resources and the environment and require various governmental agencies to heed the recommendations of these "global oversight" institutions. The specific recommended programs cover so many activities in the U.S. and abroad that we will not even try to characterize them. We wish to focus attention, however, on the last of the ten sets of recommendations, those which Global Future classifies as "Institutional Changes: Improving Our National Capacity to Respond."

"Recommendations" (quoted from Global Future): The United States should:

> Establish a government center as coordinator to insure adequate data collection and modeling capability as the basis for policy analysis on long-term global population, resource, and environmental issues.

Improve the quality of data collection and modeling for global issues and promote wider access to data and models.

Establish a Federal Coordinating Unit, preferably in the Executive Office of the President, to develop federal policy and coordinate ongoing federal programs concerning global population, resource, and environmental issues. Activities should include coordinating data and modeling efforts described above; issuing biennial reports; assessing global population, resource, and environment problems; and serving as a focal point for development of policy on long-term global issues.

Adopt action-forcing devices, such as budget review procedures, a Presidential message, creation of a blue-ribbon commission, establishing an office in each federal agency to deal with long-term global issues, or passage of legislation formalizing a mandate to federal agencies to address long-term global issues and creating a federal coordinating unit and hybrid public-private institute.

Create the Global Population, Resources, and Environment Analysis Institute, a hybrid public-private institution, to strengthen and supplement federal government efforts on long-term global analyses.

Improve the budget process to make technical expertise of U.S. agencies more readily available to other countries.

Assure environmental review of major U.S. government actions significantly affecting natural or ecological resources of global importance; designate tropical forests, croplands, and coastal wetland-estuarine and reef ecosystems as globally important resources.

Continue to raise global population, resource, and environment issues in appropriate international forums; work with and support appropriate international organizations and other countries in formulating solutions.

Enlist the business community in formulating responses to long-term global problems.

Increase public awareness of global population, resources, and environment issues. (1981, pp. li-liii)

A closely related recommendation made elsewhere in *Global Future:*

Develop a U.S. national population policy that includes attention to issues such as population stabilization; availability of family planning programs; just, consistent, and

workable immigration laws; improved information needs;
and institutions to ensure continued attention to domestic
population issues. (1981, p. xxx)

The recommended government center deserves special attention.
This is the full description:

Recommendation [of *Global Future*]: A single government
center should act as coordinator for the federal government to insure availability of an adequate data and modeling capability to carry out policy analysis on long-term
global population, resource, and environment issues. To be
most effective, this center should be part of the Federal
Coordinating Unit for policy, discussed below, or at least
closely coordinated with it. The center should:

Identify long-range problems of global significance.

Promote the development of appropriate analytical tools
and data required to assess long-term implications of global problems.

Coordinate and insure preparation, at timely intervals, of
long-term projections of trends in global population, resources, and environment and carry out other studies related to these problems.

Prepare timely reports that assess the state of global modeling and data collection, evaluate these analytic activities
in the federal government, and make recommendation for
improvements.

Name lead agencies for each population, resource, and
environment subject area to decide what data should be
collected, by whom, and with what methodology.

Coordinate modeling activities of government agencies to
insure linkage, feedback, and compatibility of data among
various models.

Establish and support a nongovernmental center as part of
the public-private Global Population, Resources, and Environment Analysis Institute, discussed below, to enhance
global modeling and analysis. (1981, pp. 160-1)

*We disagree with all of these recommendations by Global
Future.* Our reasons for disagreeing lie in one or more of these
general propositions:

(1) The public will be best served both in price and availability with respect to natural resources such as copper

and oil, which are mainly produced by the private sector and whose environmental externalities can be dealt with by governmental rules in a reasonably routine fashion, if the government takes no actions at all that affect production or distribution, except for building strategic stockpiles. (We do favor continued government funding of research in agriculture and some potential energy sources such as fusion.)

(2) Scientific research and assessments of these topics should continue to be carried out independently in a variety of locations, rather than becoming more centralized than now. The government's policy tool affecting these activities is funding. We recommend against any funding for new government agencies of the sort envisioned by the Global 2000 movement by way of the Global Tomorrow Coalition or otherwise, unless that agency is able to win funding through competition in the normal research channels with peer-group review.

(3) We believe that the government should *not* take steps to make the public more "aware" of issues concerning resources, environment, and population. We consider that the public has been badly served by having been scared by a very large volume of unfounded and/or exaggerated warnings about these matters. Many of these scientifically unsupported and injudicious warnings have derived from government agencies. The results have been disastrous from the standpoint of the allocation of social resources—for example, the contracts entered into by airlines for airplane manufacturers to build new fuel-saving airliners, contracts later canceled by the airlines at high cost to all; the high price of natural gas resulting from long-term contracts to pay-or-take entered into on the assumption that energy prices would continue to rise; the federal regulations on the average fuel mileage of automobiles sold by particular makers, leading to vast unnecessary expenditures for redesign, with consequent weakening of U.S. automobile firms; and federal grants to recycling centers that process waste at much higher social cost than ordinary waste disposal; we could fill a book with examples. The results of unfounded public fears about the future of resources and the environment probably have also caused declines in morale and the will to exert effort for continued improvements.

It is a matter of great public importance that we reverse these patterns of the 1960s and 1970s. The U.S. public must come to hear the truth that conditions have been getting better rather than worse, and that enthusiastic and vigorous efforts to do even better even faster will benefit the public as well as the individuals who act economically to bring about this social progress. In our view, the world is ready to turn its back on its pessimism, and is waiting to hear some good news. All the more reason to tell the true good news that there is to tell.

(4) With respect to population growth in the U.S., whose "stabilization" is called for by the Global 2000 movement (as seen, for example, in the recommendation by *Global Future*, p. 11, and in the bills before Congress urged by the Global 2000 movement), we make no recommendation other than that government should not attempt to influence individuals' family-size decisions in any fashion. Even if there were economic advantages to cessation of population growth in the U.S., too many wider issues and values are involved to justify such a far-reaching policy; human population is not simply an economic matter. We also do not consider it our place to discuss whether our government should attempt to stimulate fertility; we see no compelling economic reason for such a policy, and many sound reasons against discussion of the matter. Immigration is an extremely complex topic that is far beyond our purview—and beyond that of *Global 2000*, which implied, however, that immigration has been too great, though *Global 2000* did not provide even the hint of a rationale for such a proposition.

Our viewpoint on population growth in the rest of the world is much the same as in the United States. Recommendations to other countries—and even more so, pressure upon them—to institute and carry out policies with respect to their population growth rates are not warranted by any facts about resources and population, and they constitute unjustifiable interference in the activities of other countries, because such policies must necessarily rest upon value judgments. Hence we consider that such recommendations by the Global 2000 movement are unfounded and unacceptable, ignorant and arrogant.

The cost of any policy recommendation should always be reckoned, even if the policy by itself might have positive effects. For example, the recommendation of the Global 2000 movement for government collection of more secondary "global" data seems unobjectionable, on its face. But there is no reason to presume that such collection or analysis of data would be done efficiently or cost-effectively. For example, the cost of *Global 2000* executed by the federal government was roughly one million dollars (Barney, 1982). The cost of *The Resourceful Earth*, carried out by independent scholars as an extension of the work they have been doing much of their professional lives, and in some cases which they have already largely completed or published in other contexts, is roughly $30,000, less than a thirtieth of *Global 2000's* cost. Our contributors were paid out of private funds at the rate of $1000 per paper, truly only an "honorarium" for persons of this caliber and for work this serious; conference travel expenses took most of the rest. (Of course we believe that at *no* price would *Global 2000* have been a purchase of value.) This comparison, which we consider typical, does not build much confidence in the government's ability to spend taxpayers' money well for activities of this sort, and it testifies against internal staff-prepared reports on subjects that are essentially scientific.

It does not follow that, because we are not proposing new things for governments to do about resources and the environment, we therefore think that nothing needs to be done. Much is being done spontaneously, by individuals, by nongovernmental bodies, and by governments; and much more needs to be done. We believe, however, that it is a mistake to presume that the government usually handles these tasks better than, or even as well as, persons outside of government; sometimes government does better, sometimes worse. The case against government action is especially strong where there are relatively few difficult externalities, as is the case with the production of food, energy, and other natural resources.

CAPSULE CONCLUSION

The letter of transmittal of *Global 2000* to the President of the United States said:

> Our conclusions, summarized in the pages that follow, are
> disturbing. They indicate the potential for global problems
> of alarming proportions by the year 2000. Environmental,

resource, and population stresses are intensifying and will increasingly determine the quality of human life on our planet. These stresses are already severe enough to deny many millions of people basic needs for food, shelter, health, and jobs, or any hope for betterment. At the same time, the earth's carrying capacity—the ability of biological systems to provide resources for human needs—is eroding. The trends reflected in the Global 2000 suggest strongly a progressive degradation and impoverishment of the earth's natural resource base.

We radically rewrite the statement as follows:

Our conclusions are reassuring, though not grounds for complacency. Global problems due to physical conditions (as distinguished from those caused by institutional and political conditions) are always possible, but are likely to be less pressing in the future than in the past. Environmental, resource, and population stresses are diminishing, and with the passage of time will have less influence than now upon the quality of human life on our planet. These stresses have in the past always caused many people to suffer from lack of food, shelter, health, and jobs, but the trend is toward less rather than more of such suffering. Especially important and noteworthy is the dramatic trend toward longer and healthier life throughout all the world. Because of increases in knowledge, the earth's "carrying capacity" has been increasing throughout the decades and centuries and millennia to such an extent that the term "carrying capacity" has by now no useful meaning. These trends strongly suggest a progressive improvement and enrichment of the earth's natural resource base, and of mankind's lot on earth.

1. Paragraph adapted from Kahn and Schneider (1981). Various other material adapted from Simon (1981).
2. Luther J. Carter, "Global 2000 Report: Vision of a Gloomy World," *Science*, 209, August 1, 1980, pp. 575, 576.
3. *Time*, August 4, 1980, p. 54.
4. *Newsweek*, August 4, 1980, p. 38.
5. Champaign-Urbana *News Gazette*, July 24, 1980, p. 1.
6. For additional material on *Global 2000's* factual errors and internal inconsistencies, see Simon (1981).
7. Ned Dearborn, one of the three *Global 2000* staffwriters, stated in the abstract of a public talk he gave at the 1982 meeting of the American Association for the Advancement of Science:
   By deliberate political choice, only part of the *Global 2000 Report to the President* was featured in the Report's summary vol-

ume and press releases—the part containing the Report's projections. The other part, while not suppressed, was barely mentioned in the official material receiving the widest distribution.
8. In addition to the inconsistencies pinpointed in the chapters here, one might consult Simon (1981).
9. Action for World Development. Alan Guttmacher Institute. American Farm Foundation. American Institute for Biological Sciences. American Society for the Prevention of Cruelty to Animals. Aubudon Naturalist Society of Central Atlantic States. Bolton Institute for a Sustainable Future. Carrying Capacity. Center for Law & Social Policy. Concern, Inc. Conservation Foundation. Defenders of Wildlife. Environmental Coalition of North America. Environmental Defense Fund. Environmental Fund. Environmental Policy Center. Environmental Policy Institute. Federation for American Immigration Reform. Friends of the Earth. Greater Caribbean Energy & Environment Foundation. International Institute for Environment & Development. Izaak Walton League. League of Women Voters. Monitor International. National Aubudon Society. National Family Planning & Reproductive Health Association. National Wildlife Federation. Natural Resources Defense Council. Negative Population Growth. New York Zoological Society. Ohio Conservation Foundation. Overseas Development Council. Planned Parenthood of New York City. Population Crisis Committee. Population Communication. Population Institute. Population Resource Center. Population Services International. Rachel Carson Council. Renewable Natural Resources Foundation. Scenic Shoreline Preservation Conference. Sierra Club. Texas Committee on Natural Resources. Trust for Public Land. U.S. Association for the Club of Rome. U.S. Women's Health Coalition. Wilderness Society. Windstar Foundation. World Population Society. Zero Population Growth.

REFERENCES

Ascher, William (1978), *Forecasting*. Baltimore: Johns Hopkins Press.
Barney, Gerald O. (1982), "Improving the Government's Capacity to Analyze and Predict Conditions and Trends of Global Population Resources and Environment." Manuscript dated March 24.
Carter, Luther, J. (1980), "Global 2000 Report: Vision of a Gloomy World." *Science*, 209, August 1, pp. 575, 576.
Champaign-Urbana *News Gazette*, July 24, 1980, p. 1.
Clark, Colin (1957), *Conditions of Economic Progress* (3rd edn.). New York: Macmillan.
Clawson, Marion (1981), "Entering the Twenty-First Century—The Global 2000 Report to the President." *Resources*, 66 (Spring), p. 19.
Council on Environmental Quality, United States Department of State (1981), *Global Future: Time to Act*. January, pp. 1-209.
Dearborn, Ned (1982), Address to American Association for the Advancement of Science, January.
Dubos, Rene (1981), "Half Truths About the Future." *Wall Street Journal*, May 8, editorial page.
Global 2000 Report to the President, Vols. I, II and III. Washington, D.C.: U.S. Government Printing Office, 1980.

Gwatkin, Davidson R. (1980), "Indications of Change in Developing Country Mortality Trends: The End of an Era?" *Population and Development Review,* 6 (December), pp. 615-44.

Hamilton, C. F. (1982), Memo from Command and Control Technical Center, Defense Communications Agency.

Holdgate, Martin W., Mohammed Kassas and Gilbert F. White (1982), *The World Environment, 1971-1982.* Dublin: Tycooly.

Kahn, Herman and Ernest Schneider (1981), "Globaloney 2000," *Policy Review,* Spring, pp. 129-147.

Kumar, Jogingden (1973), *Population and Land in World Agriculture.* Berkeley: University of California Press.

Mayr, Ernst (1982), *The Growth of Biological Thought: Diversity and Inheritance.* Cambridge, Mass.: Belknap Press of Harvard University Press.

Morawetz, David (1978), *Twenty-Five Years of Economic Development 1950-1975.* Baltimore: Johns Hopkins.

Myers, Norman (1979), *The Sinking Ark.* New York: Pergamon.

Myrdal, Gunnar (1975), *Against the Stream—Critical Essays on Economics.* New York: Vintage Books.

New York Times, January 31, 1983, p. 5.

Newsweek, August 4, 1980.

Simon, Julian L. (1981), "Global Confusion, 1980: A Hard Look at the Global 2000 Report." *The Public Interest,* 62 (Winter), pp. 3-21.

Time, August 9, 1980.

U.S. Department of Commerce, Bureau of the Census. *Social Indicators: 1976.* Washington, D.C.: U.S. Government Printing Office, 1977.

U.S. Department of the Interior, National Park Service, *Information Relations to the National Park System,* June 30, 1944.

Wall Street Journal, September 15, 1980, p. 32.

Wall Street Journal, April 1, 1983, p. 13.

Willson, Pete (1982), Memorandum, The Alan Guttmacher Institute, September 17.

FIVE

The Goal Is Not to Describe: A Review of Nicholas Wolterstorff's *Until Justice and Peace Embrace*

RICHARD JOHN NEUHAUS

Nicholas Wolterstorff is professor of philosophy at Calvin College, Grand Rapids, and is viewed as a respected mover in what some of us perceive as a neo-Calvinist renascence in American religious thought. While situated within that vast and vague world called Evangelicaldom, the neo-Calvinists are distinguished from evangelicals of the Anabaptist tradition and are at a far remove from the evangelicalism that edges over into what is more properly designated as fundamentalism. Indeed it is questionable whether the neo-Calvinists should be called evangelicals. They are called that, one suspects, because they do not fit easily into the Protestant liberal mainstream and have to be put somewhere for taxonomical purposes. Unlike the Roman Catholics or Lutherans, they are not big enough to warrant a category of their own. Then too, many assume that evangelical connotes "conservative," and the neo-Calvinists are that,

---

RICHARD JOHN NEUHAUS is prominent as a Lutheran pastor who for many years has been active in inner city ministries, civil rights, and Christian ecumenism. He is editor of *Lutheran Forum* and the author of nine books including *In Defense of People*, *Theology and the Kingdom of God*, *Christian Faith and Public Policy* and *The Naked Public Square: Religion and Democracy in America*. The following review of Nicholas Wolterstorff's *Until Justice and Peace Embrace* is reprinted from *This World* magazine, No. 9.

at least in the sense that they self-consciously work out of a classical theological tradition.

Much of the work emerging from centers such as Calvin College, however, cannot be accommodated to conventional categories of "right" or "left." It is marked by an innovative approach to Christianity and the social order, an approach shaped by the thought of Abraham Kuyper, Dutch theologian and statesman. One thinks, for example, of the Association for Public Justice, headed by James Skillen in Washington, D.C., or of the very suggestive work of education by Rockne McCarthy, Gordon Spykman, and their colleagues (Society, State and Schools, 1981). This school of thought, to the extent it is a school, has been viewed by some as a promising alternative to the tattered liberalisms, conservatisms, and radicalisms that have dominated religious social thought in recent years. It is therefore with high hopes of engaging a fresh and carefully reasoned treatment of society and politics—especially since these are the Kuyper Lectures for 1981, delivered at the Free University of Amsterdam—that one comes to Nicholas Wolterstorff's *Until Justice and Peace Embrace*.

The book comprises eight chapters, two "interludes," and postscript. They range widely across the terrain of our contemporary situation. The author's "project in this book," he explains, "is to ask how Christians should insert themselves into the modern social order." The answer given is that they should insert themselves radically. The Christianity Wolterstorff espouses is "world-formative," as distinct from "world-avertive," the latter being the Augustinian and, most particularly, the Lutheran disease: "There is an apothegm of Karl Marx that has become so worn with repetition that one is embarrassed to cite it, and yet it puts the point forcefully: *The goal is not to describe the world but change it*" (italics his). Luther and other "avertive" Christians persisted in the mistake of thinking of social structures as God-ordained, says Wolterstorff, "rather than as something created by us to be rearranged if that seems desirable." Wolterstorff claims forcefully that rearrangement is not only desirable but imperative.

The "modern world-system" is inherently unjust and at the heart of the injustice is capitalism, argues the author, who convincingly demonstrates, at some length, that there are many poor and hungry people in the world. The idea that they can be included in the economic world-system through a process of global modernization is a cruel illusion promulgated by the rich and greedy: "It is time for us to cease inventing excuses [for global poverty] and start admitting that modernization theory is bankrupt." The truth about economic injustice, he believes, is illuminated by theorists such as Immanuel Wallerstein, who argue that the relationship between core and peripheral societies is inevitably and designedly exploitative. Says Wolterstorff, "Those in the periphery of the world increasingly see us as predators rather than benefactors . . . My own conviction is that the Third World is largely right on this issue and that we are wrong." As he elaborates this point, however, the qualifying "largely" is largely forgotten.

The author considers two quite different analyses of "the modern world-system": liberation theology as represented by Gustavo Gutierrez, and neo-Calvinism represented by Herman Dooyeweerd and Bob Goudzwaard (both Dutch thinkers in the Kuyper tradition). Wolterstorff has little argument with the social, political, and economic theories of liberation theology, but suggests Gutierrez should be clearer about the connection between liberation and salvation, and thinks he is altogether too enamored of freedom as the goal of human life. (In political theory, Wolterstorff says, the critical differences are between those who put happiness first [Aristotle] or freedom first [the Enlightenment] or order first [Plato]. Wolterstorff wants it understood that he is emphatically in "the happiness tradition.") As for the neo-Calvinists, the author appreciates the idea of "spheres of sovereignty" within which various societal functions are to be respected (state, economy, church, education, etc.), but he criticizes the neo-Calvinists for not understanding that, under the capitalist world-system, economics has gotten out of hand, breaking out of its own sphere and thereby subsuming and distorting all the other functions of society.

The most fundamental distinction—and on this the liberationists are right (assisted by "Marxist analysis," which, it is emphasized, does not mean they are Marxists)—is between the rich and the poor, the oppressor and the oppressed. And the most fundamental Christian proposition is that God is on the side of the poor and oppressed. We are told repeatedly that it is only our selfishness that blinds us to that distinction and that proposition, and to the revolutionary imperatives that they inescapably imply. The remaining chapters are devoted to the evils of nationalism, particularly that of the Afrikaners in South Africa and most particularly that of the Zionism and "the injustices that Israel has wreaked and continues to wreak on the Arabs"; to the disaster of modern cities which are "deserts of aesthetic ugliness"; to the wicked privatization of life represented by the "private automobile"; and finally (and some may think surprisingly) to the importance of liturgical renewal among Calvinists.

It is hard to know what to make of the book. The tone is so shrill and the claims so apodictic that one is inclined to make nothing of it. It might easily be dismissed as a screed produced by the excitations of an academic philosopher taking his first plunge into the turbulent waters of political and economic theory. And yet, the book comes with high praise from leading evangelical thinkers. Then too, one does not want to be dismissive of the neo-Calvinist movement, of which Wolterstorff is thought to be part.

In defense of the author, it is perhaps necessary to understand why he may feel it is necessary to shock. Throughout he describes the church in America as dismally conservative and locked into the self-serving maintenance of things as they are. It may be that he is excessively influenced by his own location in the Christian Reformed Church in Grand Rapids, and by the aggressive promotion of the market economy by leadership sectors of that world (the Amway corporation is nearby). In such a setting it may seem adventurous, even academically required, to assault the putative linkage between Christianity and capitalism. In addition, the author's stridency of tone was probably not inhibited by the audience to which the lectures were delivered at the Free University of Amsterdam, where it might take real courage to say anything positive about capitalism or America's role in the world. Were it required that philosophers be courageous, we should soon be short of philosophers.

Taking these possibly mitigating circumstances into account, the superfluity of passionately asserted simplisms is nonetheless astonishing. We are told that the U.S. and the U.S.S.R. are those "two great Enlightenment experiments" now suffering from "a deep sense of failed ideals." But we are living in dark times "because we in the First World are continuing to refuse to share the wealth of our rich, indulgent societies with those impoverished millions whom we dominate." The result is that Americans and the Soviets "have taken to terrorizing each other with the threat of nuclear bombs, arming the world, and supporting repression in their 'client states.' "

The Third World, in Wolterstorff's view, is divided between repressive regimes, typically allied with the U.S., and revolutionary movements. He wants it understood that he is not "naive concerning the reality of Soviet expansionism," but "it is sheer cynicism to label every move for reform a communist plot."

Granted. Yet the author is blithely indifferent to instances in which Soviet expansionism just might be a relevant factor in understanding revolutionary movements, and there is not even a passing attempt to distinguish between revolution and reform, or between varieties of revolution. The Third World is a world of U.S.-sponsored regimes being challenged by revolutionary forces on behalf of those victimized by the U.S.-controlled "world economic system."

Unaddressed is the conceptual complexity of "the Third World." It is not clear whether it includes the oil-rich nations of the Middle East, who here make an indirect appearance only as the poor Arabs oppressed by the nasty Zionists. And apparently the concept has no room for the nations of East Asia which, at least by most economic and political indices, are doing impressively well in collaborating with the vicious world economic system. Nor does the author treat the many and notorious instances of economic mismanagement by oligarchies and dictatorships—frequently styling themselves socialist and revolutionary—in deepening the sufferings of the poor. But perhaps it is unfair to bring up these inconvenient realities. Taking them into account can certainly take the punch, and the fun, out of issuing broadsides. And, again to be fair, perhaps the author is really not aware of facts and analyses which might nuance his assertions. This is suggested at many points in the book. For example: "Everyone who has studied the matter agrees that the pressure of population is also a decisive factor in the perpetuation of mass poverty." Presumably he is not aware of the very distinguished body of work to the contrary, most recently and cogently set forth by Julian Simon in *The Ultimate Resource*.

A reviewer's desire to find mitigating factors is strained by other items involving the author's logic and assumptions. We are told, for instance, that it is the "great and tragic" failure of Calvinists that "they failed to think through how they could live together in a just society with those with whom they disagreed." No doubt there is truth in that, but Wolterstorff throughout is disdainful of the liberal democratic ideas that have made pluralism possible. In fact, he suggests that we cannot even live together in the church with those with whom we disagree. The conflict between rich and poor "is not a conflict in which the church is to be found exclusively on the side of the exploited. *Christ* was there, and is there, but his 'body,' the church, is not—not all of it in any case. So in taking the side of the exploited, Christians will find themselves in opposition to some of those who confess the same Lord." This is of course liberation theology's notion of the "partisan church" in which fellowship is defined by socio-political allegiance rather than by religious faith or sacramental grace. It is a dubious ecclesiology in any case, but particularly surprising in a book that ends with an appeal for Calvinists to reclaim a "high" and catholic understanding of the church and its sacramental life.

Many Christians who will not be persuaded by the author's analysis of "the modern world-system" might nonetheless welcome any suggestions he has on how the misery of the world might be reduced. But here the author is coy to the point of cruelty. "It is my conviction, however, that in good measure we already know the alternatives, or can easily become acquainted with them." He tells us there are countries in the world where the evils he deplores have been overcome, but he does not tell us which. Sweden? South Korea? Cuba? It is left to us to guess. Likewise, we are told that "our contemporary academics have not been lax in producing suggestions for how things might be handled differently," but, again, we are not told which academics. One gathers that Wolterstorff would be impatient with our asking, for his argument is that the only thing that is lacking is the political will to make the world a much nicer place. And the reason we do not will it is because we are rich and really like things the way they are, our moral protestations notwithstanding. "Self-interest regularly shapes moral conviction," he concludes with an insightfulness that some might mistake as Niebuhrian.

The author's moralistic lacerations are also a cruel but, unfortunately, not unusual punishment for the good burghers of Grand Rapids and, indeed, all of us. Item: "If a rich man knows of someone who is starving and has the power to help that person but chooses not to do so, then he violates the starving person's rights as surely and reprehensibly as if he had physically assaulted the sufferer." What are we to make of this? In global terms, Wolterstorff, this reviewer, and probably every reader of this journal is rich. At this very moment we know people are starving—in Chad, Upper Volta, and too many other places. We also know (or, if we do not know, are culpably ignorant) that we have the power to transfer, in quite direct ways, our personal wealth to starving people—all of it and right now. Is it true then that our behavior is morally tantamount to physically assaulting the starving? I think not.

Nor, it would seem, does the author take his own fevered assertions all that seriously. He approves, for example, of the purchase of a Calder sculpture for a Grand Rapids plaza. When this was being discussed, "there were those who suggested that the money should instead be given to the poor." Wolterstorff was not among them, for "no one had proposed collecting this amount of money and giving it to the poor before the issue of the sculpture came up." One cannot help but wonder why Wolterstorff did not propose it. Apparently, between alleviating world hunger and alleviating the capitalistic ugliness of America's cities, some hard moral choices must be made.

The penultimate chapter is on resistance to illegitimate authority. The question is whether the church will "become an active agent of resistance to injustice and tyranny and deprivation." The Marxist idea that "the working class would become such an agent has proven to be one of the great illusions of history." So it seems to be up to the Christians. Invoking the authority of "the Reformers," Wolterstorff favors civil disobedience and says it is a "key question" whether revolutionary violence is justified. But he is adamantly certain that "the government that perpetrates injuries of an atrocious and notorious character has lost its legitimacy, and the officers of such a government have only the status of private citizens who have committed criminal acts." Does this generalization apply to the U.S. government? The author does not say. But he does say he is talking about how Christians (presumably also American Christians) should "insert themselves into the modern social order." And he leaves no doubt that atrocious and notorious injuries are systematically perpetrated by the political and economic reality that is the United States. It would seem that, by his own logic, the U.S. should have pride of place on the Christian's revolutionary hit list.

Wolterstorff does not actually say that the rule of the righteous requires American Christians to assume a revolutionary posture toward their government. The implication is near inescapable, however, and he edges up to making it explicit. Perhaps he is just being cautious, although that seems improbable since much of the book is a polemic against the caution that holds Christians back from radical commitment to justice, and Wolterstorff repeatedly depicts himself as one who is baring his anguished and enraged soul. Or perhaps he is again being coy, revealing himself obliquely to those who have ears to hear. Or perhaps he has not thought through the specifics of his sweeping generalizations, in which case stridency is matched by vacuity. But, as noted earlier, it is hard to know what the author has in mind.

This overwrought book is, to be sure, frequently uninformed, and its analysis of the causes of human misery is depressingly unoriginal. Yet it would be a mistake to let this disappointment dim one's hopes for the contribution to be made by the budding neo-Calvinist renascence. It would be a mistake because, *inter alia*, there is a very real question whether Wolterstorff should be considered, or considers himself, part of the Calvinist tradition with respect to social thought. He admires what he calls the "totalism" which marks Calvinism, "with its insistence that there is nothing at all in our experience that is not—so far as is necessary and possible—to be subjected to the will of God." Unfortunately, in his view, Calvinism suffered a failure of nerve in adopting a too limited view of what is necessary and possible.

Following Michael Walzer's understanding of the religious origins of radical politics, Wolterstorff finds himself drawn to "bands of men who surveyed the whole structure of society, judged that structure to be fundamentally wrong, and then undertook for reasons of conscience to seize power in order to alter the structure." Not for him are the careful distinctions, probity and sense of limits associated with classic Calvinism. Impatient of the eschatological hope in which justice and peace embrace, the professor of philosophy, eager for action, joins Anabaptism's "revolution of the saints" in embracing at least one version of justice. "Against the Anabaptists the Calvinists threw up a great flurry of arguments, far more than I can here review," he tells us in an historical aside. "The truth, I think, is that, on this issue especially, social realities shaped the thinking of the Calvinists." Apparently only now—in communities elected to immunity from "social realities," communities such as Calvin College and the Free University of Amsterdam—is it possible to recognize that the Anabaptists were right from the start. Far from being part of a neo-Calvinist renascence, *Until Justice and Peace Embrace* is a premature declaration of bankruptcy on behalf of Calvinist social thought. Fortunately, there are other Calvinist thinkers, more careful and more imaginative, who better appreciate their tradition's potential contribution to both describing and changing the world.

Suggested Reading

P. T. Bauer, *Equality, the Third World and Economic Delusion* (Cambridge: Harvard University Press, 1981).

> Highly reknowned economist P. T. Bauer convincingly challenges and rebuts the widely held views of economic development, colonialism, the foreign aid process, the goal of egalitarianism, and the "population explosion."

Lloyd Billingsley, *The Generation That Knew Not Josef* (Portland: Multnomah Press, 1985).

> Billingsley admonishes Christians to learn the lessons of history. Historically ignorant Christians are easy prey for the utopian promises of the Marxist-Leninist prophets. Billingsley gives us a sampling of Christians in our century who have been taken in by the utopian visionaries, as well as a sampling of others who have seen through the false prophets. Written with wit and historical insight.

Warren T. Brookes, *The Economy in Mind* (New York: Universe Books, 1982).

> Presents a balanced Christian perspective of economics. Brookes regards economics as a metaphysical rather than a mathematical science, in which intangible spiritual values and attitudes are at least as important as physical assets. He argues eloquently that the current decline in U.S. economic and strategic strength ultimately may have more to do with a decline in our morality than with the failure of specific policies. Extremely well written and thought-provoking.

John A. Howard, editor, *On Freedom* (Greenwich, Conn.: Devin-Adair, 1984).

> A collection of essays by a prestigious and thoughtful group of leaders and intellectuals including Paul Johnson, Richard

John Neuhaus, and Leopold Tyrmand. This fine book discusses the philosophical basis for freedom, the merits of the free market, and the cultural outworkings of freedom.

Rael and Erich Isaac, *The Coercive Utopians* (Chicago: Regnery Gateway, 1983).
An explosive exposé of the left and other utopian thinkers who have colluded to lead America down the Socialist path. The Isaacs bring to light the leftist coercion of the extreme environmentalists, bureaucracies, giant foundations, and the media. Fascinating reading.

Paul Johnson, *Modern Times* (New York: Harper & Row, 1983).
This dramatic and comprehensive narrative history of the modern world covers all the great events, ideas, and personalities of the six decades since the end of the First World War. Vivid and provocative, incisive and stimulating, this book combines fact, anecdote, incident, and portrait into a full-scale analysis of how the modern age came into being and where it is heading.

Charles Maurice and Charles W. Smithson, *The Doomsday Myth* (Stanford: Hoover Institute Press, 1984).
Maurice and Smithson demonstrate with great lucidity how pervasive the fear of impending doom and economic crisis has been throughout recorded history. Exploding the "doomsday myth" is a vital step toward humanitarian concern.

Ronald Nash, editor, *Liberation Theology* (Milford, Mich.: Mott Media, 1984).
A timely series of essays and criticisms of one of the most destructive theological and political trends in recent history—liberation theology. Authors Michael Novak, Carl Henry, Clark Pinnock, Harold O. J. Brown, and others dismantle the theological, economic, and moral premises of the Marxist approach to Christianity.

Ronald Nash, *Social Justice and the Christian Church* (Milford, Mich.: Mott Media, 1983).
A brilliant defense of capitalism and free enterprise in direct answer to the "evangelical left." Nash points out the fallacies of their simplistic utopian solutions.

Richard John Neuhaus, *The Naked Public Square* (Grand Rapids: Eerdmans, 1984).

Neuhaus eloquently argues for the necessity to articulate a "public framework for moral reference." A rebuttal to the argument that politics and religion do not mix, the book challenges mainline Protestantism's social and political creeds which have replaced the true gospel.

Michael Novak, *The Spirit of Democratic Capitalism* (New York: Simon & Schuster, 1982).

Gives a strong defense of traditional Western political and economic systems. Novak demonstrates how democratic capitalist societies, through the "recognition of the errant human heart, whose liberty they respect . . . follow the example of the Creator who knows what is in humans—who hates sin but permits it for the sake of liberty, who suffers from it but remains faithful to his sinful children."

Jean-Francois Revel, *How Democracies Perish*, trans. William Byron (Garden City, N.Y.: Doubleday, 1984).

Having retreated from his former Marxist stand, Revel has written a convincing and articulate defense of Western democracy. He argues that in order to survive against the expanding Soviet power, the Western democracies must actively and fervently defend their economic and political systems.

Francis A. Schaeffer, *The Great Evangelical Disaster* (Westchester, Ill.: Crossway Books, 1984).

Discusses the how, where, and why of evangelicalism's compromise. Tracing the history of evangelicalism and fundamentalism from the 1920s to the present, the book explains why evangelical leaders have been silent and apathetic in the face of the evils of our culture.

Herbert Schlossberg, *Idols of Destruction* (Nashville: Thomas Nelson, 1983).

A complete analysis of the distinction between a Christian and a secular perspective of economics, wealth and poverty, political systems, scholarship, government, and a range of other areas of life. Well-researched and highly readable.

Julian L. Simon and Herman Kahn, editors, *The Resourceful Earth* (New York: Basil Blackwell, 1984).

A powerful refutation of *Global 2000*, the report which pushed the panic button of the doomsayers. An impressive group of contributing authors document the facts about population, natural resources, pollution, and ecology. Far from predicting the death of planet earth, their findings reassuringly suggest "a progressive improvement and enrichment of the earth's natural resource base, and of mankind's lot on earth."

Julian L. Simon, *The Ultimate Resource* (Princeton: Princeton University Press, 1981).
Destroys the "we're running out of everything!" myth of the hysterical left. Simon proves that far from running out of resources, the earth still provides abundant resources, many as yet untapped. Well-documented and highly informative.

Thomas Sowell, *Civil Rights: Rhetoric or Reality* (New York: William Morrow, 1984).
As a black economist, Sowell argues convincingly that in the civil rights revolution too much was assumed and accepted in the early euphoria—and we are paying the price today. There are danger signals today that American society is drifting toward the kinds of disasters that have overtaken—and sometimes destroyed—other multiracial societies around the world. This danger alone may make this one of the most important books of our time.

R. Emmett Tyrrell, Jr., *The Liberal Crack-up* (New York: Simon & Schuster, 1984).
An amusing and witty analysis of the New Age Liberals in America. Tyrrell picks apart piece by piece the ideologies and leading personalities of the left, leaving no stone unturned in revealing the inconsistency, naiveté, and even downright hypocrisy of the liberals in their critique of America and the world.

Commentary magazine.
A monthly journal which seeks to understand the world from a traditional orthodox Judaic perspective. Read by many influential leaders, this magazine discusses foreign affairs, national policy, and a variety of other subjects.
Subscriptions: $30 per year. Address: 165 East 56th St., New York, NY 10022.

The American Spectator magazine.
Conservative, trenchant, humorous. Contributors include leading writers and satirists. With a unique combination of humor and analysis the magazine routinely covers issues

such as arts, manners, letters, politics, scholarship, books, movies, social trends.

Subscriptions: $21 per year. Address: 102 W. 6th Street, P.O. Box 1969, Bloomington, IN 47402.

This World magazine.

A scholarly journal with a Christian perspective which provides in-depth analyses of thought and culture. Editorial board includes Michael Novak, Peter Berger, James Finn, Robert Nisbet, Paul Ramsey, and George F. Will.

Subscriptions: $16 per year. Address: 320 Massachusetts Avenue, N.E., Washington, D.C. 20002.